THE
FIFE BOOK

Books Edited and Written by Donald Omand

The Caithness Book, Inverness 1972
The Moray Book, Edinburgh 1976
Red Deer Management, Edinburgh 1981
The Sutherland Book, Golspie 1982
The Ross & Cromarty Book, Golspie 1984
A Kaitness Kist (with J.P. Campbell), Thurso 1984
The Grampian Book, Golspie 1987
The New Caithness Book, Wick 1989
A Northern Outlook: 100 Essays on Northern Scotland, Wick 1991
Caithness Crack, Wick 1991
The Borders Book, Edinburgh 1995
Caithness: Lore and Legend, Wick 1995
The Perthshire Book, Edinburgh 1999
The Argyll Book (forthcoming)
The Orkney Book (forthcoming)
Caithness: Historical Tales (forthcoming)

Monograph

The Caithness Flagstone Industry (with J.D. Porter), University of Aberdeen 1981

THE
FIFE BOOK

Edited by

Donald Omand

Birlinn

First published in 2000 by
Birlinn Limited
8 Canongate Venture
5 New Street
Edinburgh
EH8 8BH

www.birlinn.co.uk

ISBN 1 84158 023 6

British Library Cataloguing-in-Publication Data
A catalogue record for this book is available from the British Library

Typeset by Textype, Cambridge
Printed and bound by Creative Print and Design Ebbw Vale

CONTENTS

SECTION ONE

Section Two

LIST OF PLATES

LIST OF FIGURES

LIST OF TABLES

Conversion: Metric/Non Metric

1 metre = 3.28 feet	1 foot = 0.30 metres
1 kilometre = 0.62 miles	1 mile = 1.61 kilometres
1 hectare = 2.47 acres	1 acre = 0.40 hectares

Acknowledgements

Chapter 2 – The Early Peoples (C. Wickham Jones)

Peter Yeoman is to be thanked for reading through the text. His knowledge of the archaeology of Fife is far superior to my own, and any faults that he did not spot must rest with me. Reg Candow also read through the text and it has benefited from his great knowledge of Fife. Figure 4 was drawn by Mary Kemp Clarke for Headland Archaeology Ltd and both are to be thanked for permission to use the drawing. Figure 5 was drawn by Sylvia Stevenson, also for Headland Archaeology Ltd. Figures 6 – 8 were drawn by Alan Braby and are reproduced with his kind permission as well as that of BT Batsford and Historic Scotland, the copyright belonging to Historic Scotland. Figure 9 is re-drawn from Gordon Barclay's 1998 book: *Farmers, Temples and Tombs.* Figure 10 is reproduced with kind permission of Gordon Barclay, David Hogg the artist, and Historic Scotland, who hold the copyright.

Chapter 17 – Other Industries and Chapter 18 – Towns and Villages (P. Martin)

The author would like to thank Fife Council for kindly supplying information about industries in Fife today. Dr. Douglas Lockhart of Keele University very kindly read and commented on the section on planned villages, and generously provided other information. Dr. Colin Martin of St Andrews University and Professor Christopher Whatley of the University of Dundee read and commented on the text of both chapters. The author would like to thank them both for their helpful comments.

Chapter 19 – Place-Names (S. Taylor)

The author would like to thank Dr. Barbara Crawford and Dr. Thomas Clancy for their helpful comments on earlier drafts of this chapter. All errors in interpretation of the material are of course my own responsibility. I would also like to thank the Anderson Research Fellowship, University of St Andrews, for support while writing this chapter.

Donald Omand would like to thank the following for suggestions for chapter inclusions in *The Fife Book*:

Dr. Barbara Crawford
Professor Chris Morris
Dr. Richard Oram
Mr. Eric Simpson
Dr. Cornelius Gillen

Finally, many thanks to Mrs. Janet Mowat of the Centre for Continuing Education, University of Aberdeen for valuable secretarial assistance.

Figure 1
Map of Fife

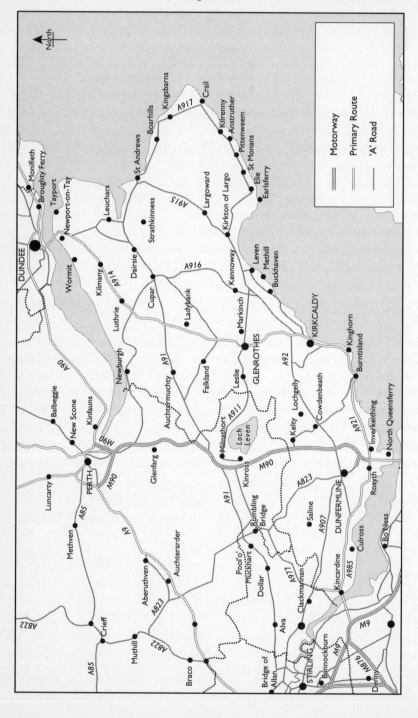

INTRODUCTION

The peninsula of Fife is surrounded by the North Sea, the Firth of Forth and the Firth of Tay. Because of its underlying rocks and glacial deposits Fife has fertile soils that support one of Scotland's most productive and intensively farmed regions.

The Kingdom of Fife (*c.* 350,000 people and 134,000 hectares) with its pleasant climate, rich agricultural land and celebrated coastline is one of Scotland's most favoured counties. The significance of its coastal zone was stressed by a Stuart monarch who referred to the Fife peninsula as a 'beggar's mantle fringed with gold'. One could only concur that the seaboard is adorned with attractive settlements, colourful cottages and their crow-stepped gables.

The picturesque settlement of Crail, made a royal burgh in 1178, is one of the East Neuk towns which stud the coastline between St Andrews and Culross. Culross, with its white-washed cottages, red pantiled roofs and cobbled streets is a 17th-century gem.

St Andrews, a royal and episcopal burgh founded in 1140 and named after Scotland's patron saint, is an outstanding example of a planned Medieval town whose high walls still surround the precinct of both cathedral and priory. At one time St Andrews was the focal point of the religious life of the nation. Its toothy cathedral (plundered in the Reformation) and St Rule's tower lord over the old town, the home of golf. Here, founded in 1411, is the oldest University in Scotland, with its elegant old buildings, quadrangles and gardens.

Dunfermline is the old capital of Scotland. The town is redolent of its historical past: the Abbot House, Royal palace and ancient abbey, the final resting place of Robert the Bruce. Many of the kings and queens of Scotland were laid to rest in Dunfermline, the town that gave birth to the industrialist/philanthropist Andrew Carnegie.

The ancient burgh of Kirkcaldy, 'the lang toun' whose name was at one time synonymous with linoleum, was the birthplace of the distinguished economist Adam Smith, writer of the treatise, *The Wealth of Nations*.

There is evidence of human activity in Fife from the Mesolithic period through Bronze and Iron Age times to the Picts (e.g. Wemyss Cave), 12th-century Inchcolm Abbey (The Iona of the east), the powerful 14th-century Kellie Castle and the sophisticated 16th-century Royal Palace of Falkland, a favourite of Mary, Queen of Scots.

The rise of the great fishing and coal-mining industries in Fife gave the area a powerful economic base. Their demise led to employment difficulties which have been tackled with vigour and new commercial ventures have been attracted to the area whose good internal communications and links across the Tay and Forth augur well for the prosperity of the Kingdom of Fife.

SECTION ONE

ONE

ROCKS AND LANDSCAPES

INTRODUCTION

Within Fife, the grain of the land runs roughly south-west to north-east, including the main coastline features (except St Andrews to Fife Ness), the Cleish Hills, the Lomond Hills and the North Fife Hills. Geologically, Fife is part of the Midland Valley of Scotland, and the rock types and history of formation closely resemble those in the Lothians on the other side of the Forth. The rocks are of two types: sediments deposited by rivers or laid down by the sea, and volcanic rocks poured out at the surface from numerous vents or intruded into underground strata. Most of the solid rocks are between about 400 million and 300 million years old. Lying on top of the bedrock is a veneer of loose sediment laid down by glaciers and by rivers flowing from the melting ice sheets around 13,000–14,000 years ago. Peat, soil and dune sands then accumulated on top and are still in the process of formation. Beach sands are constantly being moved by the wind and by currents in the estuaries and offshore.

Table 1
Geological Timetable for Fife

Geological Period	Rock Formations	Thickness (metres)	Igneous rocks	Age (million years)
Quaternary	River alluvium, peat bogs, fluvioglacial outwash, till	Variable and extensive	None	1
Tertiary and Mesozoic	None formed	Intense erosion	None	225
Permian	No sediments formed		Late volcanic vents	290
Carboniferous	Coal measures	1200	Plugs, sills and dykes intruded over a long period	296
	Passage Formation	270		
	Limestones	1000		
	Sandstones	2500	Burntisland lavas	350
Devonian	U. Old Red Sandstone	600		
	Lower ORS	2400	Thick lavas	400

1

ROCKS

The Midland Valley of central Scotland is situated between two great NE–SW parallel faults in the Earth's crust: the Highland Boundary Fault which runs from Stonehaven to Helensburgh, and the Southern Uplands Fault which runs from Dunbar to Girvan. Between these faults, central Scotland sank down about 400 million years ago to form the Midland Valley, with very high mountains to the north (the Highlands) and lesser mountains to the south (the Southern Uplands). Lavas were erupted from volcanoes close to the Highland Boundary Fault, forming the North Fife Hills and the Ochil Hills. In total, around 2400 m of lava flows piled up one above the other, each flow being around 10 m thick. Weathering took place between each flow, to form a softer reddish rock (a type of fossil soil) between each hard lava and the result of the erosion of the different hardnesses has produced a step-like pattern to the landscape. Most of the lavas are of an igneous rock called basalt – very dark and fine-grained and a related lava type known as andesite, rather more purply-brown in colour. When they weather, these rocks take on a khaki-brown appearance, and it is often possible to see vertical cracks which are cooling joints due to shrinkage of each lava flow after it was erupted onto the land surface. Earth movements around 380 million years ago forced the lava rocks up into a great arching fold that runs NE–SW, so that the North Fife Hills have steep slopes facing the Firth of Tay and gentler slopes to the south-east. The steep slopes are usually bare but the gentle slopes are covered in good quality soil.

The period in earth history when these lavas formed is known as the Devonian, after Devon in south-west England. After the lavas were folded into an arch, they were eroded and worn down, together with the rocks of the Highlands. As a result, thick deposits of sandstones formed as rivers brought sediment into the low-lying Midland Valley. Scotland in the Upper Devonian period, 360–375 million years ago, was situated south of the equator in the subtropics. Most of these sediments are reddish to dark-brown, and in Scotland they are known as the Old Red Sandstone. In Fife they form a band south of the North Fife Hills from Tayport to Leuchars, Cupar, Falkland and skirting round the Lomond Hills to Kinross and Loch Leven. The sandstones were laid down by east-flowing rivers, and they reach a maximum thickness of 600 m. Pools formed occasionally in the broad river valleys at the foot of the mountains, and freshwater fish inhabited these pools and shallow lakes. The fossilised remains of these fish were once found at Dura Den, but the site has now been worked out. Also present are thin limestone bands, shales (originally mud) and desert sandstones with rounded grains. The presence of lime in these rocks has yielded good, fertile, well-drained soils.

When the Devonian period ended 350 million years ago, the Midland

Valley was gradually flooded by a warm, clear, shallow tropical sea in which corals and bivalves flourished. This heralded the start of the Carboniferous period, which lasted for some 50 million years and culminated with the formation of the Coal Measures – rocks formed from fossil soils and trees that grew in dense forests in swampy tropical deltas. Their remains piled up and were rapidly buried, forming coal seams. Carboniferous rocks make up most of Fife, and in places they can be as much as 4000 m thick. During this 50 million year time span, Fife slowly subsided to allow these sediments to accumulate. Volcanoes were active during this period, forming lavas as at Burntisland and Kinghorn with its spectacular pattern of columnar jointing, in addition to volcanic rocks and plugs, well seen at the Rock and Spindle near St Andrews. East and West Lomond are later examples. The Rock and Spindle is a volcanic formation consisting of a vertical 'chimney' of ash, angular lava blocks and debris, intruded by the 'spindle' – a cylinder of dolerite or whinstone forced into the ash, which then cooled and formed a rosette pattern of cooling joints, rather like the spokes of a spinning wheel. Most of the vents in Fife are deeply eroded and do not form particularly prominent landscape features. Many examples are to be seen on the coast of the East Neuk, especially at St Monans and Elie, where extensive outcrops on the beach can be found of black bedded volcanic ash, cut by thin vertical lava sheets or 'dykes'. Some of these vents were responsible for bringing up fragments from the base of the earth's crust during explosive eruptions. In fact the East Neuk is studded with extinct volcanic plugs and this region must surely have been one of the most volcanically active parts of Europe. Another igneous feature was the formation of flat sheets known as sills which were forced into the beds of sedimentary rock underground. When they are exposed at the surface today, they form prominent landscape features. The biggest of these sheets is the Midland Valley Sill which is of enormous extent and forms Bishop Hill, the Lomonds and North Queensferry headland. Impressive vertical cooling joints can be seen on the approach road to the Forth Bridge. It is the same dolerite rock or whinstone on which Stirling Castle and the Wallace Monument stand. Carboniferous volcanic activity was extensive in Central Scotland, and other features of the same age and clearly visible from Fife include the Bass Rock, North Berwick Law and Arthur's Seat. In places, the abundance of hard igneous rock impeded the search for coal, as many of the bodies were forced in as sills parallel to the beds of sediment.

By now Fife had drifted northwards and lay on the equator, and the environment gradually changed from shallow open sea to rivers and coastal swamps, interspersed with volcanic islands. The sedimentary material that filled the Midland Valley basin was brought in by large slow-flowing rivers from the north. An important feature of the Carboniferous period is the way in which the beds of sedimentary rocks repeat over and over again in a series of cycles – limestones with shells and corals on the sea floor, followed by silt, clay and mud rocks, then sands from the river deltas, and finally soil and coal seams. This alternation happened numerous times and represents fluctuations in sea level during 50 million years, possibly related to ice ages elsewhere on earth, with ocean water being locked up in glaciers which grew and then melted. The scene would have been one of rivers advancing by deltas into the shallow sea with forests growing on the swampy hinterland, then drowning as the sea advanced again, and once more a delta being built.

These sedimentary rock cycles consist of coral limestones with fossil reefs as at St Monans, followed by shales and coal seams, including the Cowdenbeath and Lochgelly coals. The most important coal-forming stage was the upper part of the Carboniferous, termed the Coal Measures, from 310 to 300 million years ago. Beds of this age occur around Dysart, Leven, Kirkcaldy and Burntisland and include the opencast and underground mines and those offshore. Westfield was the biggest and most famous of the Coal Measures fields and produced 20 million tonnes in its lifetime from 1959 to 1987. Mining, surface subsidence and waste dumping with subsequent infilling and landscaping have caused enormous changes in the landscape and scenery of industrial Fife. Coal has been used in Fife for centuries – it was mentioned in the charters of Dunfermline Abbey in the 12th–13th centuries. Initially, working was local and rather primitive, and much of the output was used by the monks for heating the salt-pans to produce sea-salt crystals, important for preserving food.

TOPOGRAPHY

Topographically, Fife displays a relatively straightforward pattern of alternating high and low ground, reflecting the underlying geology. The North Fife Hills and the Sidlaw Hills are made of resistant Devonian lavas. These two ranges run south-west until they meet in the Ochil Hills. In the central part of the peninsula is the Howe of Fife which was previously a poorly-drained basin with forests and marshlands. This narrow strath continues westwards to the Loch Leven basin. The valley is filled with thick glacial sediments and was a major outlet for glacial meltwaters. A glacial loch which existed in a hollow at the centre of the Howe of Fife was drained in 1745. Settlements are found mainly around the edges of the Howe of Fife, on slightly higher ground made of boulder clay. The Lomond Hills form the western limit of the Howe of Fife, and between East Lomond and the promontory of Fife Ness north of Crail is a broad ridge of undulating high ground referred to as the 'Rigging of Fife'. In the Rigging are found old lead mines, limestone quarries and lime kilns (referred to below), and ancient upland peat bogs. The rigging ends at Largo Law (290 m), its highest point, and the eroded remnants of a late Carboniferous volcanic neck.

Generally speaking, the highest ground in Fife is formed of igneous rock: lavas, sills and volcanic plugs. Between St Andrews and Leven, most of the high ground is formed by dolerite sills, and again the 'peaks' of Kellie Law, Largo Law and Kincraig are volcanic necks.

NATURAL RESOURCES

In addition to coal, the Carboniferous rocks have yielded other economically valuable products in Fife, in particular agricultural lime from the limestone bands, ironstones which were worked at Cowdenbeath and Lochgelly in the 19th century, building stones from the sandstones, and roadstones from volcanic basalts. The sandstone often has a carbonate cement which erodes easily in rainwater and traffic fumes, so that considerable damage has been done to buildings in St Andrews, for example, where the narrow lanes are not well ventilated by the wind and acidic water sticks to the buildings. Like the former coal mines, limestone and sandstone quarries are now derelict and mostly filled in, but there are still some active roadstone quarries, including one at Lucklaw Hill near Leuchars with its conspicuous pink felsite rock which probably forced its way in as an irregular sheet cutting the Devonian (Old Red Sandstone) lavas. There were once extensive limestone workings, for example, in the East Lomond area (Charleston limestone) and at Drumcarro (Ladeddie) and Kinghorn to Seafield, with old lime kilns, some of which have been restored.

Mineral deposits are rare in Fife. South of East Lomond Hill there is an ancient lead and silver mine which operated for a brief period at the end of the 18th century and produced galena (lead sulphide). Another galena vein at Blebocraigs was worked at the same time, but also yielded little. The so-called 'Elie rubies' from the Elie Ness volcanic vent are actually tangerine-coloured garnets, which are very attractive but not really precious stones. These crystals formed at high pressure in the Earth's mantle beneath the crust and were brought to the surface during explosive eruptions. They can be found in the fine black volcanic ash beds in the low cliffs beneath Elie lighthouse.

Oil shales of Lower Carboniferous age (340 million years) used to be mined at Burntisland, but the industry has long ago ceased to be viable, with the advent of North Sea Oil. The shales were formed in shallow, stagnant muddy lakes, rich in algae, bacteria and plant debris. Oil was extracted by crushing the shale and heating it to 500 °C.

FOLDING AND FAULTING

Reference was made earlier to the arching of the lavas (the NE–SW Sidlaw anticline) that make up the North Fife Hills as well as the Sidlaws and Ochils.

After the Carboniferous rocks were formed, they were also affected by movements in the Earth's crust and were folded into a series of arches (anticlines) and downwarps (synclines). These folds run north–south (e.g. the Cowdenbeath syncline and Burntisland anticline) and the beds of sediment are therefore inclined (or dip) to the east or west. In East Fife the fold trend is more NE–SW. Coal Measures are best preserved in the basin-like synclines as in the Central or Clackmannan syncline in West Fife, and the Leven syncline east and north of Kirkcaldy. Folding is well displayed at Kinkell Braes (St Andrews), and St Monans. Also at Kinkell is a dome-shaped fold near the Rock and Spindle. Here the Carboniferous sandstone beds can be seen in a set of rings, with the sediments dipping everywhere away from the centre. Relaxation of the crust after the compression that caused the folding led to cracks or faults opening up in an east–west direction, a particularly striking example being the Ochil Fault (which is best seen at Stirling Castle). Another major fault, not seen on land, is the Firth of Forth fault which is an extension of the NE–SW Pentland fault in the Lothians. There is a 3 km-wide zone of crushed rock offshore between Anstruther and the Isle of May and the rocks may have been dropped down by around 450 m. The shape of the East Fife coastline from Elie to Fife Ness runs exactly parallel to this fault.

The final geological event to form solid rocks in Fife occurred 290 million years ago at the end of the Carboniferous period, when a number of vertical dykes, horizontal sheets (sills) and as many as 100 volcanic plugs pierced the older rocks. Prominent examples of plugs of this age are the East Lomond and West Lomond Hills. The Isle of May is a volcanic sill made of a rock known as teschenite (a basic rock related to gabbro) which was intruded approximately 295 million years ago.

Thereafter, Fife was subjected to almost 300 million years of erosion, with vast quantities of rock being removed and transported into the North Sea area by large rivers that drained eastwards, when the land surface was tilted 60 million years ago by the forceful intrusion of the north-south chain of volcanoes in the Hebrides, from Skye, Rum, Ardnamurchan and Mull to Arran and Ailsa Craig. The North Sea acted as a basin, which slowly sank to receive this huge accumulation of sediment. Scotland continued its northward drift and found itself in the northern tropics with a hot, humid climate, causing rapid erosion and torrential rain that removed the loose deposits in rivers which, once established, remain today flowing in more or less the same direction.

LANDSCAPE DEVELOPMENT

By two million years ago, Scotland had reached its present position, i.e. close to the North Pole. Climatic change led to the rapid onset of cold conditions in the northern latitudes and widespread sheets of ice became established on the continental landmasses, giving rise to the great Ice Age which lasted until around 10,000 years ago. During that period, four successive cold and warm events affected Scotland. Effects of the last glaciation from 26,000 to 14,000 years ago are seen in Fife. Ice cover was probably at its maximum 18,000 years ago when Scotland was buried under a sheet possibly 2000 m thick. The main centre of the thickest ice was the Rannoch Moor – Loch Lomond area. Traces of older glaciations in Fife were practically obliterated as this last ice sheet moved east into the Firth of Forth and the North Sea. During the main glaciation, the lower valley of the River Tay was deepened and the estuary developed by the scouring action of the ice as it advanced eastwards.

Whilst the ice was moving, loose boulders and rocks were picked up and transported at the base of the ice sheet, causing scouring and scratching of the bare rock surface. When the ice melted, these blocks were deposited over the ground, together with finer clay and sand particles. This sediment is referred to as till and the obliterating cover of glacial and fluvioglacial material is known as drift. Most of lowland Fife is covered by this blanket, and where the proportion of clay is high, the ground can be boggy due to poor drainage. Some large blocks were carried far by the ice – e.g. at Wormit Bay there are blocks which were transported from Comrie, nearly 70 km away to the west.

Loch Leven, just outside the western boundary of Fife, was formed at the end of the Ice Age as a depression, left in the relatively soft Old Red Sandstone bedrock. Blocks of stagnant ice lying on top of and within glacial sediments created kettle holes when they melted and these hollows can form deeper zones in the floor of the loch. Boulder clay (or till) in upland Fife gave rise to poorly-drained tracts of land, including lochs and swamps around Falkland (Loch Rossie), which were not reclaimed until the agricultural improvements of the mid-17th century onwards. Heath, moorland and peat bogs are now quite rare in Fife. The contrast between the rich, easily farmed soils around the coast and the wetter clay soils of the higher parts was probably the reason that Fife has been described as a 'beggar's mantle fringed with gold'.

Extensive sheets of sand and gravel, known as fluvioglacial deposits since they were formed by meltwater rivers from the ice, cover much of lowland Fife. These have been and are still economically important as sources of building materials. However, excavation has meant that many of the landform features such as esker ridges, formed in tunnels under the ice, have now been destroyed. The sand from these deposits is very clean, having been washed by fresh water in the glacial rivers. Rapid melting and the transport of pebbles at the edge of the ice often meant that temporary rivers could cut deep gorges into the underlying surface, to produce the now dry, wooded 'dens'.

The enormous weight of the 2000 m thick ice sheet caused the earth's crust to be depressed for 2 million years, but melting occurred relatively rapidly and the sudden outpouring of meltwater caused a rise in sea level at first, leading to flooding in Strathtay. Strathearn, the Carse of Gowrie and Flanders Moss were also inundated.

Once the ice had completely melted, the land surface began a slow process of recovery or rebound, and this gradual rise is still continuing today, more particularly in Scandinavia, but also in parts of Scotland although not in Fife. Uplift took place in a series of pulses over the last 8000 years as the land regained its previous level and the sea again retreated. This has given rise to a series of raised beaches around the coast, some of which are quite extensive including those at Kincardine and Kirkcaldy, most of the East Neuk coast and from St Andrews through Leuchars to Tayport. Examples of raised beaches include those at Elie, where four different levels can be seen, and just outside St Andrews, where caravan parks are sited on successively higher raised beaches. During higher water levels, cliffs and caves formed, as at Wemyss, and these are now slightly inland from and above the present-day highwater mark. Pebbles and shells can be found as raised beach deposits. Around 6000 years ago there was a major marine transgression in eastern Scotland, causing flooding and resulting in the deposition of clays in the firthland estuaries. The clays are referred to as 'carse' from a Norse word 'kjerr' meaning marshy ground. Since that period, uplift of the land has continued, but today that rise has stopped and for at least the last 200 years, no change in sea-level has been recorded for Fife.

POST-GLACIAL CHANGES

Soon after the main melting of the great ice sheets 13,000 years ago, Fife was clear of glaciers, although ice remained in the west and in the Highlands for several more thousand years. The bare landscape was rapidly colonised by trees, shrubs, mosses, lichens and grasses. Conditions initially would have been similar to the Arctic and sub-Arctic tundra found in northern Canada and Scandinavia. Dwarf willow, birch and juniper were the first trees to invade. At around 11,000 to 10,000 years ago, there was another sudden deterioration in the climate and in the Highlands ice reappeared in the valleys. This period has been called the Loch Lomond Readvance. Trees in Fife were killed off and the arctic tundra landscape was re-established for another thousand years. Thereafter, the climate improved and average temperatures rose steadily, resulting in the reappearance of birch and hazel. The period around 7500–5000 years ago was one of climatic optimum for tree growth throughout Europe. Conifers were the first migrants to arrive, followed by broad-leaved woodlands with birch and hazel, eventually giving way to oak and elm, and areas of coniferous forest. Even upland Fife, then, would have been tree-covered. The Lomond Hills are known to have had birch and hazel woods.

From about 5000 years ago, the decline of elm and the rapid spread of blanket peat, heath and grassland over previously forested areas can be connected with a climatic deterioration to cooler, wetter conditions, and the effects of humans who started to clear the native forests. By around 3000 years ago it is likely that most of Fife's forest cover had gone, virtually forever.

HUMAN ACTIVITIES

Thus the landscape of Fife has been modified by humans in deforestation, and by agricultural methods and by industrial processes, particularly mining and quarrying. Land subsidence and surface collapse have been caused by coal mining, and mining waste has been dumped extensively on land and around the coast. Reclaimed land west of Torry, where ash and cinders from Longannet have been dumped, has been done at the expense of naturally-occurring coastal mudflats. Quarries and mines have been filled in and new artificial landscapes created, sometimes as recreational lochs. Kilconquhar Loch, for example, is on the site of old peat cuttings and Lochore Meadows has been reclaimed from surface subsidence and coal waste on the site of earlier mining. Widespread drainage, field improvements and the growth of towns and the construction of wide carriageways have also contributed greatly to the changed scene of Fife. The intense network of old railways related to mining is another important man-made landscape feature.

RIVERS

The land area of Fife is drained by three main rivers, the Eden (31 km long), the Leven (21 km long) and the Ore (19 km long), each with a large number of tributaries. All of these flow eastwards. In addition there were a number of deeply incised, densely wooded dens, often now dry valleys, which were formed at the edge of the melting ice sheets by rapid down-cutting. The River Ore flows out of Loch Ore which is a landscaped artificial loch on the site of coal workings, as mentioned previously. All the surface water in Fife flows through farms, industrial and urban areas and abandoned mines, with negative consequences for water quality. Several lochs in Fife have been severely enriched in nutrients from farm runoff, resulting in profound changes in the plants and associated wildlife.

MOORS

Moorland in Fife exists on the higher slopes in the west, as in the Lomond Hills, the Cleish Hills and Benarty Hill, at elevations above about 200 m. The soils are generally acid, peaty and poorly-drained and low in natural nutrients due to the underlying rocks and the wetter, cooler climate at higher elevations.

Heather and low shrubs occupy the upland moors, with occasional rowan trees and Scots pine. Blanket peat bogs form on water-logged hilltops, especially in the Cleish Hills, although artificial drainage has led to the loss of most of these bogs. Moorland areas in Fife have been drastically reduced by land management schemes and reclamation to increase farmland since the end of the Second World War. Lowland heath and raised bogs are now very rare and are practically restricted to the North Fife Hills. Much was lost when the Tentsmuir and Edensmuir areas were planted with forest. Raised bogs occur on lowland ground covered by poorly-drained till (boulder clay) left since the last Ice Age. One example, in Moss Morran, is Fife's largest raised bog, with substantial deposits of peat up to 8 m thick.

THE COASTLINE

A profoundly important landscape feature of Fife is the coast, which extends from Newburgh to Kincardine for some 170 km and forms two-thirds of its boundary. Coastal landform types include the raised beach cliffs and caves referred to above, rocky wave-cut platforms, boulder beaches, sandy beaches, landward dunes, salt marshes and mudflats in the estuaries of the Tay, the Forth and the Eden at Guard Bridge. The rocky coast occurs between the two main estuaries. Offshore currents and onshore winds ensure that the coast is continually developing. The Tentsmuir sand dunes are still growing; and the sand bars and sand spits offshore from Tayport (the Abertay Sands and the Elbow, extending out for 7 km from the edge of the land) are constantly shifting due to the interplay between sea currents and the outflow from the Tay – which has the greatest discharge of water from any river in Britain.

The constant interaction between natural forces and human intervention means that the landscape of Fife, as elsewhere, will continue to evolve in the future. Two imponderables are the effects of agricultural practices in 'set-aside' periods, and the predicted change in climate related to global warming and the greenhouse effect. Of these, the former will affect inland regions, while sea-level changes associated with climate warming will obviously be more important around Fife's coast. Enlightened conservation efforts currently underway mean that much of Fife's natural landscape features will be preserved for future generations.

Figure 2
Physical Features of Fife

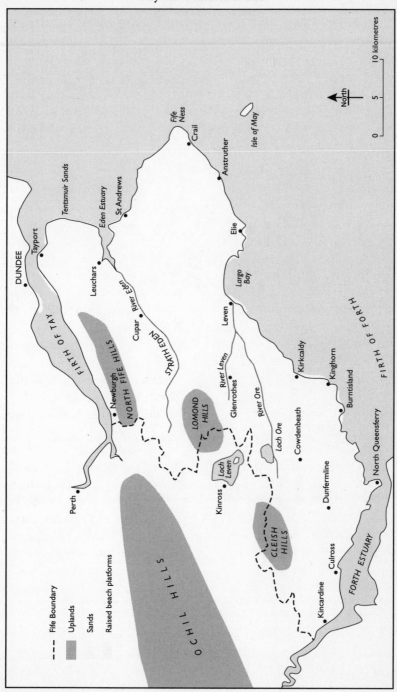

Figure 3
Geological Sketch Map of Fife

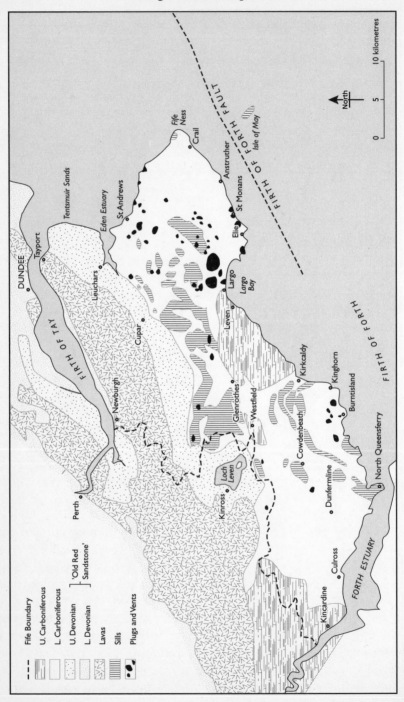

Two

The Earliest Peoples

Figure 4
Map of Main Sites Mentioned in Text

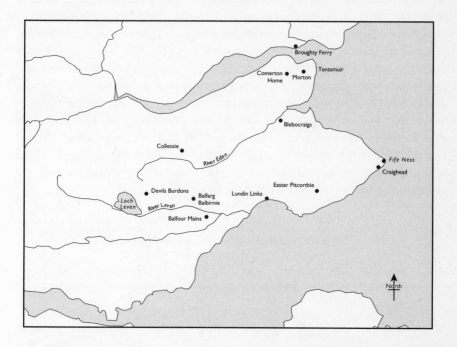

We do not know exactly when the earliest peoples arrived in the area that we now call Fife. But we do know that they were established by some 9600 years ago, when a small band of hunters, possibly only two or three people, settled briefly on the flat land above the sea at Fife Ness. Their stay at Fife Ness was short, possibly only a few days, and they left little trace of their passing, just a hearth and some pits. They may have erected a shelter from the north-east winds (Figure 5), and they were using stone tools: several were discarded during their stay. We will never know for certain why they chose that headland, nor what exactly they were doing there. These were people who had to seek out and catch all of their food, and it is likely that this small group were after migrating birds or other coastal resources. They certainly lit a fire; there is considerable evidence for heat, including many burnt fragments of stone tools which are scattered throughout the pits, and one possible explanation is that they were collecting, processing and drying meat for the winter. The exciting implication of this is that there must have been other people living not far away. Whereabouts was the main settlement where the rest of their group waited anxiously to see that the Fife Ness hunters did not return empty-handed?

These earliest peoples of Scotland are known as Mesolithic; they used stone tools (Figure 6) and obtained food from hunting, fishing and gathering. They lived a nomadic lifestyle, moving from place to place in small bands in order to make use of the various resources on offer at different times of the year. Some settlements may have been relatively long term and home to several families, others were short term and used by only a few people. Fife Ness seems to have been the latter type of site. This nomadic life means that their houses and possessions were geared towards mobility: they were light and easily portable and Scotland's acid soils have made sure that there is rarely much left on a Mesolithic site. The traces of the earliest inhabitants of Fife are often represented by no more than a collection of tiny stone tools and a burnt hearth site. Mesolithic remains are generally so ephemeral that they are hard to find and archaeologists have to employ a wide suite of techniques in order to excavate and make sense of what they have found.

Figure 5
Artist's Reconstruction of the Site of Fife Ness

Figure 6
Classic Mesolithic Stone Tools from the Site at Fife Ness

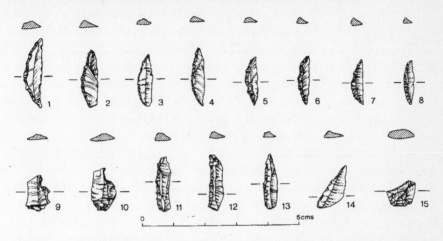

Nevertheless, collections of Mesolithic flint tools have been found at several locations across Fife (e.g. at the Devil's Burdens, Strathmiglo, and at Blebocraigs near Kemback), but little is known about most of the sites because few of them have been systematically excavated in recent times. The Mesolithic way of life lasted for at least four thousand years, and there are few remains to provide the details of Mesolithic Fife throughout this period. Much of what is known about this period has come from sites on the west coast of Scotland, where a series of recent archaeological projects has increased our knowledge greatly. This information may be referred back across Scotland to add to the interpretation of the sites in Fife.

Fife in Mesolithic times was a generally wooded land. Birch, hazel and elm trees were all well established by 8000 years ago, and oak and pine were not far behind. The woodlands were mixed and interspersed with more open areas of grass and shrubs. The lower lands and water courses may well have been relatively boggy, but the rivers were important both as routeways for transport by canoe and on foot along their pathways and as sources of food: not only for fish but for the plants that thrived beside them and for the animals that congregated along water courses. The rivers provided access into the uplands where summer and autumn could be used to hunt deer and gather a rich supply of berries. Sea levels were still oscillating as the land settled after the removal of the weight of ice that had lain upon it for millennia. This meant that the coastal lands gradually changed. Nine thousand five hundred years ago the sea may have lain much lower revealing sandy spits and bays from which to gather shellfish; 8000 years ago the water level had risen by as much as 10 or 15 m in some areas so that the coastal lands disappeared and other coves and inlets came into play. Gradually the sea has reached its present level, but it is not yet stationary, though the pace of change has slowed.

The Mesolithic hunters did not erect permanent homes or monuments. Their relationship with the land was one of mobility and their houses reflected this. No doubt they gave adequate protection against the elements, but they would be regarded as flimsy today. The evidence suggests that they may well have been bender type structures made on a framework of poles and covered with skins, bark, or brushwood. Tools were commonly made of stone, such as hard siliceous rocks like flint which could be flaked into sharp knives and arrowheads. These could be found as pebbles in the river, as beach gravels and as outcrops such as quartz in the uplands. Other materials such as bone, antler and hide were also important and could be saved from the hunt, while wood for a variety of purposes was abundant in the local forests.

One important east coast site has done much to advance knowledge of the period and this is Morton to the south of Tayport. Stone tools were first discovered at Morton in 1957 by Reg Candow, a local archaeological field-walker. He carried out a systematic collection for archaeological finds from the area of the site for many years, and then it was excavated in the early 1970s by a team lead by John Coles from the University of Cambridge.

Morton today is an unprepossessing site, a low rise in the corner of a field surrounded, on most sides, by trees. The sea lies about 4 km to the east, across the woodlands of Tentsmuir. Eight thousand years ago, however, it was a very different place. Sea levels were higher and the main Fife coastline lay on the other side of the site, to the west, about 1 km away. The low rise that we see today jutted out as a small peninsula and it was probably completely cut off at high tide. A group of Mesolithic hunters came here and built shelters on the island: the excavations found traces of several small huts and windbreaks (Figure 7). We have unusual detail of their time on the island because the soils at Morton are not as acid as elsewhere and so the remains of organic refuse such as bones and shells have been preserved.

The people at Morton were exploiting the resources of the coastal lands; their rubbish heaps included the remains of shellfish as well as coastal birds and fish. Apparently, they were also fishing in deeper waters because there were bones from deep-sea fish such as cod. It is unlikely that they stayed on the island all year round, and bones of red deer, wild cattle and pig suggest that some of them, at least, spent part of the year hunting farther inland. This impression is supported by the types of stone that they used for their tools. As well as small pebble flints that might have been collected locally they were using cherts that came from the west, along the southern shores of the Tay, and pieces of a carboniferous stone that could be collected farther to the south towards St Andrews and the southern Eden valley.

The settlement at Morton was not large. The structures were quite flimsy, and it is likely that the remains built up over a series of repeated visits to the

Figure 7
Artist's Reconstruction of the Site at Morton

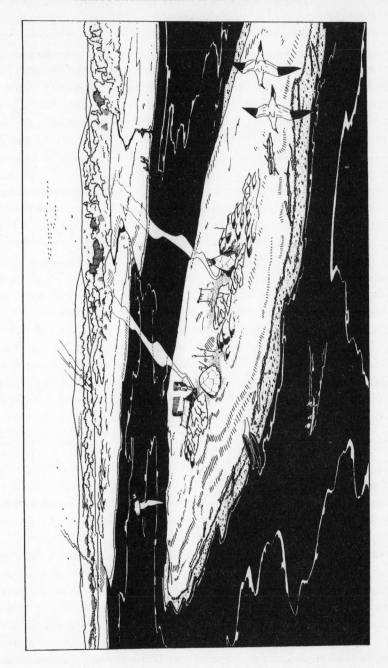

island. Nevertheless, it is possible to reconstruct a little more detail about the way in which the people used the site. There is some difference in the types of finds from the individual parts of the site which has been used to suggest that they carried out different activities in separate areas (similar to the way in which we use our houses today). Their shelters were built in one area, away from the midden deposits. This area was also used for the manufacture of stone tools, both to be used locally and apparently for use elsewhere, perhaps in hunting and fishing. There were many tiny stone microliths from this area. The processing of food and other resources, however, such as hides and bone, seems to have taken place elsewhere on the site around the midden and the stone tools that were found here were very different. There were hearth sites in both areas.

The remains from Morton did not include any boat fragments, but it is unlikely that these would have survived. We know that boats must have been around because of the remains of cod that were caught from the deeper inshore waters, and there is also the likelihood that access to the settlement would have been restricted by the action of the tide. Finds elsewhere suggest that the Mesolithic settlers used both dug-out canoes and skin boats, though there are no securely attested boat remains from Scotland and most information regarding boats is derived from Scandinavia.

The inhabitants of Morton used raw materials that were drawn from various locations and from them the excavator was able to draw a picture of a group who ranged across diverse habitats. At different times of the year they seem to have travelled west through the higher lands of the Ochils, south to the riverine lowlands of the Eden, and north to the salt marshes and shallows of the Firth of Tay. These people may only have been a small part of a larger community, joining with other groups at times to live in central settlements, and splitting into yet smaller sections as bands of hunters left in order to pursue the deer, while others left for the coast to harvest shellfish. It has been possible to carry out some environmental work on the material from the Morton middens and this suggests that the island was mostly inhabited during the winter, though the bird remains and some shellfish indicate that visits also took place in the spring and summer.

If the site at Morton functioned as we think it did (and archaeological theory is always changing) it raises the interesting possibility of a number of other Mesolithic sites, all related, across a fairly wide area of Fife. As with Fife Ness, it is likely that the remains of a larger base camp lie within this area, together with smaller more specialised sites, not unlike that at Fife Ness itself. It is easy to see that the known Mesolithic remains from Fife are but a tiny part of the picture, though many sites must have been destroyed through time.

The Mesolithic inhabitants of Fife lived at a time of great change. Sea levels were mobile and the climate, too, was changing. At first, their world was slightly warmer than today, as conditions improved after the great Ice Ages, and then it became gradually stormier and wetter, as well as cooler. About 7000 years ago the Mesolithic population had to cope with a major disaster when the coastlands of Fife were hit by a tsunami, a massive tidal wave, that travelled across the North Sea and must have caused great devastation and loss of life. Traces of the turbulent sand layer laid down by this event have been recognised above the settlement remains at Morton and at Broughty Ferry on the north coast of the Tay, as well as in numerous small sites along the coasts of Fife. No doubt they adapted and dealt with all of this, as human populations have been wont to do. But, about 5000 years ago there came a great change that was to have more impact on them, and this was a change brought about by the people

Figure 8
Neolithic Artefacts: 1 stone axe head; 2 bone polisher; 3 bone awl; 4 bone pin; 5-6 flint scrapers; 7 pot; 1-6 from Skara Brae village, Orkney; 7 from Quanterness tomb, Orkney

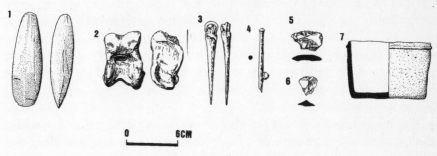

Figure 9
Artist's Reconstruction of a General Neolithic Landscape as the Woodland is Cleared to Make Way for Farming Settlements

themselves: the introduction of farming.

Farming meant great changes to life (Figure 8). It meant more reliable, and controllable, sources of food. It meant that the old, mobile, way of life was laid aside as people settled down in order to tend their crops and animals. Houses became more substantial, and everyday goods no longer needed to be light and portable: fragile pots made from local clays became commonplace; different types of stone tool were developed; and even clothing changed to take advantage of new materials and new technologies. Populations grew as nutrition improved and increased stability meant that communities developed a different view of the land. People could change and domesticate the land, as the woods were cleared and seeds sown and tended (Figure 9). Monumental architecture sprang up to mark out special places for celebration and to provide a home for the ancestors. The community's roots in the land were strengthened. This new phase in the development of Scotland is known generally as the Neolithic.

Of course, the Neolithic did not appear overnight, nor were its life-style changes all-embracing. The Mesolithic way of life persisted among some communities, and elements persist today: most towns still have shops that cater for fishing and hunting as well as a supermarket. It is also difficult to trace the very beginnings of the introduction of agriculture. By the very reason of being partial, the first tentative steps towards farming lie hidden within the Mesolithic world in which they took place, and it is hard to spot the traces of Scotland's first farmers.

The animals and crops that provided the mainstay for the farmers must have come to Britain from continental Europe by boat. Once here it is likely that they spread rapidly, partly as human curiosity allowed for the local adoption of newfangled ideas and partly as people then spread out, moving off with their new ways to look for space in which to clear forest and establish settlements. The earliest dates for Neolithic activity in Scotland come from the site of Balbridie in Aberdeenshire where excavations have revealed a massive wooden building dated to about 5800 years ago. The function of this building is uncertain; it may have been a communal centre of some sort or it may have been the dwelling place for an extended family. However it was used, the evidence shows that the community were farmers: there were bones from domestic cattle together with grains of charred wheat and barley, as well as pottery and new style Neolithic stone tools.

In Fife, the earliest dates for farming activity come from a complex site at Balfarg (Figure 10). Balfarg is important today for the information it has provided towards the interpretation of the Neolithic in Scotland, but it was also clearly important in early prehistory. Several seasons of excavation have revealed the remains of a large Neolithic ceremonial centre here, but the site was in use even before this when, some time around 5700 years ago, a group of

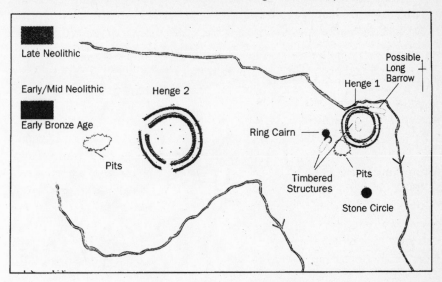

Figure 10
Plan of Ceremonial Centre at Balfarg, after Barclay 1998

shallow pits was dug. At least one of these pits was carefully and deliberately filled with pieces of characteristic early, round-bottomed pottery which were placed around the edge. The reasons for this action have long been lost, but similar pottery deposits within pits have been discovered on other sites that were later to have ceremonial structures and they suggest that the site was already an important ceremonial centre from early on.

The later structures at Balfarg included at least two timber enclosures, built between 5700 and 5300 years ago, to house a series of wooden platforms. These have been interpreted as the remains of an excarnation site where the bodies of the dead could be laid out for birds to remove the flesh (Figure 11). They were not, apparently, both used at quite the same time, and the site of the later structure was finally covered over with earth and enclosed by a shallow circular ditch. Pottery sherds found in the ditch show how pot styles were evolving; they are of a later, flat-bottomed type known as Grooved Ware, from its distinctive decoration.

The excarnation enclosures at Balfarg were long, with rounded ends, and it has been suggested that they mimic house styles. There is little evidence for Neolithic housing from Scotland, with the exception of Orkney, where many stone-built structures have survived (such as Skara Brae and Knap of Howar). Elsewhere, buildings seem to have been of wood which has meant that little remains. Excavation suggests that dwellings were generally straight sided with rounded corners, and this is supported by the existing buildings in Orkney. There are no definite Neolithic house remains in Fife, though the excavation of a small trench into a roughly circular enclosure at Kinloch Farm, Collessie, has

Figure 11
Artist's Reconstruction of an Excarnation Enclosure at Balfarg

produced dates indicative of Neolithic activity and this site has been interpreted as possibly domestic. Elsewhere in Fife there are extensive and varied cropmarks which include similar sites to those excavated at Balbridie and Neolithic settlements elsewhere. Cropmarks comprise the patterning seen from the air when a ripening crop grows over a field that contains archaeological remains.

The circular structure that was raised over the enclosure at Balfarg seems to have comprised another type of monument: a henge. Henges are well known from elsewhere in Scotland and indeed across Britain. They are circular in plan and consist of an inner platform surrounded by a ditch with an outside bank (the latter two are usually more marked than at Balfarg). The precise function of the henge sites has been lost, but they have been interpreted as gathering places where an extended community could come together for ceremonies that may have included marking the passage of death as well as calendrical and other occasions. Many henges have evidence for complex structures on the inner platform. The Balfarg henge was not large (about 20 m in diameter), but it dates to about 5100 years ago, which makes it one of the earliest henges known in Scotland. There is unusual detail relating to the ceremonies here from one of the potsherds on which a burnt encrustation had survived. This contained traces of henbane which is a powerful hallucinogenic.

After the first henge another, and larger, henge was built at Balfarg, a few hundred metres to the west. This seems to have been a much more complex structure with a more marked ditch and bank enclosing a series of timber circles built on the platform. The largest circle comprised 16 posts and internal variation among them shows that even these wooden circles were not simple structures. It has been estimated that the tallest timbers, on the west side, may have stood up to 4 m high – no small feat of engineering. Finally, the timber circles were replaced by stone settings. Evidence for at least one ring of 12 stones was found within the main Balfarg henge, and a further setting of 24 stones has been suggested. Finds within the circles included both Grooved Ware pottery and flint implements.

Balfarg was in use over a long time, and, not surprisingly, the structures were modified over this period. A burial at the centre of the henge seems to mark the last years of the complex in the early Bronze Age. The skeleton of a young person was placed in a pit, accompanied by a Beaker pot and a flint knife and covered by a particularly large stone, which weighs about two tons.

There were also stones set up outside the Balfarg Henge; one survives today by the north-west entrance causeway and a smaller circle of 10 stones was built close by at Balbirnie to the south. This henge included a rectangular kerbed area inside the stone circle, and sherds of Grooved Ware pottery like that from Balfarg were deposited in one of the stone sockets. The nature of the ceremonies that took place here could not be deduced from the remains, but much later, this circle seems to have been made into a burial place with two cists built into pits which cut the central setting. Other cists were found away from the centre. The precise date of these cists is uncertain, but it may indicate activity on the site into the Bronze Age. Enigmatic cup-and-ring marks on two of the cist slabs are likely to date to the end of the Neolithic, or early Bronze Age period. The cut-down nature of these decorated slabs has been used to suggest that the stones may previously have been in use elsewhere. One cist contained the identifiable cremated remains of a woman and child, together with pottery and stone tools, but the others were too disturbed for their contents to be certain.

The site at Balbirnie was finally covered with stones to make a small cairn which continued as a place of burial. At least 16 individuals were cremated and then laid to rest here, in small pits dug into the cairn material. At the same time as this activity was taking place here, there was also further activity at Balfarg with the digging of various ring-ditches and cairns for burials. Sherds of Bronze Age Beaker and Food Vessel pottery were found on both sites.

Both Balbirnie and Balfarg may be visited today, though the remains are reconstructed and at Balfarg they give little impression of the prehistoric grandeur of the site. The original site of Balbirnie was completely destroyed, but the reconstruction lies just to the south-east of its original location.

There is other evidence of Neolithic activity in Fife, but nothing as exciting, or as comprehensive, as the remains at Balfarg and Balbirnie. Fife is rich in cropmark sites and many must be later than the Neolithic; but some include sites reminiscent of Neolithic structures elsewhere. Among these is a circular enclosure that has been interpreted as a possible henge site near Pitlessie, though there has been little excavation here and no trace of the complex of structures uncovered at Balfarg has so far been found. Occasionally, archaeological work in advance of construction will turn up Neolithic material, such as at Craighead north of Crail where pits with late Neolithic pottery were uncovered during the construction of the new golf course. At Comerton Home, south of Newport, pits and other features with Neolithic finds have been interpreted as the remains of settlement dating from the Neolithic into the Medieval period, but this work can only offer a tiny snapshot of past activity and it is hard to interpret such traces. Elsewhere, fieldwalkers past and present occasionally uncover collections of flint tools including neolithic types of arrowhead together with pottery which point to the activities of the early farmers, though in the absence of excavation it is impossible to interpret exactly what was going on. Sites with lithic and ceramic finds such as these include the fields around Balfarg, various locations within Tentsmuir Forest, and the Devils Burdens, Strathmiglo.

Remains elsewhere in Scotland show that Neolithic society was complex and seemingly relatively stable. This was a time of great woodland clearance as the forest trees were felled to make way for fields and grazing land as well as settlements. Small villages of timber houses sprang up, and across Scotland there is a suite of burial monuments as communities designed and built great marker tombs to stand proud in the land and house their dead. Some tombs lay under earthen mounds, others under stone mounds, but so far there are no certain Neolithic burial mounds from Fife. The archives of the National Monuments Record in Edinburgh hold records of two possible Neolithic long barrows at East Friarton and Balfour Mains, Markinch, though neither has been investigated in detail. In addition, there are records for numerous cairns and barrows across Fife and while many of these must relate to the Bronze Age, or other periods, it may well be that some of them represent a peculiarly Fife tradition of burial in smaller monuments during the Neolithic. We may not be certain just how the dead were buried in Fife in the Neolithic, but we can be certain that there were dead to bury.

We have seen the great ceremonial centres that developed in the Neolithic, of which Balfarg is a particularly important example. The stone circles that were incorporated into the design of these monuments mark a continuity of use into the Bronze Age. Fife is rich in standing stone settings, most of which probably relate to Bronze Age activity, though it is quite possible that some mark sites that were already important. This chapter is not the place for a detailed discussion of Bronze Age Fife, but there was, of course, great continuity in many ways with the Neolithic, and this is perhaps epitomized by the standing stones. One of the most impressive groups is that at Lundin Links at Lower Largo on the northern shores of the Forth where a group of three huge stones may be seen. Also in southern Fife is Easter Pitcorthie, where a single stone has been decorated with cupmarks on its south face. Many of the stone settings concentrate in south Fife such as those at North Glassmount, Kinghorn, or Bandrum, Saline.

The Bronze Age stones mark the passage of time and changes in the lifestyle. Throughout the Mesolithic and Neolithic the population of Fife had been growing and consolidating its hold on the land. With the introduction of metal further changes were to be added to the prehistoric lifestyle and it is the place of the next chapter to discuss these developments.

THREE

LATER PREHISTORY

INTRODUCTION

The arrival of bronze and iron technology affected only a minority of the population for much of the two thousand year period which archaeologists divide boldly into Bronze Age and Iron Age, for life in general did not alter a great deal during this long period. We now know the main areas for settlement, defence and burial in Fife during the Bronze Age, though Iron Age burials have proved harder to find. We have begun to develop an understanding of society and its skill base, although much of the information has been gathered opportunistically. As there are no documentary data for any part of this period, we do not know what people, places or artefacts were called and so, by default, we have to use modern terms.

THE ENVIRONMENT

When they came to Fife, the early settlers found themselves in a landscape of enormous variation. Dominating the area were the East and West Lomond hills – fragments of highland mountain in a lowland setting – visible from great distances, which, with other hills, such as the Cleish Hills and the Ochils, were useful landmarks, as well as settlement and defence opportunities. There were few natural routes across the peninsula and the sides of the hills and hilltops would have been more attractive than the wet, lower ground. By following the rivers and burns it would have been possible to reach into the heart of Fife, however. The River Eden meandered eastwards across the Howe of Fife and opened onto a wide, shallow estuary, while from Loch Leven the River Leven wound its way southwards to the Forth. Both rivers overflowed their banks onto the undrained land sufficiently often for the surrounding land to be boggy and difficult to settle, with few dry places for houses and farms in an area of scrub, including hazel, alder and birch. Studies of pollen, from lake beds, peat cores and archaeological deposits have provided data on prehistoric environments and climate as well as ancient farming and settlement patterns. They show increasing influence on the land by 3000 BC, long before the first articles of copper and bronze reached Fife, around 2000 BC. Although many stone and flint axes of the earlier, Neolithic period were of imported stone, often brought in as completed tools, suitable stone was available for the skill to be learned locally. By contrast, in Fife, as in the rest of Scotland, the new bronze technology introduced a dependency on external specialists and traders, especially as tin had to be brought from Cornwall and smiths were required to manufacture bronze.

CONTINUITY AND CHANGE

Life for the people in Fife would have changed little at first, since metal would have been available only to community leaders of the Early Bronze Age people. Houses and fields of this time are scarcely identifiable in the landscape today, but burial cairns and ceremonial monuments are. Stone circles, spanning the Neolithic and Early Bronze Age periods, survive at Lundin Links and Balbirnie, while at Dunino in East Fife there is a record of another. None is complete, although Balbirnie was almost intact when excavated. Surprisingly, only a small number of henges has been found in Fife, all discovered from the air, including Balfarg in 1946 and, recently, one at Balmalcolm. Henges are circular monuments comprising a platform on which a timber circle was set, surrounded by a ditch and enclosed by a bank; there could be one entrance or two, through a gap in the bank and ditch. Most henges are small, but a few, including Balfarg are extremely large. Balfarg was a multi-period site starting in the Neolithic and continuing in to the Early Bronze Age. In what appears to have been the final use of Balfarg, a single burial of a young man was placed in a deep grave near the centre of the monument. This burial, accompanied by an unusual, handled Beaker of the Early Bronze Age, provided evidence for change at this complex, thousand-year-old site.

Balfarg henge sits within a complex of other monuments, stretching across several hundred metres of the landscape and includes remains near Balfarg Riding School as well as the Balbirnie stone circle, the longest-lasting component of this entire group of sites. Here, earlier burials in short cists were later covered by a cairn, using the stone circle as a kerb. A number of token cremation burials associated with urn fragments was inserted into this cairn. Taken as a whole the range of monuments at Balfarg–Balbirnie, with the array of ancillary remains points to an area of great ceremonial significance during the long period from before 3000 BC to after 1400 BC.

Many henges, including Balfarg, are situated where they can be overlooked from slightly higher ground, which is one clue to their ceremonial rather than defensive purpose. The henge would have required substantial labour to build and rebuild over several centuries. This observation has led to debate not only about the nature of ceremonies held there, but also about the size of the population and the nature of society. Stone circles and henges have been interpreted as astronomical centres and it is generally agreed that phases of the moon were significant for their layout, but it is not possible today to find out how the sites were used.

Interpretation is fraught with problems, but size, and rarity of sites such as Balfarg henge, do imply not only a well-organised society, with highly-skilled leaders, but also a wider community, whose members would travel considerable distances to help with construction and to take part in ceremonies on the appropriate festive or ceremonial occasions. Any society capable of expending energy and time in ways such as these must also have been producing food surpluses, to feed workers during the construction periods as well as those members taking part in the celebrations. The comparative rarity of henges such as Balfarg suggests tribal affiliations well beyond the immediate environs of the monument. However, we know nothing of the settlements of the builders or of the leaders who would have had the knowledge to organise construction or lead ceremonies at Balfarg or at similar sites throughout the country. The importance of these monuments may be recognised, however, since sites such as Balfarg were in use for some fifteen hundred years, almost twice as long as the oldest cathedrals in Britain.

DEATH AND BURIAL

Although houses and fields of the Early Bronze Age have left little visible trace on the ground, the round cairns and tumuli for the dead are prominent throughout Fife. They can be seen on hilltops, such as Greenhill or Harelaw, and on prominent knolls, some coastal, like Barns Farm, others inland, like Cairnfield or Foxton. The majority lie between 50 m and 170 m OD, but that on West Lomond is at 522 m OD. Some cairns seem to have been built to be seen from long distances. Harelaw cairn, for example, sited at 122 m OD, on the modern local authority boundary east of Lochore, has extensive views and can be seen from considerable distances. The cairn on top of West Lomond Hill is the largest cairn in Fife and also the highest. Many others have been placed on contour promontories, such as Pitcairn and Norrie's Law, each with fine views to the Firth of Forth.

Some cairns were used over a long period and it can be seen even from incomplete early excavations that there was great variation in construction and contents. Some covered a single cist burial. Others seem to have been built only after a number of burials had been deposited, as at Barns Farm, Dalgety Bay, where graves and short cists covering inhumations and cremations were found below the cairn. However, not all burials were covered by cairns. At Briary Gardens, on the west side of Dalgety Bay, three cists, comparable in date with those at Barns Farm, seem not to have been covered by a mound, perhaps because further burials were expected to take place before the mound was raised. The mound-building phase of most cairns probably represents the closure of the monument. While many mounds and cairns apparently were simple, one-period monuments, others were more complex, such as Pitcairn and Collessie, which were surrounded by a kerb, while Norrie's Law was built of earth and covered by a stone capping. Some sites, Balbirnie, for example, were reused at a later date.

Taken together, the evidence of the cairns suggest a very different society from that of earlier monuments. Where Neolithic tombs and henges were originally used for ceremonial purposes, with communal burials, Bronze Age burial mounds covered cists or graves of individuals, sometimes with several such graves below one mound. In contrast to the earlier period, access to these burials was not intended. Certainly the artefacts deposited in graves show considerable changes, with the introduction of new pottery types, such as Beakers and Food Vessels and the first metal objects. Early artefacts found in a cairn or mound appear to be residual, brought to a site in the soil or dropped during construction. Otherwise, later burials may be inserted into a cairn.

Burial in short cists, whether or not below a cairn, was normally of one individual, with the knees drawn up towards the chin. Burials were placed with the head at either end of the cist, sometimes on the left side, sometimes on the right. Orientation varied, but east–west was not unusual. Often beautifully built, with well-chosen stones, there were, nevertheless, many variations in detail, one of which was the sealing of the corners with clay. While many burials appear not to have grave goods, others included artefacts. Analysis of all the elements of burial suggests that these communities were wealthy, since conspicuous expenditure is represented by the richness and range of resources involved, as well as in the effort required for cist and cairn building, especially on larger sites. Although large numbers of short cist burials have been found in Fife, as in the rest of Scotland there is no evidence to suggest that the entire population was buried this way.

URNFIELDS AND CREMATIONS

Short cist burial gave way to other styles of burial, sometimes in pits in the ground and often reusing cairns. Throughout Fife and dating from before 1800 BC to around 1400 BC cremations in urns have been found, generally by accident, since there is rarely any surviving above-ground identification. They are found singly or in small groups as well as in cemeteries known as urnfields. These urns are large hand-built pottery vessels, up to 40 cm high and often as wide at the mouth, with small bases. There are many variations, including collars, or heavy rims, usually decorated with impressed designs, created by string, twigs, hazelnuts, pointed objects or finger-nails. Others have added strips of clay as cordons. Decoration normally is confined to the rim and the collar at the top of the urn. These urns are particularly interesting technically, because they were still hand-built, of a coarse fabric, top heavy and fired in an open fire or in a fire pit. Drying them without cracks developing before firing would have been only one of the many skills required to ensure these special pots survived manufacture, to be used for burials. When fired they were used as containers for the cremated bones of one or more individuals and buried, usually inverted, in a small pit.

Artefacts found among cremated bones are not numerous, but burnt flint tools and bone pins occur as well as, in a few cases, decorated oval bronze razors with a tang for a handle. Two of these were found at Lawhead, near St Andrews where a cemetery of at least eighteen cremations in urns was found more than a century ago. Extensive urnfields were found at Southfield and Brackmont in north Fife and at least fifty urns were found during sand quarrying over a twenty-five-year-period at Brackmont.

Evidence for the method of cremation has been found at a small number of sites. Cremated remains could be placed in an urn, deposited upright, with a flat stone over the mouth of the pot; at other times the urn was filled with the burnt bones and covered, perhaps by cloth, before being inverted and buried in the vicinity of the funeral pyre, if not actually among the ashes. Sometimes the urn sat on the ground, while at others a pit was dug for the deposit. Because they were inverted it has been assumed that there were cloth or skin covers over the mouth of each urn, but evidence for this seldom survives, although sometimes an earth 'plug' has been found. Not all cremations were placed in urns, but might be placed in a prepared hole. If an organic container was used instead of a pot this would not survive. At Westwood, near Newport, the ashes seemed to comprise burnt twigs and straw, as well as charcoal from larger wood. One important aspect of these cremations is the impact they must have had on the landscape. Any cremation required large quantities of wood for the pyre and, where evidence has been recovered, sizeable wood was used, rather than only the small twigs and branches used at Westwood. Taken together with the evidence for timber houses, cremation represents a considerable amount of woodland clearance, as well as management of woodland, even in areas where sustainable coppicing and pollarding probably may have been the norm.

TECHNICAL SKILLS

Among the many artefacts from Early Bronze Age burials are Beakers and Food Vessels, as well as urns, all of hand-built pottery. While no two pots are the same, individual pots belong to groups of similar form and decoration, none unique to Fife, and found all over Britain. There has been much debate, however, about whether these pots were made locally and whether they were made by specialist traders. Whichever is the case, they were primarily intended for burial rather than domestic use, although Beaker sherds have been found in a domestic context at Brackmont and possibly at Balfarg Riding School.

Daggers, like one from Collessie, belong to a series of thin copper or bronze blades of which about a dozen have been found in cists in Fife, including Masterton, near Dunfermline and Ashgrove, at Methil. Others have been found elsewhere in Scotland and the rest of Britain. These date to around the 15th century BC and although almost all differ in detail they clearly exhibit great similarities of form, decoration and manufacture. Like flat copper axes they are amongst the earliest copper or bronze artefacts found in Britain; such items could have been owned only by relatively few people – and yet they were placed in graves, many apparently without ever being used. At Ashgrove the dagger was complete, with horn hilt, whale tooth pommel and bark and skin sheath. Personal possessions placed in Fife cists included beads of cannel coal or shale (often called 'jet'), all finely made and highly polished. At Masterton a multi-strand necklace of small, washer-like jet beads was found in a cist with two massive bronze armlets, together with evidence of two individuals. At Strathairlie, another multi-strand crescentic jet necklace comprised tubular beads, with elaborately perforated large flat spacer beads. Buttons, both conical and others similar to toggles of jet, are evidence not only of craft skills, but also of woollen clothing. Although many burials have been found we really do not know how many people lived in Fife, from before 2000 BC to the end of the Bronze Age, around 500 BC, since the proportion of the living to buried population at any one time must remain a matter of conjecture.

AGRICULTURE, FISHING – AND BREWING

Where conditions were favourable unexpected survivals offer unusual insights to the skills of the living, as at Ashgrove and Barns Farm. In the Ashgrove cist traces of animal fur, fragments of plants and pollen were all recovered. The wealth of pollen, particularly of meadowsweet and lime, has led to the suggestion that this was evidence of a deposit of flowers as well as of an alcoholic drink, such as mead, placed in the Beaker. One burial at Barns Farm was in a coracle, a small boat suitable for paddling around and fishing in sheltered river and coastal waters. Such use is suggested by a deposit of salmon bones placed at one end of the coracle at Barns Farm. Animal bones, sometimes found in burial deposits, show that pigs and sheep/goats as well as cattle were farmed. At Collessie, scientific study of the dagger sheath showed it had been made of cattle skin, with black hair surviving. This was interpreted as similar to the skin of modern Shetland cattle. Impressions in pottery of grain and of string made from twisted straw, as well as pollen grains of cereals from soil show that barley was the main cereal and that little wheat was grown.

Bronze Age fields and houses are hard to identify, even from the air, although traces survive below later, Medieval fields, for example at Leuchars.

Recent excavations at Drumoig, north of Leuchars, have revealed a landscape of settlement, houses, field boundaries and artefacts, although much damaged by centuries of later agriculture. Immediately to the north of Drumoig, on Cowbakie Hill, settlement evidence seems even more dense; much of this could be of Bronze Age date. In fact aerial photography offers a view of Fife where small settlements of circular timber houses, with their associated fields, was the norm throughout much of the prehistoric period. Few land boundaries are known in Fife, but Harelaw cairn appears to lie on an ancient boundary in an area where old field boundaries could also survive. A cairn at Foxton lies on a contour above the Eden valley, a site visible from long distances and with extensive views. This site lies almost on the eastern boundary of Cupar parish, which perhaps reflects an ancient boundary.

MORE NEW TECHNOLOGY

Until recently there were few finds in Fife of artefacts of the later Bronze Age, dating from about 1000 BC to about 500 BC. A few sunflower-headed bronze pins were found near Burntisland and on Tentsmuir and two bronze axes survive from an early hoard find at Gospetrie. A ribbed, looped, socketed axe from near Gauldry, socketed spearheads from Lordscairnie and Kinghorn and a sword dredged from the Tay many years ago were the main objects known and the impression was of an area where little bronze was available. However, while evidence for early bronze manufacture may still be lacking in Fife, there have been new discoveries, which show that the new technology was available, if only to a few. Metal objects seem to have been imported rather than manufactured locally, but future excavation could revise this view.

A deposit from the hillside south of St Andrews, in a garden in Priestden Place, has dramatically changed our perceptions of the Late Bronze Age in Fife. The Priestden Hoard comprised over a hundred metal objects and fragments, including tools, weapons, ornaments and scrap metal all found with jet bracelets, amber beads and boars' tusks, packed into a parcel, perhaps wrapped in a bag or basket, and clearly deposited with the expectation of the owner returning to retrieve them. In addition, fragments of wood from the socketed weapons and tools were recovered, as were woollen cloth and skin fragments, the remains of individual wrappings. One item, of French origin, is of particular interest. It is a small, ribbed bracelet with a 'hook and ring' fastening which had broken in many tiny fragments. This was found, like the amber beads and most of the wood, cloth and skin fragments, as a result of sieving the soil from around the find spot. Most of the objects are similar to others from hoards of various kinds found in Scotland and at Heathery Burn in Durham. Many, like Priestden, were chance discoveries, but Priestden has proved spectacularly informative about a wide variety of skills and contacts of the Bronze Age people.

Interest in the Priestden Hoard extends beyond the artefacts and the technology they represent, bringing Fife into the mainstream, modern development of the time. Some of the items were of French origin and were, therefore, imports. Here, for the first time in Fife, is a sword fragment, with part of a chape from a scabbard. Though old and broken, possibly a trade-in for a new weapon, it is the first such weapon found in Fife, although another was dredged from the Tay at Mugdrum. The hoard included a number of socketed spearheads which could be put to several uses, for ceremonial, hunting and war, for example. Among other bronze items were tools, including tweezers, gouges and chisels and a number of socketed axes, all different and all with side loops, to tie them onto their hafts. As with other, smaller hoards, this one also contained a mixture of personal items, including razor fragments, bronze and cannel coal bracelets, spiral and other finger rings, dress pins with sunflower-shaped heads and amber beads. Other rings, of various sizes, included several tied together with string to form short chain links, possibly some kind of horse harness. Most remarkable is the preservation of organic materials that rarely survive – woollen cloth and skin from containers and wood fragments from the hafts of weapons and tools. When the research on all this material has been completed, pollen trapped among the fibres, detailed analyses of the types of wood, and cut marks on the wood-tips will offer new insights to the Late Bronze Age and perhaps hint at where the artefacts were made or brought from.

The Priestden artefacts, many brand new, seemed to have been destined for trade. In the present state of knowledge of east Fife it is not clear where the owner of the hoard would have gone to trade, since no settlement is known in the St Andrews area itself, although cremation burials at several places within the burgh and at Lawhead may be close to undiscovered houses. However, air photographs do show an unenclosed settlement about 2.4 km inland, on wester Balrymonth hill, others to the east at Cambo and several north of the Eden at Drumoig and Pickeltillum, while urnfields found generally throughout the area must indicate local settlements.

The Arrival of Iron

There was no clear-cut change from the Bronze Age to the Iron Age, but around 500 BC is generally accepted as the start of the Iron Age. This new technology was not developed locally in Scotland and the earliest finds must have been imported. In Fife, artefacts of early Iron-Age date are few and lack of excavation means that there is little additional information about either structural remains or artefacts.

The settlement and farming lifestyle of the later centuries of the Bronze Age and the earlier years of the Iron Age are virtually indistinguishable at unexcavated sites and it is probable that some hillforts could have been built initially in the later Bronze Age. At Down Law fort the rampart overlies a series of pits, some of which may be seen in good light conditions. Excavation could reveal traces of a Bronze Age palisade phase, prior to the construction of the Iron Age fort, as in some Border forts. Continuity is entirely possible at most sites, as seen at the Scotstarvit Covert homestead where there were two main phases of development, the earlier a timber roundhouse of the Late Bronze Age and a later house, only slightly different in size, identified as Iron Age from the pottery sherds found within it.

The number of known sites of the Iron Age has been augmented almost annually since the introduction of aerial surveying, with sorties over ripening grain crops as well as over hills and so-called marginal land, often in advance of pre-development surveys. This increase in numbers of sites has, however, hardly changed our understanding of settlement distribution. Settlement knowledge has developed, however, usually by comparison with similar remains elsewhere. Hilltop forts are prominent and numerous, but only on selected hills. East Lomond Hill has a fort, while West Lomond does not. To the east there are no major hilltop forts, but, on the north side of the Ochils is a string of defended sites, notably Clatchard Craig and Norman's Law, as well as Castle Law, Abernethy, just in to Perthshire. Down Law, to the south of the Howe of Fife, has a fort, while Largo Law does not. On the Forth is Dunearn fort, while in west Fife, Saline and Cult hills both have forts, as do Dumglow and Dummifarlane, but Wether Hill does not.

All these sites have ramparts and ditches. Little excavation has been undertaken and interpretation is based mainly on comparison. Generally, however, where there are two sets of defences, there is a tendency for the larger enclosures to be earlier and for the smaller remains on the summit to be later; these are often referred to as citadels built after the Roman phase of the Iron Age. Other important sites, such as the broch on Drumcarrow Hill, Cowden homestead, Dunshelt earthwork and souterrains are discussed in the next chapter.

At the end of the prehistoric era the Romans had reached Scotland, and from references by classical writers it has been possible to map some of the territories of a number of tribes, including a group called the Venicones, who occupied Fife and the immediately adjacent area. These local people were the traders, farmers, house- and fort-builders of the later prehistoric period and they were the people who lived through the Roman period to emerge into the early centuries of the first millennium as the Picts.

Four

Living with the Romans

Introduction

Documentary and archaeological evidence for the Venicones, in what is now Fife, Clackmannan and Kinross remains limited. Roman activity must have affected the people, but life probably continued much as before. It has become conventional to refer to the Celtic Iron Age as before the arrival of the Romans and the Roman Iron Age for the early centuries AD, with a high degree of continuity of settlement in much of the country. In the first half of the chapter the continuing Iron Age is discussed, followed by the Roman evidence, including the surprising number of Roman artefacts from east Fife. By the end of the period the people of Fife emerge into the historic era as one of the groups known collectively as the Picts. Some sites may have continued in occupation during the Roman period, while others were abandoned, apparently to be reoccupied after the departure of the Romans, although this has not been shown by excavation in Fife.

Strategy?

The fort on Castle Law, Abernethy, just beyond the Fife border, is a spectacular monument in the landscape even today. Clearly visible from long distances in all directions, this fort occupied a conspicuous position on the high ground above the Rivers Earn and Tay. It also overlooked the pass through the hills towards the south, into the Howe of Fife. Few forts have been excavated, but that at Abernethy was extensively investigated in 1898, producing only Iron Age material. The walls were found to stand at that time more than a metre high and the horizontal timbers used in their construction had been preserved as voids, showing that timber-strengthened walls were being built in pre-Roman times. No Roman artefacts were recovered, but a safety-pin style brooch, of a type known to archaeologists as La Tène 1c, probably from the south of England, but ultimately European in origin, was among the numerous Iron Age artefacts found. Such brooches can be closely dated in the south of England and so the Abernethy brooch provides a time marker for events in Scotland, as well as evidence for contact between England and Scotland in the pre-Roman period.

Several other forts were built along the Tay, in similar prominent locations to the one at Abernethy. Clatchard Craig overlooked the Den of Lindores, which also gave access to the Howe of Fife. Little is known of the early fort at Clatchard Craig, which seems to have been incorporated into the later Dark Age stronghold. However, several sherds of Iron Age pottery were recovered from scraped up material in the lowest levels of the ramparts and other sherds were in the upper rampart levels, suggesting that early deposits had been disturbed when the ramparts were constructed. Reused Roman tile and other fragments were found in the latest phase of Clatchard Craig showing later development, but there is no sign of Roman occupation of this or any fort. As most of the hill has been destroyed by quarrying the fort now can be interpreted only from early air photographs and the limited excavations of many years ago.

It is difficult to identify territorial areas from the locations of these and other multi-rampart forts, although Abernethy and Clatchard Craig do lie on either side of very long-lived boundaries, still in use, but perhaps originating far back in prehistory. Norman's Law, also on the Tay, at 285 m OD, was part of the string of defences along the north of Fife. Other major sites are on East Lomond, overlooking the Howe of Fife, and Dunearn above the Forth. Smaller and less impressive, but no less strategic forts, with single ramparts, are known on Down Law, Green Craig, Saline Hill or Cult Hill, for example, all of which enclosed substantial areas of hill top. Few of the Fife forts include more than one or two circular houses, while some, such as East Lomond seem too small for even one building. Moreover, the distribution of these defended hilltops is difficult to interpret. We do not know if forts were contemporary with one another, whether single or multiple phase or in sequential use. Nor do we know how hilltop sites related to other forts and defended homesteads in less prominent locations in Fife. Many hills lack any kind of defensive site and so detailed study will be necessary of size, complexity, distribution, proximity to other forts, groups of settlements and possible territories before even excavation might offer serious information about the society to which these forts belong. It is also possible that some sites were not defensive, but were important meeting places or even religious centres, their ramparts serving as focal points.

There are other defended enclosures, often sited on a spur rather than on a hilltop, as at Links Wood, Lady Mary's Wood or Maiden Castle. Without excavation it is not clear whether such sites should be described as small forts or as defended homesteads or whether they were look-outs for a more important site. Promontory forts, or defended farms, may survive above ground or only as cropmark sites. Examples are Waulkmill, Crombie, with a Roman camp below, Trench Knowe, Culross, overlooking a loch, Purin, high on East Lomond, Myres castle on low lying ground near Auchtermuchty and Randerston on the east Fife coast. Cowstrandburn in the west is a low-lying defended homestead, enclosed within a substantial bank; Scotstarvit Covert may be similar, though on a terrace overlooking the River Eden, while on the summit of nearby Tarvit Hill is an enclosed homestead. These sites represent only a small proportion of known defended sites and little is known about them, apart from their form and location. However, many were defended houses, which were not unlike the later, medieval tower-houses in purpose, built in a defensive location and set among farmland, each perhaps the centre of a small estate.

Scotstarvit Covert is of particular interest, since it has been shown to date from the Late Bronze Age and the Iron Age, one of few sites to have been excavated. Situated on a terrace, the earthen-bank of the enclosure surrounded the remains of a single large timber roundhouse, of about 26 m diameter. This had replaced an earlier, slightly smaller house of some 20 m diameter. Both had been built of timber posts, with double outer walls, an inner circle of uprights to support the roof and a central hearth. Sherds of Iron Age pottery suggest that the later house dated to the centuries immediately before the Romans came to Edenwood camp, on the riverbank just below the site. On the adjacent Hill of Tarvit an oval earthen enclosure surrounds a single, undated house. This site occupies a particularly strategic position and is visible from considerable distances; on the west it overlooks Scotstarvit Covert and Lady Mary's Wood fort, both on the north of Walton Hill. These three sites, all close together could represent different elements of a single estate or their juxtaposition could be successive. All, however, overlooked good farmland.

An apparently contemporary roundhouse, though unexcavated, was set on a promontory, defended by multiple defences at Randerston on the east Fife coast, while the similar site at Waulkmill utilised a contour promontory above a burn, again near the sea and at Myres Castle the promontory was an area of firm ground in a marshy area. These seem to be defended farms, set on the edge of their fields, but the triple bank and ditch arrangement suggests a considerable need for defence or social display.

Other sites, such as Wester Balrymonth, visible only from the air, include numerous groups of timber roundhouses, without any form of enclosing earthwork, perhaps forming open 'villages', although we do not know if all the structures were contemporary with one another. These are probably of the Iron Age, but without excavation there is no dating evidence and some remains could be Bronze Age. Drumnod in north Fife is a small open settlement of three round stone-walled houses, while an excavated example, one of three houses, lies on the saddle west of the Drumcarrow summit. The excavated Drumcarrow house proved to be a substantial structure, with thick stone walls, a wide doorway, paving near the door and an off-centre hearth. Pottery from the house and an adjacent small rectangular barn was dateable to the pre-Roman Iron Age. On Ormiston Hill, north Fife, another stone roundhouse of similar date was excavated, and roundhouses are known on Lomond Hill and on the lower slopes of other hills.

Souterrains, long, underground curved stone chambers, often associated with round timber houses were built in the first and second centuries AD, usually on sandy ridges, where the drainage was good. These underground structures have been variously interpreted, but their association with houses does suggest storage as a probable use. For a long time only a few had been recognised in Fife, but aerial photography has revealed the position of several others, all in east Fife. On the Fife coast, the Ardross souterrain is typical, with its stone roof slabs intact. It lies on a sandy ridge and could well be associated with a ploughed out timber house.

One anomalous site is Drumcarrow Broch, the only example of these round defensive towers in Fife. Broch towers are normally found in the north and west of Scotland, with only a small number in the south and east. All are in strategic locations and all are on the edge of the best local agricultural land. Drumcarrow broch has not been excavated, but its thick walls have been identified and the entrance is partly visible through the fallen rubble. At 217 m OD it was not only highly defensible, it was widely visible. More significantly, perhaps, it overlooks the whole plain from the Tay and the Eden to St. Andrews and eastwards towards Fife Ness. This site overlooks its farming landscape, a location typical of the majority of brochs. Without excavation the broch cannot be dated, but like most brochs it probably was built in the first or second century AD. This structure is unlikely to have been built by local inhabitants, unless they sought help from the north, where brochs were common. North of the Tay another broch was built within The Laws, a fort above Monifieth. This is visible from Drumcarrow, and together, perhaps, they suggest reaction to Roman activity in the area.

BURIAL

Few Iron Age burials have been found in Fife, partly because no ceremonial burial monuments have been identified and individual burial sites are difficult to recognise. Long cists may have been used at this time, as suggested by the cemetery on the shore at Lundin Links, excavated some years ago. There, extended burials were in oriented long cists strung out along the beach, some in low cairns under round and square barrows of a type found elsewhere to be of Pictish date. One iron object was recovered, and a radiocarbon date of between the 4th and 5th centuries AD for human bone, suggests a late Iron Age date for at least some of the burials. Occasional individual long cists have been uncovered, as at Balfarg farmhouse and these could be of early date. Two burials at the Early Christian site on the Hallow Hill, St Andrews contained Roman objects of the 2nd century AD. Differing in construction from each other and from the later long cists, they date to the pre-Christian native, late

Iron Age, but whether these were traditional burial monuments is not known. These examples show the wide variety among the few burials known so far in Fife, but they certainly do not represent the wider population and on this limited basis it is not clear where larger cemeteries or groups of burials should be sought. More probably burials would be found if fort and settlement sites were excavated, as happened in East Lothian at the Broxmouth fort, where burials were in the ditches. No shrine sites are known, with the possible exception of the Hallow Hill, where the possible chapel could have been built near the site of an earlier shrine. Because of the general lack of excavated burial sites we know little of the burial practices of Iron Age society in Fife.

Some writers see Fife as belonging culturally to a southern province during the Iron Age, partly because of the open settlement pattern. However, others consider that the early timber-laced forts, such as those at Abernethy and Clatchard Craig show northern characteristics. These are similarly constructed to others in the North East, excavated at Cullykhan, on the Moray Firth. More realistically, then, as now, Fife might well have maintained contacts with both north and south.

ROMAN IRON AGE

Agricola was the Roman leader in the late 1st century, while Severus was emperor in the the 3rd century. Both were active in Scotland and the few Roman sites in Fife have been attributed to their attempts to conquer the north. In the Agricolan period the Roman military route to the north lay well to the west of Fife, and Agricola focused his attention there. One reason he is thought to have by-passed Veniconian territory is because it is claimed that the Venicones posed no threat to the army. However, the route to the north avoided the marshy estuary of the Forth and so access to Fife could well have been easier by sea than across the land.

Ptolemy's 2nd-century map of Britain, although cartographically difficult, does include the tribal name *Venicones* and a small number of place names possibly in Fife, although the locations of Orrea, Alavna and Victoria have not been identified. These names do not shed light on the relationships between the Romans and natives and much work has yet to be undertaken on this, especially in Fife. One geographical feature on Ptolemy's map, however, may be instructive. Ptolemy's placing of a river, the Tina, between the Forth (Boderiae), and the Tay (Tavae), has puzzled Roman scholars for many years. Numerous arguments have been put forward, suggesting the Tina was a transposition of the River Tyne to the north instead of to the south of the Forth. However, it is entirely possible, and more probable, that the Tina was correctly located by Ptolemy and represents the mouth of the Eden.

Known Roman contact with Fife was primarily coastal and one of the most dangerous areas for ships plying from the Forth to the Tay would have been the estuary of the Tina, which gives every appearance of leading to a major river. Instead it is the mouth of a minor river, its estuary an extremely shallow sandy bay with dangerous, shifting sand bars, its narrow channel difficult to locate. It seems reasonable, therefore, to equate the Eden with the Tina. As Ptolemy's map presumably included the most up to date information for mariners, his inclusion of Tina between the Forth and Tay makes complete sense, warning ships not to turn too soon, but to keep out to sea until they actually reached the Tay.

Contact by sea also offers an explanation for the location of the three temporary camps in east Fife. That at Bonnytown, a small camp of 14 ha, near Boarhills, has been identified as Agricolan. Its location, less than 4.8 km from the sea, not far from a small but safe harbour, looks more appropriate to a Roman incursion from the sea, than to a camp constructed after an overland march across the difficult terrain of inland Fife. Communication between Bonnytown camp and the sites at Abernethy and Carpow, for example, could have been easier by sea than overland in the 1st century AD, Agricolan period. It has been suggested recently that Agricolan troops crossed Fife on the way north in AD 82, but there is little physical evidence for this. The only other Agricolan camp known in the area at present is the large, 40-ha camp at Abernethy on the south bank of the Tay, just over the modern boundary in to Perthshire and at some distance from the forts of Strathearn. A short distance to the east of Abernethy lies the fort of Carpow, which is now thought to have originated in the Agricolan period, although its main period of occupation was in the 3rd century, during the Severan campaigns. The Abernethy temporary camp and Carpow fort could have controlled Abernethy Glen and several other routes into central Fife. Such Roman presence could well have led to the abandonment of the native fort on Abernethy Hill, if not of others in the area.

The two other camps known in east Fife, at Edenwood and Auchtermuchty are thought to be Severan, 3rd century, rather than Agricolan. They, too, could have been approached from the Tay down the glens leading through the Ochils, rather than by an inland route from the west. A third camp at Waulkmill, west of Dunfermline, lies almost on the coast of the Forth. Since no other camps have been identified in that area it is difficult to work out the possible military strategy for west Fife either in the Agricolan or the Severan periods. To the east there could be a string of undiscovered camps to reach Bonnytown or a fort at the mouth of the Eden, but a link by sea around north-east Fife to the Tay at Abernethy and Carpow is equally plausible.

Military activity during the 2nd century was concentrated to the south of the Forth, but by the late 2nd and early 3rd centuries the Severan army was active along the Tay and had penetrated into central Fife, a detachment of soldiers from the Severan fort of Carpow on the Tay responsible, perhaps, for constructing the temporary camp at Auchtermuchty. Assuming the Ochils to be safe, troops could have followed one of several routes through the hills to the strategically-situated Auchtermuchty camp, which sits on a well-chosen, though sloping site, with commanding views across the boggy land of central Fife as well as to east and west. From this vantage point, or from the hill above the camp, many forts and homesteads would have been visible. A route to the east from the camp at Auchtermuchty could have followed high ground, not far from the present road network, turning south again along an access similar to the minor road today, to reach the Eden at a relatively easy crossing point, where Edenwood camp was constructed on the south side of the river. From Edenwood, if these sites were all contemporary, access to the coast and to Bonnytown would have been feasible.

Unlike the Auchtermuchty camp, Edenwood can never have had an extensive view in any direction. However, it, too, is well-placed, although not perhaps in a typical temporary camp location. It lies on the south bank of the river Eden, on a flat, well-drained terrace, with rising ground to the south. From there access to the coast and the mouth of the Eden is relatively easy, along a route similar to that taken by the modern road, on higher, well-drained ground above the river. Edenwood camp was strategically well-placed, whether in relation to a putative camp near the Eden mouth or in relation to the many native forts and homesteads in the area. The relationship between the Roman presence and the local inhabitants is not known. However, Edenwood camp was built on cleared agricultural land, and this presumably would have affected native farming in the vicinity. Aerial photographs show many features enclosed by the camp, some of which could be Roman rubbish pits or tent lines, but others that could relate to native occupation of the site.

Temporary camps are by their nature not solid constructions, but they are still easily studied from air photographs, which clearly show the defences as colour differences in a growing crop. A few sites survive above ground, however, and Edenwood is one of that small group. Part of the line of the ditch is traceable in woodland and at the south-east corner a short length of bank survives as well. This was tested in a small-scale excavation in the late 1970s, shortly after it was discovered, revealing the usual bank and V-shaped ditch. Two further excavations have confirmed the line of the ditch as well as short, external ramparts, designed to protect the entrances. The feature was called a *tutullus* and is characteristic of many forts and camps. No artefacts have been recovered. Less is known of the other camps. Part of the Auchtermuchty camp has been built over and so far limited excavations have not provided evidence about the camp or the soldiers who built it. No work seems to have been carried out at Bonnytown or Waulkmill.

ACCOMMODATION OR SUBJECTION

Largely because of the silence of the classical writers it has been suggested that the Venicones posed no threat to the Roman army. However, it can also be argued on archaeological grounds that this seems indeed to be the case, although there has been little excavation. Although there were several large forts along the Tay, Norman's Law and Clatchard Craig being among the most important, they seem not to have been in use during the Roman interlude. Other forts were irregularly situated, not clearly guarding any specific territory and several hills were not defended, including the entire south side of the Ochils. Largo Law, for example, a particularly distinctive and prominent hill, was not fortified. Forts generally have been interpreted as having been abandoned during the Roman period. Evidence is restricted, but at Norman's Law and Clatchard Craig, houses were later constructed over the degraded ramparts. More conclusive, however, is the evidence that at the latter site Roman building materials, possibly from Carpow, were used in the Dark Age fort.

Little is known of the status of settlements, but the few that have been examined, near St Michael's in north Fife, near the broch on Drumcarrow Craig and at Scotstarvit do not show signs of burning or deliberate destruction. Probably farms would have been left alone, as long as they contributed their levy of grain, which was so urgently required by the Roman army, but there has not been research to examine this possibility. Certainly, however, study of pollen from peat and lake mud samples confirms that the landscape was open, with mainly agricultural land and relatively little woodland, except in the wet areas, where wet-loving trees and bushes throve.

ROMAN ARTEFACTS

A Roman presence may have proved difficult to identify in Fife, because of lack of structures. However, artefact studies show that at least some Romans were in the area. Interestingly, the artefacts all date closely to the late 1st and early 2nd centuries. As long ago as 1914 excavations in two caves, Kinkell Cave near St. Andrews and Constantine's Cave at Fife Ness, uncovered important Roman artefacts, but little attention has been paid to them until recently. At Kinkell there was a bronze jug handle as well as Samian and coarse pottery, while at Constantine's Cave part of a glass bottle, wine amphorae and Samian sherds were uncovered among numerous other artefacts of earlier and later dates. Similarly, there are two rare, high quality Roman glass cups, one complete and the other fragmentary found in a grave in the 1860 excavations at the Hallow Hill, St Andrews. However, excavation of the long cist cemetery on the Hallow Hill in 1975 resulted in the discovery of another grave with Roman artefacts of similar, 2nd-century date to the glass cups found previously. This new grave contained more high status objects, an enamelled seal box, an enamelled brooch, part of a silver snake-head bracelet and a minute Samian sherd, among other artefacts. A Samian sherd was excavated at Clatchard Craig. The brooch, sword and spears, found many years ago in the burial at Merlsford, and an enamelled mount from Kinglassie, are all of 2nd-century date, as were two hoards of 2nd-century coins, one from Pitcullo and the other from nearby Craigie Hill. To these can be added a number of casual items of value uncovered recently in north Fife, all of comparable date. A button-and-loop fastener, part of a tankard handle, three headstud brooches and a number of coins have been found. The single coins are difficult to interpret, since they were largely dug up in gardens, but the other items, although not all from excavated sites do show a degree of similarity. They are high status artefacts. The circumstances of deposition for most finds, including those in the three grave deposits, are not known, but they are widespread across the area, and undoubtedly they are not the only such items. These artefacts, for most of which we lack secure archaeological contexts, can be interpreted in different ways, but the one clearly identifiable thread is that there must have been Roman contacts with local people. The number of finds is too small and too scattered to allow of firm conclusions, but such rich finds warrant closer analysis. Many scenarios can be proposed, based on known Roman behaviour patterns elsewhere. For example, in addition to troops there could have been scouts, emissaries and traders, all in Fife for differing reasons. The coastal items could have come from sailors or even shipwrecks. Some individuals could have lost their possessions while travelling, some could have died, others been robbed, but on present evidence none of these can be confirmed and only when additional Roman artefacts and sites have been discovered will it be possible to identify the context of at least some of these artefacts.

After the departure of the Romans because of pressures on the army, circumstances of life for the local population generally remained much as before. However, there were changes. Classical writers mentioned the tribal groupings ranged against the Roman army, among them from the 3rd century, the Picts and other Caledonians, who occupied a wide territory, including Fife, and who seemed by this time to represent an amalgamation of the many tribes recorded earlier.

FIVE

THE PICTS AND THE EARLY MEDIEVAL PERIOD

INTRODUCTION

The peoples of eastern Scotland were known to the Romans by a variety of tribal names, including the Maeatae, the Caledonians and the Verturiones. By late Roman times the *Picti* and the Caledonians were recorded as the dominant tribes in the north, but it is not known if *Picti* was a real name or, as usually assumed today, a nickname, relating to painting, either themselves or their belongings. In Ireland the Picts were known as the Cruithne, which could have been their name for themselves. Today the name Picts is used to refer to those people who lived predominantly in eastern Scotland during the first millennium AD and it is this half of the country that is Pictland. Pictland itself was divided by the mountains known as the Mounth into a northern and southern kingdom, with a king in the vicinity of Inverness and another in the south, where the Forth was the southern boundary. The southern centre could have been at Dunnichen in the 7th century, but by the 8th century Kinrimond, modern St Andrews, had emerged as the power centre in the south.

Pictish tribes occupying the lands north of the Forth as far as the Mounth included the Dicalydones and the Verturiones. Their power centre in Strathearn became known as *fortriu* or *fortrenn* in the early historic period, while the associated name *fif* referred to what is now Fife. Few documentary records of the Picts have survived apart from king lists and occasional references in annals, particularly in Ireland. Nevertheless, knowledge of the Picts has greatly increased in recent years using these sources and archaeological, place name, linguistic and other studies. The Picts were farmers, warriors, artists and craftsmen. Initially they were pagan, but by the 6th century many had become Christian. In late and immediately post-Roman times, when the Picts were in eastern Scotland, early historic sources suggest that raiders and settlers, mainly the *Scoti* from Ireland had become established in the west of Scotland, forming the kingdom of Dal Riata in what is now Argyll. It is argued that Gaelic, the precursor of that spoken today in the west of Scotland and in Ireland, was introduced by these *Scoti*. In addition, from the 6th century Irish missionaries, following St Columba's foundation of his abbey on Iona, spread into Pictland, particularly into the north. Ultimately the *Picti* and the *Scoti* were united under Kenneth MacAlpin, who became king of a united kingdom known as Alba.

SETTLEMENT AND FARMING

There is little difference in Fife in settlement patterns between the post-Roman phase and the previous era and many families presumably continued to live on the same farms as before in houses set among their fields. Many early farm sites can be recognised from the air and it is also probable that old-established Fife farms are on the same sites as predecessor Pictish farms, often on south-facing sites, beside high quality farmland. Until systematic excavations have been carried out detailed knowledge of Pictish houses will remain elusive, however. So far, only two settlements in Fife have been excavated, at Easter Kinnear and Hawkhill. The chosen sites were selected for several reasons and because the farmer had shown great interest in the numerous large green 'circles' in his ripening grain fields, visible from the hill above the farm and from the air. Most importantly, as well as the circular cropmarks, several were of a form not previously examined anywhere. Unusually, they appeared to be sub-rectangular or square with rounded corners and on air photographs a thin line, suggestive of a ditch could be seen around these. The Scottish Field School of Archaeology was working in north-east Fife and excavated these sites as well as researching the early documentary background of the Kinnear estate which, therefore, became the focus of research for several years.

The lands of Easter Kinnear lie on a well-drained gravel ridge sloping down to the west bank of the Motray Water. Two areas were selected for study. In 1989 one site was excavated east of the modern farm of Easter Kinnear and in 1990, a second excavation took place, in the adjacent field, at Hawkhill. The Easter Kinnear site was a single, large sub-rectangular structure, with revetted dry-stone walls set in a scoop or hole, dug in the ground, thus presumably forming an underground store, or cellar. The structure measured 12 m east–west, 10.5 m north–south and it survived to 1.1 m below the subsoil. No floor or associated features were found inside the structure, which had been filled up with soil, to allow for rebuilding on the surface. The date for this structure is not known, but a hearth built in the partly in-filled remains has been radiocarbon dated to the late 6th to early 7th century and the structure must have gone out of use and been infilled by that date.

It has been suggested that this scooped structure was used for underground storage, presumably of grain from the surrounding fields, but perhaps also for meat and dairy products. A timber building had originally stood over the walls. It appears to have fallen down or been destroyed and the underground chamber was deliberately filled in. Subsequently, a series of up to five buildings was constructed on the same site, all of similar dimensions as the original remains, but now with associated surrounding ditches. Some of the wooden buildings, which had been built of wattle and daub, were burned down. Radiocarbon dates of the mid-6th to 7th centuries were again recorded from charcoal samples. Few artefacts were found during the excavation, but fragments of disused querns, of a type that went out of use during the early centuries AD had been incorporated into the revetting walls of the structure. There was a lack of other finds, except 12th-century pottery, which was recovered only in the plough soil. This implies that the presumed cellar and its timber houses had been abandoned by the 11th or 12th centuries.

At Hawkhill, in the field adjacent to the first site, a series of four similar scooped structures with revetted stone walls was uncovered. One of these was slightly smaller than that at Easter Kinnear, but was built in the same way. It, however, had a sloping ramp entrance passage, with a stone threshold, where presumably there had been a door. The floor of this chamber was roughly paved, but there was no trace of a hearth. This structure had been deliberately in-filled and not reused. However, partly over the in-filled underground structure, a complex set of remains representing more than one building was uncovered. Finally, a rectangular structure was built, 10 m by 4 m, with straight stone walls, although only traces survived. This building has been interpreted as the remains of a Medieval long-house of perhaps the 12th to 15th centuries. Finds at Hawkhill, as at Easter Kinnear, were mainly residual stone quern fragments, although at Hawkhill a whetstone, part of a stone lamp and a spindle whorl were also found. An iron knife and part of a bronze pin from Easter Kinnear were in such poor condition that they could not be used for dating. Few animal bones were recovered and other artefacts, including pottery sherds, were mainly residual from earlier periods. The paucity of finds has been taken to suggest that these were not high status buildings but were used for storage purposes, probably for grain and other products.

In concluding this summary of these two Pictish domestic sites, mention should be made of their contemporary environment. The burnt fragments of twigs and various seeds recovered suggest that the site lay close to rich woodland, with oak, hazel, birch, willow and alder, these latter presumably from the bank of the nearby burn. Pollen of grassland plants suggest open land as well as arable, finds of grain showed that barley and wheat were grown. Seeds of bramble and raspberry, as well as a bulbil of sand leek, somewhat similar to but milder than garlic, offer hints of food. Traces of heather and peat were too few for detailed interpretation, but it is possible these materials were used for thatch or perhaps for draught-proofing woven lath walls. Future research using air photographs will undoubtedly reveal more domestic sites, similar to the two summarised above, as well as other building types that may be attributed to the Picts.

The 6th- to 7th-century sites at Easter Kinnear and Hawkhill may be the earliest Pictish houses so far identified in Fife, but numerous other sites are known from air photographs and from place names, although the latter are of later, probably 9th-century date. Names with *pit-* are compound and have long been recognised as of Pictish origin; they are found throughout Fife as well as the rest of Pictland. *Pit-* seems to indicate a share of land, usually in a well-drained location, often south-facing and is usually descriptive, as in Pitliver, 'share of the book', Pittencrieff, 'share of the tree', or Pittenweem, 'share of the cave'. In all these examples the second element is Gaelic in origin. The shares, or farms, seem not to be large and many names imply subdivision of an original farm, as in the Angus Pitmedden, 'middle share'. Research into most aspects of place names and archaeological study is in the early stages, but it is possible that taken with the evidence of small farmers at Easter Kinnear, the *pit-* names may represent the settlements of ordinary people working the land, while the Gaelic second element of the names, which are often personal or descriptive words, may be a sign of increasing integration of the Picts and the Scots by the 9th century. A Gaelic word, *bal-*, meaning a small farm became common in the 9th century, sometimes interchangeably with the *pit-* element, perhaps an indication that *pit-* and *bal-* had a similar meaning.

POWER CENTRES

As well as farms there seem also to have been defended sites. The key sites in Fife seem to have been Clatchard Craig, East Lomond, and possibly Norman's Law and Dunearn. Although the excavations at Clatchard Craig were limited, evidence was found for at least one of the ramparts being ruinous by the 8th century AD, with Dark Age artefacts scattered on the nearby ground. These included clay moulds and other metalworking finds earlier in date than the remains of a probably Medieval rectangular building which overlay the area where many of these finds were uncovered. The clay moulds had been broken to release the objects. This has been interpreted as evidence for metalworking, although the actual working areas were not found. The moulds were for penannular brooches of various types and sizes, for several styles of pins as well as rings and other ornaments, all personal items of which the penannular brooches are of 8th-century forms and are the first recovered from southern Pictland. In the far north St Ninian's Isle, Shetland, and Birsay, Orkney, are two sites where comparable objects have been recorded. Other finds included iron-working slag, a silver ingot, fragments of 5th-century glass, a glass bead and sherds of imported pottery, known now as E-ware. The few sherds of this type of pottery known at present in Scotland are all from high status Dark Age forts, but this distribution pattern could be modified if more excavations were carried out. In her report of the excavations and related finds at Clatchard Craig, Close-Brooks suggests that the upper fort, with the personal finds seems to have had a domestic focus, while the sheep, pigs and cattle were kept on the lower slopes, within the outer enclosure walls. While such uses have often been proposed, this is a rare opportunity to relate the suggestion to actual finds, and, of course future excavations should clarify spatial activities within other forts of the period.

One factor all of these Fife forts have in common, and share with similar sites elsewhere, is that the latest periods of construction utilised the highest part of the hill, on which a comparatively small citadel was built. This can be seen particularly well on Norman's Law, East Lomond and Dunearn Hill. Lack of excavation at these sites means lack of information. We do not know whether these were tribal centres, designed to be seen more than to guard, whether they were for ceremonial or religious use or as meeting places for fairs and trading. We assume they were forts in a defensive sense because of the ramparts and the location on hilltops, but at present there is little evidence for warbands or their weapons. We also lack evidence for the tribal territories associated with these forts, although the forts overlook agricultural land and must surely have been significant centres for the local population. The only other fort in Fife to have produced an unequivocal Pictish find is East Lomond, where a stone was found with a Pictish bull incised on it.

CARVED STONES

Carved stones have been found all over Pictland, with a small number in the west and in the Hebrides. They have always been the most recognisable legacy of the Picts, the most discussed and the least understood in detail. For convenience of discussion Pictish carved stones have been classified in three sets, Class I, Class II and Class III, but a few do not fit into this classification. The Classes are roughly chronological groupings, although some decorative symbols may be found on stones of more than one class. Normally Class I stones are unshaped boulders and the symbols, which are not Christian, have been cut or incised into the surface. Class II stones are trimmed to shape, often with symbols incised on one face and a Christian cross with interlace decoration in relief on the other. Class III stones are normally also shaped but the Pictish symbols have been abandoned, although the same carving styles and interlace detail were still used. Old Testament scenes were often used and more sophisticated interlace decoration is on the crosses.

The meaning of the symbols on the Class I incised stones is not known, though they are beautifully designed and expertly cut, but apparently randomly placed. They are thought to have been grave-markers, meeting places or boundary stones, among other interpretations. Some, presumably, had (pagan) religious or ritual significance, but what the symbols and their sites meant to people at the time of their erection is not known. Class I stones have been dated to the 5th–6th centuries, but some could be even earlier. Most commonly a stone has two or more distinct symbols, abstract designs, including rectangular and circular forms, double disc and Z-rod and crescent and V-rod. Other symbols seem to be representational, for example, incised bulls, deer, eagles, salmon and serpents. The so-called elephant or Pictish beast is mythical, with remarkable consistency of form wherever it occurs. Representations of artefacts include items such as mirrors, combs, hammers, anvils and pincers. These identifications and all the interpretations are modern, partly to aid discussion, but also as part of the efforts to understand them.

SYMBOL STONES OF FIFE

The catalogue of Class I stones from Fife is limited but to these should be added the graffiti on the walls of the Wemyss Caves and the symbols on some of the silver from the Norrie's Law hoard. One stone, originally at Lindores, incised with abstract symbols, including a crescent and V-rod and a mirror, is now housed at Abdie Kirk. A fragmentary stone from Walton Farm, Cults, is clearly from a large slab; it has a bird's head above a possible mirror symbol. This is an interesting find spot, as it is fairly close to the Roman Camp of Edenwood. Another stone, found at Westfield Farm, Strathmiglo, carved with two symbols, including a long-necked deer with spiral terminals, has been moved recently to outside the graveyard of Strathmiglo Church. Two other fragments from Westfield have abstract designs; they are now at Falkland Palace. Another, which can be included with Fife examples now stands at the foot of Abernethy Tower, close to the Fife border.

The stone from the East Lomond Hill and that from Newton of Collessie are the remaining examples. These Class I stones are from a restricted geographical area in central Fife and none has been found to the west or to the east. The stones are all different, exhibiting the broad range of symbols, but two stand out, one from Collessie and the other from East Lomond Hill. The Collessie stone is particularly important since it represents a human figure and it is one of the few still in the field, although not exactly *in situ*. It fell over and its site was excavated before the stone was re-erected. There was no indication of its purpose, although on air photographs probable Pictish square barrow graves have been identified in the same field. The carving depicts a tall, thin man, with a prominent nose and large ears, apparently clean shaven and with short hair. He is carrying a shield and spear and beside the figure is a horseshoe design. As with most Pictish figures the man appears to be wearing pointed shoes, but detail on the stone is faint and there can be no certainty, any more than with the subject of his dress – or lack of it, but a break in the incised line of his forward leg could represent the end of a trouser or legging.

A CULT CENTRE

The incised bull on the East Lomond stone is simpler and more natural than other similar carvings, such as those from Burghead, in Morayshire, perhaps because it is of earlier date. The bull has a long extended tail and heavy thighs, the muscles picked out simply, without the prominent Burghead curls. His hooves are not shown in detail, as if the design was not entirely finished. This stone was found on the ground within the fort, but not during an excavation, and it may be assumed that it had lain there since the hill-fort was abandoned. Burghead, where six bull carvings survive and there were many more originally, has been interpreted as a cult centre or shrine and it is feasible that East Lomond Hill could also have been a cult or tribal centre. Other such centres could have existed in the caves on the Fife coast, which were in use regularly from early times. Among these the Wemyss Caves have particular significance because of the carvings on the walls. Not all of the Wemyss Caves are accessible now but Jonathan's Cave is the easiest to visit, with a large number of identifiable Pictish designs. A range of abstract figures, including double discs, arches, rectangular shapes and a fleur de lys are incised on one wall, along with fish, birds, a lion and other less intelligible designs. A boat with oarsmen on the opposite wall may be Pictish, but could be earlier or later, as its date of carving is not known. Later additions to the suite of carvings include several crosses and related designs.

INTRODUCTION OF CHRISTIANITY

One Fife stone, known as the Skeith Stone, at Kilrenny, differs from all others in southern Pictland. It sits beside a path, on the highest point of a relatively flat field, about 30 m above sea level, and is possibly in its original position, although it could represent the replaced top half of a broken slab. This stone bears a large circle in relief on one face and within the circle, also in relief, is an equal-armed Maltese-style cross. This cross has a *chi-rho* sign to the right of the top, only recently recognised and similar to those from the south-west of Scotland, around the Whithorn area. The *chi-rho* is a symbol of the early church and this stone at Kilrenny may be the earliest identifiable indication that a missionary monk had brought Christianity to Fife from the British Church at Whithorn. In that area it would be dateable to the 5th–6th centuries. Around Kilrenny church a large enclosure ditch, extending well out into the fields to the west, is an interesting recent discovery. The Skeith Stone lies outside the enclosure, but it is on the approach track, leading into the enclosure. This has provided a context for the Skeith Stone, for the church at Kilrenny itself and for recently discovered fragments of another cross slab. The present, and perhaps an earlier church, is situated on an ideal site for an early church, on a low promontory, on a bend above a deeply cut burn. The enclosure could be the remains of an early monastic site of the British Church.

A change in the carved stones all over Pictland provides evidence that missionaries of the Church were at work, from the 6th century, while south of the Forth there were influences from Northumbria as well as from Whithorn. In Fife the Class I carved stones gave way to stones with Pictish symbols on one face and a decorated cross on the other. These are Class II stones, serving a dual purpose, partly to introduce Christianity and probably to maintain some aspects of the old religion as a means of conversion. The stones combine Pictish symbols with cross designs, the most important symbol of all for Christians and are generally attributed to the 8th century. Sometimes a Class I stone was modified with the addition of a cross on its other face. At others both faces seem to have been carved as a holistic design. Unlike the unshaped Class I stones, these sandstone slabs were selected for their fairly regular flat surfaces and they were trimmed to a rectangular form. An often elaborately detailed, equal-armed cross set on a shaft, sometimes with a base stone in outline was carved on one face of the slab. The entire cross was completed with intricate interlace panels, a design which seems to have come from the west, Ireland and Iona, although there crosses were free-standing and not on a slab. While the cross was heavily ornamented so too was the background of the rest of the slab. At first the spaces beside the shaft and in the upper corners were filled with animals straight from the Class I repertoire. Later, interlace decoration was employed to emphasise these carvings. Initially the carving was incised, but later the technique changed and the design was carved in relief; occasionally, both techniques were used. Often a frame around the outer edge showed the original thickness of the stone and how much was cut away as the cross and other patterns were carved.

Although Fife has relatively few Class II stones and no two are alike all fit the general pattern. The Largo Stone, of local rich dark red sandstone, has been broken and mended and has been under a shelter at Largo Church for some years. Carved in relief on one face is the outline of a high base and shaft, surmounted by an elaborate equal-armed cross with square hollows at the armpits and an encircling ring. Only faint traces of interlace survive on the lower arm of the cross and the top of the shaft, but initially it would have been completely covered in interlace. To the right of the cross-shaft intertwined sea-horses can just be made out, but the remainder of the carving is too faint to see. On the other face of the slab is that favourite of Pictish stone carvers, three horsemen with hounds; a double disc and Z-rod and a Pictish beast interrupt the flow of the design. Not far from Largo was the Scoonie Stone; now incomplete this stone is in the Royal Museum of Scotland. It is also a slab, beautifully carved. Sadly, the cross in relief on one face is now indecipherable, but the scene on the other side is still sharp. Part of a large, incised Pictish beast survives at the top of the stone, with a hunting scene below. The horses and riders are depicted in intricate detail, with hounds and a magnificent stag. Near the base of the stone is a small incised cross, possibly an addition of later date. An inscription in ogam, an early form of writing, translated as 'Ethernon', has been cut down the edge of the stone. The vertical base-line of the inscription lightly crosses the stag's muzzle but appears to respect its raised front leg. Below this the third horse's head abuts the lettering. The impression is that the hunting scene and the ogam were contemporary but, as in many other cases, this cannot be shown conclusively. Two recently discovered fragments of a carved stone are on display in Crail Museum. One fragment is of the upper arms of the cross and the other is part of the shaft. Rich interlace decoration fills the cross, and a spiral terminal completes the design on one fragment. To the right of the shaft on the other fragment, also in relief, is a dog-like animal. Originally from Kilrenny, the fragments survive from a large ringed-cross slab, which seems to have been broken up many years ago to use as building stones. As the stone had been split at that time the other face does not survive and there is no indication of what could have been carved there.

Theories abound about these stones, but, as in the rest of Pictland, the symbols of the old regime or religion were eventually displaced by the Christian symbol of the cross that filled such a prominent place on many Class II stones. In Fife these stones were all found in coastal locations. It has often been claimed that the Picts in Fife lived away from the coast, but they certainly set up their first Christian stones in coastal areas.

SUPREMACY OF THE CHURCH

Class III stones were carved from the 10th century, by which time the early Pictish symbols had been completely abandoned and the Christian cross was the only symbol, although the interlace infill continued in use and Biblical as well as hunting scenes still occurred. A number of these later stones survive in Fife, mainly in coastal locations as with the Class II stones, and there are two large groups of stones, at Abercromby and at St Andrews, which represent a significant development and sophistication in carving and content.

An important Class III stone is on private land at Mugdrum, near Newburgh in north Fife. Unlike most of the Fife stones this one survives to 3.5 m tall and is a free-standing cross. Its west face has lost its carving because of wind erosion, but the east face has survived better and neat, small panels of horsemen can be seen with three deer and three dogs in the lowest panel. Scrolled vines have been carved up the sides. Unfortunately there is nothing to indicate what the top of the cross looked like, but the shape of the shaft and its height suggest a free-standing cross similar to examples from the west of Scotland and Ireland. Although the horsemen indicate that the Mugdrum Stone may have wider connections, the design of the carved panels is clearly

Pictish. Remains of another free-standing cross is the Dogton Stone, which still stands on its original base, in a sloping field a short distance north of the River Ore, some 8 km from the coast at Kirkcaldy and one of only two not found near the coast. A third, now in the Cathedral Museum at St Andrews was dug up in the graveyard at Dunino.

The Sauchope Stone, from a farm on the coast to the east of Crail, has been re-erected in the Victoria Gardens, Crail. Both faces of this stone have an outlined frame and, although the designs are now faint, panels of horsemen can be seen on the front in bright, raking morning sunshine, while on the other face, in mid-afternoon sunlight, an undecorated ringed cross can be seen, standing on a base, with animals flanking the shaft. Another stone, from Inverkeithing, now lost, had panels of horsemen on one face and a cross on the other, perhaps not dissimilar in concept from the Sauchope Stone. Other stones have been found, two on Inchcolm Island, including a hogback tomb which, unusually, is carved with a cross integral with the design. A heavily-decorated, but worn, stone is in Crail Church.

Two collections of stones complete the catalogue of carved stones from the early Christian Church in Fife. One group of five small fragments has been built into the 13th-century church at Abercromby, a mile inland from St Monans. Some stones have crosses without decoration but with interlace on the sides and filling the background behind the cross, while another is a complicated, undecorated cross, perhaps unfinished, since there are empty panels around the cross. Only one stone in this group includes figurative elements, with two animals resembling a lion and a boar above a man.

The second collection of stones is at St Andrews and, like those from Abercromby, includes a number built into a later church, in this case into the foundations of the Cathedral. Others were found in excavations at the chapel of St Mary on the Rock. For the most part the stones are Class III, with interlace decoration of extremely high quality and little figurative work. The number of stones alone implies an important and long-lived clerical community. Fragmentary documentary information shows its longevity and importance, all prior to the building of any of the known buildings on Kinrimond, 'the head of the king's ridge, or muir'. In an age when writing was reserved for church use and when historical events were recorded almost by chance, the first reference to the monastery at Kinrimond is to AD 747, when the death of the Abbot, Tuathalan, was recorded in Irish Annals. Clearly the monastery had been established some time before this date and there is no indication that Tuathalan was the first abbot, merely that he was of sufficient importance for the information to be conveyed to Ireland. This offers a context for the 8th-century St Andrews Sarcophagus, a magnificently-carved stone coffin, on display in the Cathedral Museum at St Andrews. Although in the form of a stone shrine, of which two sides and part of a third survive, together with three corner posts, the decoration on the sarcophagus resembles that on the carved stones found elsewhere in Fife, although it is more elaborate. The corner posts with slots for the side panels are richly ornamented with finely detailed interlace, as is the cross on one end, where there are insets with opposing carved bosses and animals and a central boss. On the main panel of the sarcophagus a large, royal figure is depicted rending the jaws of a lion, a smaller figure, on foot, represents a shepherd, while the third, also a royal figure, on horseback is portrayed as a hunter, defending himself against a lion. These figures are interpreted as the Old Testament king, David, involved in important kingly activities, appropriate to the patron who commissioned the carving and the sarcophagus. The theme of David occurs on a number of Pictish stones throughout Pictland, but this is the finest example.

The superior carving on the sarcophagus is a reflection of the sculptor's technical skill and detailed knowledge of Old Testament themes. The sculptor and his patron must surely both have seen illustrations of these themes either in manuscripts or on religious artefacts. Such models would have been available at Bede's monastery at Jarrow in Northumbria, in Iona and in Ireland, for example. European courts may also have been visited and could have provided source material for the ideas, but the skills of the sculptor were rooted in Pictish tradition and especially in his understanding of animals and the natural world. We do not know who commissioned the sarcophagus, but Isabel Henderson, in her recent study of the sarcophagus has shown that Oengus, son of Fergus, who died in 761, is a candidate.

PICTISH BURIALS

Burials of pagan Picts have been difficult to recognise in the landscape and only recently have sites been discovered which are comparable with those recognised as Pictish in northern Pictland. At Garbeg, Inverness, for example, a cemetery of small low cairns or barrows, some square, others round, with a slight ditch around have been shown to be Pictish; one cairn utilised a symbol stone in its construction. Another such site, also with a symbol stone as a cover slab, was excavated some years ago at Dunrobin, Sutherland, while only in 1999 a substantial cemetery of this type was excavated near Red Castle in Angus. Aerial photographs have shown a number of similar sites in Fife, some in large groups, others apparently single and no doubt further examples will be found in future sorties. Several such square barrows have been identified in the same field as the Collessie stone, for example, and there are others in the vicinity of the excavated houses at Easter Kinnear. Dates for these sites are few at present, but as more sites are excavated these barrows probably will be found generally to predate and to overlap with long cists. This seems to be the case for a group of square and round cairns excavated some years ago at Lower Largo, for which newly published radiocarbon dates fall in the 4th and 5th centuries.

THE EARLY CHURCH AND LONG CISTS

Although the monastery at Kinrimond was established by the 8th century, there are indications that the Church was active in Fife from a much earlier date. Burials of individuals without grave goods in graves lined with stone slabs, known as long cists, have been found in East Lothian and around the Fife and Angus coasts. Others have been found to the north, but the majority of such burials are from this eastern zone. For the first time large numbers of individuals were buried close together, in long cists, lying approximately east to west and with their heads at the west. This is distinctly different from pagan burials, which may be accompanied by grave goods, but rarely show close conformity in layout or orientation. The long cist cemeteries vary from half a dozen cists through to many hundreds. Evidence is generally lacking for association with a church or chapel, but in Fife several sites seem to have such an association. At the Hallow Hill, where a mixture of earlier graves was uncovered among some 130 long cists surviving from possibly an original 400–500 burials, there was slender evidence of a small structure that has been interpreted as a chapel or early church. Support for this was found in a 'lost' place name, *eglesnamin* meaning the 'church of the saint' or the 'church of the old shrine'. Another site where long cists and an early church were found is Mare's Craig, opposite Clatchard Craig. A Celtic bell was found there, lending credence to the idea that this was an important early church site. In the vicinity of Kinrimond there could have been at least one, or perhaps two early foundations, as two small long cist cemeteries are known from the St Leonard's College site. St Bonoc's Church lay immediately west of the present church at Leuchars and associated with this early church was a long cist cemetery. Dates for a number of the burials at the Hallow Hill fell almost entirely within the 7th century, and other dated examples appear to be of approximately similar date. No Pictish stone has been found in association with long cists in Fife, another reason for concluding that long cists are of Christian origin.

CONCLUSION

In conclusion, as Fife approached the end of the 1st millennium AD, life for the majority of the people had not changed a great deal. As place-name evidence implies, there were incoming settlers from among the *Scoti*, on present evidence from Dal Riata, but possibly directly from Ireland, inferred perhaps from by the influx of Gaelic place names in Fife, particularly *Bal-* names. The work of the church should not be forgotten. There could have been some earlier influence from the British Church of south-west Scotland. Moreover, the contact with Irish missionaries, following Columba had been extremely influential. There must have been sculptors willing and able to create the wealth of carved stones. Pilgrims were already travelling to St Andrews and there were traders, too, as implied by foreign finds from excavated sites.

The importance of Fife in national developments from this time lies outside the remit of this chapter, but the importance of St Andrews, which had become the principal church in the country ensured continuing wealth and prosperity. The political climate was changing. By the 9th century the integration of the Pictish and Dalriadic royal families through dynastic marriages had reached the point where, in AD 847 Kenneth MacAlpin, already king of Dal Riata, became king also of Pictland. This political union of Scots and Picts continued the integration that had been taking place for years and brought together the original tribes who had occupied the country from before the Roman period. It is often claimed that the Picts disappeared, but the common language and background of Picts and Scots seems only to have led to the loss of the nickname *Picti*. This was more than a tribal amalgamation. It represented the formation of the first Scottish State.

SIX

FROM THE WAR OF INDEPENDENCE TO THE UNION OF THE CROWNS

Late 13th-century Scotland has been dubbed the 'Golden Age', and Fife enjoyed the benefits of these decades of peace wrought during the reigns of Alexander II and Alexander III. Church foundations flourished and the Fife estates of the feudal barons and prelates who were representatives within the Community of the Realm prospered. Yet Fife was to witness directly the tragedy that was to plunge Scotland into a spiral of violent decline. On 19 March 1286, Alexander III, the last of Scotland's Celtic kings, fell to his death from the cliffs above Pettycur Bay Sands on Fife's shores of Forth on his way to join his wife Yolande de Dreux at Kinghorn Castle. Adding tragedy to disaster, Alexander's heir Margaret 'The Maid' of Norway died aged four on her sea journey from Norway. Scotland's throne now became open for competition amongst 13 claimants. Scenting the main chance, Edward I of England chose John Balliol, ingloriously nicknamed 'Toom Tabard' (empty surcoat), as King of Scots in 1292. This followed the protracted competition that had rejected the only other serious contenders, John Hastings, great-grandson of David, Earl of Huntingdon, and Robert Bruce, Earl of Annandale. The consequences of this choice were to be reflected in Fife.

By the 13th century, Fife had two locational focal points: St Andrews and Dunfermline. This meant that Fife evolved from the Middle Ages into political, economic and commercial alignments north-east to south-west around these burghs. Both had become prominent and prosperous through the presence of holy corporeal relics; those of the Apostle and Martyr Andrew of Bethsaida in Galilee at St Andrews, and the remains of Margaret, educator and social reformer, queen of Malcolm II, King of Scots. Malcolm had made Dunfermline his capital, and Robert I, the Bruce, recognised Dunfermline as a burgh dependent on the Benedictine abbey, which had given it birth, around 1320. As time passed Dunfermline assumed all the obligations due to a royal burgh and was admitted to the Convention of Royal Burghs in 1555 and to the Scots Parliament in 1549. St Andrews developed from its settlement around the Celtic monastery to its status of chartered burgh of the Anglo-Norman Bishop Robert some time between 1140 and 1150, to become the ecclesiastical capital of Scotland until the Reformation. Its university of 1410–12 enhanced its status and influence.

In many ways the history of these two locations was the history of Scotland in the Middle Ages, for by the 13th century the influence of the clerics of Fife, for instance, was well established in Christendom. Fife was the hub of an episcopal diocese that stretched from the eastern borders with England at the Tweed, to the Dee at Aberdeen; with an expanse towards Stirling in the west. The diocese (of St Andrews) was exempt from metropolitan authority (although that of the archdiocese of York always claimed superiority) and functioned at the direct mandate of Rome. The status of the diocese in particular and Fife in general was enhanced when Pope Sixtus IV elevated the diocese into an archdiocese on 13 August 1472.

Following Edward I's brutal sacking of Scotland's largest port burgh of Berwick-upon-Tweed in March 1296, John Balliol renounced his homage to the English king. The English army marched north and on 27 April the Scots army of the seven earls was defeated at Dunbar, and the English continued to Elgin almost unopposed. On their way back Edward I entered Fife and visited the region's key locations of St Andrews and Dunfermline. He is known to have crossed into Fife at Abernethy, and via a visit to the abbey of the French Benedictine order of Tiron at Lindores, he progressed to St Andrews, thence by Markinch to Dunfermline. Here he made clear to Scots nobles that the nation was ruled from Wick to Berwick by the writ of John de Warenne, Earl of Surrey and Lieutenant of Scotland, and Hugh Cressingham, Treasurer of Scotland.

During the period 1296–1318, which historians dub the years of English Occupation and Scottish Recovery, the English royal house held the castles of St Andrews, Cupar and Crail which were most puissant during 1296–1306. Until the Scots re-took Berwick in April 1318, the English crown administered Fife through the already existing structure of keepers and lieutenants. The burden of administration of Fife during English overlordship fell upon the Chancellor and Chamberlain at Berwick, a stronghold held as a source of troops for the military rule and supplies to back up the martial infrastructure.

Fife was to be represented in the title *Comes de Fyf* (Earl of Fife) from the days of Malcolm III who intended the earldom to be an appanage to the Crown; that is a provision for maintenance of the monarch's younger child. Specific lands such as Ramornie, in Kettle parish, Largo in its eponymous parish, Mountquhanie, in Kilmany, as well as Auchtermuchty, and castles like Myrecairnie, in Kilmany, and Denmiln, in Abdie parish, formed a part of the extensive territory and possessions of the earls. The first to be so named in extant documents was Dufagan who, in 1114, signed the charter for the foundation of the abbey of the Augustinian canons at Scone. The title persisted until 1425 when its holder Murdoch, son of Robert, 2nd Duke of Albany, was executed by the command of James I. The title was attained and not revived in the medieval period. Nevertheless in 1567 James Hepburn, 4th Earl of

Bothwell, was created Marquis of Fife and Duke of Orkney; by December 1567 he had been attained and his titles and estates were forfeit. It is interesting to note that when James VI decided to marry Anne of Denmark in 1589, he proposed to bestow upon her the 'morrowing' (pre-nuptial) gift of 'the Erldome of Fyff, wt the palice and castell of Falkland'.

Local regional control was enacted in Fife through the sheriffdoms with the nuclei of power being again at St Andrews, Cupar and Crail. Cupar Castle, which once stood on the eminence of School Hill, was one of the strongholds of the Thanes of East Fife since the 12th century, and there was access to the sea from the port on the water of the Mottray Burn. Edward I secured the castle and the port in 1296, and his son the Prince of Wales (later Edward II) occupied it in 1303. There had been confirmed royal property at Crail since the days of David I; this Edward I seized along with its trading revenues. The local landowners did homage to Edward, including Isabel de Vesci, who on 29 December 1296, had lands in the area restored to her by Edward. At St Andrews Edward occupied the castle which had been founded in 1200 by Bishop Roger de Beaumont. When Edward revisited St Andrews in 1303–4 he caused the castle to be refurbished with royal chambers, and the building remained in the hands of the English until 1305.

During his first visit to Fife in 1291, Edward received the four sheriffs of Fife at Dunfermline Abbey, where he quartered his troops; here the sheriffs acknowledged him 'as over and immediate Lord of the Kingdom of Scotland, and made fidelity, and swore, some of them upon the high altar of the Abbey, and some in the Chapter'. He extracted the same 'superiority' on Balliol's defiance, and in 1303–4 he fired the monastery at Dunfermline as a warning against incalcitrance.

Fife's Medieval sheriffs had bases at the 'royal castles', and theoretically were the heads of the district administration. Responsibility for the military organisation of the area was also amongst the sheriffs' duties. Castles had to be kept in repair and local lairds were pressed to keep in readiness their quotas of armed men for future requirements. The training of these men was monitored by the sheriffs at *wappenschawings*. Sheriffs also had to oversee the collection of 'crown monies'. To these were added the fines in the individual sheriff courts through which the sheriffs dispensed local rulings as administrators of civil and criminal justice, and that of their superior the Justiciar, the supreme legal head. Until the title was attained in 1425, the Earls of Fife held the rank of sheriff, with local barons as deputies; after the title's extinction the office of sheriff in Fife was made hereditary and was conferred on a Fife nobleman of superior rank. Thus for three hundred years the office was held by the Leslie family, Earls of Rothes.

Parliamentary representation for Fife is associated with the rise of the burgesses into the Third Estate of the Realm in the early part of the 14th century; before that Fife was represented by its diocesan bishops, abbots, priors and provosts. From the Great Council, held at Cambuskenneth Abbey, 15 July 1326, Fife was known to be represented at separate locations and from 1357 to 1603 there are named Members of Parliament for ten areas; Cupar, Anstruther Easter, St Andrews, Pittenweem, Inverkeithing, Kinghorn, Crail, Burntisland, Kirkcaldy and Dunfermline. From time to time the Scots Parliament was held in Fife. For instance, during the 1303–4 visit Edward I held a parliament of both nations and received homage from the leading Scots nobility and local lairds like Sir John de Randolfstoun (Randerston in Kingsbarns parish), at St Andrews and Dunfermline. While at St Andrews, Edward and his second wife, Queen Margaret, gave money for the embellishment of the reliquary arm of St Andrew at the cathedral whose shrine was always a point of call of royal peregrinations in Fife. In 1461 Mary of Guelders, the widowed queen of James II, gave an 'offering to the relics in the cathedral of St Andres x ss'. Such oblations to the relics of one who had supposedly walked with Our Lord was a powerful act of self-justification which kept Fife's pilgrim routes busy.

By the 12th century the hunting forests of Fife were well established, an early location being the *Cursus Apri Regalis*, the run of the royal wild boar. This parcel of land stretched from the precincts of the Augustinian Priory at St. Andrews to the village of Boarhills, then westward to include Cameron and Kemback, and the land south of the river Eden to within sight of Cupar. When Alexander I regranted the *Cursus* to the clerics of St Andrews he presented them with a pagan hunting artefact, a set of 16-inch boars tusks, which were fixed with silver chains to the altar of St Andrew. At Lindores the mitred abbots enjoyed their hunting forests, as did the Cistercian brother abbots at Balmerino; like local barons the abbatial lairds could mark off restricted areas for the hunt at will. By 1286 Cluny, in what was to be the parish of Kinglassie, was developed as a hunting forest land from the gift of the land to Dunfermline Abbey by Sybilla, Queen of Alexander I. The Earls of Fife, among others, feued this land for hunting down the centuries until in 1466 such favours were granted to the Wemysses of Rires. In 1538 James V united Cluny and its hunting runs to the barony of Pittenweem as a gift for services rendered in France by Patrick Wemyss of Pittencrieff.

Yet, it was to be at Falkland, ancient Kilgour, where the most famous of Fife's hunting grounds were sited. Certainly the policies of the Castle of Falkland, the precursor of the palace, was a hunting ground for the Macduff family, first as Thanes, and then as Earls, of Fife. Here they hunted both 'greater game' (red deer, roe deer, and boar) and 'lesser game' (fox, rabbit, wild cat, marten and hare) by the king's permission. In time the Macduffs let off 'herbage' or 'foggage' to tenants to rent, to graze cattle and fill a modest pot with fauna. Since the early years of Scottish land tenure the sovereigns of the day claimed forestry and hunting rights (mostly for 'greater game') over the whole of Scotland, and most tinkered with the Scots law, as did Edward I who tried to bring it into line with English law. At Freuchie, in Falkland parish, James II divided the lands amongst 12 proprietors with the proviso that they upkeep the hunting forests in good order and plant 'eschis, sauchis, aller, easp plane, and birk trees' and cultivate broom, lintseed and hempseed beyond their kitchen gardens. This proviso was repeated in charters up to the end of the 16th century.

Daily administration of hunting lands was in the hands of foresters, but royal forest law was enforced by local justiciars. At Falkland an interesting pattern of hunting administration was developed. In 1371 Isabel, Countess of Fife, resigned the family earldom to her brother-in-law Robert Stewart, Earl of Monteith (brother of King Robert III) and the castle of Falkland and its rich hunting grounds became a Stewart possession. Again, through the political machinations of the period the whole became Crown Property and by 1455 James II is describing his possession as a *palatium* rather than a *castellum*. It was under James IV, James V, Mary, Queen of Scots and James VI that the forests of Falkland were the most used for hunting, or the 'drives' as they were known. A large number of the sovereign's staff 'drove' the animals from the forests and hills into the path of the huntsmen.

The 'Forester of Falkland' was for centuries an important office within the Scottish Court, with the prerogatives of 'the deid timber' and those 'unrooted or cassin-doun by the wind'. Falkland still reflects the relics of the accommodation needed by the large numbers of retinue which came on royal visits, and the permanent staff of foresters, falconers, dog handlers, hostlers, and game bird tenders (some of the royal game birds were reared on the island of Inchkeith); the bird tenders were also taxed with the monitoring of Scotland's Game Laws, which from 1427 regulated the seasons in which wild fowl could be hunted. The hunting forests of Falkland ensured a regular progress of royal visits to Fife, and no more keen visitor was there than Mary, Queen of Scots, particularly during 1563–65. This sport she passed on to her son James VI who gave Falkland 'the acme of its glory' before he disappeared down the road to England. Some falconers rose to great prominence; one such was George Moncrieff, 'Master of the Hawks' to Prince Henry, son of James VI. Before he died in 1638, Moncrieff had established for himself (a now vanished) mansion at Reedie and lands at Layngswaird.

Down the centuries royal associations with Fife were further sustained through a pattern of residence, births, and land apportionments to heirs and supporters. Dunfermline was to be a favoured location for royal births and residence. For example, David II was born here in 1324 and his queen, Joanna, was a frequent resident as were Robert III and his queen Annabella; James I was born here in 1394, as was Elizabeth, Queen of Bohemia, in 1596, and Charles [later Charles I] in 1600, both offspring of James VI & I. At Inverkeithing tradition has it that Robert III's queen Annabella Drummond had her residence at the house known as 'The Inns', and here she died in 1406; the old mercat cross at Inverkeithing displayed her arms.

The north-east Fife seaboard parish of Leuchars offers examples of royal land acquisition and apportionment. Several Fife estates were variously forfeit to the Crown. John Comyn, 3rd Earl of Buchan, was declared traitor by Robert I, the Bruce, and his Leuchars estates, including the important port on the Mottray Burn, were divided amongst Bruce's supporters. At a later date Robert II gave the castle of Leuchars and its policies to his son Robert, Earl of Fife, and in 1497, James IV gave Earlshall and lands thereabouts to Sir Alexander Bruce. Nearby Brackmont had been given in 1372 by Robert II's wife, Euphemia of Ross, to her son David, Earl of Strathearn, as a 'fee' for protecting her castle at Lochleven.

During his 18 years' imprisonment in England, after he was captured by English buccaneers off Flamborough Head on 22 March 1406, James I was attended by one Robert Coxwell. When he returned to Scotland in 1424 James brought Coxwell with him and conferred a pension on him and a large part of the estates of Auchtermuchty, with Myres castle, which he held until his death in 1453. Because of its abutment to Falkland, Strathmiglo's land charters show royal favour too. Under James III the royal baker, Patrick Purdy, enjoyed land-rent privileges, transferred to the royal squire John Ramsay on Purdy's death in 1480. Further, as a condition that he kept St Andrews-born James III's navy in good repair, Sir Andrew Wood (d. 1515) received a long lease on property at Largo on 28 July 1477. Wood was to win fame as a courageous seaman with his repulsion of the English in 1481 and as commander of the royal vessel *Flower* in James IV's summer campaign in the Hebrides of 1495.

Fife was deemed a healthy location as well as the site of fine royal sport and entertainment. The apothecaries of Madeleine, first wife of James V, considered Balmerino 'as having the best airs of any place in the kingdom'. Although Madeleine died before she could enjoy the efficacy of the 'airs', James V and Mary, Queen of Scots, were able to enjoy the abbey's supposed salubrious environs regularly.

The county was also to see episodes of royal violence and court skulduggery. Robert, Duke of Albany, second son of Robert II, who held land at Rosyth and Leuchars was long denounced as murderer of his nephew Prince David, Duke of Rothesay. Sir Walter Scott was to make the supposed guilt of Albany an important plot skein in his *The Fair Maid of Perth*. It is averred that Albany starved to death his rival Rothesay at the castle of Falkland in 1402. Rothesay was given a magnificent funeral though, and interment in the choir of Lindores Abbey, where his cadaver lay undisturbed until the tomb was prised open by reforming hands in 1559.

In 1496 Fife was to witness aspects of an intrigue that was to bring 'long suffering' to Scotland. By the reign of James IV, 1488–1513, enmity between England and Scotland continued and James opened negotiations with Margaret, Duchess of Burgundy, sister of Edward IV. Margaret's court was a hive of Yorkist plotting and she had welcomed therein a strange royal pretender newly expelled from the court of Charles VIII, King of France. In 1492 Perkin Warbeck had appeared in Ireland and France calling himself Richard, Duke of York, son of Edward IV and claimant to the throne of Henry VII of England. It seems that Irish malcontents suggested that, because of the startling likeness of Warbeck to Prince Richard (who had supposedly been murdered in the Tower of London by the orders of Richard III) he should impersonate the prince. As an enemy of Henry VII, James IV of Scots took up his cause and sumptuously entertained him in Scotland. So taken with Warbeck was James IV that he installed him at Falkland palace for the greater part of 1496 and gave Warbeck his cousin Lady Catherine Gordon, daughter of the Earl of Huntly, in marriage.

Fife was one of the counties levied for a special tax to pay for the invasion of England in Warbeck's cause. James IV assembled his troops at Falkland, and commanded that the bakers of Strathmiglo prepare eight *chalders* (some eight quarters of grain) of bread at £2.82 for the army's sustenance at Falkland. The Scottish army was then mustered and marched into England. It was to be a rehearsal for the future disaster at Flodden Field. Warbeck's pretentions were rejected, particularly by Scotland's neighbour lairds in Northumberland, and the Scots army returned humiliated and James IV stung with his own credulity. Warbeck was executed for his presumptions in 1499.

A truce was now forged with England and James married Henry VII's daughter Margaret Tudor in 1503, a move which ultimately led to the Union of the Crowns, but years of suffering in Scotland were to intevene with a scattering of Fife bones as James IV, surrounded by the 'flower of Scottish manhood', fell to the swords and arrows of the army of Thomas Howard, Earl of Surrey, at Flodden Field on 9 September 1513. At Falkland Margaret Tudor received the widows of those who had fallen with the king like George, Earl of Rothes and Sir Michael Balfour of Mountquhanie. At St Andrews cathedral the mangled cadaver of James IV's illegitimate son Alexander Stewart, Archbishop of St Andrews, was interred by the Altar of the Relics.

Because of its important political and economic position in Scotland Fife was to see its fair share of public executions. A whole range of religious martyrdoms was enacted from Paul Craw's execution at St.Andrews in 1433 to that of Henry Forest in 1533. Yet, there was inspiration for the romantic balladeers too. The French poet and swaggering galliard Pierre de Boscose de Châtelard had arrived in Scotland in the entourage of Mary, Queen of Scots, in 1561. He formed an infatuation for her and secreted himself in her bedchamber at Holyrood. Discovered and admonished, Châtelard followed the queen to Fife on her visit of 1563 and once more secreted himself in her bedroom at Rossend Castle, Burntisland. This time he was deemed to have committed severe *lesé majesté* and was brought to trial at St Andrews; here he was executed for his ardour on 22 February 1563.

The name of Somerset was to be added to those feared in Fife. Already Edward Seymour (*c.* 1506–52), Earl of Hertford, now Duke of Somerset and Lord Protector on the death of Henry VIII, had caused Scottish anguish in his notorious campaigns of 1544 and 1545 within 'The Rough Wooing' of the infant Mary, Queen of Scots. From Fife's Forth coastline nervous Fifers had watched flames engulf Edinburgh and Leith, and in 1547 Somerset was back to order an attack on Fife, following the defeat of the Scots regent James, 2nd Earl of Arran, at the battle of Pinkie, east of Edinburgh. While Admiral Sir Andrew Dudley secured Dundee for Somerset, Vice-Admiral Thomas Wyndham, with a force of 300 infantry and harquebusiers attacked the Cistercian abbey of Balmerino on 25 December. Apprised of a possible attack, Abbot Robert and his chapter had secured guns (described in their charters as 'harquebusses of croke') and had formed a small mounted band of local tenants. Somerset's soldiers easily defeated the abbot's small force and the abbey was put to the torch. There followed the pillage and burning of neighbouring hamlets and stockyards and the purloining of 'a great deal of corn'.

Fife was to witness a microcosm of all the events, ideals, politics and economics of the Scottish Reformation. Yet the emotions stirred up in Fife had more to do with an anti-clericalism and outright secular greed for church assets than in a movement towards church reform or the expansion of protestant Lutheranism. Thus, active Protestantism had little effect in Fife as a whole, and seems to have been confined to a few county lairds and to the port burgh of St Andrews. It is true to say, however, that St Andrews with its university colleges was markedly involved in religious activity which spilled over after the death of the Lutheran preacher Patrick Hamilton on 29 February 1528. Once the Feast of the Faculty of Arts at St Andrews was an occasion to promote brotherly love and friendship. Yet, as it was celebrated with a sung Mass and an overtly religious procession, it was dispensed with in 1534 as confrontational for several collegiate fellows. By and large the students at the university looked on church reform as a good thing, but did not riot in its name. To most in Fife, by 1539 Protestantism was a hard to define doctrine outside the credo of the committed and the fanatical, and there was no mass grassroots network of 'heretics' against the Medieval Church. What stuck in the craw of the intelligent was the Medieval Church's use of idolatry, supposed (or trumped up) miracles, blackmail by excommunication, financial malfeasance and the sexual immorality and venality of the clergy.

During the Reformation, and the years immediately preceding the reformers' attacks and sackings of such abbeys as Lindores (1543 and 1559) and Balmerino (June 1559) and St Andrews cathedral (14 June 1559), many Fife-based noble families were directly involved in the foremost political events of the day. One politically motivated Fife landowner, who by political expediency achieved much economic gain, land tenure and title by backing the reform movement, was Henry Balnavis of Easter Collessie (then called Hallhill). A student at St Andrews and Cologne, Balnavis studied law. His prominence in court circles won him the position of Ordinary Lord of Session in 1538, a short while after James V's foundation of the College of Justice. Balnavis was Secretary of State under the regency of James Hamilton, 2nd Earl of Arran, but was dismissed from his post for his devotion to Protestantism. He became a close friend of John Knox and was an arch plotter in the assassination of Cardinal David Beaton, Archbishop of St Andrews, on 29 May 1546.

When the reformers surrendered the castle of St Andrews in 1547, Balnavis was taken to France as a prisoner, to be incarcerated at Rouen, and his estates at Auchtermuchty and Hallhill were forfeited to the Queen-Regent Marie de Guise-Lorraine. On his return to Scotland, Balnavis took up once more his proselytising of Protestantism and in 1563 was restored to the bench and regained his Fife estates as Lord Hallhill. His support of the Regent James Stewart, Earl of Moray, earned him more Fife lands at Letham. In 1575 he resigned as Lord of Session and died in 1579.

Of all Scotland's monarchs until the Union of the Crowns, the one with the highest profile in Fife was James VI, born 19 June 1566, son of Mary, Queen of Scots, and Henry Stewart, Lord Darnley. He was one year old when he ascended the throne of Scotland, and 36 when he assumed the throne of England. The charter chests of Fife were rich in the land and title privileges granted by James, who confirmed a wide range of established burgh prerogatives. An example was the granting of a new charter to Auchtermuchty on 28 October 1591; at the same time he set anew local feus and rents and reallocated grants of Crown lands to such as his court cup-bearer Sir David Murray (later Viscount Stormont) of Gospetry. James was also busy consolidating Crown properties in Fife, conferring upon his wife, Anne of Denmark, a huge portion of pre-Reformation ecclesiastical, and secular, land in Fife, as well as Dunfermline Abbey and its temporalities.

James VI's jealous rage over a matter concerning his queen brought another violent episode to Fife. The estate of Donibristle was the principal residence of James Stewart, Earl of Moray, the 'Bonnie Earl O'Moray' of ballad fame. At Donibristle House, on 7 February 1592, the Bonnie Earl, the darling of the Protestant cause, was murdered by George Gordon, Earl and Marquis of Huntly, the leader of the Roman Catholic party. The Bonnie Earl had earned the jealousy of the king; balladmongers linked the handsome Moray with the queen:

He was a braw gallant,
And he played at the glove.
And the Bonnie earl o' Moray,
Oh, he was the Queen's love.

All that, and Moray's association with the king's enemies, was enough to sign his death warrant.

Fife was to witness aspects of the witchcraft delusion that infected Scotland largely from the Protestant Reformation of 1559 to the Union of the Parliaments in 1707. In all this activity James VI was to be a keen student, producing his own prejudices against witchcraft in *Daemonologie* (1597). During the period 1542 to 1604, witchcraft cases were recorded in St Andrews, Dunfermline, Burntisland, Crail and Kirkcaldy. The *Rentale Sancti Andree* records how witches were brought frorn Dunfermline (and Edinburgh) in 1542 for trial, sentence and execution by burning at St Andrews castle. Until the end of the 16th century St Andrews was the main centre for witch prosecution of high and low with many a 'show trial'. In 1569 (records the *Historie and Life of King James the Sext*) Sir William Stewart, Lord Lyon King of Arms was tried before a civil court and hanged 'for dyvers poynts of witchcraft and necromancie'. While in 1572 James Melville records in his *Diary* that John Knox himself spoke out against 'the witch' Richard Bannatyne who was burned in this year.

The earliest case of Fife witchcraft recorded in the High Court of Judiciary of Scotland occurs in 1563, wherein Agnes Mullikine, alias Bessie Boswell, was 'banised and exilit for wichecraft'. The Presbyterian clergy of the coastal villages of Fife seem to have been particularly hypersensitive to the witchcraft delusion at this period. In Crail in 1599 the *Register of St Andrews Presbytery* records how the minister Andrew Duncan had one Geillis Gray taken from his custody accused of witchcraft to be 'torturit' by the laird of nearby Lathockar. At Kirkcaldy they were not quite so violent towards witchcraft suspects for the *Records of the Burgh of Kirkcaldy* cite in 1604 the case of Dorathie Oliphant a 'wagabond', who was condemned 'to stand at the Tron with a paper on her head' declaring her infamy as a witch before being banished from the town.

By and large the Medieval Church in Fife cared nought for supposed witches, and the county never had the like of the famous sustained witchcraft cases of 'The Aberdeen Witches' of 1597, or the 'North Berwick Witches', 1590–92. Yet as late as 1704 the 'Pittenweem Witches' case showed how the Church of Scotland bigotry fanned the flames of witch persecution for nigh on two hundred years.

When James VI removed his court to London, on the death of Queen Elizabeth I on 24 March 1603, many of his Fife retainers went with him, like his falconer George Moncrieff. James also recruited widely from his Fife lairds for his new dual court. Among those he chose were Sir William Anstruther of Easter Anstruther and Sir John Learmonth of Birkhill, who was appointed a Scots commissioner to organise the administration of the Union of the Kingdoms of 1604. He died in the same year as the king, 1625.

Further, several Fife exiles returned to their family estates to pursue new preferments. One of these was Sir Robert Aytoun, the poet, whose family controlled the properties of Souther Kinaldy, in Dunino parish. Aytoun was to become a prominent courtier as Gentleman of the Bedchamber and roving ambassador to European courts. He also served the monarch as Privy Councillor and retained court office until his death at the Palace of Whitehall in 1638.

Although St Andrews ceased to be the ecclesiastical capital of Scotland at the Reformation, and Edinburgh thereafter assumed its place of singular importance in the realm, Fife continued to retain a distinctive position within the mainstream of Scottish life up to and beyond the Union of the Crowns. During the years from the Wars of Independence, Fife had kindled a strong perception of local identity within Scotland; it was never to be extinguished.

SEVEN

FROM THE UNION OF THE CROWNS TO THE UNION OF THE PARLIAMENTS: FIFE 1603–1707

The period of just over a century between the two great turning-points in the history of early Modern Scotland was a time of prolonged revolution in all aspects of life in Fife. The nation-wide religious and political upheavals which had commenced in the mid-16th century rumbled on until 1689 and even then left a bitter legacy which haunted Scotland into the mid-18th century. Religious conflict and war, both civil and foreign, changed forever the complexion of national politics and the shape of Scottish political society at all levels. Rather than chart a chronological narrative through this century of discord and debate, this chapter focuses in turn upon the processes of religious, socio-political and economic restructuring which underlay, drove, or were driven by, the momentous developments in the political life of the kingdom as a whole.

THE CHURCH – PRIESTS AND PRESBYTERS

Central to the turbulence which characterises Scotland's history throughout the 17th century is religion.[1] Contrary to the popular view of a Reformation achieved by parliamentary decree in 1560, with Presbyterianism replacing the Medieval hierarchy, the structure of the reformed Kirk was not established until the 1690s. Support for Protestantism varied from region to region, with some among the upper nobility, who still provided leadership within their territories, adhering to Catholicism in the face of pressure from the Kirk. Within Fife, however, Reformation penetrated deeply and its Protestant noble and lairdly classes provided Presbyterianism with some of its most committed supporters. Here, too, the reorganised Kirk gained a firm footing, aided by the flow of highly educated, articulate and politicised graduates into the ministry. This new ministry emerged rapidly in the late 16th century as a rising professional class who, with the lairds and lawyers, effected a revolution within conservative Scottish society.[2]

The religious battle-lines of the 17th century originated in late 16th-century controversies. Ultra-Presbyterian zealots, like Andrew Melville, principal of St Andrews University, sought to exclude lay authority from ecclesiastical affairs.

The king, however, favoured episcopacy. He viewed bishops as essential for his management of both secular and ecclesiastical government. Between was a range of opinion which favoured, in general, Presbyterianism. Along with Edinburgh, Fife was a centre of religious radicalism, focused on St Andrews University. General Assemblies meeting in St Andrews, therefore, were dominated by Melvillians and the radical Fife ministry, who used this situation to resist royal policies. James circumvented this inbuilt opposition by moving assembly meetings to conservative centres, such as Dundee or Perth, and by the late 1590s had contained the ultra-Presbyterian threat. When he headed south in 1603, he left behind a Church in which episcopacy sat uneasily within an otherwise Presbyterian organisation. However, after 1606, when radical ministers encouraged riots in Edinburgh and James seized the opportunity to summon Melville to London where he was imprisoned in the Tower until 1611, the most vocal opposition to royal ecclesiastical policy was stifled.

James proceeded with his plans, in 1610 re-introducing diocesan bishops on the pattern of the Medieval episcopate. Beneath them, however, the Kirk maintained its post-Reformation organisation. A shift to more thorough-going Episcopalianism came in 1618 with the 'Five Articles of Perth' – observance of the main dates of the Christian year, the right to private communion and baptism, the introduction of kneeling at communion, and the introduction of confirmation by the bishops – all of which ran against the grain of the Presbyterian tradition. These were imposed at a time when James was also tinkering with the liturgy, the two episodes together uniting opposition to his religious policies. In Fife, half of the ministers rejected the changes and faced expulsion, but confrontation was avoided through the moderation of the Archbishop of St Andrews, John Spottiswoode. Nevertheless, there remained little enthusiasm for the new practices amongst the majority of the ministry, for whom the alternative to compliance was expulsion.

Spottiswoode faced an uphill struggle, even within Fife, to effect a general Episcopalian reconstruction of the Kirk. Resentment of the bishops' intrusion into lucrative and influential posts in government – Spottiswoode was chancellor from 1635 – alienated the consequently excluded nobility. Furthermore, until Charles I persuaded the Duke of Lennox to surrender the former estate of St Andrews priory and settled it on the archbishopric, he lacked the resources of his predecessors. His power and authority, although founded on the principle of episcopal hierarchy, therefore, depended entirely upon the king. Despite these handicaps, Spottiswoode was an energetic diocesan and strove to reconstruct the Kirk within his diocese. The changes in liturgy made this literally a physical reconstruction, as the layout of parish churches required adaptation to provide a liturgical east end for the celebration of the more elaborate communion rites. Spottiswoode led the way in this, building at Dairsie in 1621 what he intended to be a blueprint for rural parish church planning. The conscious medievalism of its Gothic revival design perhaps stressed religious continuity over the upheaval of the previous decades.[3]

Spottiswoode's limited achievements collapsed in 1637–8 in the backlash against Charles I's policies which coalesced into the Covenant. It is ironic that one of the men who framed that revolutionary document, Alexander Henderson, was minister of Leuchars, his church within sight of the archbishop's see. The overthrow of episcopacy was followed by a sustained effort through the 1640s to purge the Kirk of men whose doctrinal beliefs or lifestyle did not conform to the standards of the Covenanters and to fill vacancies with suitably qualified men. Amongst them was James Sharp, a regent in St Leonard's College at St Andrews, who enjoyed the patronage of both Henderson and the leading lay Covenanter, the Earl of Rothes.[4] With their support, he secured the backing of a third prominent Covenanter, John, 1st Earl of Lindsay, who held the patronage of Crail.

As minister of Crail, Sharp entered the ministry at a defining moment for the Kirk, as it and the traditional political leadership with which it had worked in partnership since 1638 parted company. The deciding issue was the Engagement, an agreement between the nobility and Charles I whereby in return for Scottish assistance in regaining control over England, the king would impose Presbyterianism there for a trial period of three years. To many in the Kirk, this was a betrayal of the Solemn League and Covenant of 1643, in which those same nobles had pledged to assist the English parliament against Charles in return for the establishment of Presbyterian church government in England. The Engagement was denounced by the General Assembly and when the Scottish army was defeated its failure was presented as Divine judgement on an ungodly act. Its moral authority boosted by this apparent vindication of its stance, the Kirk imposed punishments on the supporters of the Engagement and succeeded in a petition to parliament for an act abolishing lay patronage, a move which reduced ministers' dependence on the nobles and gentry who had presented them to their charge.[5]

In the perfervid spiritual climate of the late 1640s, the Kirk enjoyed unprecedented influence over national life. Sharp's abilities established him at the heart of religious politics and by July 1650 he had been elected to the Commission of the General Assembly which, together with the Committee of Estates, governed Scotland. He was, however, no radical and aligned with the moderates in the ministry and the Committee of Estates who wished to allow the new king, Charles II, more freedom in government. Their success led to a breach with a substantial minority of radical ministers, who denounced any dilution of the theocracy established by the events of 1648. This breach persisted throughout the 1650s when, following the conquest of Scotland in

1651 and union with England in 1653, both factions sought the support of the Cromwellian government in a struggle for control over the Kirk. In Fife, despite its past radicalism, it was the moderates who were in the majority, well represented by four of their number who were arrested in September 1653 for praying for the exiled king.

Throughout this struggle, Sharp was regularly resident in London as representative of the moderate clergy and was, thus, able to observe the death throes of the Commonwealth regime in 1659–60. With the likelihood of a restoration of the monarchy strengthening, Sharp was instructed to involve himself in the negotiations with the exiled Charles II and extract guarantees for the Presbyterian structure of the Kirk. His elevation to the Archbishopric of St Andrews in December 1661, at the head of a restored episcopacy, was therefore greeted with horror, outrage and denunciation by his fellow clerics.

Within Fife, Sharp found few allies in either Kirk or community. Few ministers attended his installation at St Andrews and personal alienation was further embittered by news that the 1649 act abolishing lay patronage had been rescinded. Ministers were now obliged to approach the restored patrons of their parish for a fresh presentation and then get collation from their bishop. As in 1618, they were faced with the alternatives of compliance or expulsion, but the fact that only around one third of incumbents in Fife stood by their principles indicates the pull of both conformity and aversion to secession.[6]

Although the new religious settlement quickly won a general, if often grudging, acceptance, particularly amongst those who had fallen foul of the worst excesses of the radical Covenanters, there was still a substantial minority who opposed any form of episcopacy. The main support for Presbyterianism was amongst members of the gentry and minor landholders who had been politically empowered in the 1640s. Although their activities were most pronounced at first in Galloway and the south-west, by 1668 illegal meetings known as conventicles had spread to Fife. Attempts at conciliation with the non-conformists having failed to curb the escalating violence associated with these meetings, Sharp sought government support for their military suppression. By the late 1670s, the moderate clergyman of the 1650s had transformed himself into an agent of repression and advocate of increased severity towards the conventiclers.[7]

1679 saw a virtual military occupation of Fife, which had become one of the chief centres of conventicle activity. Discipline was lax and the widespread violence and extortion inflicted by the soldiers upon the population, regardless of their religious sympathies, fuelled support for the radicals. In this increasingly lawless situation, groups of independent radicals formed to mete out rough justice on individuals whom they regarded as agents of repression. It was one such group, comprised of two lairds: David Hackston of Rathillet and John Balfour of Kinloch, six sons of tenant farmers and a weaver from

Balmerino,[8] who chanced upon Sharp in his coach near St Andrews. Secure in the self-justification that they were instruments of divine justice, they dragged him from his carriage on Magus Muir and murdered him.

Sharp's death, despite its semi-mythological status in the narrative of the religious struggle, changed nothing. Government repression failed to curtail or contain the activities of the non-conformists, but the latter, equally, were unable to attract the political support necessary to achieve yet another religious revolution. Indeed, it took another action outwith the control of the Scots, the English revolution of 1688, to overturn the settlement of 1661–62. That nearly two-thirds of the ministers in the country were deprived of their charges after 1690 when Presbyterianism was restored is indicative of how deeply entrenched Episcopalianism had become in the fabric of the Kirk and within society in general. Despite significant continued support for episcopacy in some parts of the country, the Presbyterian sympathies of the new political regime in Edinburgh determined the final character of Scottish church government. But, despite the triumphant return of some surviving ministers of those ejected in 1662 and the expulsion of Episcopalian die-hards to make way for suitably Presbyterian clergy, this fresh upheaval was a politically directed act and no return to the radical theocracy of the 1640s was to be permitted. Influential though the Kirk was to remain in Scottish society, it stood as just one other political interest amongst several. Never again was the General Assembly to wield powers which could challenge parliament itself. It was the last religious revolution of the 17th century.

POLITICS AND SOCIETY

Plundering the Temple: Lords of Erection

From the first, the Reformation had profound implications for the social and political fabric of the kingdom. Although some principled Reformers had hoped that the resources of the old regime would be diverted to the uses of the new, much of the wealth of the old hierarchy passed into the hands of secular lords. Central to this process was conversion of monastic properties into temporal lordships, begun soon after 1560. Laymen who had been awarded control of a monastery as commendators before 1560 sought to exchange temporary tenure for permanent possession as hereditary lords through the conversion of the spiritual lordship of the monastery into a temporal lordship. It was a slow process and few monasteries passed permanently into hereditary possession before the end of the 16th century. The rich monasteries of Fife represented an important source of patronage for James VI, who used grants of commendatorships of defunct religious communities to reward crown servants and favourites. The first development was in 1589 when James gave the Dunfermline estate to his new wife, Anne of Denmark. The chief beneficiary in Fife, however, was James's kinsman, Ludovick Stewart, Duke of Lennox, for whom St Andrews priory, the richest monastic estate in Scotland, was converted into a temporal lordship in 1592. At Lindores, Patrick Leslie's commendatorship was erected into a lordship in 1600. At nearby Balmerino, the beneficiary was James Elphinstone, a key figure in royal administration, Secretary of State 1598–1608 and Lord President of the Court of Session from 1605, who was created Lord Balmerino in 1603. In 1609 the two remaining substantial ecclesiastical properties in Fife, Inchcolm and Culross, were erected into lordships for Henry Stewart, son of Sir James Stewart, Lord Doune, the former commendator of the abbey, and Sir James Colville.

Although these creations marked a significant change in national political society and in the character of the governing elite, they had little impact upon local patterns of lordship. In Fife, the former ecclesiastical estates rarely formed compact blocks upon which to base territorial influence, a situation further aggravated by the trend towards feuing by ecclesiastical landlords after 1500. By the 1600s, while many of the new men had succeeded to the privileged jurisdictions of the former monastic proprietors and possessed extensive superiorities, their position was founded on money – the residual rents and rights to teind enjoyed by their predecessors – not on the ties of kinship or lordship which underpinned the social and political leadership of the traditional nobility.[9]

These 'lords of erection', as they were termed, formed an aristocracy of service central to James's administration of Scotland subsequent to his departure for London.[10] Representing the emerging class of professional administrators and judges and drawn largely from the ranks of the lairds and lesser barons, often younger sons, they lacked the kin-based networks of the older nobility. It was their closeness to James which gave them their power but, equally, it was on him that they were utterly dependent and therefore entirely amenable to his will. While they may not, at first, have carried much weight amongst the traditional aristocracy, by 1625 the king's new creations had triggered changes within the fabric of noble society which signalled the emergence of money and access to political patronage as the keys to power.

A good example of the new class was Edward Bruce (*c.* 1549–1611). A member of the lesser aristocracy, he held the commendatorship of Kinloss in Moray from 1583 and rose in royal service, being made a Lord of Session in 1597 and serving as James's ambassador to England in 1594 and 1601, before finally being created 1st Lord Kinloss in 1603.[11] With the exception of a scattering of property around Culross, Bruce held little by way of land or superiorities in Fife. However it was there that he based himself, within reach of Edinburgh, the political hub of the kingdom where he exercised his power and influence, rather than on the northern estate from which he derived his title. This separation of landed lordship from the exercise of power was marked by the architecturally advanced Culross Abbey House, built, unlike the residences of the traditional nobility at the hearts of their complexes of landed estates, as a symbol of Bruce's social elevation and political influence in an area where he possessed little significant property.

Crisis of Leadership

The already limited lordship of the new lords was curtailed in 1625 by Charles I's Act of Revocation. This unpopular act, framed largely with the advice of the rising lawyer, Sir Thomas Hope of Craighall near Ceres, who in 1626 was created Lord Advocate, clawed back Church lands and revenues which had been alienated to the nobility, in part to provide a much-needed supplement to royal income but also to augment the incomes of the parish ministry. While lords of erection and members of the traditional nobility who had received Church property were generally permitted to retain lands which they exploited directly, they lost what they did not actively exploit. In effect, feued land was removed from the superiority of the lord and was placed instead under crown superiority.[12] While intended to win support from the feuars, it was perceived widely as an assault on the powers of the aristocracy and alienated support amongst the political elite.

The proliferation of lordships and earldoms as rewards for service to the crown reflected a general lowering of the status of these titles throughout Britain. The new titulars derived their influence from closeness to the king, a weakness revealed graphically by Charles I who did not enjoy any rapport with his father's creations and who preferred bishops as his key agents in government. The sons and successors of James VI's lords of erection, moreover, rarely followed in their fathers' footsteps in the executive of government. As a consequence, most of the new titles faded into the political twilight, a truer reflection of their social significance. One exception was John Elphinstone, 2nd Lord Balmerino, who emerged as a prominent critic of Charles's policies and was tried for treason in 1634 for involvement in a supplication protesting against the king's misgovernment. His dissenting credentials thus well established, in 1638 he stood as one of three leading nobles at the forefront of the Covenanting movement.[13]

The political lead in the confrontation with the king was provided by another Fife-based nobleman, John Leslie, 6th Earl of Rothes. He had opposed royal policies since 1621 but, like many of the nobles drawn into the Covenanting movement, his motivation was perhaps the opportunity offered for personal gain rather than any high legal or religious principles. Faced with sharply falling incomes as the economy went into protracted decline in the later 1630s, men like Rothes sought to offset this with lucrative offices or crown pensions. But here they collided with the new nobility of service and with the political episcopate who controlled the key offices of state. The only remedy for this impasse lay in revolution.

War with Charles afforded Rothes and his peers the opportunity to restake their leadership in the guise of warlords and as the dominant group in the 'Tables', the committees set up to organise the political opposition to the king.[14] By 1645, however, their domination of the Covenanting enterprise was in tatters. The military leadership which these amateur commanders had assumed for themselves in 1638 was gradually transferred to professionals who had gained practical experience in the European wars. Men like Alexander Leslie, who although created Earl of Leven in 1641 had started his career as a landless bastard, or David Leslie, nephew of the Earl of Rothes, who was created Lord Newark in 1661, shared more in common with the lairdly and professional classes who shouldered the running of the war than with the noble warlords.

While the great lords indulged their military fantasies and went in pursuit of office and power on a national level, the administration on which the regime was founded fell into the hands of men of lesser rank. The lairdly class had progressively gained in importance throughout the 16th century as they staked a claim in political and religious decision-making, but it was not until the events of 1637–38 that the extent of their influence became apparent. By 1640 the lairds had gained recognition as a separate estate in parliament and in 1641 secured nine seats on the privy council. It was at a local level, however, that the power of the lairds was most evident, particularly in the civil presbyteries and shire committees of war set up to facilitate local government and the raising of revenue for the Covenant. In Fife, lairds and gentlemen, like Sir John Scott of Scotstarvit, Arthur Erskine of Scotscraig, Michael Balfour of Denmiln, or William Scott of Ardross, and burgess leaders such as Bailie James Sword and John Leiper of St Andrews, were prominent in these courts and committees which underpinned national government. Many, such as Balfour, were lawyers and played a key part in the legal pursuit of royalists[15] and in the enforcement of political and religious conformity.

The functionaries of the civil presbyteries and committees of war were heritors, men whose status depended upon possession of heritable property rather than feudal superiority. Their position was reinforced after the collapse of the Engagement, which discredited the moderate Covenanting lords. Their defeat in 1648 pitched power into the hands of a radical minority, whose authority was reinforced by the 1649 Act of Classes. This disbarred from public office all men who did not adhere to rigid Covenanting principles, political, spiritual or moral. Its effect was to purge the army of all but a handful of senior nobles, sweep away men who had held on to high office since 1638 and thereby cement the lairds and burgesses in their domination of local government, and deprive the nobility of influence within the Kirk, where they had previously fulfilled the role of ruling elders. Indeed, it has been remarked that by 1650 the ruling elder 'was more likely to be a tenant farmer than a lord'.[16]

These developments undermined the bonds of kinship and lordship which had sustained noble power throughout the Middle Ages, not least because heritors as a class operated within the framework of a shire community rather than a network of kin. Religious belief, moreover, proved more powerful than ties of kinship and marriage or the demands of 'feudal' lordship in determining the political activities of the middle orders of society. Conscience and conviction led men to choose different political paths from their heads of kin or superiors, thereby severing social bonds which had provided the basis of aristocratic political power for centuries.

The assault on aristocratic domination of the political community continued after 1651 under the Cromwellian regime. It looked to 'the meaner sort' to form its administration and to serve as Justices of the Peace, the latter entrenching men of moderate means into positions of authority within the shire communities. More substantial lairds who demonstrated loyalty to the regime, like Sir Andrew Bruce of Earlshall, could likewise expect advancement to positions where their local influence could benefit the occupiers, in Bruce's case to the post of sheriff-conjunct of Fife. While there was an aristocratic backlash in the administration established after 1660, which saw many noble rights lost in the past two decades restored, thereby returning some degree of local power to the old nobility, it was clear that the pattern of authority in Scotland was irrevocably changed. Political survivors, like Sir Alexander Gibson of Durie, who had embraced the Commonwealth in 1652 and represented Fife as a commissioner for union in 1653, MP and, from 1656, as a JP, secured their position by serving as a commissioner in the deputation sent to London in 1660 as preparations for the return of Charles II gained momentum.[17] Pragmatism and hypocrisy underlay men like Gibson's declaration of loyalty and readiness to serve the king, but their behaviour in 1660 was that of thoroughly political animals for whom service in government was automatic and exclusion unthinkable.

The Civil Wars and the Cromwellian occupation left many nobles in deep financial embarrassment. For some, the financial rewards of high office offered redemption. The 7th Earl of Rothes was particularly successful in this. An Engager, he had been captured at Worcester in 1651 and remained imprisoned until 1658 and, therefore, politically emasculated while his Fife estates were plundered to pay the fines and taxation imposed on the nobility. His recovery after 1660 was rapid: President of the Privy Council in 1660, Treasurer and Royal Commissioner to parliament in 1663, and Chancellor in 1667. Others were less fortunate. One prominent Fife casualty was the Elphinstones, the 2nd Lord Balmerino leaving heavy debts on his death in 1649 which were met only by his son, John, 3rd Lord Balmerino, selling off much of his landed inheritance. At a stroke, indebtedness all but removed this political family from the social landscape of Fife. This, coupled with erosion of their traditional leadership role, prevented many from regaining the prominence in political life which their predecessors had enjoyed and forced them to concentrate on the reconstruction of their estates.

The financial straits of the nobility are reflected in the dearth of new, large-scale building, the traditional medium for projection of power and status, undertaken by this class between the 1640s and 1670s. The Elphinstones continued to reside in the small mansion formed by the old cloister buildings at Balmerino, while the two Leslie generals, Alexander, Earl of Leven, and David, Lord Newark, simply refurbished the older castles which they had acquired. At Balgonie, bought by Leven in 1635, limited reconstruction was undertaken in the 1640s,[18] and further limited remodelling, including a staircase by Robert Mylne, carried out under his successors after 1661. Sixteenth-century Newark, whose ruins totter on the cliffs east of St Monans, saw similarly limited remodelling, revealed in the remains of a fashionable curvilinear roof-line and enlarged windows broken through the original fabric. None, it is clear, had the resources or inclination to mark their social elevation through architectural patronage.

Where major building took place in the decades following the restoration of Charles II, it was the rising 'middling sort' who were making their mark. The Hopes of Craighall typified this trend. Ambivalent in the 1630s, Lord Advocate Hope had emerged as a supporter of the Covenant. His eldest son, John, a prominent judge, had conveniently fallen from favour in 1651, so rendering him attractive to the English administration: he became president of Cromwell's Committee of Justice after 1652. Thus, he avoided the punitive fines and taxation which ruined many of his Fife neighbours. Indeed, he was appointed a trustee to administer some forfeited estates. By the 1660s, the Craighall estate was turning over £12,500 *per annum*, much being spent on redevelopment of the Hopes' mansion near Ceres. The main expenditure here was in the 1690s when the architect, Sir William Bruce, was commissioned to redesign the house for a family whose many branches had by then penetrated the ranks of the higher nobility and formed a veritable legal dynasty at the heart of the Edinburgh establishment.

The most striking example of lairdly success is in the houses built by Bruce for himself. Bruce, the son of a laird, received a baronetcy in 1668 and in 1671 was appointed the king's Master of Works. His rise was marked by the provision of a suitable architectural expression for his new status at his house, Balcaskie near Anstruther. This, like Balgonie and Newark, was not a fresh build but took an existing tower as its core. Unlike the Leslies, however, Bruce completely transformed the old house. Balcaskie, however, was just a stepping-stone to greater things, with Kinross House, a completely new building on a virgin site, outstripping in scale and modernity the residences of many of the greater nobility even although shortage of finance forced some retrenchment on his original plans.[19]

For the great families of Fife, the three decades after 1660 were a watershed. For them, power no longer lay in the localities but depended upon the offices of state and pensions in the gift of the clique which managed Scotland for the crown. To men like Rothes, Fife was simply the location of the estates from which he derived his titles. It was no longer the seat of personal, political, or after the 1640s military, power: local government was the preserve of lesser men. Feuds between the political elite were no longer settled through private wars in the localities, but were fought out in the committees of the faction-ridden government in Edinburgh. While all but bloodless, these rivalries had their casualties.

Amongst these was George Leslie, 4th Lord Melville, who succeeded to the family's Fife estates in 1643 as a seven-year-old. In the 1670s he had carved himself a political niche and was active against the Covenanters in 1679 following Sharp's assassination. Good marriages were secured for his sons, his heir, David, marrying the heiress to the earldom of Leven, to which he succeeded in 1681. Another branch of the Fife Leslies appeared to have secured entry to the highest ranks of the nobility and guaranteed its place in the elite of government, perhaps even aspiring to step into the shoes of the Earl of Rothes, who had died in 1681. This, however, was followed by a rapid reversal of alignment and fall from grace: by 1683 Melville was associated with the supporters in Scotland of the radical Protestant English Whigs who plotted to assassinate the king and his Roman Catholic brother. On the discovery of the plot, Melville fled to Holland and joined the growing band of Presbyterian exiles there. His support in 1685 for the rebellion raised by Argyll against James VII resulted in forfeiture and ensured his permanent adherence to the political and religious opposition. When James was toppled from power in England in 1688, Melville's return from exile in the train of the triumphant William III and Mary was followed by rapid promotion in the new government in Scotland.

Unlike the muted response made by the financially straitened nobility in the 1660s, the new political establishment of the 1690s made its presence felt immediately in the landscape, commissioning major building works which symbolised their triumph over the old order. In Fife, George, Lord Melville, created Earl of Melville and Secretary of State by William and Mary, almost immediately commenced work on Melville House, sited, perhaps symbolically in view of the recent overthrow of episcopacy, on the former archiepiscopal property of Monimail. Isolated within its walled policies and separated from the community around it, it encapsulated in stone the final detachment of the upper nobility from the landed power and local political domination which had been the basis for the authority of their forbears.

THE ECONOMY

Fife in 1600, like the rest of Scotland, was still a primarily agricultural society. Its population, set in the Medieval mould which prevailed until the onset of intensive industrialisation in the late 18th century triggered the rapid growth of the south Fife towns, was overwhelmingly rural-based and dependant upon agriculture for income and employment. The burghs which fringed the Forth exercised an economic domination over their rural hinterland out of all proportion to their size, a product of their near monopoly control over trade. This pattern had been established in the 12th century, at which time the burghs had received their privileged status, and had remained effectively static down to the 16th century. The Scottish economy, however, was not impervious to change and before the end of the 1500s northern European economic development had stimulated some restructuring here.

Amongst the most marked of these developments in Fife was the proliferation of coal-mining and saltpan complexes along the northern shore of the Firth of Forth. Both originated in the medieval period, but the later 16th century witnessed an intensification and commercialisation of the operations. At the forefront in these fields was Sir George Bruce (d. 1625), who developed saltpans and coal mines at Culross.[20] His famous mine, developed with German technological expertise to overcome problems of drainage, struck out under the Forth and rose via a shaft to an artificial island – Preston Island – from which the mined coal was loaded directly on to ships. Early accounts of the mine – visited in 1617 by James VI – indicate that it was regarded as an engineering marvel.[21] But the fame of Bruce's operation should not obscure the fact that the early decades of the 17th century saw a general development of such deep mining around the Forth estuary. At Wemyss, for example, the Earl of Wemyss developed a combined coal and salt-panning centre comparable to Culross. This was profitable business, with exports possibly climbing from around 7000 tons a year in the 1590s to about 60,000 tons in the 1630s,[22] offering substantial returns to investors, such as the Edinburgh merchants who sank considerable capital into the development of the Fife mines.

The expansion of coal production was linked to the commercial development of salt-pans from the mid-16th century.[23] Sir George Bruce had 44 salt-pans at Culross, the evaporation process fuelled by dross from the mined coals. The remains of the 18th-century complex at St Monans indicate the scale of production. Rectangular depressions below the raised beach mark the site of firing beds beneath the iron-pans in which sea-water was evaporated. Above them, the stumpy round tower on the edge of the raised beach is the remains of the windmill which pumped sea-water into the pans, the pipe-channel still visible cutting through the shelving rocks below the high-tide line.[24]

The growth of the salt export trade from the 1570s had stemmed largely from disruption occasioned by warfare affecting traditional European production centres and the associated carrying trade. Scottish merchants met the shortfall in both fields. Bruce's investment in what was a high-cost activity demonstrates the profits to be made from the poor-quality Scottish product in a market where demand for this essential commodity was outstripping supply. By the 1630s the value of exported salt exceeded that of coal,[25] but overseas trade declined in the 1640s as European producers and their low-cost, high-quality salt restaked their market share and the Dutch reclaimed their dominance of the carrying trade. Scottish producers sought to protect their grip on the domestic market, threatened down to the 1660s by cheaper and finer imports. Competition, however, did not deter further investment, with the Earl of Wemyss in the 1650s commencing works at Wemyss and Methil which, by the 1700s, were two of the largest in Fife.[26] Such investment paid off after 1665 when the Privy Council introduced punitive levels of duty on imported salt, other than high-quality salts intended for the fish- and meat-curing trades. Armed with this effective monopoly, Scottish producers were by 1670 able to dispose of around 40% of their output within Scotland, rising to around 69% by 1706.[27]

While coal and salt offered substantial profits to owners and merchants, competition between these men for skilled labour, coupled with difficulty in attracting workers into these dangerous and unpleasant operations, resulted in deterioration of the levels of personal freedom of their workforce. Legislation which permitted vagrants to be bonded for life to employers provided an opening for mine-owners in Fife to impose bondage on their employees. This achieved formal legality in 1606, when colliers and salt-workers were made into serfs by act of parliament. The rights of owners over their workers were steadily extended throughout the 17th century, with an act of 1672 empowering them to seize vagrants and press them into labour.[28]

The buoyant early 17th-century economy had a profound impact on the townscape of the coastal burghs. The rambling structure at Culross, known as 'The Palace', charted the growing wealth of Sir George Bruce, its piecemeal development between 1597 and 1611 being determined by progressive buying-up of parcels of land to consolidate into the single plot occupied by his house-cum-business administration centre.[29] While externally architecturally unpretentious, other than in its scale, its once rich internal fittings and decor reveal the significance of the commercial elite as artistic patrons. Others, though, also benefited from the success of Bruce's business and the expansion in trade at Culross, a situation reflected in the surviving buildings of the 'new town' which developed along the foreshore. Indeed, much of the construction work was undertaken in the period *c.* 1590–*c.* 1630 when the burgh's involvement in the coal and salt trade was at its peak.

Whereas Culross was, in effect, a new burgh built on industry, the older Fife coastal communities, with their established overseas trading links, also experienced an upsurge in prosperity at this time. Shipmasters were major beneficiaries of this economic revival, the profits of business being reflected in such fine early 17th-century houses as the so-called Mary Somerville's House at Burntisland, built by the ship-owning Watson family. Their involvement in the timber trade may have provided them with materials for their house and the money to employ the skilled artist, James Workman, who probably produced the remarkable painted ceilings which graced its principal rooms.[30]

A decline in overseas trade from the mid-1630s, particularly in carriage of salt, affected the Fife ports badly. This is marked by a slackening in building activity around this time and a decline in the quality of materials used. Roofing materials are a key indicator of prosperity and reveal striking patterns of economic decline, or continuing prosperity, around the Fife coast. Red pantiles, nowadays regarded as typical of East Neuk ports such as Crail and which give Culross its character, were a cheap commodity and considered inferior in all ways to slate. The widespread use of pantiles in Fife from the mid-17th century onwards, therefore, signals the downturn in segments of the regional economy around that time.

The demands of warfare after 1638 added to the financial plight of the burghs. The Covenanting regime introduced a rigorous scheme of taxation to finance its armies throughout the 1640s, extracting monthly payments of £108,000 Scots from the shires. This was a heavy burden at a time of declining trade. Figures from 1645 detailing two months' levy record the demands on the burghs and provide broad comparisons of wealth.[31] St Andrews heads the list, assessed for two months at £1,080 Scots. Close behind was Kirkcaldy at £828, reflecting trade through its port and valuable local mining and salt-panning ventures. Then there is a significant drop to Anstruther Easter and Dysart at £558 and £540 respectively, then to Crail and Cupar, both assessed at £432. Then come the also-rans: Burntisland at £288, its low position consequent on decline in the shipping trade, Pittenweem at £270 and Kinghorn at £252. At the foot of the league Dunfermline and Culross paid £108, the low positioning of the latter indicating the collapse in its trade following the flooding of Sir George Bruce's mine in 1625, followed by Inverkeithing at £90 and Kilrenny at a mere £52. Together, the burghs contributed £2,520 Scots monthly, approximately one third of the contribution of the rural districts of Fife. This disparity emphasises how, despite the growth in commerce into the 1630s, the wealth of the region remained in the agricultural hinterland.

Cromwell's forces entered Fife in the summer 1651 and, after defeating the

Scots at Inverkeithing on 20 July, traversed the shire mopping up resistance. Although damage was limited, fines were levied on burghs which resisted demands for surrender, such as the £500 sterling – equivalent to £6,000 Scots – taken from St Andrews. More serious for the wider community, however, was the obligation to provide free quartering and maintenance for the occupying army, converted once the occupation had become established in an area – after August 1651 in Fife – into a monetary impost known as cess. The levy was two and a half times higher than the Covenanters' tax but was based upon their system which used parishes and presbyteries as collection units. Kirkcaldy presbytery, for example, paid cess for the maintenance of the garrison in Burntisland, while St Andrews contributed to the fort at Perth.[32]

The occupiers understood that the country was too impoverished after twenty years of warfare, economic decline and repeated outbreaks of plague to pay the sums demanded. Although the level of cess was lowered and garrison costs subsidised from the English exchequer, Scotland was in a perilous state. The removal of the occupying army with the fall of the Commonwealth did not see any quick easing of these economic woes. Wars with the Dutch in the 1660s and 1670s slowed the recovery, further hindered by the ending of the pan-British free trade regime of the Cromwellian union, and the decline of trade with traditional partners, most notably the French. Nevertheless, the late 1670s saw a quickening pace of recovery, marked in particular by revival in the carrying trade with a resultant increase in the volume of shipping.[33]

While coal and salt continued to dominate Scotland's overseas trade, a significant element in this recovery was the export of grain. The dominance of agriculture in the domestic economy of Fife in the earlier 17th century, despite the intensification of industry in some zones, has already been noticed in respect of the levying of cess and this weighting was maintained into the later 18th century. An expansion of arable agriculture was well advanced by the 1660s, when falls in grain prices indicate over-supply of the market. This surplus was not the product of improved techniques, although some estate-owners had been experimenting on their lands in the early decades of the century. Some intensification of agriculture had resulted from noblemen seeking to recover from the crippling burdens of debt which the wars and punitive fines of the mid-17th century had brought, but this generally involved enforcement of old rights rather than experimentation. Indeed, the low grain prices were a disincentive to improvements,[34] and the export of cereals from Scotland was a product of the lure of higher profits rather than long-term over-supply of the domestic market. The boom, however, was short-lived and by the 1680s increasing protectionism in traditional European markets was squeezing the domestic economy.

Fife in many ways characterised key deficiencies in the 17th-century economy. The proliferation of small ports, all competing for trade, generated insufficient revenue to permit development of large, specialist facilities. The private enterprise of Lord Wemyss, who built a new harbour at Methil to serve his coal- and salt-producing ventures, was a significant exception but failed to encourage similar investment in the established burghs. Their small harbours could not accommodate the large vessels used in the international carrying trade and, conversely, deterred Scottish merchants from investing in larger ships. While there was an increase in the volume of Scottish shipping, this was almost exclusively to service exports to traditional markets. Few Scots broke into the lucrative international carrying trade, in part a consequence of conservatism and a reluctance to bear the risks involved in penetrating new markets. While locally significant, Fife-based merchants were minor players by international standards and lacked the access to capital or credit with which to expand. Geography, too, was against them as the Atlantic trade began to develop: the Fife ports were left to compete for a diminishing share of northern European traffic. The decline was long term and permanent. In 1612 they had contributed 9% of the burghs' share of taxation, by 1705 they barely registered 3%.[35]

The final blows to this declining economy came at the close of the century. The French wars of William III and Anne, although primarily English affairs, closed off this traditional Scottish market after 1689. In the 1690s, the domestic market went into sharp reversal, triggered by the disastrous harvests of the so-called 'Seven Ill Years' of 1695–1700 which saw widespread famine and forced the import of grain with a consequent outflow of cash.[36] In the midst of this, the Scots launched the ill-fated Darien venture, seeing the development of colonial trade as the panacea for their domestic woes. Ill-conceived, ill-planned and ill-fated, between its launch in 1698 and collapse in 1700 it is estimated to have consumed around a quarter of Scottish capital. It was a body-blow which brought the already failing national economy to its knees and forced the Scots to make hard choices about their future direction. After a brief, bitter backlash which directed national fury at the failure of the Darien scheme against the English and which for a while threatened the severing of the Union of the Crowns, in 1706 the economic realists saw an incorporating Union of the Parliaments as the only viable way forward.

By 1707, the shire had been transformed beyond all recognition from that which had faced the opening of the 17th century. War, religious conflict and natural disasters had all played a part in breaking down and remodelling old patterns inherited from the Medieval past and had revealed the inadequacies of the traditional structures. Fife in 1707 could look back on a century which had seen it stand at the heart of all the spiritual, religious and economic upheavals which swept the kingdom and see a social landscape littered with the wreckage of failed regimes and a faltering economy. By turn a hot-bed of religious radicalism, political opportunism and economic entrepreneurialism, by 1707 the fires in each field appeared to have burned themselves cold. While Edinburgh mobs and a handful of political ideologues looked upon the Union with horror, in the country at large there was more positive hope and expectation, and amongst the commercial classes of Fife not a little desperation that the future might hold brighter prospects.

REFERENCES

1. See Chapter 14.
2. See M. Lynch, *Scotland: A New History* (London, 1991), chapter 15.
3. B. Walker and G. Ritchie, *Exploring Scotland's Heritage: Fife and Tayside* (Edinburgh, 1987), 114.
4. J. Buckroyd, *The Life of James Sharp Archbishop of St Andrews 1618–1679*. A Political Biography (Edinburgh, 1987), 12–15.
5. G. Donaldson, *Scotland: James V to James VII* (Edinburgh, 1965), 339.
6. Ibid., 365–6.
7. Buckroyd, *James Sharp*, 104–5.
8. Ibid., 106.
9. Some idea of the nature of these temporal lordships can be gained from the 1561 rental of Dunfermline Abbey and the subsequent register of infeftments and alienations in monastic property: *Register de Dunfermelyn* (Bannatyne Club, 1842), appendices ii and iii.
10. For a general discussion of their role, see R. Mitchison, *Lordship to Patronage. Scotland 1603–1745* (reprinted Edinburgh, 1990), 10–11.
11. Donaldson, *James V to James VII*, 220–221.
12. A. I. Macinnes, *Charles I and the Making of the Covenanting Movement* (Edinburgh, 1991), 54–7; Mitchison, *Lordship to Patronage*, 33.
13. M. Lynch, *Scotland*, 248.
14. D. Stevenson (ed.), *The Government of Scotland Under the Covenanters 1637–1651* (Scottish History Society, 1982), xiv–xvii.
15. Ibid., e.g. 52–3.
16. Lynch, *Scotland*, 251.
17. Dow, *Cromwellian Scotland*, 40, 47, 239, 259, 263.
18. R. S. Will and T. N. Dixon, 'Excavations at Balgonie Castle, Markinch, Fife', *PSAS*, 125 (1995), 1109–1118.
19. Walker and Ritchie, *Fife and Tayside*, 75.
20. I. D. Whyte, *Scotland Before the Industrial Revolution. An Economic and Social History c. 1050–c. 1750* (London, 1995), 277–8.
21. G. Donaldson, *Scottish Historical Documents* (Edinburgh, 1970), 183–4.
22. Whyte, *Scotland Before the Industrial Revolution*, 278.
23. C. A. Whately, *'That Important and Necessary Article'. The Salt Industry and its Trade in Fife and Tayside c. 1570–1850* (Dundee, 1984), 26–7.
24. Whately, *Salt Industry*, 16 and plate 3.
25. Whyte, *Scotland Before the Industrial Revolution*, 278.

26. Whately, *Salt Industry*, 28.

27. Ibid., 29.

28. For a general discussion of serfdom in these trades see Whatley, *Salt Industry*, 43–56; Whyte, *Scotland Before the Industrial Revolution*, 165–7.

29. Walker and Ritchie, *Fife and Tavside*, no. 49.

30. M. R. Apted, 'Two Painted Ceilings from Mary Somerville's House, Burntisland', *PSAS*, xci (1957–58), 144–76.

31. Stevenson, *Government Under the Covenanters*, 43–4.

32. F. D. Dow, *Cromwellian Scotland 1651–1660* (Edinburgh, 1979), 23–4.

33. Whyte, *Scotland Before the Industrial Revolution*, 282.

34. Mitchison, *Lordship to Patronage*, 93–4.

35. Donaldson, *James V to James VII*, 391.

36. Whyte, *Scotland Before the Industrial Revotion*, 291.

EIGHT

FIFE IN THE MODERN ERA

INTRODUCTION

To any one vaguely familiar with Scottish Lowland history the story of Fife over the last three centuries will have a familiar ring. The themes of industrial development, changes in agricultural practices and the increase in population with its concomitant expansion of urban settlement loom large. Yet Fife's particular geographic location and topography, previous historical development and its abundance of natural resources provided it with a unique blend of ingredients with which to enter and proceed through the modern era. This chapter will explore some of the changes that have occurred in social composition and economic fortunes over the last three hundred years, highlighting transformations that have had an enormous influence upon the landscape and the people in the past and continue to affect the Fife of today.

SETTLEMENT AND POPULATION

During the last 250 years the population of Fife has increased fourfold. Most of that increase took place between the mid-19th and mid-20th centuries when the number of residents doubled. This increase is significant in itself but the prominent feature of Fife's population history is the contrast in fortunes that can be found between the eastern and western portions of the region.

At the beginning of the modern era Fifers were living in a landscape dominated by a number of minor settlements punctuated with small, predominantly coastal, burghal developments. The urban developments of most importance were Royal Burghs; settlements that had acted as collection, distribution and small scale manufacturing centres for a considerable period of time. The location of Fife's 18 Royal Burghs (all but five were on its southern coast) reflect the importance that maritime trade to northern Europe and proximity to the capital had on the Fife economy. Although there were, by Scottish standards, a significant number of burghs located within its boundaries it would be wrong to describe the area as urbanised at this period in time. The number of residents in the burghs was small by today's standards. The earliest population figures, compiled in 1755 by Dr Webster, indicate that few parishes, let alone burghs, could muster a total above two thousand souls. Those that did exceed this figure, six out of the ten most populous, were located west of the Lomond Hills, mainly on the northern shore of the Firth of Forth. Despite having the larger urban centres the western part of the county accounted for slightly less than half (48%) of the total population. This small disparity was reversed by 1801, considerably widened within forty years and had become a gulf by 1931.

Table 2
Total Population of Fife 1755–1991 (selected years)

Year	Population
1755	81 570
1801	93 743
1851	153 546
1891	187 346
1901	218 837
1911	267 733
1921	292 925
1951	306 778
1991	351 200

Table 3
The Ten Largest Settlements in Fife (with population figures)
1991 and 1891

Settlement	1991	Settlement	1891
Kirkcaldy	47 930	Kirkcaldy	27 155
Dunfermline	43 670	Dunfermline	19 647
Glenrothes	39 440	St. Andrews	6 583
Methil	15 850	Burntisland	4 993
Buckhaven	15 850	Cupar	4 792
St. Andrews	14 050	Leven	4 577
Rosyth	13 100	Anstruther	4 268
Cowdenbeath	10 360	Cowdenbeath	4 249
Leven	8 440	Lochgelly	4 133
Dalgety Bay	8 070	Buckhaven	4 006

The changing status, function and populations of the ancient burghs of Dunfermline and St Andrews throughout this period mirror many of the shifts that have taken place in their respective hinterlands. Prior to the modern era their respective monarchical, ecclesiastical and, in the case of St Andrews, educational connections, had provided them with powerful economic and political standing. The fast approaching era of production and manufacture would challenge and erode these positions to the economic detriment of St Andrews. The distribution maps of the ten most populous Fife settlements in 1755, 1891 and 1991 show that St Andrews is the only eastern burgh to still command a place in the lists. In 1755 St Andrews had half the population of the then largest settlement of Dunfermline. In 1891 it was slightly more than a quarter and by 1991 it had less than a third. St Andrews faired slightly better than the eastern part of the Kingdom as a whole. By 1931 only 22% of a considerably enlarged population lived in this part of Fife, a figure that was to become 20.5% in 1991. Indeed, the huge disparity between west and east Fife becomes clear when the total population size of the respective areas during the period 1755 to 1951 is examined. During this period the eastern area increased by 50% from 42,000 to 63,000 and that of the west rose from 39,000 to 244,000, an increase of over 500%.

The underlying causes of growth in the west are largely attributable to economic expansion via, initially, textile manufacture and the successful development of the coal and associated industries from the mid-19th century onwards. The result of these changes can be witnessed in the sprawling urbanisation of the south-western coastal district. The previously separate towns of Leven, Methil and Buckhaven have become all but one, coming under the heading of Levenmouth. Farther along the coast the town of Kirkcaldy has swallowed up the ancient burghs of Dysart, Linkstown and

Figure 12
Fife Population Distribtuion 1755: Ten largest by parish

Figure 13
Fife Population Distribution 1891: Ten largest by settlement

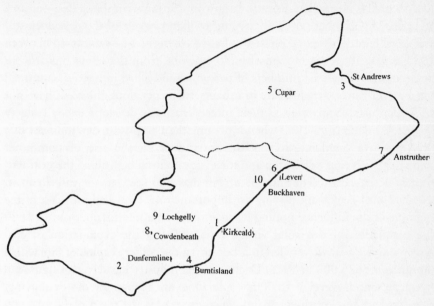

Figure 14
Fife Population Distribution 1991: Ten largest by settlement

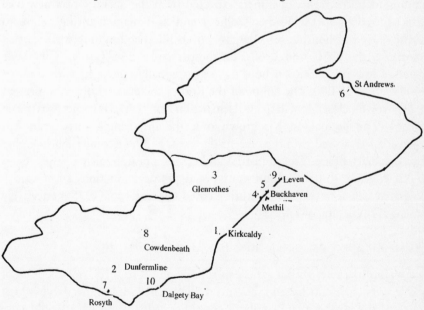

Pathhead, along with the villages of Sinclairtown and Galatown. Other coastal growth points during the 20th century have been the planned settlements of Rosyth and Dalgety Bay. Rosyth, begun in 1909, was initially laid out as a 'Garden City' to house the military and civilian workers of the new dockyard and naval base. This initial phase was halted when the base was closed between 1925 and 1938. A resumption of building work, from the 1950s onwards, to accommodate increased numbers of personnel and allied industries continued until recent times. The increase in urban settlements along the coast have not all had industrial expansion as their antecedents. The development of Dalgety Bay largely dates from 1962 when it became the first private development of a new town in Scotland. It was the forerunner to the rise of commuter settlements, serving Edinburgh and the eastern central belt, along the northern shores of the Forth. The interior of Fife has also seen an increase in town dwellers with coal again playing an important role. Cowdenbeath is a prime example of the influence mining has had on population distribution. In 1850 the population of this rural village was 1000 but the exploitation of coal reserves in the near vicinity led to it becoming the colliery capital of Fife with a population of 25,000 in 1914. Decline in the industry has seen this figure fall to the present day level of 10,000 people. One other expansion of urban living, that has had and continues to influence growth, is the town of Glenrothes. Established in 1948 as the second of Scotland's new towns Glenrothes was to accommodate the influx of miners expected from the opening of a new coal seam centred upon the Rothes Colliery and as a manufacturing centre to provide jobs and housing for Glasgow's overspill. The building work carried out during the 1950s and 1960s, on the principles of a 'Garden City' style layout of low rise suburban housing, was originally envisaged with a target population of 55,000. The failure of the Rothes colliery and the commitment to new towns closer to Glasgow itself has meant that this target was never reached. The population has grown over the intervening forty years but expansion has slowed with the present-day peak of 39,440 only slightly higher than the 1981 figure. The industrial and economic supremacy of the west is reflected in the shift of administrative and political functions from rurally integrated Cupar to the manufacturing based Glenrothes in 1975 – effectively making it the capital of Fife.

TRANSPORT AND COMMUNICATIONS (SEE ALSO CHAPTER 20)

In a region like Fife, with a variety of topographical features, not the least of which were small lochs and bogs, travelling the 34 km overland which separated the northern and southern coastlines at its widest point could pose numerous problems for our recent ancestors. It is not surprising to find that the 185 km of coastline still contains remnants of over sixty slips, landing places and harbours. In the past one suspects there were a considerable number in excess of this figure. No canal systems were ever constructed, although a number of schemes were envisaged, notably the canalisation of the Eden between Cupar and Guardbridge. The history of transport and communications in the Kingdom is inextricably linked to its peninsular location between Dundee (the north) and Edinburgh (the south). It has not been the building of roads and railways across the landscape that has defined transport developments in Fife but the crossing of the Firths with links that were formed by the utilisation and application of new technologies and innovations to improve and enhance the commerce and trade of the region.

The proliferation of coastal settlements led to a great number of maritime developments from an early period. A lack of good reliable inland communications made coastal shipping the only viable means of importing and exporting goods and raw materials. From the mid-18th century new works and improvements to existing facilities can be found in a number of locations, many for specific purposes. The building of a pier at Balmerino in the 1750s was to ship lime from the Fife hills to the Carse of Gowrie. Two decades later Charlestown harbour was built and the existing facilities at Limekilns improved to ship lime from the new kilns erected by the Earl of Elgin. Much earlier in the century both Kingsbarns and Pittenweem had small piers erected to aid local fishermen; Crail followed their example in 1760. The 19th century witnessed a considerable number of building and improvement schemes. On the Tay new piers at Newport, Tayport and Newburgh were constructed during the first two decades. On the Forth a new pier was built at Leven in 1833; similar works had already been carried out at constructed at Inverkeithing in 1805 and Aberdour in 1811. As the century progressed the size and number of vessels calling at the ports increased; this led to a flourish of enlargement programmes. The already noted improved facilities at Leven were further enhanced by a wet dock in 1880. Near neighbours Methil had carried out similar work in 1871 and would do so again in 1887 and 1907; these were developments that led to the reduction and eventual demise of trade at Leven. Other ports that also embarked upon substantial improvements to their maritime infrastructure during this period include Burntisland in 1848, 1870, 1875 and again in 1881, Buckhaven in 1851, Anstruther, for the fishing fleet, in 1831 and Pittenweem, for the same reason, during the 1850s. Kirkcaldy embarked upon considerable change to its harbour in 1841 and again in 1909. The last major maritime development on the Fife coastline was begun at Rosyth in 1909 when a naval base was constructed; one that has undergone numerous changes to its layout and facilities up to the present day. Apart from the now privately owned and operated maritime complex at Rosyth there are only a small number of ports and harbours still in use. The three ports of Burntisland, Kirkcaldy and Methil still function as export and import facilities for industrial and agricultural goods and raw materials. Inverkeithing and St David's harbours are used for ship breaking and water borne leisure pursuits are catered for at Dysart, Elie, St Andrews, Tayport and Woodhaven. The now greatly diminished fishing community can still find refuge at Crail, Cellardyke, Anstruther and St Monans but home is the principal fishing harbour of Pittenweem which also houses Fife's fish market. The chief role of many of the harbours and landing places noted have been supplanted by changing methods of freight transportation throughout the modern era. These changes have encompassed an improved road system, the introduction of a national rail network and the ever increasing size of ocean going vessels along with the advent of containerisation and juggernauts. At a time when the road haulage of freight is seen as the most efficient and economical mode of transport it is difficult to envisage a period when movement of goods overland was carried out by carts and packhorses.

At the beginning of the 18th century the road system consisted mainly of a few poorly maintained natural land routes between the important Medieval inland Royal Burghs and ecclesiastical centres. There were two great roads: one was part of the nationally important route between Edinburgh and Aberdeen via the ferries at Kinghorn and Woodhaven and the other was the Great North Road from Edinburgh to Inverness by Queensferry, Kinross and Perth. Improvements in agricultural practices and the exploitation of natural resources from the mid-18th century were to lead to demands for an im-proved internal road network. The need for a systematic road building and maintenance programme had been recognised in 1699 with the passing of the Statute Labour Act. This Act put the onus on landowners to supply men and materials to maintain the roads in their district. The need may have been recognised but the system was not sufficiently co-ordinated to bring about substantial improvement, nor expansion, to the existing network. If the 18th century witnessed only minor changes to overland routes, the first fifty years of the next century saw an extended period of improvement that transformed communications within the Kingdom. The passage of the 1790 and 1797 Turnpike Acts led to a number of road building schemes in both the eastern and western portions of the region. Further Acts passed between 1802 and 1842 brought the total of proposals for turnpikes to over eighty, the majority of which were instigated. The resultant combination of new and upgraded roads led to a network that would be familiar to the present day traveller. An important aspect of the road developments was the increased access it provided to the various ports, harbours and the all important crossing points on both the Forth and Tay estuaries.

The phrase 'since time immemorial' can be found in many documents pertaining to the crossing points that have operated from the Fife shoreline. Existing records bear witness to the fact that these crossings were not simply for passengers but carried all manner of goods and livestock. The existence of a large number of ferry points reflects their importance to the economy of not just Fife but the east coast as a whole. It should be noted that the alternative to using the passage boats between Edinburgh and the north was a very long overland detour via Stirling Bridge. The modern era has witnessed the rationalisation, modernisation and demise of these ferry services as new forms of transport and modes of communication have been harnessed.

There were five crossing points operating during the 18th and early 19th centuries across the Tay estuary. The most easterly of these was South Ferry Port on Craig which was to become known as Tayport by the mid-19th century. Others were located westwards from here at Newport, Woodhaven, Balmerino and Newburgh. The latter two were local services whereas the three lower estuary crossings were of national importance. The crossing at Tayport is reputedly one of the oldest in Scotland. Its location at the narrowest part of the estuary on an old land route between the ancient ecclesiastical centres of St. Andrews and Arbroath lends credence to this view. During the 18th century one particular commodity that contributed to the profitability of the passage was the movement of cattle from the north of Scotland to markets farther south. This was a trade that, according to the author of the Old Statistical Account, was severely curtailed by the bridging of the Tay at Perth in 1771. The fortunes of Tayport were to take another downturn when a new ferry terminal was constructed upriver at Newport in 1822. This terminal also led to the end of services from Woodhaven, a place that had been the premier crossing point thirty years earlier due to the construction of a road between it and the county town of Cupar. The introduction of steam ferries and the decision of the Ferry Trustees to build a new pier combined to make Newport the main crossing point to Dundee and the North East until services were abandoned in 1966. However, all was not plain sailing for the ferry operators throughout this period. Its supremacy was first challenged when the Edinburgh and Northern Railway bought the rights of passage at Tayport and embarked upon the construction of new harbours, both here and on the north shore at Broughty Ferry, which would transform the fortunes of this crossing for a few decades. From 1851 until the opening of the first Tay rail bridge in 1878 the ferries plying between these two harbours were purpose built vessels able to carry train wagons and their passengers. The collapse of the first rail bridge led to a further eight years of prosperity until the second Tay rail bridge was opened in 1887 and the rail ferry was abandoned. The purpose built rail ferries may have been removed but the crossing stayed active in the form of a passenger service until the mid-1960s. Although the Newport to Dundee service fell on lean times with the introduction of rail services it managed to continue and indeed flourished with the rise in popularity of motor transport. In the end, increased use of the motor car led to the building of a new road bridge across the Tay and this led to the demise of the Fifies, a mode of transport across the Tay that had been around in one form or another for some eight centuries.

The southern crossing points shared a similar history to those in the north. The numerous ferry services that existed between Largo and Torryburn throughout the 17th and 18th centuries gradually became concentrated in fewer and fewer harbours. At the end of the 18th century the principal crossing on the Forth was at Pettycur, where nine boats were stationed. Other places from which it was possible to hire passage included Kirkcaldy and Kinghorn, all of which were collectively known as 'the broad passage'. The narrow passage was situated at North Queensferry and had been in use since at least the 11th century. Like Tayport in the north, Burntisland was to become the boom ferry for a few decades. In 1850 the first rail ferry in the world, the *Leviathan*, came into operation, linking Burntisland and Granton on the opposite side of the Firth. This crossing was to be in service until the opening of the Forth Railway Bridge in 1890. After this date the only crossing that was fully maintained was the one operating between North and South Queensferry, a link with the distant past that was severed in 1964 when the Forth Road Bridge was opened to motor vehicles.

The initial bridging of the Firths by railways was the culmination of a transport revolution that had started 45 years earlier in 1845. In that year 16 projects were lodged with the authorities concerning the building of railway lines across the region. The victor was to be the Edinburgh and Northern Railway Company which opened their main line from Burntisland to Ladybank, with branch lines to Cupar and Lindores, in 1847. A year later they completed the links to Perth and Tayport and opened a line to Dunfermline. It was this company, having changed their name to the Edinburgh Perth and Dundee Railway, that was to operate the train ferries across the Firths. By the early 1860s it had become part of the amalgamated North British Railway Company that was to finance the bridging of the Firths. In the 1890s Fife was criss-crossed by 421 km of line that was considered to be 'very complete, no important place being left unconnected with the main line'. The railway connections remained very complete until the 1960s when rationalisation led to many of the country lines being cut.

Present day Fife retains the road and rail bridges. Apart from the construction of both road bridges improvements to communications in the last few decades have resulted in the building of the M90 to Perth from the Forth Road Bridge and a west Fife highway that connects the growing towns of Kirkcaldy and Glenrothes with this main transport artery. Although another road bridge across the Forth has been endorsed by many, Fife Council included, it remains to be seen if such a project will materialise. The main east coast railway line still connects Fife with Aberdeen and Edinburgh but more frequent services north of Kirkcaldy and a station at the Fife end of the Tay Bridge would improve the service considerably. The instigation of a Fife commuter service to Edinburgh in the early 1980s and the opening of a new station at Thornton, for Glenrothes, in 1994, provides evidence that the railway can provide a viable transport option to travellers going both north and south.

INDUSTRY AND COMMERCE (SEE ALSO CHAPTERS 15, 16 AND 17)

The industrial and commercial activity associated with Fife has often been portrayed as a combination of mining, fishing and farming. It is without doubt that these three industries have played an important role in the economy but they are by no means the only ones that have provided employment and wages to its residents. Textile manufacture, both spinning and weaving, was once central to the wealth of the area. Salt making, lime burning, brick and tile manufacture, pottery, shipbuilding, paper-making, electronics and services are but some of the enterprises that have contributed to the diverse industrial and commercial base of the past and in the present.

At the beginning of the modern era Fife had a limited range of industries operating on a modest scale. Coal-mining was one, allied to which was the quarrying and burning of limestone and the extraction of salt from sea-water. These concerns, by their very nature, were confined to specific areas where the raw materials were abundant. In general the salt-pans were located on the southern coastline, with coal-mining in the south-west and lime quarries on a number of coastal and upland locations. The manufacture of textiles, mainly but not exclusively linen, also operated on a small scale, at household level, in nearly every community, whilst agriculture and fishing remained the staple of many a parish. The pace of industrial change began to quicken in the early decades of 19th century, accelerating remarkably from the 1850s until the outbreak of World War One. For a long time the textile trade continued to underpin much of the economy but by 1870 coal-mining and its allied heavy industries were beginning to play an increasingly important role. The old stalwart of the economy, salt, had diminished greatly in importance by 1830 and the new, lime, would contract considerably a decade or so later. The introduction of steam power to the manufacturing process changed the social and economic landscape, whilst agricultural improvement and increased mining activity altered the physical one. Their combined effect would result in the expansion of the textile towns and mining villages and create a clear demarcation between rural and urban economic activity. The inter-war years were characterised by uncertainty and strife whereas the immediate post-war era boomed. The last thirty years has been a period of reorganisation and reorientation as the economy shifted away from its traditional roots to a predominantly service orientated one.

The extraction of coal from the landscape was not new to Fife in the 18th century. The monks at Dunfermline and Culross were digging for coal as early as the 13th century and Sir George Bruce of Culross had sunk a mine into the waters of the Forth in the 1600s. The increase in output during the 18th century can be attributed to an increased domestic and export trade, the expansion of the salt and lime industries and the creation of an iron industry. Most of the coal used in the early decades of the century was mined from seams on or near to the coast to cater for the salt and coastwise export trade. By the end of the 1760s new techniques in mining, allowing deeper shafts to be sunk, and the building of wagonways from nearby pits to the coast were linked to a growth in production stimulated by exports and an expansion of the local lime industry.

Like salt-pans the lime-kilns required large amounts of coal to make small amounts of lime. Unlike the salt industry lime-kilns were eventually spread throughout much of the region from the shores of the Forth to the hills near Strathkinness. The widespread nature of the raw material gave a boost to a number of small inland coal fields that had not hitherto been considered economical. The majority of lime workings, of which there were over thirty around 1800, were modest in scale but there was one impressive exception; the lime works at Charlestown on the Forth. A limited amount of lime had been quarried from this area since the early 17th century. As demand grew throughout the 18th century, the 5th Earl of Elgin greatly expanded the scale of operations. During the 1770s, in addition to constructing fourteen draw kilns, the largest group in Scotland, he improved the harbour and laid out an entirely new village. By 1790 80,000–90,000 tons of lime were being quarried and the port was handling 1300 cargoes a year. In the early years of the 19th century superior grades of lime from the north of England became available to customers in Scotland, thereby competing with local producers. This competition accounted for the closure of many Fife quarries by the middle of the century. The continuing operations of the Cults Lime Company, by Cupar, maintains a modern-day link with an industry that once flourished in many parts of the region.

Lime was also an ingredient, along with coal, of another industry with Fife associations. The setting up of the Carron Iron Company, near Falkirk, in 1759, had an effect upon Fife almost immediately. Coal was needed for the furnaces and lime for the fluxing process, both of which were imported from workings in Fife. The company also worked ironstone mines around Dunfermline from about 1771 and imported the more readily available clay band ores from as far afield as St Andrews. The initial processing of iron ore in Fife began at the turn of the 19th century with the founding of the Balgonie Iron Works, a venture that lasted until 1815. It would be a further 35 years before the industry was revived for an other short lived period. One of the first new ironworks was at Dunfermline where the Transy Ironworks operated between 1846 and 1855. Those at nearby Oakley survived a little longer until 1869, whilst the Lumphinnans and Lochgelly ventures remained in operation into the 1870s. With nine furnaces in production in 1850, thirteen in 1870 and none within a further five years, the revival of the trade lasted only a decade or so longer than the initial venture. It is not for its short lifespan that this industry is notable but in its contribution to the concentration of industrial development near to the coal fields, a trend that continued well into the present century.

As the demand for coal increased during the 19th and 20th centuries, mining in Fife expanded to cater for the need. Employment in the industry increased from 3000 in 1851 to 27,000 just prior to the first world war. Output during this period also rose from a few hundred thousand tons to nine million, the bulk of which was for export. In consequence, coal became the mainstay of the economy, displacing textiles and agriculture that had been the main earners throughout the previous century. Cowdenbeath and Lochgelly, at one time surrounded by productive pits, became the hub of the coal industry. During the inter-war years output and numbers employed fell considerably; the peak of 1914 was never to be reached again. Nationalisation of the industry's 33 collieries in 1947 and the decision to further exploit the Fife reserves led to a short-lived period of high expectations. The failure of the Rothes Colliery project, due to flooding, and the resultant blow to the development programme was a precursor to the contraction of the industry during the 1980s that saw the numbers employed fall by over 50% between 1981 and 1991. An industry that once dominated Fife's economy now has fewer than 2000 employees working at the last remaining deep mine, Castlebridge, as well as a number of open-cast sites.

The mainly localised nature of industrial concerns in the 18th and 19th centuries made the number of participants in them small when compared to the textile industry of the same period. During the course of these centuries Fife became one of the main textile counties of Scotland. The already established trade links with the Baltic provided access to the raw flax upon which the industry was based. The import of lint seed enabled home cultivation of flax and was therefore a factor in the widespread distribution of the industry. Prior to the introduction of the factory system, especially spinning mills, it was not uncommon for the cloth to be grown, spun, bleached if necessary, and woven by the same family. The linen industry encompassed a number of finished products from napkins to sails and Fife looms produced a host of different items. As early as 1733 the importance of table linen to the economy of Dunfermline Parish was noted. Within a few decades Inverkeithing became engaged in similar production, whilst Pathhead and

Dysart had dual manufacturing interests in table linen and the checks and ticks that were identified with close neighbour Kirkcaldy. Other textile towns and villages, Cupar, St Andrews, Falkland, Auchtermuchty, Leven and Leslie were associated with the production of coarse cloth, especially osnaburghs. Indeed, the village of Dairsie in north-east Fife was originally named after this type of linen. The finished products were purchased by merchants from the main towns who would then sell them to the English and American markets. The introduction of water power led to the erection of a number of spinning mills on the watercourses of Fife. These new mills provided the yarn that made hand-loom weavers the aristocrats of the industry until the widespread introduction of steam power to the manufacturing process during the second half of the 19th century made them redundant in favour of factory operatives.

The rise of the factory system led to the concentration of manufacturing in towns. At the beginning of the 20th century Kirkcaldy and Dunfermline looms dominated the trade. However, there were still mills to be found in many of the smaller urban centres: Leven, Leslie, Auchtermuchty, Cupar, Newburgh and Tayport amongst them. Initial contraction of the industry can be traced to the loss of American markets during the inter-war period. The immediate post-war era saw nearly forty firms still engaged in an industry that now numbers barely a handful. The penetration of markets by industrialising nations, the introduction of man-made fibres and the concomitant cost of upgrading plant and machinery has resulted in the closure of most of those firms. The textile manufacturer Scott and Fyffe Ltd in Tayport is one firm with a long history that has weathered the storms of the recent past and remains in production today.

Another process that has links with textiles and remains in production, albeit a shadow of its former self, is the making of linoleum. A product that has its roots in sails and floor cloth manufacture, it was first produced in 1877 by Nairn of Kirkcaldy. The product soon found a ready market from homes to battleships and in consequence a number of other firms were started in the town. Although Kirkcaldy is recognised as the home of Scottish linoleum, and remains the only place in which it is manufactured, it was also made at factories in Newburgh and Falkland until it went out of fashion in the early 1970s in favour of vinyl and fitted carpets. In recent years an increase in environmental awareness has led to a revival of this combination of natural substances.

It has already been noted that the harnessing of water as a power source was an important development in the expansion of the textile industry. This is also true of an industry that remains a significant component of the economy: the firms of Tullis Russell, Fettykill, and Culter Fine Papers remain as links to a paper-making industry that was first introduced in 1806 on the River Leven. Within twenty years there were a further three mills in production, two on the

Leven and one on the Eden at Guardbridge. Further developments in the industry led to Fife containing the third largest concentration of paper mills in Scotland by 1890. In the 1950s seven mills were in production and a healthy future was predicted for the industry. In reality international competition and new technology has led to rationalisation in the industry, which has resulted in the closure of firms and the specialisation of production for those that remain. Water or to be more precise, the sea, has long had a bearing upon two other Fife occupations: fishing and ship/boat-building.

During the 18th century the majority of Fife fishermen were participating in the white fishery trade. Using open boats in coastal waters they cast long lines of bated hooks for cod and haddock. The markets for the fresh and dried catch were the larger towns and burghs of the area, along with Dundee and Edinburgh. The shellfish that abounded – cockles, whelks and mussels mainly – were also gathered and brought to market. For some of the Forth coastal communities the market for lobster and crab became an important source of revenue. There is evidence that Crail participated in the North Sea herring trade in the early decades but for most of the fishing communities it would be late in the century before they became involved. The movement of the shoals into the Forth, along with improved government subsidies, were the catalysts. In the Firth of Tay and on the rivers Eden and Leven the salmon fishing became an increasingly important source of employment and revenue from the middle of the century. Although the trade was dominated by Perth merchants, they frequently used local ships, especially the smacks belonging to Newburgh. The main market was London, with southern European cities also being catered for. By the end of the period a thriving national and international trade in ice-packed fresh and par-boiled fish was being conducted.

The various branches of the fishing industry have met with differing fortunes since the opening of the 19th century. The salmon trade that was a feature of the previous century was dealt a blow by legislation passed in 1812 that banned the use of fixed nets. Although this diminished the overall size of the catch, the export of the fish remained an important source of revenue throughout the century and well into the next. Indeed the despatch of local salmon to the London market ceased relatively recently. Another venture pursued by local fishermen had a far shorter life span. Ships from Kirkcaldy and Burntisland joined in the hunt for the whale for a short period during the early part of the 19th century, but diminished returns meant that these ventures were few and far between and by 1835 the industry was in decline. The vast majority of the coastal villages associated with fishing were not involved in either of these pursuits. The fleet based along the Forth, especially in the East Neuk, pursued the herring and the white fish, cod, ling and haddock. Prior to the increased export of coal from ports along the Forth there were few places not engaged in the fishing. In the 1860s the number of fishing ports on the Fife coast numbered at least twenty-four, stretching from Newburgh on the Tay to Limekilns on the Forth. Anstruther and near neighbour Cellardyke became the home of the Fife herring industry by the end of the century with a fleet of over two hundred boats which included most of the steam trawlers. The boats engaged in the white fishing invariably called at Pittenweem, a port that accounted for over 66% of landings during the 1930s. The third most important port in the East Neuk was St Monans which drew custom from both the white and herring fishing industries. The total absence of the herring shoals in the Forth from 1948 resulted in a reorientation away from inshore to deep-sea fishing. The resultant costs led to a considerable decline in the size of the fleet which has been ongoing ever since, a situation exacerbated in recent years by declining stocks and EU quotas. Fishing no longer retains the importance it had to the Fife economy a generation ago, although it remains a significant factor in the economic health of the East Neuk. Within the last twenty years it can be argued that the Fife fishing industry has come full circle and is again a village industry carried out by small boats. Today the industry is centred upon the village of St Monans where the present fleet of thirty-five vessels is located.

When vessels were first built on the Fife shoreline is difficult to trace, but at various times throughout the 19th century wooden sailing vessels were built and repaired on the Tay at Newburgh, Woodhaven and Tayport. The Forth ports of Kirkcaldy, Kincardine, Kinghorn, Limekilns, Charlestown, Dysart and Inverkeithing witnessed similar activities. By the 1890s shipbuilding could be found at only two locations, both on the Forth. One was at Abden, near Kinghorn, where iron steam-vessels were constructed, and the other at Inverkeithing where timber remained the preferred building material. The year 1918 saw the founding of the last shipbuilding yard in Fife at Burntisland. The Burntisland Shipbuilding Company built numerous steam and diesel driven bulk carriers before the company ceased operations. Many of the skills associated with this industry remain in use at the newly privatised Rosyth dockyard and the breakers' yards operating at Inverkeithing and St David's harbours. These same skills have also been utilised at Methil in connection with the North Sea oil and gas industry. On a lesser scale, but just as important to its customers, has been boatbuilding, an industry carried on in the past at a number of fishing ports from Tayport to Kincardine. In the early part of the 20th century there were five boat-building companies operating in the East Neuk and the decline of the fishing fleet is mirrored in the fact that now there are none.

The poor and inefficient state of agriculture in Fife during the 18th century is commented upon by almost all the writers of the *Statistical Accounts* in the 1790s. The introduction of new crop varieties and methods of farming would appear to have been slow, if not non-existent, in much of the region; but changes there had been. Enclosures are noted in a number of parishes as is the introduction of turnips, clover and potatoes. That these changes were not yet widespread and that much of the inland area was still unimproved is the probable cause of such negative commentary. Whatever the actual state of the land it is without doubt that Fife was an exporter of agricultural produce from at least the 1760s. The ports of Balmerino, Newport, Newburgh, St Andrews, Kirkcaldy and Elie were some of those involved in the grain trade to London and the west coast via the Forth and Clyde Canal.

Improvements carried out in the next century were to fashion the landscape we know today. The *New Statistical Account* abounds with reference to new farming techniques, road improvements and the construction of farm buildings. The introduction of root crops to the newly drained and limed land meant that land that had been of poor quality was now productive. The improved conditions and new breeding techniques led to a rise in exports of cattle, grain and potatoes throughout the century. In the present century farming has undergone more change with mechanisation and a loss of international markets resulting in a steady decline in numbers employed. The drop of 20% recorded between 1881 and 1931 saw the numbers employed fall to 8000. That number has continued to decline to a figure of 2479 people involved in farming in 1997. The number and size of holdings has also changed over this period. In 1867 there were 1109, the 1947 count showed 2179 and presently the number stands at 1089. A trend from larger to smaller back to larger average size of holdings can be detected but there are other reasons for the decline in overall numbers since the 1950s. Fife was once a landscape dominated by mixed farming, with dairy cattle also prominent. Since the 1970s there has been a shift away from this to an industry dominated by a variety of crops. In the last two decades oilseed rape cultivation has gone from little or nothing to 10% and vegetables have increased to 22%. The old staples of wheat, barley and other cereals still dominate the landscape but their acreage is shrinking. The number of farms has been reduced by over 2% per annum since 1985; of those that remain many are also operating alternative enterprises on their land. Despite these changes agriculture still accounts for over 5% of Fife's GDP with an annual turnover in excess of £100 million. This figure does not include the revenue from land that has been taken out of production and changed to recreational use. In the last ten years there has been a marked increase in such activity.

Economic activity in Fife at the end of the 20th century no longer revolves around the traditional postwar occupations of coal mining, farming and fishing. The 1970s and 1980s saw the collapse of these industries as significant sources of regional employment. During the same period manufacturing has also declined sharply but remains important due to the development of an electronics sector. Glenrothes has become the centre of this activity with a variety of companies providing considerable diversity of activity. However, the industry is dependent upon an inward investment strategy that has led to 42.5% of employment in foreign-owned plants. These plants are extremely susceptible to the vagaries of the world market. The decision by the Korean electronics giant Hyundai not to occupy a major site outside Dunfermline underlines this fact. Despite this setback electronics is expected to continue being a major component of the manufacturing sector for the foreseeable future.

Since the 1980s the service sector has become the foundation of Fife's employment structure, accounting for over 60% of jobs. An increasingly important segment of this sector is tourism, accounting for expenditure in excess of £250 million per annum and employing over 6000 people in the 1990s. The town of St Andrews is the focal point for visitors, especially golfers, along with the picturesque coastal settlements along the shores of the Forth. During the last decade a number of interpretative/visitor centres have opened their doors to an increasing number of visitors. These developments have meant that alongside the natural beauty and numerous historic attractions of the area tourists can also gain access to information about Fife's natural, industrial and social past.

CONCLUSION

The description of Fife as a 'beggar's mantle fringed with gold' attributed to James VI may have had some validity in its time but within a hundred years the mantle had become the blue of the flax field. Since then the developments outlined above show that Fife has played an important role in Scotland's modern social and economic history. This is a role that she continues to play in the present and is poised to maintain as we enter another century and new millennium.

SECTION TWO

NINE

PATTERNS OF LORDSHIP, SECULAR AND ECCLESIASTICAL
c. 1100 – *c.* 1300

The monolithic block of the former shire, county or region of Fife is an instantly recognisable feature of the political map of modern Scotland, occupying the promontory between the firths of Tay and Forth. Its unity is often presented as ancient in origin, dating from its existence in the Early Historic period as a Pictish sub-kingdom – a memory preserved in 'The Kingdom of Fife' label – and continuing through the Medieval period in the form of the premier earldom of the kingdom of the Scots. Yet it is a thoroughly false presentation, for throughout the Middle Ages Fife never constituted a unitary political entity, but was home to a shifting pattern of lordships, secular and ecclesiastical, albeit largely under the social leadership of the Earl of Fife. The qualifying 'largely' must be emphasised, because the earls did not monopolise lordship within the peninsula, for within the region there were two other great lords, the Crown and the Church, of which the Crown was by far the greatest in the early Middle Ages. Under this triumvirate, the landscape was broken up into a patchwork of lesser lordships, whose existence is hinted at by the scattering of mottes, the earthen mounds of timber castles which served as the seats of power of the territorial nobility in the 12th and 13th centuries, and the ruined monastic complexes which formed the nerve-centres of sprawling ecclesiastical estates.

A pattern of secular estates of Pictish origin but surviving under new masters through the 9th and 10th centuries, and beyond, has been posited by Simon Taylor to be fossilised in the distribution of *pit-* place-names.[1] This apart, however, there is no documented evidence for the structure of landholding in Fife before the later 11th and 12th centuries, when the earlier arrangement can be reconstructed backwards from information recorded in royal and aristocratic charters. The foundation of a priory of Benedictine monks at Dunfermline by Malcolm III and St Margaret in the early 1070s points to the existence in the south-west of the region – the district formerly known as Fothrif – of a block of important royal estates from which the king and his immediate successors provided a substantial endowment for tbe monastery.[2] These royal properties, a network of agricultural settlements grouped into small administrative units known as shires, stretched along the north shore of the Forth from Clackmannan to Newburn on the eastern slopes of Largo Law. Whole shires, such as those of Kirkcaldy, Gellet and Goatmilk, were gifted to the monks for their support, but the Crown retained control of important centres, such as Dunfermline itself west of the Pittencrieff Burn, or the blocks of property subsequently developed as the royal burghs of Inverkeithing and Kinghorn.[3] North-east Fife contained further royal estates, one block in the East Neuk centred on Crail and a second, more dispersed complex, extending from Auchtermuchty and Falkland to Forgan at the north-eastern extremity of the region. Here, too, lay the core of the sprawling estates of the bishops of St Andrews, centred an St Andrews itself. Finally, running through the centre of Fife from Markinch to Cupar and south to Largo, Elie and Ardross lay the complex of properties controlled by the earls of Fife and their kin.

MONASTIC LORDSHIP

The pattern of lordship was not immutable and as it emerges in the course of the 12th century can be seen in a state of continuous development. A key feature of this change was the rapid growth of the major ecclesiastical lordships of the bishop of St Andrews, the priory of St Andrews[4] and Dunfermline Abbey in the early 12th century, and the more compact and localised holdings built up by the priory on May Island,[5] the East Lothian nunnery of North Berwick[6] and Inchcolm Abbey.[7] Two newcomers in the early 13th century, the abbeys of Culross and Balmerino,[8] while never enjoying the scale of endowment of their 12th-century brethren, nevertheless secured significant landed interests in their own localities, but a third, Lindores, had its main properties other than its home estate outwith Fife.[9]

The chief component of these early monastic lordships was land. At Dunfermline, for example, the 11th-century priory had been endowed by Malcolm III and St Margaret with properties largely clustered around the original church of the Holy Trinity within what would become Dunfermline parish (at Broomhill, Urquhart, Pitcorthie, Pitbauchlie and Pitliver), plus the shire of Kirkcaldy and the adjacent lands of Bogie, and lesser Inveresk across the Forth in Lothian. Subsequent endowments saw a consolidation of this original pattern: Duncan II added the towns of Luscar some 4.5 km to the north-west of the monastery; Edgar gave the shire of Gellet, 2.5 km to its south; his brother Ethelred added Hailes to their Inveresk holding; Alexander I gifted Primrose, the shire of Goatmilk (now underlying Glenrothes), Pitconmark and Balwearie near Kirkcaldy, Keith (Humbie) in East Lothian, and the unidentified lands of 'Drumbenin', while his wife, Queen Sibylla, added the whole of the extensive lands of Beath 10 km north-east of Dunfermline.[10] Following what was effectively his refoundation of the community, David I added substantially to this already significant holding, bestowing on the monks the lands of Dunfermline to the east of Pittencrieff Glen, Fod 3.5 km east of the abbey, land at Kinghorn, greater Inveresk, plus properties in the royal burghs of Berwick, Edinburgh, Stirling, Dunfermline and Perth.[11] This marked a new point of departure for the monastery, and before the end of David's reign they had acquired landed interests scattered from Moray to Lothian, but the bulk of their estates remained concentrated in the southern coastal fringe of Fife.

Landed estates of this type were intended to provide the monks with means of economic support, either through direct cultivation as demesne or from rents. Although the landlords were churchmen, the rights which they enjoyed were no less inferior to those of the secular nobility. Thus, at Inveresk the monks gained control of the lordly rights to the lucrative fishings and the mill – at which all their tenants were bound (thirled) to have their grain ground, paying the monks a portion of the grain (multure) in the process. Other mills were added as the landed holdings developed, the 16th-century abbey rental listing at least fifteen meal-mills in the abbey's possession, of which three were in Dunfermline itself.[12] The multures and rents from these mills formed a significant element of the monastic income, but David I otherwise provided a substantial financial base through generous grants of portions of crown revenue: an eighth of his income from 'pleas and quarrels in Fife and Fothrif', the teind of his cain (a render in kind) and of his hunting from the same area, and so on. Most of these grants were made in what is referred to as 'free alms', where the king renounced – with some reservations – his right to the secular services due from those lands, receiving in return the spiritual render of prayers and masses said in perpetuity for the salvation of the souls of himself and his family. In effect, the kings were surrendering many of their local rights of lordship to the Church.

Landed lordship entailed lordship over men, in terms of both physical ownership and seigneurial or jurisdictional rights. The inhabitants of the abbey's landed properties, both free tenants and serfs who were tied to the land (*neyfs* or, in Latin, *nativi*, meaning literally 'born of the land'), were its men and, as such, they were obliged to perform a variety of labour services and dues to their lord, such as field-work – particularly at ploughing, sowing and harvest times–maintenance of fences, hedges and ditches, carting of firewood, and, where appropriate, military service in the royal army and labour for royal works. Such service would originally have been of great economic importance to the monks, but in the course of time there was a steady shift towards commuting labour dues for a money payment as the monks opted to rent out their lands rather than cultivate them for themselves. Nevertheless, serfs were valuable commodities, both in terms of labour and the children whom they would produce, and lords were empowered to retrieve or reclaim runaways whom they could trace.[13] In the 12th century, beneath the level of the various

grades of unfree peasants, can be glimpsed a more servile class which was
treated as disposable property by its lords. These may have originated as slaves,
whom Scottish armies were recorded as taking during campaigns in northern
England, and probably elsewhere, in the 11th and 12th centuries. Thus, about
1126, David I granted Dunfermline possession of three men, Ragewin,
Gillepatric and Ulchil,[14] and soon after 1173 William the Lion gave the monks
Gillandreas mac Suthen and all of his offspring in perpetuity.[15] The clearest
expression of this lordship over men lay in the judicial rights which the abbot
exercised over the monastic estate. By the 1130s, the abbot was dispensing
justice in his own court like any secular lord, with the Crown reserving only
certain capital crimes for trial before royal justices and the right to intervene
should the abbot be negligent in his legal proceedings. Before the end of the
13th century, these basic legal powers had expanded vastly and the abbots of
Dunfermline exercised what is known as a regality jurisdiction, i.e. the right to
try all cases except treason, free from intervention by royal justiciars or sheriffs.
This was a mark of exceptional status, perhaps reflecting Dunfermline's
position as the principal royal monastery north of the Forth, and was shared in
the 13th century by its only clear rival for that role, Arbroath Abbey in Angus.
The physical expression of this privileged position can still be seen in the ruins
of the monastic complex at Dunfermline, where the great abbey gatehouse and
the remains of the substantial precinct wall represent the material projection of
the seigneurial might of the abbot.[16] There could be no clearer statement of the
worldly power of the Medieval Church.

Within Fife, Dunfermline's only, and ultimately more successful, rival was
St Andrews Cathedral Priory. The origins of the monastic landholding there
can be traced back to the foundation of the Celtic community in the 9th
century, but most of this early estate probably came to form the core of
the bishops' lordship before the establishment of the Augustinian priory in the
1120s, while portions of it remained in the hands of the celide of St Mary
on the Rock. A major new landholding, however, had been assembled, largely
through royal grant, by the mid-12th century. Although this included
substantial properties in Gowrie and in Lothian, the core of the complex
was clustered around St Andrews.[17] The rivalry of the bishops, with whom the
priory was often in conflict, probably lies behind the lateness of the grant
of a regality jurisdiction to the canons: that privileged status was secured only
in the early 14th century. As at Dunfermline, the earthly power of the prior
was projected through the construction of substantial gatehouses and a circuit
of walls – greatly elaborated by Prior Hepburn in the 16th century – with
the magnificent 14th-century Pends gatehouse acting as a clear demarcation
between the bishop's burgh and the priory precinct.[18] By the later Middle Ages,
the priors of St Andrews were regarded as the most senior of the heads of
Scotland's monasteries, in reflection of the wealth and power of the

community over which they ruled.

THE BISHOPS OF ST ANDREWS

Powerful though the priors of St Andrews were to become in the later Middle Ages, their influence could not match that of the bishops of St Andrews, the greatest ecclesiastics in the kingdom. Details of how they accumulated the enormous complex of properties and rights which pertained to their dignity, scattered from Nigg on the south side of the Dee estuary at Aberdeen in the north to Berwick-upon-Tweed in the south, have been lost, but of what they consisted can be recovered from later records. Significant elements of the bishops' properties lay north of the Tay, especially in Gowrie, and south of the Forth in Lothian, but it was in Fife that the major block of properties was located. The core of these lay in north-east Fife and especially around St Andrews itself,[19] which lay on episcopal land and had been developed as a trading burgh by the bishops, who had secured a charter from David I permitting the holding of a weekly market there.[20] The bishops remained the superior lords of the burgh throughout the Middle Ages, royal burgh status being gained only in 1620.

The presence of the independent Augustinian priory serving the bishops' cathedral appears to have become quite early a source of friction. Before the end of the 12th century, Bishop Roger de Beaumont moved out of the cathedral precinct and began the building of the most potent symbol of the episcopal lordship, St Andrews Castle.[21] It was not the bishops' only residence, manor-houses existed at Inchmurtlach near Boarhills, at Monimail between Letham and Collessie, and at Dairsie, but it acted as the administrative focus of the sprawling episcopal domain. The layout of the original castle dictated the plan of its successors, and it is probable that the present stone curtain wall follows the line of an early earth-and-timber enclosure. From the first, however, like the stronghold of some great secular magnate, it was intended to stand as a symbol of the bishops' earthly might and a stone gate-tower in the centre of its south side acted as a highly visual projection of that authority. Like the gatehouses at Dunfermline and the priory of St Andrews, this gate-tower also proclaimed the secular power of the man whose principal residence this was, and here the bishops presided over the law-courts which gave reality to their jurisdictional lordship.

EARLS AND LORDS

Unlike the ecclesiastical lordships which were constructed in the 12th and 13th centuries, little detail survives of the complexes of secular lordly power which were built up over the same period. Indeed, it is not until the later 12th century that a pattern of lordships beneath the level of the earls of Fife can be pieced together in any detail. The earls themselves, drawn from the MacDuff kin, possibly descended from the 10th-century king of Scots, Dub mac Maelcoluim (d. 966), are somewhat shadowy figures until the middle of the 12th century when a clear succession emerges. Traditionally, the 1st Earl within our period is given as Ethelred, son of King Malcolm III,[22] who could only have held the earldom from 1097 when the Mac Malcolms returned from exile in England, but it is difficult to fit him into a chronology of succession where Earl Constantine held the title from 1095 to *c.* 1130.[23] Records of Constantine's activities as earl are scanty, but good evidence survives for his exercise of some of the functions of Gaelic lordship. The most prominent of these was as leader of the common army of his province, in which capacity he can be seen in the late 1120s,[24] a role in which other Scottish earls can be seen throughout the 12th and 13th centuries.[25] Interestingly, 'the bishop's army', composed presumably of the men from the episcopal estates and forming either a distinct entity from the host under the earl's leadership or a clearly identifiable element within it, occurs on the same occasion, underscoring the nature of the secular power of the bishops of St Andrews. When these forces first appear, however, it is not in a military capacity but in a function as a court summoned to settle a property dispute. Here, then, is the earl as social and political leader of his province, acting as both leader of its army and as president over a provincial court composed of that army.[26]

While the MacDuff kin continued to exercise many of the attributes of Gaelic lordship as late as the 1290s – 'MacDuff' of Fife, acting as head of the kindred during the minority of Earl Duncan IV, led the army of Fife at the battle of Falkirk in 1298[27] – the kin-based society over which they presided had undergone profound change as it encountered and integrated with the new styles of lordship which were introduced into Scotland by the crown after *c.* 1100. The importation of 'feudal' forms and traditions in the course of the 12th century had an early impact in Fife, where the Crown possessed a significant reservoir of land from which it could provide holdings for a colonising nobility. The process of colonisation may have begun in the 1070s when Malcolm III received a small group of Anglo-Saxon aristocratic refugees who were fleeing the Norman conquest of England. One, Merleswain, was probably the grandfather of a second Merleswain who in the later 12th century held the lands of Kennoway, where the earthwork motte which stood as a symbol of his seigneurial rights can still be seen, and Ardross between Elie and St Monance.[28] The political instability which followed the death of Malcolm III in 1093 may have put a temporary halt to such settlement and it was possibly not until the reign of Alexander I that new infeftments took place. One of the earliest of these was the grant of Lochore to Robert the Burgundian, who was in dispute with the Church of St Andrews over the boundary between his property and the churchlands of Kirkness before 1126.[29] However, it was in the reign of David I that the new tenurial forms have been presented traditionally as beginning to make significant headway in Fife, when Earl Duncan I (*c.* 1133–54) surrendered his earldom to the king and received it back as a feu held on specified terms.[30]

This conversion of the earldom of Fife into a feudal lordship held of the Crown was of great significance for the spread of feudalism into Scotland, as it is the first instance of one of the great Gaelic earldoms embracing the new forms of tenure. Research recently, however, has called into question the weight which should be placed on this act, for the degree of political or cultural change within the earldom which resulted in the short term from this new-fangled status appears to have been slight.[31] Indeed, its primary effect – and probably its intended aim – was a change in the practice of succession to the earldom, with an older, kindred-based Gaelic system of alternating succession between two segments of the ruling family being replaced by the continental method of primogeniture, where the eldest son of the incumbent lord would succeed his father. This resulted in the exclusion of the descendants of Earl Gille-Micheil (*c.* 1130–1133) from the succession but they received substantial compensation for this disinheritance. Gille-Micheil's son, Hugh, was a significant landholder in the time of David I and Malcolm IV, when he held the lordship of the former abbey of Abernethy which straddled what is now the Fife–Perthshire border and which his descendants, the Abernethy family, continued to hold until the Wars of Independence.[32] He also received the important lordship of Markinch, likewise the location of a celide community, which was in the hands of his son, Hugh, who was described as a knight when he granted its church to the priory of St Andrews.[33]

Beyond the MacDuff kin, little evidence survives for a hierarchy of Gaelic lordship within Fife.[34] The substantial lordship of Leuchars, which was evidently held of the Crown rather than the earl in the later 12th century, may have originated as a native-held property but its lord in the 1150s, Ness son of William, was the son of a man bearing a Norman–French name. This hints at one of the mechanisms used by the crown both to facilitate the spread of 'feudalism' and reward loyal service, and, consequently, thereby bolster their own authority, the marriage of members of the colonial nobility to native heiresses. The policy was used once again in respect of Leuchars in the 1160s when Ness's daughter and heiress, Orabile, was married to Robert de Quincy, one of the rising stars in the royal circle. Certainly, the Crown used intermarriage as a medium for strengthening its relationship with the earls of Fife. After 1153, Countess Ada, mother of kings Malcolm IV and William, continued to hold the complex of royal estates centred on Crail which had been settled on her at the time of her marriage to David I's son, Earl Henry. Her position as a major landholder in eastern Fife was exploited to the benefit of both her children and her de Warenne kin. One niece, Ela, married Earl

Duncan II of Fife, their marriage being marked by the gift to them by Malcolm IV of the royal estates of Strathmiglo, Falkland and Rathillet in Fife and Strathbraan in Perthshire.[35] Connections to both the royal family and the earls of Fife provided an opening for the de Warennes into Fife's landholding community, and by the early 13th century they were prominent benefactors of both Lindores and Culross abbeys.[36] They were, however, just one of several colonial families who were implanted into Fife in the later 12th century.

From *c.* 1160 onwards, the crown lands in Fife were exploited as a source of patronage, with feus being carved out of the royal demesne for favoured servants. Thus, the lordship of Lundin was granted *c.* 1161–4 to Malcolm IV's chamberlain Philip; in *c.* 1162–4 Rosyth and Dundaff were granted to Ralph Frebein.[37] Both of these grants were substantial holdings, for which Philip and Ralph were required to provide the service of one knight in the king's army in place of the old Gaelic obligations of common army service and the payment of cain and the like, but smaller grants were also made, such as those to Henry Revel of the lands of Cultra in Balmerino for the service of half a knight, or to Robert de Newham of the whole of Cambo and a toft in Crail for the service of one foot-soldier and the common army service due from that land.[38] These few surviving recorded instances of infeftment on crown lands are reinforced by a substantial body of evidence for further infeftments for which the crown charters have not survived. Thus, the Mortimers were infeft in Aberdour, the de Cameras in Fordell, and the de Lascelles in Naughton and Forgan before the end of the 12th century.[39]

While the charters which recorded these grants of land were an innovation in secular landholding in Scotland in the early 12th century – they were developed originally by the Church to preserve a record of its rights – the perquisites of lordship which they narrated were of ancient origin and had been exercised by lords for centuries. Although expressed now in overtly feudal language, the economic and juridical lordship enjoyed by the colonists may have been indistinguishable from the rights exercised by the Gaelic lords of Fife. But the cultural trappings introduced by men of largely English or northern French background were radically different from Gaelic traditions. A new vocabulary of lordship was imported along with the colonists, projected most vividly through the armoured horsemen – the knights – with whom the process of 'feudalisation' is commonly associated. Cultural change affected even the most basic symbols of lordship, the residences of power. With them, the knights brought alien traditions in defensive engineering, in particular the motte, represented by the 'inverted pudding-basin' earthen mound – as at Kennoway – upon which towered the timber-built residence of the new lord and his family, raising them literally above the level of their tenants, or the elevated platform – as at Leuchars – which would have been crowned by a cluster of buildings within a defensive enclosure. Few among the native nobility, confident in their inherited status and power, embraced these new traditions for they had no need to advertise their lordship, unlike the feudal parvenus. Indeed, it was not until the later 13th century that the earls of Fife opted for the new cachet of lordly power, the stone castle, when they shifted their seat of lordship from Cupar to Falkland, where the foundations of their great stone castle are preserved as a garden-feature to the north of the 16th-century palace. By then, however, many of the cultural distinctions which had once clearly separated native from newcomer had blurred.

While the building of castles in stone may not have been a priority for many secular lords, native or newcomer, an expression of power and status could be made in the building of a church as the spiritual focus of their lordship. Examples of this can be seen at Markinch, where the earls of Fife may have built the fine 12th-century church of which only the tower survives, or at Leuchars, where the magnificent late Romanesque church was constructed by Ness son of William or his de Quincy successors.[40] A pattern of parishes had evolved before the end of the 13th century, partly as a product of this trend, with some parishes sharing the boundary of the secular lordship of the family who founded the parochial churches. Even on estates of more ancient origin, it is evident that control of the local church often lay in the hands of the secular authority. These were, in effect, proprietary churches where lords founded and built the physical structure, provided the land from which the incumbent priest derived much of his support, and retained control of the right to appoint the priest.

As a national system of teinding developed in the early 12th century, where a tenth of the annual increase of crops and livestock was assigned to the Church for its support, many lay lords of proprietary churches found themselves in effective control of these teinds. The papacy, however, was voicing a powerful line against the perceived incompatibility of spiritual revenues controlled by lay lords. Fear of damnation and a wish to secure salvation in the hereafter prompted many lords to resign their rights over these churches. Thus, for example, Earl Duncan II resigned the churches of Scoonie, Cupar and Markinch, and Ness son of William Leuchars, to the canons of St Andrews priory;[41] and from earls Duncan II and Malcolm, the nuns of North Berwick received the churches of Kilconquhar, Largo, Logie and Aithernie.[42] These resignations transferred the right of patronage from a lay lord to a religious corporation which now became responsible for the appointment of the parish priest. Over time, this basic right was extended, with parish revenues being diverted to the controlling monastery – a process known as appropriation – with often inadequate stipends being allocated for support of the priest. This was a distortion of the papal policy of freeing parishes and church revenues from secular control, for although the revenues were being diverted for the support of the monastic communities, they were viewed as little more than income derived from lordship with little being turned to spiritual use. Control of teind became, in effect, simply another manifestation of the economic lordship enjoyed by the great monastic landlords of the Middle Ages, and one which touched directly on the lives of the population in general.

REFERENCES

1. S. Taylor, infra.
2. *Registrum de Dumfermelyn* (Bannatyne Club, 1842), nos 1–3.
3. *Regesta Regum Scotorum*, i, *The Acts of Malcolm IV*, ed. G. W. S. Barrow (Edinburgh, 1960), 41.
4. *Liber Cartarum Prioratus Sancti Andree in Scotia* (Bannatyne Club, 1841).
5. A. A. M. Duncan, 'Documents relating to the Priory of the Isle of May, *c.* 1140–1313', *PSAS* xc (1956–7), 52–80.
6. *Carte Monialium de Northberwic* (Bannatyne Club, 1847).
7. *Charters of the Abbey of Incholm*, ed. D. E. Easson and A. Macdonald (Scottish History Society, 1938).
8. *Liber Sancte Marie de Balmorinach* (Abbotsford Club, 1841).
9. *Chartulary of the Abbey of Lindores* (Scottish History Society, 1903).
10. *Dunfermline Registrum*, no. 1.
11. Ibid.
12. *Dunfermline Registrum*, appendix II.
13. e.g. *RRS*, i, no. 167.
14. *Dunfermline Registrum*, no. 19.
15. Ibid., no. 64.
16. R. D. Oram, 'Prelatical builders', in R. D. Oram and G. P. Stell, *Lordship and Architecture in Medieval and Renaissance Scotland* (forthcoming, 2001).
17. *RRS*, i, no. 174.
18. Oram, 'Prelatical builders'.
19. See, for example, *Registrum Magni Sigilli Regnum Scotorum*, ii, ed. J. Balfour Paul (reprinted Edinburgh, 1984), no. 1444.
20. *RRS*, i, no. 91.
21. Oram, 'Prelatical builders'.
22. A. A. M. Duncan, *Scotland: The Making of the Kingdom* (Edinburgh, 1978), 127 and n. 14; *St Andrews Liber*, 115.
23. A. A. M. Duncan, 'The earliest Scottish charters', *Scottish Historical Review*, xxxvii (1958).
24. *St Andrews Liber*, 117–8.
25. R. D. Oram, 'Continuity, adaptation and integration: the earls and earldom of Mar *c.* 1150–*c.* 1300', in S. Boardman (ed.), *Native Kindreds in Medieval Scotland* (forthcoming); *Jordan Fantosme's Chronicle*, ed. R. C. Johnston (Oxford, 1981), lines 471–474, pp. 36–7, appears to show the earls of Buchan and Angus operating in this role in 1174.
26. Duncan, *Making of the Kingdom*, 167–8.

27. Bannerman, 'MacDuff', 38.
28. *St Andrews Liber*, 258–9; *Regesta Regum Scotorum*, ii, *The Acts of William I*, ed. G. W. S. Barrow (Edinburgh, 1971), no. 137.
29. *St Andrews Liber*, 117.
30. G. W. S. Barrow 'The earls of Fife in the 12th century', *Proceedings of the Society of Antiquaries of Scotland*, 87 (1952–3), 51–62 at 54–5. The details of his tenure, however, do not survive.
31. J. Bannerman, 'MacDuff of Fife', in A. Grant and K. J. Stringer, *Medieval Scotland: Crown, Lordship and Community* (Edinburgh, 1993), 2–38.
32. *RRS*, ii, no. 152.
33. *St. Andrews Liber*, 216; Bannerman, 'MacDuff', 32.
34. What is evidently the social leadership in Fife was addressed by Malcolm IV *c*. 1153 x 1162 (*RRS*, i, no. 181). They comprised Earl Duncan, Merleswain, Hugh son of Earl Gille-Micheil, G. mac Slodach (possibly the son of Sluadach who led the bishop's army in the 1120s) and Ness son of William, lord of Leuchars and Alun.
35. *RRS*, i, no. 190.
36. Duncan, 'Priory of May', 74, no. 52.
37. *RRS*, i, nos 255, 256.
38. *RRS*, i, nos 147, 131.
39. *Inchcolm Charters*, nos v, xii; *St Andrews Liber*, 274–5.
40. D. MacGibbon and T. Ross, *The Ecclesiastical Architecture of Scotland*, i (Edinburgh, 1896), 193–6, 309–14.
41. *St Andrews Liber*, 241–2, 254–5.
42. *North Berwick Carte*, nos 6, 7.

TEN

PILGRIMAGE SITES

The manifestation of the reverence and honour in which a saint was held in the Middle Ages is commonly called a 'cult', a word derived from the classical Latin word *cultus* which was usually used to refer to 'worship' or to an 'act of worship'. The prime function of a saint seems to have been as an object for praise and as an example for imitation. This function developed during the Middle Ages so that saints came to be seen as intercessors whose prayers were particularly effective in obtaining benefits from God for those who venerated them. Nowhere is this seen more dramatically than in those places which were established as the focus for pilgrimage: those places to which the faithful travelled from far and near in the expectation of receiving demonstrable benefits from the earthly remains of the saints, more often than not in the form of miraculous cures from a whole host of physical and mental ailments.

Saints, both martyrs and confessors, were honoured on their anniversary days which were compiled, as lists of feast days, in calendars. Churches chose particular saints to be their patrons and intercessors. Saints were also named in the hymns of the Church's Office and in the prayers of the liturgy of the mass. Images of saints were made and venerated, and relics were produced and adored. The increasing importance of saints resulted in further developments in the liturgy to accommodate their veneration, in processions and special festal masses. The resultant influence of this increasing prominence given to saints was noticeable on both art and architecture. Churches and religious houses fostered the cults of individual saints often, though not invariably, with local connections. The promotion of centres of pilgrimage came to involve laity as well as the clergy, as finances became increasingly important for the maintenance of a respectable cult.

The very architecture of surviving Medieval churches in Fife can be of interest if one can look beyond subsequent alterations and envisage a church in its actual Medieval form. It is clear from some churches that the very layout was designed with pilgrimage and the cult of a saint in mind. Churches were sometimes designed with consideration shown for where a saint's reliquary, altar and image would be, and in recognition of the need for processions of clergy and pilgrims to pass those parts of the church. Objects more directly related to saints and their cults have not survived from Fife churches. Statues which adorned the outside of churches, and images from within, have been lost

116

as a result of time and reform. We know that such things did exist along with other trappings of the worship of saints such as reliquaries, the relics themselves, bells and such-like objects associated with saints. In certain cases we can look to surviving examples from other parts of Scotland such as the Monymusk Reliquary and the Perthshire relics associated with St Fillan, and assume that similar trappings existed at Fife pilgrimage sites. Most of these things were lost at the time of the Reformation. So great was the zeal of these reformers, and so effective were they in the pursuit of their aims, that little survives for us to study today. The reformers attacked those failings in the life of the Church which were most widespread and most well-established. That the trappings of the cult of saints were so thoroughly destroyed may be seen as an indication of just how popular devotion to the saints and the practice of pilgrimage had become by the middle of the 16th century.

The region of Scotland now known as Fife seems to have attracted missionaries and ascetics from earliest Christian times. Little survives by way of sites in Fife associated with the very early Church, but by the 12th century we begin to see how a few simple cells and cave retreats along with the stone crosses and simple chapels, which had been used for worship, had increased and multiplied into the complex system of religious houses and parish and collegiate churches which really made Fife the ecclesiastical centre of Scotland and put it on a par with similar regions in Northern Europe.

Caves, hills and islands were popular haunts for early hermits and missionaries seeking solitude and spiritual refreshment. As churches came to be built, these associations were neither forgotten nor neglected, but missionary zeal and the need to be where communities were settled led to the establishment of churches all over Fife. From the founding of Dunfermline Priory in the second half of the 11th century to the first half of the 16th century somewhere between forty and fifty religious houses were founded in Fife.

The Church in Fife had its origins in the Celtic Church but it kept abreast of developments in the life of the Church Catholic. It is a region which was open to external influences yet it did not dismiss its roots and traditions. Medieval Fife was populous and was active in politics and commerce. It was a major ecclesiastical and educational centre incorporating churches of all types. Above all, however, it was the people who made up the Church. It was the people of Medieval Fife who constituted the worshipping communities which adopted, nourished and needed saints, their cults, and their pilgrimage sites. Fife represents a cradle of saints and is acknowledged as one of the major European centres of pilgrimage. We may dismiss the Middle Ages as an era of superstition but we should consider, carefully, the difficulties associated with a supposedly credulous, ignorant and largely illiterate people and the influential few who manipulated them until such time as the destructive zeal of the

Reformation, which was fired by new religious thoughts from the Continent, brought some semblance of relief.

The foremost pilgrimage centre in Medieval Scotland was the cathedral church at St Andrews, which ranked as one of the most prestigious and popular places for pilgrimage anywhere in Europe. In adopting St Andrew as national patron, the Scottish Church hierarchy was doing more than asserting ecclesiastical and liturgical superiority. After all, St Andrew was the brother of St Peter, the Prince of the Apostles and the Rock on which the Church was founded. The Scottish Church had been subject to the metropolitan see of York, where the cathedral church was dedicated to St Peter, for long enough. In seeking to assert its independence from England, the Scottish Church had found a suitable ally in the man responsible for bringing St Peter to Christ in the first place, his brother Andrew. Although the bishops of St Andrews could not challenge the authority of the bishops of Rome, they could free themselves from the control of York and enjoy a special relationship with Rome itself. In fostering the cult of St Andrew the see of St Andrews was being established as the capital of the Scottish Church.

The cult of St Andrew flourished in Fife, and in Scotland as a whole, at least from the foundation of the Priory of Augustinian Canons in 1144 and the subsequent establishment of the cathedral in 1160. We cannot be sure of the historical origins of the relics of St Andrew, which legends record being brought by the monk St Regulus voyaging by ship to the shores of Fife, or of when they were enshrined. It is clear, however, that these relics (comprising an arm, a kneecap, three fingers and a tooth of the blessed apostle) were responsible for the rise of St Andrews to a position of ecclesiastical superiority in Scotland. The very size of the cathedral at St Andrews indicates the popularity of this pilgrimage centre, whilst the presence of hostels, hospitals and other churches indicates that provision was made for the physical and spiritual welfare of those who flocked to the city in the hope of being blessed and cured at the shrine of St Andrew. The expansion and development of the city itself suggests that the cult was popular with the local faithful and with merchant travellers as well as pilgrims. These pilgrims were responsible for increased trade and the subsequent rise of St Andrews to a position of importance as a mercantile centre may be seen as a further offshoot of the development of the pilgrimage site. Such things as lists of visitors to the shrine or accounts of miraculous cures do not survive, but they are not needed for the grandeur and size of St Andrews speaks volumes about the success of the cult of St Andrew.

Simple Medieval faith in the efficacy of the prayers of St Andrew and in the beneficial properties of his bones must have made the scene at Scotland's national shrine somewhat like that at the shrine of Lourdes in France today, even down to the souvenir tokens or medallions taken home by contented

pilgrims. The rubrics for the services on the Feast of St Andrew on 30
November, as laid down in the *Aberdeen Breviary*, give us some idea of what
would have occurred at such a major national festival. In the instructions for
the procession to the altar of St Andrew, for example, we read that the priest
was to be preceded by acolytes bearing candles, a thurifer with burning
incense, and a boy carrying the Bible; and he was to be followed by a robed
choir. If this was part of the liturgy to be celebrated in churches throughout
Scotland, how much greater would the ceremony have been in St Andrews
itself! The processions would have been lengthy and grand within and without
the cathedral. Scores of priests and monks must have led the faithful in
procession to the shrine. Relics and sacred books were carried with great
honour and accompanied by lights, incense and glorious music. Although the
Aberdeen Breviary contains the words used, it cannot convey the sense of the
liturgy. In Fife, the cult of St Andrew enhanced the standing of the city which
bore his name, gave Scotland a focus for its national identity and met the needs
of the credulous faithful.

Fife did not only boast the shrine of Scotland's national apostolic patron,
however, but also that of St Margaret, Queen and Patroness of Scotland.
Margaret was seen as a mother figure and as an intercessor for the Scots people
rather than simply as some distant pious patron. Her cult in Fife seems to have
become popular soon after her death although it did not reach its climax until
the time of her formal canonisation and the translation of her relics from her
original grave in 1250. The shrine of St Margaret at Dunfermline was the focus
of the cult of Scotland's second patron saint.

Margaret was born around the year 1045, probably in exile in Hungary.
Having been brought to England in 1057, she found refuge in Scotland after
the Norman Conquest. Margaret became Queen of Scotland when she married
Malcolm III around 1070. Her biography was written by her confessor, Turgot.
Margaret is remembered for her personal piety, her charitable acts and religious
foundations, and for having produced two daughters and six sons including
her particularly saintly successor, David. Margaret and Malcolm Canmore
founded Dunfermline Abbey, with Benedictine monks, around the time of
their marriage; and they were both buried there in 1093.

Medieval chronicles and charters record important early pilgrims to the
shrine of St Margaret, including King William the Lion. The *Dunfermline
Register* mentions that in 1250 the Earl of Fife did homage to the Abbot of
Dunfermline for his lands of Cluny on the day of the translation of Margaret's
body in Dunfermline Abbey, before King Alexander III, seven bishops and
seven Scottish earls. Quite a gathering!

A miracle is recorded in connection with the translation ceremony whereby
the bearers of St Margaret's relics found the bier to become so heavy that they
could not carry it farther until it was realised that the saint's husband, Malcolm

Canmore, should also be buried with due honour. Following their exhumation, Margaret's relics were placed in a costly shrine of gold and precious jewels.

Accounts of the monastic seals from Dunfermline would seem to indicate that we may be able to gain some impression of what the shrine was like, at least to the extent of visualising some form of canopy supported by six columns and with a candle burning on either side. The churches and topographical features associated with St Margaret in Fife and elsewhere in Scotland are evidence of the enduring popularity of her cult which, although based in Dunfermline, received national, and indeed international, support.

One writer has recorded the richly ornamented reliquary containing the relics of St Margaret:

> which consisted of her skull, with 'the auburn flowing golden hair still on it, along with certain bones'. Particularly on her festival day, St Margaret's day, these relics were exposed to the view of admiring pilgrims and other devotees, who had come to humble themselves and make their adorations before the shrine.

From 1250 the charters in the *Dunfermline Register* refer to the church of Dunfermline being under the patronage of the Holy Trinity and of St Margaret. Indeed, the cult of St Margaret flourished in Dunfermline from the time of the translation of her relics and the establishment of her new shrine. The town became a very popular pilgrimage centre and we know that on 8 October 1290 Pope Nicholas IV agreed that those pilgrims who visited her shrine would benefit from an indulgence of a year and forty days penance – a much-desired guarantee of relief of the time to be spent purifying the soul in purgatory.

There is evidence of the persistence of the cult of Scotland's patroness up until the time of the Reformation and her name is attributed to various places and objects. There was, not surprisingly, a St Margaret's altar in Dunfermline Abbey which, in the later 15th century, was patronised by the burgh magistrates. There are frequent references in the *Dunfermline Register* to the lights at her shrine and in 1468 Richard of Bothwell, Abbot of Dunfermline, made provision in his will for a candle of one pound of wax to be kept burning during Divine office at the high altar near the picture of St Margaret. These same records have a reference to St Margaret's Bell. Margaret, Queen and Saint, is represented on the seals of the burgh, chapter and abbot of Dunfermline, and her name is linked with various topographical features such as St Margaret's Stone, St Margaret's Oratory or Cave, St Margaret's Well, St Margaret's Hope, and the place-names North and South Queensferry. All these are in the vicinity of Dunfermline where there was also a Fair of St Margaret. Far from being restricted to the south of Fife, however, there are indications that the cult of St Margaret was fostered throughout pre-Reformation Scotland.

Although she may not owe her natal origins to Scotland, having been its Queen, St Margaret is the Scottish saint *par excellence*. We are fortunate in that we know so much about her as a person and it is so much more satisfying that we are able to trace the later history of her persistent cult. She was the object of particular devotion both for the people of Fife and for pilgrims from much further afield. It is fitting that her shrine and the focus for pilgrimage were in the abbey church which was her foundation. Dunfermline in some ways mirrors St Andrews as an ecclesiastical and pilgrimage centre at the opposite side of Fife. With these two great centres of pilgrimage for Scotland's apostolic patron and the national patroness it is small wonder that Fife should be considered a centre of national importance in terms of pilgrimage and the cult of saints.

Two saints who owed their origins to the mainland of Europe, St Adrian (or Ethernan) and St Monan, also had important, if more localised, cults in Medieval Fife. The cult of St Adrian of Fife was centred on the site associated with his martyrdom by the Vikings in 875: the Isle of May which lies, off Anstruther, in the Firth of Forth. Legend records the arrival, by boat, of the monk (and perhaps later bishop) Adrian from Pannonia (in modern-day Hungary) along with 6606 holy companions.

Recent archaeological excavations on the Isle of May, led by Fife Council Archaeologist Peter Yeoman, have revealed much of interest and caused considerable excitement. Undoubtedly the most remarkable find of all being the skeleton of a man buried before the high altar of the priory church of the Isle of May. The man's jaw was found wide open revealing a large scallop shell within. The scallop shell was a popular symbol of pilgrimage in Medieval times – the practice of pilgrims identifying themselves by carrying or wearing a scallop shell having its origins at the great shrine of St James at Compostella in Spain. Although the identity of this holy man remains a mystery, the position of his burial and his clear identification with the merits of pilgrimage may perhaps rank him as Fife's pre-eminent Medieval pilgrim.

The burghs of Pittenweem and Anstruther also had connections with the cult of St Adrian, which was probably maintained by the monastic house at Pittenweem, the successor of the priory on the Isle of May. Precisely what form the cult took we do not know although the light which was kept burning in honour of St Adrian on the May Isle did receive royal support. Medieval chronicler Andrew of Wyntoun and later traditions associate St Adrian with the Caiplie Caves on the coast between Crail and Cellardyke. The cave known today as Chapel Cave probably became the site of his shrine and the crosses incised in the walls of the caves may be seen as the enduring signs of individual acts of devotion paid to St Adrian by later generations of pilgrims. These and other caves along the Fife coast are currently the subject of intensive research by historian Liz le Bon.

The second eastern European saint to have had an important local cult in Fife was the white-robed confessor and companion of St Adrian named in the *Aberdeen Breviary* as St Monan. According to the account in the *Aberdeen Breviary*, the cult of St Monan flourished at the place which now bears his name, but was then called Inverie, where his relics attracted pilgrims seeking miraculous cures. The Breviary relates how many people sought to be healed at the shrine of St Monan. The most important of these pilgrims was King David II, who founded and endowed the church of St Monan in recognition of cures he himself had received. This royal patronage may well account for the later popularity of the saint's cult.

Another island in the Firth of Forth which has an abbey church dating from the early 12th century is Inchcolm. The dedication of the church here, according to early Latin charters, is to 'Sancti Columbe'. Links between the abbey and the cult of St Columba of Iona are strong, although some suggest that the name of both the island and the abbey is derived from an early, and otherwise unheard of, hermit called St Colm. In any case, the mainstay of the cult of St Columba in Fife and in the East of Scotland as a whole, was the island of Inchcolm (or Aemonia), off the coast from Aberdour.

Columba is perhaps the most celebrated of all Scotland's saints, and his feast is celebrated on 9 June. Having left Ireland in 563, Columba, a monk, travelled to the island of Iona, off the coast of Mull, and there he established a religious house which resulted in the evangelisation of much of Scotland and of northern England. Missionaries went out from Iona to preach the gospel in Europe, and Columba's foundation was the model for many other churches. The sanctity of the man himself was recognised early by his biographer, Adomnan, abbot of Iona, and the subsequent cult of St Columba was on a national scale. He was held in high esteem by the kings of Scotland who treated Columba as a national patron and churches were placed under his patronage before and after the Reformation.

In 1123 King Alexander I was stormbound on the island of Inchcolm and enjoyed the hospitality of the resident hermit who held St Columba as his particular patron. King Alexander invoked St Columba and, as a thank-offering for his survival from the storm, he founded a monastery of Augustinian Canons on the island. The church on Inchcolm continued to enjoy royal favour, including the granting to Aberdour of an annual fair on the feast and octave of St Columba by King James IV. As Dunkeld, Perthshire, was the resting place of Columba's relics, he was held, understandably, in particular reverence there. Nonetheless, although it cannot be said to match the importance of Iona or Dunkeld in the cult of St Columba, Inchcolm would still appear to have been a popular resort of pilgrims as they travelled between Scotland's holy places.

Another saint, who may have had Irish origins and who has enjoyed an element of enduring popularity as a focus for pilgrims is St Fillan, to whom there are a number of supposed dedications in Fife. This saint is commonly attributed with the evangelisation of part of Perthshire. That one of his relics was carried at the Battle of Bannockburn shows that his cult had continued support in central Scotland in the early 14th century. Tradition alone, however, names St Fillan as the resident and patron of the cave and holy well at Pittenweem which today bear his name. There are no surviving Medieval references to pilgrims visiting this cave shrine, although pilgrims undoubtedly did visit other caves along the East Neuk of Fife, as we have seen. That the cave was reconsecrated as a shrine by an Episcopalian bishop in the latter part of the 20th century indicates the persistence of a modern tradition. This legendary association along with some late and dubious dedications to St Fillan in Fife cannot, however, be treated as reliable evidence of a thriving cult of the saint in pre-Reformation Fife.

As small communities became important cult centres through the increased awareness of their association with local saints, or the presence of the relics of national patrons, their whole form and nature would be altered. To cope with the increase in pilgrim-visitors, churches, hostels and hospitals were founded. These pilgrimage centres became bastions of commercial and mercantile activity. The very topographical structure of such communities was transformed. One has to try to visualise what various places would have been like at the time of the Reformation if there had been no cult of saints and no desire to go on pilgrimage: the Isle of May, Pittenweem, Anstruther and Inchcolm for example and, on a larger and more national scale, St Andrews and Dunfermline. In short, pilgrimage and the cult of saints in Medieval Fife altered the structure of local communities not only in ecclesiastical terms but also from the point of view of the economy, the social structure, the architecture and the geography. Moreover, it is clear that, through land and its importance in the maintenance of a saint's cult, politics too entered into ecclesiastical affairs. In some situations the royal promotion of a saint's cult probably involved the manipulation of a saint for political ends.

With or without the patronage of the king, a cult needed a community to support it if it was to thrive. In fact, the picture we get of the cult of saints in Medieval Fife is that each saint's cult was centred on a specific religious house. In most cases the saint and the pilgrimage site would be supported by monks or regular canons. The cult of St Andrew was maintained by the Augustinian Canons, and that of St Margaret by the Benedictines; the Dominicans had that of St Monan at Inverie and the Benedictines at Pittenweem were probably responsible for maintaining the cult of St Adrian. Presumably there was some competition between various shrines and we can imagine the monks encouraging the presence of sick and infirm pilgrims at their shrine in order that they might compete in miracles of healing with rival saints' shrines. In fostering the presence of pilgrims, it is clear in the case of saints' cults in Medieval Fife that the situation of monasteries with shrines by harbours on the coast of Fife was an indication of the importance of travel by sea. In the case of the major cults, notably those of St Andrew and St Margaret, the arrangement of a particularly elaborate translation of relics and the provision of the most splendid buildings were great boosts to the pilgrimage centres. The importance of the monastic role in the cult of saints cannot be over-stressed. Monks were responsible for the establishment and the maintenance of cults and of the magnificent liturgies associated with them. Monks were further responsible for the written records which preserved the stories of the saints, and for the dissemination of information about the efficacy of the prayers of particular saints and the benefits to be gained at particular pilgrimage sites. In Fife, saints were an important monastic product which, with monastic marketing, brought indispensable monastic profits. Whilst not wishing to undermine the personal devotion of some ecclesiastics to the cult of saints at pilgrimage sites, it would be wrong to pretend that a more materialistic side did not exist.

Notwithstanding this scepticism of motivation, there is no doubt in my mind that, with the shrines of Scotland's national patrons at St Andrews and Dunfermline, and with the widespread veneration of literally dozens of other saints, Fife became the focus for a cosmopolitan assortment of pilgrims. In terms of religious activity and as a pilgrimage centre St Andrews in particular could match shrines across Europe in its splendour and popularity.

ELEVEN

MEDIEVAL CHURCHES, ABBEYS AND CATHEDRALS

SOME STATISTICS

The earlier stages of the revitalisation of the Scottish Church during the reigns of Alexander I (1107–24) and David I (1124–53) had many aspects. Amongst these were the re-establishment of the bishop's dioceses, the first stages of the formation of a nationwide pattern of parishes, and the introduction of most of the varieties of monastic life then available. Fife was an area of enormous importance for the re-energised Church, and we shall start the chapter with some statistics to illustrate this. Although the situation was by no means static, by the end of the 13th century the county was divided into some 46 parishes, most of which were under the immediate authority of the archdeacon of St Andrews and the deans of Fife and Fothrif. The majority of these parishes lay within the vast diocese of the nation's premier bishop, whose cathedral was at St Andrews, and who in 1472 became Scotland's first archbishop, though some parishes were in outlying portions of the dioceses of Dunkeld and Dunblane. Each of these parishes had its own mother church, and many in addition would have contained numbers of chapels which either served outlying parts of their territory or which were attached to the residences of the greater landholders.

Moving on to religious houses: Fife was home to the earliest site of Benedictine monasticism in Scotland, at Dunfermline, an abbey which also became the principal royal burial place in the kingdom. There was also a small Benedictine priory on the Isle of May. Of the newer orders of Benedictines, which had begun to emerge from the later 11th century, the Tironensian monks were represented at Lindores Abbey and the Cistercian monks at the abbeys of Balmerino and Culross, with a cell of the latter at Gadvan. The Augustinian canons were most importantly present in Fife as the cathedral chapter of St Andrews, and there was an abbey of the order on Inchcolm as well as a priory at Pittenweem which probably housed the later successors of the Benedictine priory of May. There may have been a preceptory of Knights Templars at Carnbee, though this is open to doubt. The friars were eventually well represented, with Dominicans at Cupar, St Andrews and St Monans and Franciscans at Inverkeithing and St Andrews. The only nunnery in Fife seems to have been a small community of Franciscan Poor Clares at Aberdour.

Looking at other forms of religious life, St Andrews had Scotland's earliest known collegiate foundation at the church of St Mary on the Rock. The same city, which was to become the seat of the nation's oldest university, had the academic colleges of St Leonard's, St Mary's and St Salvator's. There were also parochial collegiate churches in the parish churches at Crail and Strathmiglo. A number of churches were important places of pilgrimage, most notable being the shrines of St Andrew at St Andrews, of St Margaret at Dunfermline, and of St Adrian (or Ethernan) on the Isle of May. In addition, mention should perhaps be made of a number of holy caves, including that associated with St Serf at Dysart and that of St Fillan at Pittenweem; Christian symbols carved on the walls of caves at Caiplie, Kinkell and Wemyss suggest that they may also have been places of worship.

Religious life could find many expressions and, as well as offering prayers on behalf of the world, most of the monastic communities had charitable functions. However, there were also a number of hospitals founded to serve particular purposes. The needs of the poor were met by hospitals or almshouses at Ardross, Dunfermline, Kinghorn and St Andrews, and there was in addition a hospital for lepers at St Andrews. Some of these also catered for pilgrims, while hospitals at Inverkeithing, North Queensferry and Uthrogle met a variety of other needs.

All of these foundations required buildings, some of which we know were planned on a magnificent scale. Inevitably, many of them have been lost: some when the functions they housed were abolished at the Reformation, others as a result of later changes of requirements, and yet others through the inevitable processes of wear and tear. Nevertheless, far more survives than is often thought. Parish churches still in use for worship which still incorporate substantial Medieval work include those at Aberdour, Crail, Cupar, Inverkeithing, Kilrenny, Kirkcaldy, Leuchars, Markinch and St Andrews. There are in addition parts of the monastic churches of Culross, Dunfermline and Pittenweem, the friary church of St Monans, which now serve parishes, while the collegiate churches of St Leonard and St Salvator at St Andrews continue in use for worship. Many other Medieval churches and monastic buildings survive as ruins in varying states of preservation, and considered all together these buildings tells us a great deal about the ecclesiastical architecture of Medieval Fife.

PATRONS AND CRAFTSMEN

The massively increased requirement for church buildings which had emerged from around the 1120s onwards called for larger numbers of masons to build them than had ever been required before, and to meet this need patrons necessarily had to look beyond Scotland. Lowland Scotland's closest links were with England, which was where David I had spent much of his young adulthood, and it was also from England that many of the leaders of the church were brought. For example, Bishop Robert of St Andrews came from Nostell in Yorkshire and Abbot Geoffrey of Dunfermline came from Canterbury. It was therefore natural that those requiring new churches should send to England for people to design them and to train up masons who would be able to continue their work. The first masons who designed Dunfermline Abbey and Leuchars Church probably came from Durham Cathedral, with which the Scottish royal family had well-established connections. Extensions to the church known as St Rule's at St Andrews were perhaps carried out by masons who had earlier worked on some of the Yorkshire churches for which the prior of Nostell had responsibility. But Scotland soon became an equal partner in this exchange of architectural expertise, and by the time that St Andrews Cathedral was being built masons working in Scotland were contributing as much to the pool of ideas as were their counterparts south of the Border.

The situation was to change markedly in the later Middle Ages, however, as for much of this period England and Scotland regarded each other as enemies. In the 14th century we know that the tomb of Robert I was made in Paris and that a Paris-born mason worked at St Andrews Cathedral, while in the following century it is recorded that the founder of St Salvator's College bought his mace from the goldsmith of the heir to the French throne. There were thus clearly close artistic links with France. But there is good reason to conclude that ideas were also being sought from the Low Countries, which had become Scotland's main trading partner. Archbishop Scheves arranged to have his tomb made in Bruges, for example, while one of the archdeacons bought tiles for his chamber floor from Flanders. All of this shows us that the patrons of major buildings were in close contact with the continent, and probably drew some of their architectural inspiration from there; the Late Medieval architectural scene becomes far more cosmopolitan as a result.

THE TWELFTH CENTURY

One of the most important first steps in the 'modernisation' of the Scottish Medieval Church took place in Fife. By the late 11th century it seems that the state of the nation's Church was at a rather low ebb, at a time when elsewhere in Europe there were the beginnings of a phase of renewal spearheaded by the monastic orders. Most of those orders followed a rule compiled by St Benedict of Nursia as long ago as the early 6th century, and in about 1070, St Margaret introduced a small group of Benedictine monks from Canterbury to a church that she built at the place where she had married King Malcolm III shortly before. This church was later replaced by a much larger one, but we know something of its basic plan from excavations. It seems it was first built as a small two-compartment structure in the form of a nave with a tower over it and a chancel within which the monks held their services. Later, perhaps in about 1100, it was extended when a larger choir was added at its east end, and this terminated in a semicircular projection known as an apse as the backdrop to the principal altar.

A surviving building which helps us to understand something of how this first church at Dunfermline may have appeared is the church usually referred to as St Rule's in St Andrews. This church had an enormously tall western tower, a rectangular nave, and probably a choir to the east of that. The plan and a number of the details of St Rule's have suggested to some writers that it may be of a similar date to the first church at Dunfermline, but on balance it seems more likely that it was built after Bishop Robert was appointed to the diocese at the request of King Alexander I in 1124. It was almost certainly Robert who extended the church with additions to both east and west when he introduced Augustinian Canons as the cathedral's chapter in 1144. Those extensions have been lost, but the arches which opened into them remain, and from those we can see that it is likely that the masons came from the Yorkshire estates of Nostell Priory, where Robert himself had originally been a canon.

The most striking feature of both phases of the building at St Rule's Church is the superb quality of the masonry, which is of large blocks of finely cut stone. Very similar masonry may be seen at a number of other churches under construction in Fife in the early 12th century. Amongst these are the small island priories for the Augustinian order of canons at Inchcolm and Loch Leven, and the tower of the parish church at Markinch. At Inchcolm the priory later became a full abbey, and the church was extended on a number of occasions, though the fine masonry of parts of the original nave may still be seen; but at Loch Leven the tiny nave of its church survives through having been put to later use as a fishing bothy. At Markinch the tower is the only part of the medieval church not to have been rebuilt, and it is now surmounted by an imposing 18th-century spire. The similarities of Markinch's masonry with that at St Rule's are probably explained by the fact that the church had become a possession of St Andrews in the early 12th century, and masons from there may have built it.

By far the most important building campaign to be started in the early 12th century was at Dunfermline. In about 1128 David I decided to re-establish his mother's small Benedictine priory as a full abbey; it was her burial place, and David clearly intended it to become the dynastic mausoleum of the Scottish royal house. He brought up a fresh group of Benedictine monks from Canterbury, though to design and build the great abbey he almost certainly took advantage of a pause in building works at Durham Cathedral and recruited masons from there. Although only half the size of Durham, Dunfermline manages to give a sense of scale out of all proportion to its actual size.

Only the nave of Dunfermline survives, because that was the part retained for worship after the Reformation, but we know the basic layout of the rest of the church from excavations. Like Durham, it had a cross-shaped plan, with transepts projecting out on each side at the junction of an aisled nave and choir, and with an apse at the east of the choir; there were three towers, two over the west end of the nave, and a third over the crossing of the four arms. Internally, like most major churches at that time, the church was three storeys high, with arcades of arches opening into the vaulted aisles, tall galleries above the aisles, and an upper row of windows known as a clerestory. It is at the lowest level that the links with Durham are most clear, in the decoration of the aisle walls and arcades, and the finest single feature is the processional doorway through which the monks passed from the cloister into the church. By the time the upper parts of the nave were reached, it seems that the original master mason may have returned to England, and the design of the much simpler later parts was probably in the hands of a mason from elsewhere.

A building which shows a similar degree of enrichment as the earlier parts of David I's Dunfermline, albeit on a far smaller scale, is the parish church of Leuchars. Only the chancel and apse of the original church survive, and they are remarkable for the quality of their decoration. Externally they have two levels of decorative arcading, that along the lower levels of the chancel having intersecting arches. Internally, the arches which divide the parts are finely detailed and the apse is covered by a ribbed vault. But few 12th-century parish churches could afford to be as lavishly decorated as Leuchars, and at Aberdour we see a church which is probably more typical. In its original form, before the later addition of an aisle, a porch and a post-Reformation laird's aisle, Aberdour consisted simply of a rectangular nave for the lay people and a rather smaller rectangular chancel for the high altar (and priest), both of which were lit by small round-headed windows. Nevertheless, the quality of the masonry is very high, perhaps because it was built for the canons of Inchcolm, to whom it belonged. The church at Crail may once have been of a similar layout and scale, though only the much-altered remains of the original chancel have survived through later extensions.

In the second half of the 12th century new architectural fashions began to spread across Europe. Under the influence of ideas that had originated in France, massively constructed round-arched architecture with a high degree of surface enrichment, like that at Dunfermline, began to be replaced by architecture of a different kind. Increasingly, the visual weight of the wall was reduced by the use of more slender mouldings and by a growing preference for pointed arches. The most important building in Scotland in which these changes began to be introduced was the new cathedral at St Andrews, which was started by Bishop Arnold soon after 1160. In the Middle Ages, just as now, buildings were an important way of making a statement, and it was through the scale and quality of their cathedral church that the bishops of St Andrews set about reminding their brother bishops that they were the leaders of the Scottish church. The new cathedral was laid out on a vast scale, with a choir of eight bays and with transepts which projected three bays to each side. The nave was probably originally intended to be 14 bays long – though, when it was eventually nearing completion over a century after the start of work, the west front was blown down in a storm and it was completed with only 12 bays.

From the fragmentary remains of the cathedral we can reconstruct much of its original appearance and can see that it must have been a prototype for a number of other important buildings, amongst which were Jedburgh and Arbroath abbeys in Scotland, and the priories of Hexham and Lanercost in England. At this period there is a strong sense that, whatever the political boundaries, Lowland Scotland and northern England were essentially parts of a single architectural province, and that Scotland had become an equal partner in the relationship.

THE THIRTEENTH CENTURY

Some of the ideas that made St Andrews Cathedral different from what had gone before had reached Britain through the medium of the architecture of one of the newer varieties of Benedictine monasticism, the Cistercian order. This order, which placed stress on a particularly austere way of life, had originated at Cîteaux in eastern France, from where it spread rapidly across Europe. In order to ensure the maintenance of its original standards, many of the architectural solutions that had been first employed in its monasteries in eastern France were exported elsewhere, and these included pointed arches, delicate mouldings and an altogether more simply 'engineered' approach to design. A particular plan type was also favoured. Surprisingly enough, in view of the rigid attitudes of the Cistercians, both the architectural details and plans they introduced proved to be very influential, perhaps because they were so different from what had gone before and fitted in with the spirit of the times.

In Fife we have the remains of two Cistercian abbeys of the early 13th century. That at Culross was founded by the Earl of Fife in 1217, while that at Balmerino was founded by Queen Ermengarde and her son King Alexander II and was intended as the queen's own burial place. Both abbeys appear to have been designed to the same plan, with a small rectangular presbytery for the high altar, transepts with a pair of chapels on the east side of each, and a long aisle-less nave. One reason for this plan, apart from its simplicity, was that early Cistercian churches were not open to the public, and the long nave was divided into two choirs, one for the monks themselves, and the other for the group of lay brethren who carried out most of the work of the community. At Culross the eastern parts of the church survive almost complete, because they were taken over as the church of the parish after the Reformation, and they represent one of the best surviving examples of such a Cistercian plan anywhere in Britain. At Balmerino, however, only fragments survive. In both cases there were later alterations to the original plan: at Culross a tower was added over the nave, in defiance of the original Cistercian ban on bell towers, while at Balmerino a single aisle was added against the nave, on the side away from the cloister.

The influence of the Cistercians on other orders is seen very clearly at Lindores Abbey, which had been founded for the Tironensian order in about 1190 by David, Earl of Huntingdon, a grandson of David I. Although Lindores was founded before Culross or Balmerino, it may have been built around the same time, and it appears to have had a very similar first plan as them, although with three rather than two chapels on each of the transepts. As at Balmerino an aisle was later added on the side of the nave away from the cloister, but in this case it seems that a free-standing bell tower had already been built on the north side of the nave, so that the aisle could not extend the full length.

At all of these abbeys there are fragmentary remains of the monastic buildings which, as was usual, were arranged around three sides of a square open space, known as the cloister, with the nave of the church forming the fourth side. Usually the church was on the north side so that it did not block the light from the cloister, and this was the case at Lindores, Culross and St Andrews. At Balmerino, however, perhaps because of the location of the water supply, the church was on the south side of the cloister. There would have been covered walkways along all four sides of the cloister, interconnecting the various rooms around it. The most important room, after the church, was the chapter house, which was the business room of the community, and which was always placed in the east range. On the floor above it was the dormitory, where the monks or canons slept, and which was connected to the cloister and church by stairs, one for use during the day and the other giving direct access to the church for the night-time services. The second most important room was the refectory, which occupied most of the range facing the church. The rooms on the west side of the cloister usually contained store rooms, but might also have a residence for the head of the community or accommodation for visitors.

The most intact example of monastic buildings in Scotland is at Inchcolm, where all three ranges are complete and still roofed. The mid-13th century chapter house there is particularly lovely, and is one of only three octagonal chapter houses known to have been built in Scotland. The other monastic buildings are rather unusual, since the cloister walks occupy the whole of the ground floor of each range, with the refectory and guest house on the upper floor, like the dormitory. However, in their present form those buildings are probably of the 15th rather than the 13th century. One other remarkable feature at Inchcolm, which is of the early 13th century, is the tower built over the original choir at the same time that the choir was extended eastwards. In the two arches through its lowest storey are the remains of the stone screens which were built to separate the canons in the choir from any layfolk in the nave. The eastern screen was of three arches, while the western screen was of two, and the counterpoint between the two screens when they were both visible must have been a delightful feature.

Another abbey where large-scale works were again in progress was Dunfermline, reminding us that there would have been few times when building work was not being carried out at a major religious house. Many of Dunfermline's monastic buildings were destroyed in 1303 on the orders of King Edward I of England though, from the surviving lowest storey of the dormitory range and of the latrine block that ran parallel to it, we can still see that those parts were essentially of the later 13th century and thus survived the English devastation. Perhaps the most significant works at Dunfermline of the 13th century were those aimed at providing a more suitable chapel for the remains of St Margaret. An abbey or cathedral which possessed the remains of an important saint was indeed fortunate, not only because of the added aura of sanctity that they gave to the church, but also because the pilgrims who came to seek the saint's assistance would leave generous offerings. It was therefore usual to try to give particular prominence to the saint by housing him or her as splendidly as possible, and at Dunfermline this was done by extending the original choir a little to the east and projecting a rectangular chapel out from it to contain the shrine. The chapel was completed in 1250, and the royal saint was duly placed there. The lower walls of the chapel and the base on which the shrine was set are still to be seen.

As will by now be evident, by far the greatest expenditure on church building in Fife during the 13th century was on the various abbeys that were under construction, as well as on the continuing work at the cathedral. Some of the funding for these operations came from diverting endowments that had originally been provided for the parishes, and an inevitable consequence of this was the growing impoverishment of many parishes. Nevertheless, parts of Fife were relatively wealthy and could still afford to build churches on a large scale. The best surviving illustration of this is the 13th-century nave and tower of Crail. The nave has an aisle on each side, with arcades carried on five cylindrical piers, and there was also a row of clerestory windows, which are now hidden within the later roof. Elsewhere, however, churches were increasingly aisle-less buildings set out as a single rectangular space, with no differentiation between nave and chancel, as can be seen in the ruined churches at Carnock, Dalgety and Abdie. Yet, despite the simplicity of their plan, all of these churches are carefully proportioned, with well grouped windows, and we must assume that they would have contained a number of fine items of liturgical furnishing, including a timber screen to separate the chancel from the nave, a well as altars and a font.

THE FOURTEENTH CENTURY

The long years of warfare that followed the outbreak of the Wars of Independence in the 1290s greatly limited the opportunities for church building for much of the 14th century. Nevertheless, during the periods of relative peace several fine ecclesiastical buildings were raised in Fife. Amongst the earliest and most magnificent was the refectory range at Dunfermline Abbey, which seems to have been rebuilt with the help of Robert the Bruce shortly before his death and burial there in 1329. Only the south and west walls survive to full height, but these are enormously impressive, because the steep fall of the ground meant that the refectory hall itself had to be raised on two storeys of undercrofts. A particularly attractive feature is the way the pulpit, from which readings were delivered to the monks as they ate, is carried on an arch between two of the soaring buttresses.

In a later pause of hostilities, following King David II's return from English captivity, he built one of Fife's most delightful churches on the coast at St Monans. The king had been almost fatally injured by an arrow at the battle of Neville's Cross, and he believed that it was due to the intervention of St Monan that he was able to recover. The church, which was built in thanksgiving for his recovery between 1362 and 1370, was planned as a cross-shaped structure with a central tower and spire, though the nave, to the west of the tower, was never built. The church was extensively remodelled after James III established a Dominican friary within it in 1471, and it is by no means clear what dates from 1362 and what from 1471; it is likely, however, that the basic shell is essentially of the earlier campaign.

Towards the end of the century another major campaign had to be started at St Andrews Cathedral after it had been ravaged by a fire in 1378, and rebuilding extended well into the following century. According to an inscription at Melrose Abbey, St Andrews Cathedral was one of the buildings on which the Paris-born mason John Morow had worked. There are certainly aspects of the design of the new windows in the west front and of the new nave arcade piers which could be a result of French influence though, rather unexpectedly, they are not very like what we know of John Morow's work elsewhere.

THE FIFTEENTH AND EARLY SIXTEENTH CENTURIES

A striking feature of the religious life of the later Middle Ages was that individuals increasingly wanted to have a more direct hand in their own salvation, instead of leaving it to the prayers of monks and canons behind the walls of the cathedrals and abbeys. One result of this was a great increase of endowments for chantry masses, by means of which priests were paid to pray for the welfare of the living and the salvation of the dead, and thus reduce the risk of their eventual damnation. As the setting for these prayers, large numbers of additional altars were founded, most commonly in the churches where individuals had worshipped in their lives rather than in some distant cathedral or abbey. The very wealthy might go further and establish a college, in which an incorporation of priests was to pray for their founders' souls for all time to come and, again, this was usually either in an existing local church or in a new church close to where the founder lived. All of this meant that local churches began to be much more of a focus of attention than before and, although the cathedrals and abbeys were still able to be major architectural patrons, there was far more building at parochial level than before. However, one other group which greatly benefited from the trend towards a more personal form of religion was the friars, who had always placed great emphasis on preaching and administering to the urban population, and were therefore perceived as being more in accord with the times.

Fife acquired a number of very fine late Medieval parish churches, particularly in the richer coastal burghs. One of the best was the church of the Holy Trinity in St Andrews, which was moved away from a location within the cathedral precinct to its present site at the heart of the burgh in about 1410, at least partly in order to reduce the cathedral's control over the parish. There may eventually have been as many as 30 altars within that church which had been founded by individuals or by trade guilds. Although much of what is now seen at Holy Trinity dates from a restoration of 1907–9, it is an impressive structure with an aisle running along the full length of each side and with a handsome bell tower over the west end of the north aisle. It became quite common to have a bell tower set to one side in this way, and a similar arrangement is to be seen at Cupar, where rebuilding was started in about 1415. Only the tower and part of the north aisle wall now survive at Cupar. At Dysart, where much of the ruined shell of the church still stands, the tower was over the west end of the south aisle. This tower, which probably dates from the middle decades of the 15th century, is an unusually massive structure, and the shot holes at its lower level demonstrate that it was designed with defence as well as bell ringing in mind. Amongst other good late Medieval church towers to survive are those at Kirkcaldy and Kilrenny.

Moving on to collegiate churches, it should be remembered that most had charitable as well as chantry functions, since great stress was placed by the church on the value of good works as an aid to salvation. Of the eight or so collegiate churches founded within Fife, over half were attached to the University of St Andrews and their charitable functions were, of course, educational. The best surviving academic chapel is that of St Salvator, which was founded by Bishop James Kennedy in 1450, and which is an aisle-less rectangular building with a polygonal apsidal termination to its east end. This type of apse, which was probably new to Scotland at St Salvator's, was to be copied in many other churches. Bishop Kennedy, who had received much of his training in mainland Europe, and had spent a great deal of his time as bishop in travelling across Europe on ecclesiastical or diplomatic missions, possibly took the plan of his own chapel from one of the French university chapels he saw. The finest surviving feature within the chapel is his tomb, on the north side of the altar, it is a towering structure surmounted by intricately carved tiers of what is known as tabernacle work.

Finally, we must briefly consider the physical remains of two of Fife's friaries: the Franciscan friary at Inverkeithing and the Dominican friary at St Andrews. Friaries have not survived well because they were usually on prime urban sites that were quickly redeveloped after the Reformation; so these are rare survivals. At Inverkeithing, where the friary was possibly established around the 1380s, there are the substantial remains of a range of buildings which may have been the guest house. It is attractive to remember the many pilgrims who must have stayed there after crossing by the Queen's Ferry on their way to the shrine at St Andrews. At St Andrews itself the Dominican friary may not have been established until around the 1460s, and it seems to have been entirely rebuilt in about 1514 with money left by Bishop Elphinstone of Aberdeen. Only a laterally projecting north apsidal chapel of the church survives, but it is a particularly interesting fragment in which the loop-like tracery of the windows is very like tracery of around the same date in the Netherlands. Since the Scottish Dominicans had been recently advised on how to reform their way of life by their brethren of the Congregation of Holland, and the new friary at St Andrews was the flagship of the order in Scotland, it seems possible that architectural as well as religious advice had been taken from the Netherlands. We can thus see that, on the eve of the Renaissance, the Church in Fife was already in close contact with continental Europe.

Twelve

Medieval Burghs

Burghs were one of the most important institutions in Scottish Medieval society. A 'burgh' was both more and less than a 'town': it was a place, or community, with quite specific legal privileges. Burghs were 'made' and did not emerge, as they were endowed by the king, or with the king's permission by an important churchman or nobleman, with certain specific rights. Their first mention in Scotland is in the early 12th century; but, usually, it was an existing township or settlement that was elevated to burghal status.

The first burghs we hear of in Fife are Dunfermline, which David I (1124–53) referred to as *meus burgus* very early in his reign, so it was probably given burghal status some time between 1124 and 1127; St Andrews, a burgh known to have existed from before 1144; Inverkeithing, a burgh by at least the early 1160s; Crail, probably established between 1165 and 1171; and Kinghorn which makes its first appearance between 1165 and 1172.

Cupar appears as a burgh by 1327, along with Kirkcaldy some time between 1315 and 1328 and Falkland in 1458. Falkland was, however, never represented in parliament or at the Convention of Royal Burghs and never paid stent or taxes, as did most other burghs. It came to be recognised as one of four small non-functioning royal burghs of Fife, the others being Auchtermuchty, first noted as a burgh in 1517; Earlsferry; and Newburgh, sometimes called Ferryport-on-Craig or South Ferry, although, as a settlement dependent on the Abbey of Lindores, it had been granted a weekly market as early as 1266.

During the 16th century, a number of new burghs appeared in Fife. Many of these were established as burghs of barony, with a local lord as superior, rather than the crown or an important ecclesiastical or lay magnate. Pittenweem, for example, was a burgh of barony before 1526, although it was elevated to a royal burgh in 1541, as was Burntisland which had anciently belonged as a town and harbour to Dunfermline Abbey. Four other burghs to become royal in the 1580s and 1590s were Anstruther Wester, Anstruther Easter, Culross and Dysart. A number of burghs of barony founded in the 16th century, however, remained dependent on the local lord. Aberdour or Aberdour West, for example, was established as a burgh dependent on the Abbot of Inchcolm in 1501. Other such Fife burghs, with various burghal Superiors, included Strathmiglo, Wemyss or Wester Wemyss, Balnald, Corshill-over-Inchgall, Drummochy, Pitlessie, Newbigging, St Monans, Kilrenny and Elie. These later burghs, however, did not function in the same way as the historic burghs founded in the 12th, 13th and 14th centuries, doing so largely in name only.

It is not surprising that David I chose to elevate Dunfermline as one of his first burghs, and granted that Robert, Bishop of St Andrews might so honour St Andrews, as both were already established settlements with strong religious connections. Inverkeithing, Crail, Kirkcaldy and Kinghorn, along with St Andrews, were to set a pattern for several later burghs, importantly placed on the east coast of Scotland, strategically situated to have close links with Scotland's trading partners, the Low Countries, the Baltic, northern France and England. Their important, but small harbours and havens played a vital role in the Scottish economy.

One of the most important privileges gained with burghal status was economic. The burgh was a community organised for trade. To judge from the percentage of clauses dealing with mercantile matters in early burghal legislation, it was recognised as such as early as the 12th century. In practice, this brought several advantages. Perhaps of most significance to burgesses, the freemen of the burgh, was the freedom from payment of toll to the owner of a market, thus enabling a burgess to travel at will around the country buying and selling. Also, the burghal community gained the right to have its own market, at which it could exact toll on others.

In time, burghs gained the authority to have their own councils and courts. The most important were the three annual head courts, which all burgesses were obliged to attend. They were also permitted to appoint their own municipal officers – the *prepositus*, later called provost, and bailies – and were granted control of their own finances. The burgh seals, representing the authority of the community of the burgh, and the right of royal burghs (along with important ecclesiastical burghs, such as Dunfermline) to sit as the third estate in parliament also enhanced their powers. All gave burghs a status and importance in the realm unknown to other settlements and organisations, for the community of the burgh was freed from all feudal ties, other than to the Crown and the burgh superior.

Medieval burgh records illustrate the priority placed on marketing matters in urban life. Control of the market, the standards of selling and the quality and quantity of supplies were clearly the major secular preoccupation. So that all dealings should be seen to be open and fair, selling was to take place at the market cross or in official booths in the market place; and the town weights were the only officially recognised standard. Forestalling, the purchase of goods before they reached market so avoiding the payment of toll to the burgh, and regrating, buying in bulk and possible hoarding in order to sell at an advantageous price when prices were high, were both met with stiff fines or even banishment from the town. Quality and price control were maintained not only by the rulings of the burgh and guild merchant courts, but also by officials, such as the ale and meat tasters, chosen annually at the Michaelmas head court. Also, all burghs imposed bans in times of shortage on essentials being exported outwith the town. The purpose of all these measures and penalties was to ensure an adequate supply of good quality commodities for the most important consumers – the burgh community.

Some burgh charters make specific reference to a more radical and far-reaching privilege, which was a very real potential power base: while burghs were to have a marketing monopoly, many of them were granted the sole right to trade over an extended rural hinterland. This obliged all inhabitants in a specified landward area to market their goods in the burgh of their locality. The consequent relationship of a town with its surrounding countryside and the extent and prosperity of this rural neighbourhood were, therefore, to have a profound influence on the economic success of the town. In 1363, for example, David II (1329–71) decreed that the four regality burghs of the abbey of Dunfermline – Dunfermline, Kirkcaldy, Musselburgh and Queensferry – should have the sole right to trade throughout the full confines of the regality of Dunfermline. In practice, this meant an apportioning of the monopoly area by the four burghs, Kirkcaldy and Dunfermline having distinct commercial hinterlands in Fife. Neighbouring Inverkeithing had its hinterland defined as early as the reign of William I (1165–1214), to be confirmed by Robert III (1390–1406) as between the water of Leven and the water of Devon and with its north-eastern boundary marching with the jurisdiction of Cupar. Such an overlapping of territorial economic rights meant inevitable clashes between Inverkeithing, Dunfermline and Kirkcaldy (Figure 15).

The importance of this patchwork of monopolistic trading privilege throughout Fife and the rest of the country was not whether it was ultimately enforceable in fine detail, but rather the economic influence it bestowed on particular burghs, an influence that these urban communities valued highly and fought to maintain against the encroachment of ambitious burghal neighbours.

Drawing the people from the surrounding coutryside, as well as the townsfolk, market days were noisy, busy and hectic. The market place would be lined with the booths of the merchants; and hawkers and pedlars would also set up their stalls. All sorts of commodities were bought and sold – fish and meat, home-grown produce, ale, wine, eggs, butter and gathered fruits, as well as the products of the local craftsmen, such as leather shoes and jackets, bone combs and tools, wooden stools and, sometimes, imported luxuries such as spices, exotic fruits and fine materials. The sense of bustle and noise was intensified by the bellowing and clucking of animals brought for sale, the jostle of traders, purchasers, children and scavenging dogs, hens and pigs; and the raucous laughter at the taunting of miscreants placed in the stocks or held fast by the neck to a pillory, or nailed by the ear to the tron, the town weighing beam, for all to ridicule.

Trade did not benefit the town only. Burghs were an important source of income to the burghal superior, whether he was the king or a wealthy nobleman or cleric. A further asset was that overseas trade was granted as a monopoly to the royal burghs and wealthy ecclesiastical burghs. 'Great custom' was levied in the 14th century on wool, hides and woolfells; to these James I (1406–37) added cloth, fish, salt and skins; and this was taken further by James III (1460–88), who made all exports subject to duty. By the 1530s, Pittenweem, Anstruther, St Monans and Crail paid over 50% of Scotland's

Figure 15

Burgh Trading Liberties: Dunfermline, Kirkcaldy, and Inverkeithing *c.* **1500. This illustrates not only the extensive economic juridiction of burghs; but also highlights the difficulties of enforcing attendance at a burgh's market over such a large area; and likewise the potential for dispute between burghal neighbours. (Courtesy of E. Patricia Dennison)**

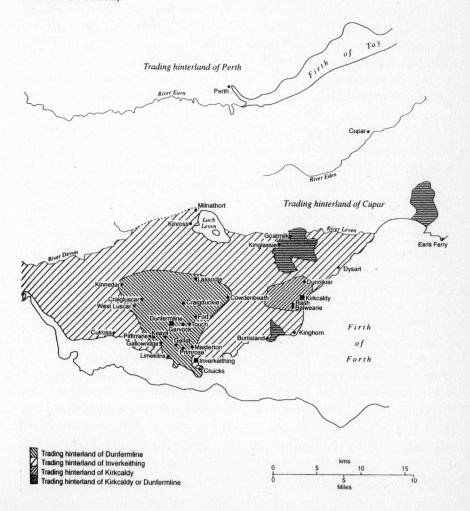

custom on cod; Dysart in the 1490s held 73% of the export of salt and by the 1590s Culross produced 89% of all Scottish salt exported. Burghs, partly through the resourcefulness of their overseas merchants, became the economic backbone of the Scottish nation, often giving them a power quite disproportionate to their size.

Burghs were not large places. We would now consider them more as villages – in most cases just a few hundred people. Fewer than one in ten of the Scottish population lived in towns, but towns were a distinct feature on the landscape. They were often formally laid out, typically as a single street. Kirkcaldy is a fine example of a single-street town, with its curving High Street running to this day from south-west to north-east. Kirkcaldy is also an interesting reminder of how natural phenomena influenced the first lay-out of a burgh, whether in Fife or elsewhere in Scotland. Kirkcaldy's High Street was deliberately laid out along the edge of a natural ridge, at the 10 m contour line. This was one of a series of postglacial raised beaches that extended westwards from the sea, so placing constraints on the site and delineation of the first main thoroughfare, by preventing expansion westwards, until modern times. Raised beaches were to impact on the lay-out of a number of Fife east coast burghs.

St Andrews and Crail, as many other burghs, eventually developed more complex town plans; but, just as in Kirkcaldy and so many other Fife burghs, the Medieval lay-out is still detectable today. The laying out of the burgh was not random: official liners were appointed to measure out the burgh land. So important was this task that official planners, with experience from other burghs, might be brought into the town to formally lay it out. One Mainard the Fleming, for example, was brought into St Andrews after probably planning Berwick-on-Tweed.

Lining the main street were the burgage plots, specifically measured out by the liners. The frontages in Dunfermline, for example, were 22½ ft (6.9 m), with at times a variant of between 20 ft 9 inches (6.4 m) and 25 ft (7.6 m); and great care was taken here, as in other Fife burghs, that these measurements should be respected and maintained. The plots ran back in herring-bone pattern from the street frontage. The houses of the burgesses were usually set at the frontages of the burgage plots or tofts, each toft in the earlier part of the Middle Ages normally housing only a single tenement, with a long garden at the rear. In time, these backlands housed workshops, middens, wells and outhouses, as well as being used as gardens and space for animal rearing. Some of the burgage plots on the edges of towns remained gap sites well into the Medieval period – which is also an indication of the small population sizes. This was not the case in the market centre, where pressure for space encouraged further building at the rear of plots. It was usually the poorer members of the community who lived to the rear, but they still needed to come and go through the foreland; this insistence on access resulted in the central cores of many towns becoming jumbles of closes and tiny vennels. Visitors to many Fife burghs can still experience these old vennels and detect the Medieval burgage plots in the townscape. The rears of many properties still bear the imprint of the medieval burgage plots: Inverkeithing, Cupar, St Andrews and Crail offer fine examples. Kirkcaldy perhaps is one of the most fascinating urban lay-outs. Over the centuries, the burgesses dug their way into the raised beach that first impeded expansion westwards, and to the rear of the dwellings at the north-east end of the High Street, one may see to this day, as one could in the 19th century, the elongated, terraced burgage plots.

Burghs psychologically distanced themselves from the surrounding countryside, with ditches and wooden pallisades, although a few burghs, such as Inverkeithing, may have had an element of stone walling. Stone walls did not become common, however, until the 16th century or later. The official entry to the town precincts was by the town ports or gates. These were closed for the night at the curfew at dusk and when danger threatened. As well as acting as collection points for tolls, equally important was the control of undesirable persons likely to be a burden or source of annoyance to the townspeople, particularly during the times of epidemic diseases such as plague. Kirkcaldy, for example, shut its gates in 1585 at the approach of plague – unsuccessfully, as it turned out: about 300 inhabitants died of plague and a Kirkcaldy man was blamed for transporting it to Leith! Dunfermline believed it was faced with a 'troublous world' in 1559, when the Protestant Lords of the Congregation were in retreat through Fife, pursued by French troops. The town shut its gates and the merchants of the guild divided up the costly and spiritually precious adornments of their Holy Blood Altar for safe-keeping from both sets of unwelcome visitors.

Most town gates throughout the Middle Ages were simple wooden barresses. As time went on, some of these were replaced with prestigious stone entrances to the burgh precincts. The West Port of St Andrews still stands, but there are clues to the siting of town gates in the placenames of towns to this day: Crail's Westgate, Falkland's East Port and Dunfermline's East Port are merely a few examples. Burgesses also had ready access to and exit from the town through their backlands where their rigs abutted onto the burgh boundary, and many burgage plots had their own small back gates out of the town.

Burghs being communities established for trade, the most important urban landmark was the market cross. Set prominently in the market place, along with the tolbooth, or townhouse, and the tron, it was the symbol of the community's authority and of the importance of the burgesses and their senior officers, the provost and bailies. The tolbooth was the collection point for market tolls and the repository for the town's weights, and also functioned as the meeting place for the burgh council and housed the town jail. Remnants of Medieval market crosses and tolbooths can still be seen in Fife. For example, the Medieval cross-shaft of Inverkeithing's market cross, supporting a sundial and unicorn, which replaced the medieval figure of Christ in the 17th century, stands near to its original site in the High Street. Crail's tolbooth, likewise, has early lower courses, dating to the 16th century and still houses a fine Dutch bell made in 1520.

In Cupar, Crail, Falkland, Auchtermuchty and St Andrews, the open market places still survive. Inverkeithing's market area, at the north end of the High Street, has been replaced, or colonised, with buildings, a process called 'market repletion'. Kirkcaldy and Dunfermline, however, never had open market places. Geology meant that Kirkcaldy had a long High Street, with little or no scope for a widening out to house a market. As a result, the market occupied much of the length of the 'lang toun'. Dunfermline, also, had a linear market. Its tolbooth stood at the west end of the High Street, facing up towards the market cross, which is still sited in its original position at the foot of Cross Wynd. The townscape of Dunfermline, just as that of Kirkcaldy, was determined by natural phenomena: the High Street runs along a spring line, tucked below a natural ridge and, beyond, marshy land.

The tolbooths of most of the Fife burghs, being the most prestigious secular buildings in the towns, were usually by the 15th century of stone and slated, as were the parish churches. Most other Medieval buildings, however, were of wood. The very earliest urban dwellings were basic hut-type houses made of stakes and inter-woven wattle with free-standing posts to support the walling, and roofs thatched with cut heather or turves of growing plants which offered water resistance. From the late 13th century, there is growing evidence of an increasing sophistication in house building, with stakes set in wooden ground sills, later replaced by stone sills, and exterior walls given extra strength by a reinforcement of heavy clay, dung, mud or peat cladding. Larger wooden buildings were roofed in colourful pottery tiles and some in slate. Such was the improvement that, when Pedro de Ayala visited Scotland in 1496, he reported that 'the houses are good, all built of hewn stone and provided with excellent doors, glass windows and a great number of chimneys'. This was, undoubtedly, an exaggeration, but does at least show that improvements were being made in the townscape. A number of burghs still have late Medieval standing town houses that illustrate how prestigious some urban dwellings had become: for example, the 'Roundel' and others in South Street, St Andrews, 339–343 High Street, Kirkcaldy, and the so-called 'palace' at Culross. A disastrous fire in 1624 not only wiped out most of Dunfermline, however, but also is a sure indicator that most houses, at least above ground floor level, were of wood.

The records, however, make it clear that the Fife burghs were anxious to maintain their communication routes. Roads and bridges received constant maintenance, as did the all-important harbours. Crail and Kirkcaldy, as all other east coast ports, invested hugely in time and money in upgrading and rebuilding their harbours. Some burghs, by the late 15th century, maintained elaborate water supplies and primitive, but functional, sewage systems. That in Dunfermline was particularly impressive; and may have been the result of the influence of the Benedictine abbey.

Dominating the townscape of most towns, along with the tolbooths, were ecclesiastical buildings: cathedrals, abbeys, parish churches, chapels, friaries and, sometimes, monasteries. Most of these were constructed in stone, in sharp contrast to the majority of domestic dwellings. The setting of friaries gives an insight into the extent of Medieval urban settlement, as they were usually deliberately set on the edges of towns, either for peace and calm or where there was available building space; and it becomes very clear how small and closely confined were Medieval burghs. For example, the Greyfriars friary of Inverkeithing, possibly dating to the 13th century, the *hospitium* of which still stands, is close by the south end of the High Street. Most towns did not develop suburbs until after 1700.

The church dominated the town emotionally. Scottish burghs housed only one parish church; and worshipping together as a single community probably encouraged a sense of closeness. Many remnants of Medieval churches may be found in Fife. One of the largest parish churches was the 'outer' church of the Benedictine monastery of Dunfermline, still structurally intact, although its interior no longer gives clues to its former magnificence and opulence. Little St Fillan's Church on the road to Silver Sands at Aberdour dates to the twelfth century. The 15th-century tower of St Peter's parish church still stands in Inverkeithing. Church life dominated town life. Baptism brought the child into protection; the few boys who attended schools were taught by clerics; handfasting, or becoming engaged, and marriage were blessed by the church. Church festivals marked out the year and offered the only real chance of holidays – or Holy Days. Of particular importance were local saints' days. St Andrews and Dunfermline became pilgrimage centres, attracting many to worship at the shrines of St Andrew and St Margaret. The church bells regulated the daily routine of rising at dawn, work and curfew at dusk. Church attendance, prayer and the hearing of mass offered consolation in the worldly life and assurances about the after-life.

Death was never far away. Although we have evidence that townspeople made efforts to maintain an element of cleanliness, the intermingling of industrial and agricultural premises with residential, the use of straw for flooring and even bedding in some houses, lack of adequate sanitation and effluence contaminating drinking water inevitably brought problems. Many townspeople kept their animals – pigs, goats, cows and hens – in their backlands and this closeness also transferred infection. Several diseases were rife, some, such as leprosy, endemic and chronic. Medieval people understood why it was necessary to isolate victims and most major towns had a leper house set outside the town limits at a distance from the healthier, and luckier, townspeople. But medical knowledge was primitive and herded with the genuinely afflicted were many who suffered only from disfiguring skin disorders. St Andrews' leper house, which stood to the south of the town, has been partially excavated and gives a clear indication of the workings of a Medieval leper house. Skeletal, archaeological and documentary evidence has shown us that Medieval people suffered from illnessess known today, such as arthritis, tuberculosis, spina bifida, smallpox, cholera and amoebic dysentry. More common then, also, were infestations of parasites, often of worms, common to both man and his domestic animals. The most feared illness was 'pest' or plague. This was actually several diseases, bubonic, which was spread by rats, being the most common. Many people in Scotland were, however, susceptible to pneumonic plague, which was encouraged by cold and rain.

Children and women of child-bearing age had the worst death rates. It has been estimated that only one third of Aberdeen women survived the child-bearing period of their lives. But, once having achieved that, many lived much longer than men; there are many examples of women marrying three or four times as widows. Provision for the care of the sick was minimal. Many towns had almshouses or 'hospitals' but these were not genuinely open to all. Although Kinghorn had a hospital for the poor, founded around 1478, it could not house many. This was true of all Fife Medieval burghs. Self-help was essential, usually in the form of traditional medication brewed from herbs.

There were lighter sides to life. Medieval townspeople enjoyed games such as football, shooting at the butts (the Dunfermline bow butts were sited at the west end of Nethertoun Broad Street, for example), dicing and gaming, gossiping and drinking. The Holy Days were days for fun; processions through the streets on saints' days were not only days to venerate the saints, but also times to introduce some laughter into life. Strolling companies of players travelled around the country and added to the laughter with jesters, tumblers, minstrels, drummers and pipers. Secular festivities, such as the May Games and the Robin Hood entertainments, brought some light relief to the harsh working year. A number of Fife's burghs still celebrate festivities dating to Medieval times. Inverkeithing had four Medieval fairs, that of Lammas being held in August. This is still held each year, as it is in St Andrews. In 1652, the burgh records described it as a day of 'fun, frolic, fit races, ale and drunken folk'. It was probably exactly so in the Middle Ages!

Thirteen

Castles of Fife

Like most areas of Scotland, Fife contains numerous castles dating from the 12th through to the early 17th century. During these centuries, castles were home to the aristocracy and to lairds of much more modest social status.

Fife boasts no really magnificent castles; there is no equivalent of Bothwell or Doune, and, with the exception of Falkland which is really more of a palace than a castle, none of the surviving buildings is of major architectural merit. Nonetheless, they are a varied and interesting group with much to tell us about the developing society of the county. A few of them are maintained and open to the public (St Andrews, Aberdour, Balgonie, Kellie and others); many more lie abandoned and in some cases (Lordscairnie and Ballenbreich for example) their present condition is so precarious that it gives cause for anxiety: ours may be the last generation to be able to see these ancient structures.

Fortified sites had existed in Fife, as in other areas, for many centuries, but castles in the true sense were unknown in Scotland before the 12th century and, specifically, before the reign of David I (1124–53). The king had lived in England, where castle building had been known since the Norman conquest of 1066, and had himself held castles in his extensive honour of Huntingdon. Not surprisingly, therefore, he brought architectural ideas north with him. He also began to encourage knights of Norman origin who were settled in England, to come and establish themselves north of the border. So, families like the Stewarts in Annandale began to build castles.

In Fife, where there was comparatively little Norman settlement, the native earls seem to have adapted to ideas from the south and it was probably Earl Duncan I (d. 1154) who founded the castle at Cupar, now entirely destroyed and only surviving in the name of Castle Hill.

Apart from the earldom itself, other lordships were founded on the Anglo-Norman model, like Kennoway, held by Merleswain, who was probably of Anglo-Saxon origin, and Leuchars, held by Ness, son of William.

Both Kennoway and Leuchars were the sites of castles which probably date back to the 12th century. Like the vast majority of castles in Scotland (and England) at the time, these were not stone and mortar structures, but mottes, that is artificial earth mounds, surmounted by a wooden palisade or tower. At the base of the motte, there would often be a bailey or protected enclosure surrounded by a bank which might be strengthened by wooden fortifications.

Such mottes can be seen in a number of places in Fife, at Leuchars for example, where the traces are indistinct and largely ploughed out, and at Kennoway, where the motte still rises impressively beside the road. The castle at Kennoway was probably built by Merleswain or his descendants and is a typical flat-topped mound with steep sides. It has no bailey but a series of earth ramparts on the most vulnerable side, the south-east.

There is no surviving stone castle in Fife which can be securely dated before the year 1200. At St Andrews, the bishops built a castle, which was in existence by the time of Bishop Roger (1189–1202). Roger was the son of the Earl of Leicester and, given his English background and the building works being carried on in the nearby cathedral, it would not be surprising if the castle was built in stone. However, none of the surviving structure can be dated with any confidence to this period.

The castle of Aberdour has claims to be the oldest stone built castle in the county though only a small part of the present structure is early. The Mortimer family, who then held it, seem to have constructed a small hall-house around 1200. Of this a fragment remains, incorporated into the later Medieval building. It has stylistic links with work of the same period on the island monastery of Inchcolm, of which the Mortimers were patrons.

Apart from the fragment at Aberdour, the earliest stone built castles in Fife date from the period after the Wars of Independence. The late 14th century saw the beginnings of secular building on a large scale. The most ambitious project of the time was the rebuilding of St Andrews Castle by Bishop Walter Traill (d. 1401). The original castle of Bishop Roger had been almost completely destroyed during and after the great siege of 1337 when it was taken from the English garrison by the regent of Scotland, Sir Andrew Moray. Traill created a major enclosure castle, with a massive gatehouse tower in the centre of the southern range and sub rectangular towers at the four corners. Domestic accommodation, including a great hall on the eastern side, was arranged around the interior courtyard. Though much of the work has been rebuilt and ruined, it is clear that Traill's castle was a fortified palace on a grand scale, perhaps comparable with Doune in Stirlingshire, built by the Regent Albany at the same period.

The late 14th century saw other building projects. At Ballenbreich, on the north coast, the Leslie family built an impressive enclosure castle. The lands were acquired by the family during the course of the 14th century and in 1390 Norman Leslie was given a charter confirming him in possession of the lands of the Barony of 'Balnebrech'. The court was surrounded by ranges of buildings on three sides. Major rebuilding in the late 16th and early 17th century, followed by later ruination, have obscured much of this work. However, it is clear from the surviving masonry of the chapel on the first floor of the south range, which includes three elegant gothic sedilia or priests' seats, that this was a building of quality and elegance.

In the far west of the county, at Tulliallan, just north of Kincardine on Forth, another impressive castle was constructed at the same time. It was on a smaller scale than either St Andrews or Ballenbreich, but it too shows elegant masonry work. The building was little more than a fortified manor-house, a single rectangular block which was surrounded by a courtyard that may have been fortified in earth and timber. Despite its modest dimensions, the building is constructed in fine ashlar masonry. On the west end there are two projecting towers containing staircases, one half-octagonal and one half-hexagonal, both unusual shapes at a time when almost all towers were built square. Equally unusual was the position of the hall on the ground floor (rather than the more usual first floor) with fine ribbed stone vaults supported by central octagonal columns. The building history is quite obscure, but it may have been done for a member of the Douglas family who held the lands at the time.

The 15th century saw the building of a number of impressive tower-houses in the county. The tower-house is the characteristic feature of Scottish castle building in the period after the Wars of Independence. As we have seen, enclosure castles were still being built but the typical castle was now a simple, square tower with a number of floors, some with stone vaults, others separated by wood. Usually there is a spiral staircase in one corner and often, but not always, fireplaces and chimneys. The exterior is unornamented apart from corbelled machicolations around the wall head. These may be real (i.e. they have gaps between the corbels for throwing objects at assailants) or they are ornamental, being designed simply to finish the top of the wall in an impressive way.

Despite this uniformity of plan, tower-houses are in fact much more varied than appears at first sight and these variations are an indication of the date, status and wealth of the builders. The plan can be a simple rectangle or be elaborated with one or more wings. The masonry can be rubble or fine ashlar. Windows can be simple slits or much more elaborate openings. It should be remembered that the tower-houses rarely stood in splendid isolation but were surrounded by smaller buildings, often made of timber and earth. These in turn might be surrounded by a stone barmkin wall. Each tower-house is individual and tells its own story of wealth, power and taste.

Fifteenth-century tower-houses are usually simple rectangles in plan. Their walls are thick and the openings few. Internally there is often just one chamber on each floor. The most impressive example of a simple 15th-century tower can be seen at Balgonie; it was probably built in the first half of the century for the Sibbald family. The plan is very simple and the walls are thick; there are four floors, the lower three separated by massive stone vaults. The windows are small and access to the upper floors was gained by a simple turnpike stair. The design may not be elaborate but the quality of the work is high, almost entirely executed in finely cut ashlar.

Few of the other early tower-houses are as large or as well preserved as Balgonie, which always seems to have been habitable. However, Macduff's Castle on the cliff near East Wemyss was one. The original tower may have been constructed in the late 14th century, so making it the earliest simple tower-house in Fife. The tower seems to have doubled as the entrance to a yard or enclosure, with a gateway on the ground floor and living accommodation, in one single chamber, above. Most of it was apparently demolished in 1967 because it was said to be dangerous. In rather better condition is the later 15th-century tower-house at Rosyth, now within the perimeter of the Royal Naval Dockyard. It is a smart, well-built rectangular tower with a single chamber on each floor. There are four storeys separated by two stone vaults, one over the first floor and another over the second. Compared with the massiveness of Balgonie, the walls are thinner and a small wing extends from the rectangular block and helps to contain the turnpike stair.

At Balwearie, near Kirkcaldy, William Scott was granted a licence to build a castle in 1484 and part of this massive simple tower still survives. As in other 15th-century examples, the plan was simple but the building was of high quality ashlar, the bareness of the interiors being softened by fine fireplaces and those window seats which are characteristic of so many towers.

Another simple tower-house of the 15th century can be seen at Lordscairnie, north-east of Cupar. Now sadly decayed and in imminent danger of further collapse, this was once the seat of one of the most famous families in Fife, the Lindsay earls of Crawford. Popular tradition ascribes it to Alexander, the 3rd 'Beardie' Earl (1446–53) but there is no hard evidence. The present, desolate aspect of the building is somewhat misleading. The tower was surrounded by a courtyard and a barmkin wall, of which a small round turret with gun-loops at ground level survives; no doubt there were other structures in the courtyard. The marshy area which presently surrounds the castle may have been a small loch, so that the castle stood on an island site, somewhat like the great Douglas tower-house at Threave in Dumfriesshire. Apart from the small turret, all that survives now is a ruinous rectangular tower house with a small square staircase turret projecting from one corner. The masonry is rubble with freestone dressings around the openings. Above the vault which covered the ground floor, the first-floor hall was clearly an elegant chamber with large windows to the south and west. It is interesting to see that the greatest families in the land, like their more modest neighbours, were living in fairly simple tower-houses in the 15th century.

The finest example of a 15th-century tower-house surviving in all its glory, is Scotstarvit, south of Cupar, built for the Inglis family at the end of the 15th century. It shows how a building of comparatively simple plan can be elegant in proportion and classy in execution. It is a single-chamber tower with a small projecting jamb to house the turnpike stair. The fabric is an excellent ashlar and the corbels around the wall head give it a smart somewhat military appearance. Within, two stone vaults and wooden floors are used to create five storeys.

Amid the simple and massive tower-houses of the 15th century, one Fife castle stands out, both because of its architecture and the patron who built it. Apart from Falkland Palace, Ravenscraig is the only royal castle in Fife. Being a royal building, we also have firm evidence of both date and architect, unlike most of the baronial and other castles in the county. The building of Ravenscraig was begun in 1460 by King James II for his queen, Mary of Gueldres. The master of works was David Boys and the architect and master mason was Henry Merlioun who seems to have founded a small dynasty of masons that were later employed at Edinburgh Castle and Holyrood. There can be little doubt, however, that the real inspiration for the unusual design came from the king himself. James II was a great enthusiast for the new technologies of gunpowder artillery and Ravenscraig was clearly designed to be defended against cannon.

The castle stands on a rocky spit of land extending into the Forth just to the east of Kirkcaldy. The steep cliffs around the promontory meant that defence was only needed on the short, landward side. Here, a massive defended curtain was constructed from one cliff edge to the other. Instead of the rectangular towers common at the time, the entrance front was dominated by two substantial D-shaped towers whose rounded sides pointed outwards so that cannon balls would be deflected from them rather than slamming straight into the surface. Between the towers ran a substantial curtain wall with an entrance in the centre, reached by a drawbridge across the artificial ditch. The upper storeys of the two towers contained residential accommodation with large windows on the protected sides.

Unfortunately, in the year building started King James was killed at the siege of Roxburgh when a cannon exploded. Building probably continued until Mary herself died in 1463. At this stage only one of the great towers had been completed to full height. In 1470 James III granted the unfinished castle to William Sinclair, Earl of Orkney. Under the Sinclairs building continued on a much more modest scale: the fortifications were patched up, though the west tower was never completed, and a range of residential buildings was constructed in the interior. Despite its unfinished state, Ravenscraig remains an interesting exception to the general run of castles in the county.

The 16th century saw the building of many new castles in Fife and the expansion and development of old ones. With the new century, however, priorities began to change. Owners no longer put such a high price on defensive features and began to pay more attention to comfort and privacy, light and style. The castle was evolving towards the country house and sometimes the dividing line between the two is hard to define.

Security clearly remained a priority. This is not the same as military defence. Ravenscraig shows how effective defence against military attack required the building of huge stone bastions. With one exception, the castle owners of Fife were unable, or more probably, unwilling, to make this massive investment. Security, however, was still required. At a time when there were no banks, families naturally kept their valuables, jewellery, fabrics and, of course, money, at home. They also had to protect those charters and deeds which proved the ownership of their lands. Castles in the 16th century were fortified against robbery and general disorder rather than military attack.

The one exception to this was at St Andrews. In the aftermath of the defeat at Flodden, James Beaton, archbishop from 1521 to 1538, tried to fortify his castle against artillery attack. At both ends of the south facing curtain wall, the rectangular towers of Bishop Traill's castle were replaced by massive, circular block-houses, now almost completely disappeared. These were designed to mount artillery and prevent an enemy approaching the main walls. Both were badly damaged in the siege of 1546–7 and the eastern one has now been entirely lost to the sea while only fragments of the western one can still be discerned.

The archbishops of St Andrews led high-profile political lives. Most of the other castle owners in Fife were more concerned with domestic matters. They wanted to improve their castles or build new ones to reflect new concerns and priorities. Basically, there were two ways of doing this: one was to develop an existing tower-house to provide extra and more spacious accommodation. The other was to build a new design of tower-house which would satisfy within its own walls, the need for space, privacy and light. As has already been pointed out, the tower-houses of the 14th and 15th centuries rarely stood in isolation. Around them, within the protection of the barmkin walls, clustered timber outbuildings which have now disappeared. Some of the building projects of the 16th century were simply rebuilding these flimsy structures in stone, at once more durable and more stylish.

Again, one of the best examples of this can be seen at Balgonie. In 1496 the property passed into the hands of Sir Robert Lundie who held the lucrative post of Lord High Treasurer of Scotland. In the 16th century he or his heirs constructed a long hall raised on an undercroft which stretched to the east of the great tower and perhaps a range which led south from the east end of that. A wall with a fortified gate was led from the south end of the east range back to the tower, so enclosing and protecting the courtyard. Much of this work was subsequently modified when the castle passed into the hands of Sir Alexander Leslie, 1st Earl of Leven. The building continued to be developed and expanded at least until the time of the 3rd Earl, David (1691–1728), who constructed a three-storey building in the centre of the east wing. Balgonie thus developed from a grim tower-house into an elegant 17th-century country house.

1. Radiating near-hexagonal columnar cooling joints in basalt lava flow, near Kinghorn

2. One of eighteen cremation urns from a cremation cemetery at Lawhead, west of St Andrews (now in Fife Museum, Kinburn House, St Andrews)
Copyright © E. Proudfoot

3. The Skeith stone, near Kilrenny. The only example in Fife of an equal-armed cross, enclosed in a circle, with a faint *chi-rho* symbol, top right *Copyright © E. Proudfoot*

4. The St Andrews Sarcophagus main panel, showing David scenes, now in St Andrews Cathedral Museum. To the left and right are the corner posts, decorated with interlaced animal motifs *Copyright © E. Proudfoot*

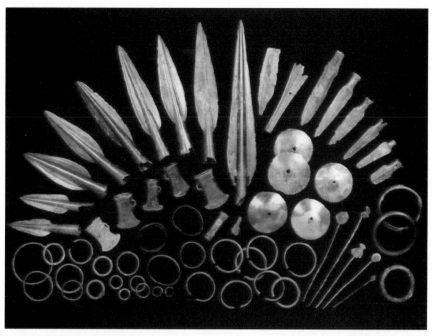

5. Priestden Place, St Andrews. View of the entire collection of artefacts from the Priestden, St Andrews hoard, after cleaning *Copyright © Trustees RMS*

6. Clatchard Craig hillfort. Aerial view showing the circular upper enclosure and the outer ramparts which follow the contours *Crown Copyright © NMRS*

7. Dunfermline Abbey, nave interior *Crown Copyright; reproduced by courtesy of Historic Scotland*

8. St Andrews, Dominican Church *Crown Copyright; reproduced by courtesy of Historic Scotland*

9. St Andrews Cathedral *Crown Copyright; reproduced by courtesy of Historic Scotland*

10. Inchcolm Abbey, the church and chapter house from the east *Crown Copyright; reproduced by courtesy of Historic Scotland*

11. Unloading herring from steam drifters at Anstruther in the winter herring fishery in the early 1930s *Copyright © W. H. Flett*

12. Kirkcaldy from the east, 1838 by an anonymous artist *Kirkcaldy Museum & Art Gallery, Kirkcaldy District Council*

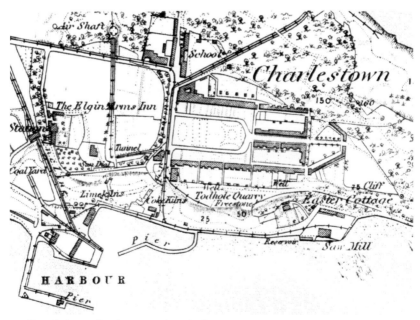

13. Detail from the first 1:10,560 Ordnance Survey map of Fife, surveyed in 1854, showing Charlestown, established in 1761 by Charles, 5th Earl of Elgin for workers in his limekilns and quarries *Reproduced by courtesy of St Andrews University Library*

14. Detail from the first 1:10,560 Ordnance Survey map of Fife, surveyed in 1855, showing Linktown of Abbotshall, a burgh of barony founded in 1633, at the southern edge of Kirkcaldy, and its adjacent Newtown *Reproduced by courtesy of St Andrews University Library*

15. United College Quadrangle, St Andrews University, showing St Salvator's Tower (1460) and the cloister on the north side of the chapel (1846) *Reproduced by courtesy of St Andrews University Library*

The enclosure at the castle of Ballenbreich was also developed. As at Balgonie, there were 16th- and 17th-century phases. The west range was developed in the early 16th century and the south front was completed, with the semi-circular projecting tower with gun-loops which is now the most conspicuous feature of the south front. In the 17th century another range was erected on the north side of the courtyard. Further modifications were made to the west wing which now has a magnificent four-storey mansion with large windows. This later work is all constructed in high quality ashlar. By 1680, when the 7th Earl of Rothes was created Duke of Rothes and Marquess of 'Bambreich', the castle must have been one of the most magnificent residences in Fife. Shortly before this, however, the Duke had started work on his great palace at Leslie House (begun 1667) which became the seat of the family and Ballenbreich was allowed to decay.

At Balgonie and Ballenbreich the residential buildings were constructed around the courtyard. At Macduff's Castle in the 16th century a different solution to expanding the tower-house was found. Macduff's Castle was essentially a gate/tower-house, presumably leading in to a fortified enclosure. After the Colville family look over the property in 1530, they decided to extend it. The gateway in the old tower was blocked up. They then matched the tower by constructing another tower some 20 m to the south to create a more or less symmetrical front. The gap was filled with a range of buildings with a new gate in the centre. An undercroft probably supported a large hall above. At the end of the 16th century, an enclosing wall, with round turret and gun-loops, was built around the whole structure. Again, we can see how a simple tower became the nucleus of an elegant mansion. Although still habitable in 1666, the castle is now in an advanced state of decay and it takes the eye of faith to reconstruct anything of its previous glory.

In contrast to the sad ruins at Ballenbreich and Macduff's Castle, at Kellie we can see an extended tower-house in its full glory, thanks to the restorations of the Lorimer family in the late 19th century. The castle began as a simple rather forbidding tower-house, built by the Oliphant family around the year 1400. It was no doubt surrounded by ancillary buildings and a barmkin wall. So matters remained until 1573 when a second tower-house, with a projecting staircase tower was constructed across the other side of the barmkin. The building of two towers in the same enclosure was unusual but not unique: there is a fine example at Huntingtower just west of Perth, and it probably reflected the needs of two separate households within the same extended family. In the early 17th century Laurence, 5th Lord Oliphant, linked the two towers with a smart new two-storey range to provide more spacious accommodation, and, for good measure, built a third tower at the south-west corner to balance the original tower of his ancestors at the north-east. John Gifford memorably describes the results as 'a mixture of incipient classicism and tower-house Indian summer' Despite internal changes, Kellie survives in its early 16th-century form, a classic example of an expanded tower-house and an indication of what we have lost elsewhere.

While old towers were being extended to meet new needs, the 16th and early 17th century also saw the construction of new ones; indeed, the second half of the 16th century was the real golden age for the tower-house in Fife. These new tower-houses were still single fortified blocks but they differed in many ways from their predecessors. The plan became more elaborate. The most typical example of this was the development of what is rather misleadingly known as the 'Z' plan. This involved adding towers or turrets to two of the diagonally opposite corners of the main tower. This provided space for staircases, which could now be wider and grander, and extra rooms for an age in which privacy was coming to seem more important. It was also useful for security reasons: all four sides of the building could be covered from gun loops in the sides of the projecting tower. Another obvious change was in the fenestration. The increasing availability of window glass combined with the lower priority given to defence meant that large rectangular windows could be used, especially on south-facing walls.

One of the first and most impressive of the new style tower-houses was at Earlshall, near Leuchars; it was built by Sir William Bruce and his family from 1546 onwards. Here the tower is rectangular rather than square, which in itself increased the living area. There are boldly projecting towers, one square and one rounded at opposite corners with a small staircase tower in the re-entrant angle. The interior is large enough to be divided into separate chambers including the second floor gallery with a superb painted ceiling, dated to 1620. There is an ancillary block across the court from the main castle which was built in the late 19th century, apparently on the site of earlier buildings. The castle and garden are surrounded by an enclosing wall. Earlshall, restored with loving care by Sir Robert Lorimer after 1890, remains one of the best examples in Scotland of a 16th-century tower house.

At Fordell, outside Inverkeithing, there is another 'Z' plan castle which is still inhabited. It was built for James Henderson from 1567 by the master masons Robert Peris and James Orrok and, despite a disastrous fire the next year, much of their work survives. The projecting towers and turrets, with pistol-holes in their corbelling, give the place a slightly military air. The windows are large and the internal arrangements spacious. An unusual feature of Fordell is the existence of two turnpike stairs, one in each projecting tower.

Another example of the 'Z' plan can be seen at Dairsie Castle, home of the Learmonth family. Probably constructed at the end of the 16th century, it is an oblong hall standing on a fine site overlooking the River Eden. There are round towers with gun loops at two of the corners. As usual there was an undercroft and a hall on the first floor with large south facing windows. Until the mid-

1990s the castle was a dismal ruin, just a shadow of its former glory, but it has since been imaginatively reconstructed and now gives a good impression of how a late 16th-century tower-house would have looked when new.

One of the pleasures of looking at these tower-houses is the variety and originality that they show. Although the basic formula is more or less the same, each has its own character and variations of the theme. At Denmylne, just south of Newburgh, hard beside the Cupar Road, the tower house is now roofless but almost complete to the wall-head. It was probably built by Patrick Balfour after 1541 as a 'T' shaped plan, with the turnpike stair in the tower which projects from the rectangular block. As with many towers of this period, there is the combination of a secured building, complete with gun loops and corbelled parapet at the wall head, and large, rectangular windows which show a desire for comfort and ease.

There are numerous other examples of 16th-century towers to be found in Fife. Some, like Pitfirrane west of Dunfermline, have always been inhabited. Others, like Pitcullo near Balmullo have been restored from ruin; others still, like Pittarthie near Dunino stand forlorn and derelict. They all combine to show the resources and aspirations of the Fife lairds of the 16th century, concerned on the one hand for security and a degree of martial display and on the other for comfort and a new sort of domesticity.

Old castles were maintained and extended in 17th-century Fife, but no new ones were built. The work of Sir William Bruce at Balcaskie in 1671 and later, and most impressively, at Kinross House, made the old traditional forms obsolete. Old towers were simply allowed to languish and decay while classical symmetry came to rule supreme.

FOURTEEN

REFORMATION AND COVENANTERS IN FIFE

REFORMATION

The Reformation in Scotland came about through the convergence of two movements, one theological and the other political. In both dramas Fife was centre-stage. This was particularly so in the theological development, on account of the part played by the University of St Andrews. Very soon after the outbreak of the Lutheran revolution, reformed literature made its way into Scotland, and the new religious ideas found favourable soil in the humanism that was gaining ground in the university. The College of St Leonard, which had been founded in St Andrews in 1512 through the efforts of the Augustinian canons, who provided the college principal, was particularly sympathetic. John Knox attributed the propagation of new theological opinion in the college to Master Gavin Logie. John Winram, who was to play a prominent part in the Reformation after 1559, sat at Logie's feet, and in his turn was a major influence in the education of the prior, James Stuart, who long before his official conversion in 1555, favoured and protected Reformers. Many leading reformers had first experienced the new teachings at St Andrews, so that the phrase 'He's been drinking at St Leonard's well' became a euphemism to denote the assimilation of Protestant ideas. Just how deeply the Augustinian Priory was affected can be gathered from the fact that after the Reformation the community provided the Kirk with a superintendent, 16 ministers, five readers, and David Peebles, who was one of the writers of music for the Scottish Psalter.

The Catholic Church, alarmed at the spread of the new ideas, reacted with heresy trials and burnings. The most renowned of these martyrdoms, Patrick Hamilton in 1527, Henry Forrest c. 1533, George Wishart in 1545, and Walter Myln in 1558, all took place in St Andrews which, as the Primate's cathedral city, was the ecclesiastical capital of Scotland. There is little need to seek ulterior or personal motives for this procedure, since it had long been the traditional manner of dealing with heresy. In fact there were fewer executions in Scotland than in most other European countries. Nevertheless the procedure was fundamentally flawed, and not at all consistent with Christian principles, and the burnings had precisely the opposite effect of what was intended so that many people were moved with pity and became much more sympathetic to the Protestant cause. One striking example was Alexander Alan, later known as

Alesius, who converted to Lutheranism on seeing the death of Patrick Hamilton, and subsequently on the Continent wrote many books in defence of Protestantism. A further tactical error was made by the Old Church when she declared interdict on the imprisonment of Cardinal Beaton at the beginning of 1543. Once again this was the traditional practice because the imprisonment of a cardinal was deemed a grievous sacrilege, but the penalty deprived Catholics of Mass and the sacraments at precisely the time when they needed them most, and in all probability Protestant style services were celebrated which would have been the only ones available during the interdict. Yet another weakness on the Catholic side was the failure to write. While Protestant tracts and books abounded, though banned by Act of Parliament in 1527, Ninian Winzet, a priest in Linlithgow and Quintin Kennedy, Abbot of Crossraguel, were almost alone in writing pamphlets for the defence of the ancient faith, although one must add John Major's *Commentary on the Four Gospels* (1529), on which he worked in St Andrews, and which explicitly part of a campaign against Lutheranism. Catholic reforming synods, which showed the existence of abuse but also a willingness to put things right, were convened in 1549, 1552 and 1559 by Archbishop Hamilton who published his Catechism in 1552. These measures, however, did not have sufficient time to take effect as the political movement advanced. To this we must now turn.

Ever since the Battle of Flodden, there had been divergence of opinion among the Scottish nobles about alliance with England. Immediately after the battle the majority were opposed to alliance with the 'auld enemy', but the intrigues and bribery of Henry VIII gradually changed the balance. Henry's policy for Scotland was not only to establish his own overlordship, but also, after his break with Rome, to join Scotland with England in the denial of Papal supremacy in order to oppose the formation of a great Catholic league. Having failed to persuade his nephew, James V, to concur with his plans against the Old Church, Henry sought to win over the Scottish nobles. James V, on the other hand, by his marriage to Princess Magdalen cemented the Scots–French alliance, and his second marriage to Mary of Guise bound the Scottish sovereign even more strongly to the Catholic cause. Cardinal David Beaton, who succeeded his uncle, James Beaton, as Archbishop of St Andrews in 1539, became advisor to the king and the champion not only of Catholicism but of union with France. It was natural for the Reformers who opposed Beaton on religious grounds to become the allies of those who opposed the French alliance. Thus the political divide became intertwined with the religious division; in general terms those who favoured treaty with England were on the Protestant side while Catholics wanted to maintain the French alliance. In Fife two very important landowners, Kirkcaldy of Grange and Leslie of Rothes were fervently pro-English and very definitely allied to the Protestant cause. Several factors made divisions more pronounced. James V, recognising the support he got from the Church, tended to favour the clergy, and thus alienated many of his nobles and drove them to Henry's side in the religious struggle. The disastrous rout of the king's forces at the Battle of Solway Moss (1542) made the situation much worse as a number of nobles, taken prisoner after the battle, were granted freedom and financial rewards in return for a pledge to further Henry's aims. Cardinal David Beaton had been the big obstacle to Henry VIII's ambitions, and had successfully triumphed in his endeavour to prevent a meeting between James V and Henry VIII. Henry had not been able to discredit Beaton with the Scottish king, and the prelate's imprisonment which Henry had contrived did nothing to promote the English cause. Having failed by all other means, Henry plotted to assassinate the prelate. Whether or not it was part of Henry's plan, the murder took place in St Andrews. On the morning of 29 May 1546, John and Norman Leslie of Rothes, Peter Carmichael, James Melvil, the younger Kirkcaldy of Grange and others pushed their way into the castle which was the bishop's residence, and advanced on Beaton's room. The Cardinal barricaded the door, but opened it after it was set on fire. The assassins burst into the room, and stabbed the Cardinal to death amidst his pleas that he was a priest. Thus the leader and champion of the Catholic cause perished. The struggle was, however, by no means over; it was to continue for a further 14 years. The murderers, finding that their deed was not so popular as they had imagined it would be, took possession of the bishop's home and locked themselves in. The castle became the refuge of all disaffected to the government, and John Knox joined them at Easter 1547 to begin his vigorous preaching. In the summer, however, the stronghold fell to the French, who had come by sea, and had mounted cannon on the cathedral roof to breach the castle's walls. Along with others, John Knox was sent to the galleys and was a galley slave for two years.

For the time being, the action moved away from Fife. An English army invaded Scotland, but despite victory at the Battle of Pinkie near Musselburgh on 10 September and the capture of Broughty Ferry and Haddington, French troops forced a complete withdrawal by 1550. The respite from fighting gave both religious sides time to attend to their internal affairs. Archbishop Hamilton, who had succeeded Beaton, convened reforming councils in 1549, 1552 and 1559. He published a Catechism in the vernacular in 1552, and ordered that it be read to the people at church on Sundays. Nowadays, both sides generally agree that his attempts at reform were sincere, but a grave tactical error was made at the 1559 council when it was decreed that all alienated church property had to be returned. This was a sure way to put all who had illegally benefited from church revenue into the Protestant camp. A far bigger mistake was the execution of Walter Myln in St Andrews in 1558. He was an old man of over 80 years and ordinary people were appalled at his burning. On the Reformers' side, their numbers were increased by preachers fleeing from the persecution of Queen Mary Tudor in England.

John Knox came back for a short time in 1555–6. He not only dissuaded many from attending Mass, but more importantly he organised leading Protestants into a coherent political and religious group, later known as the Lords of the Congregation, which was to play such a crucial role in the final struggle. This began at Easter 1559 when the people of Perth and Dundee stayed away from Mass. In May the Reformers went to Perth where after a sermon by John Knox, the mob destroyed images in the parish church, the Charterhouse and the Franciscan and Dominican friaries. Thus began the chief assault on church buildings. People in Cupar followed suit with the purging of their church. Mary of Guise was prepared to do battle, but Lord James Stewart and the Earl of Argyll, both being Protestant, deserted her, and with a small group of soldiers entered St Andrews in June. John Knox arrived from the south, having cast down the images in Crail and Anstruther on his way, and after preaching in Holy Trinity Church, St Andrews, exhorted the people to destroy all images and altars in that church and in the Cathedral. According to Spottiswoode, Bishop Lesley and Buchanan, the friaries and churches of the Franciscans and Dominicans were completely demolished, as was the collegiate church of St Mary of the Rock. The Congregation moved to Perth for a meeting on 24 June, and on the way some of them turned aside to 'purge' the Abbey of Lindores where, contrary to the terms of a truce to give time for parley, they destroyed altars, statues, vestments and missals. The Lords of the Congregation moved from Perth to Stirling, Linlithgow and Edinburgh. Bishop Lesley dated the purging of Dunfermline Abbey in July 1559, although religious life in the monastery continued. If that date is accurate, the 'casting down' may have occurred on the journey from Perth to Stirling. Mary of Guise had to retire for a short time to Dunbar, but soon was able to occupy Leith. At a chance encounter in Restalrig, the Congregation troops were mauled so badly that they had to retire from Edinburgh on 6 November, and the regent had them pursued into Fife. The French land troops went by way of Culross, Dunfermline and Burntisland to meet their ships at Kinghorn. At Pettycur, three-quarters of a mile (1205 m) to the south, there was an encounter in which six or seven Protestants were killed, and some taken prisoner, amongst them a French boy who was hanged from a steeple. Probably because he was French he was seen as a traitor, but this unnecessary cruelty could only serve to put sympathy with the other side.

The French took Kinghorn, to the elation of Mary of Guise. Knox's recounting of the regent's words, 'Where is now John Knox's God? My God is now stronger than his – yes, even in Fife!', whether it be accurate or not, shows how great a part Fife had played in the Reformation movement. Meanwhile the Congregation was joined at Cupar by Knox who preached a sermon of encouragement. Although Mary of Guise's forces were stronger, for some time the Earl of Arran and Lord James Stewart held the French at Dysart, and in one incident, William Kirkcaldy of Grange, the day after his house had been demolished by the French, ambushed a Captain Le Battu with his hundred. The French captain sought refuge in Glennis House, about a mile (1.6 km) from Kinghorn, but Kirkcaldy and Lord Lyndsay successfully attacked, killing Le Battu and 50 of his men. The French were marching on St Andrews when their supply boats were intercepted by English ships. Whereupon the French withdrew from Fife. In an attempt to stay their progress Kirkcaldy destroyed the bridge at Tullibody, but the French took the roof off the parish church and made a bridge to cross the River Devon.

In February 1560 the Treaty of Berwick was made between Elizabeth I and the Lords of the Congregation, after which England took charge of the military operations. The English fleet began the siege of Leith. Mary of Guise died in June; the French garrison was defeated soon afterwards, and the Treaty of Edinburgh was signed in July 1560. The Lords of the Congregation, with military assistance from England, had won, and the Scottish Parliament proclaimed the country Protestant in August. Continuance of the auld alliance with France was no longer a feasible proposition as it would inevitably have led to constant warfare with England, and France would have given meagre help when engaged on other fronts. To have survived in this political upheaval, the Old Church would have needed to be very strong and it would have been necessary to make a clear distinction between Church and State to allow an alliance between a Protestant England and a Catholic Scotland. The Catholic Church, however, was weak in spiritual leadership because of royal appointments to bishoprics and abbacies, and it would have been very difficult to differentiate between Church and State in a Europe engaged in religious wars and in a country where Church and monarchy had been so interdependent.

Though the country was officially Protestant from 1560, a great deal of organisational work had still to be done, and in this, Fife, under the superintendence of John Winram, former prior of the Augustinian monastery in St Andrews, led the way; his church became known as 'ane perfyt Reformed Kyrk'. It is difficult to assess how much resistance there was from the Old Church. It was certainly less than would have been expected, especially as Catholics were still a majority. Archbishop Hamilton's tardiness in protesting is hard to explain even though his brother's position on the Protestant side would have made it very difficult for the archbishop to act effectively, and it is evident that no one wanted more war. Probably, there was less clinging to the old faith in Fife than there was anywhere else. Yet a few instances can be noted. Several of the masters of St Salvator's College in St Andrews, including William Cranston, the principal, adhered to the ancient religion and left their places. In 1564, three priests, Sir Nycholl Bawerege, Sir George Tod, and Dean John Wilson were summoned to appear before the superintendent on charges of saying Mass and administering the sacraments in private houses. In 1587, a Mr James Myrton, recently returned from the continent, was suspected of being a papist, and three times summoned to appear before the superintendent at St Andrews. This is almost certainly the same James Myrton, listed in the Douai Diary as being at the Scottish seminary of Pont-à-Mousson in 1582 with the note that he did good work as a priest for some time before lapsing and going to England. Perhaps most note-worthy of all is the fact that the monks of Dunfermline Abbey were still singing the Divine Office in the monastery in 1580. By that date, however, there were very few Catholic priests left in the country, and Scotland was to remain a predominantly Protestant nation.

THE COVENANTERS

The earliest Protestant Reformers in Scotland were Lutheran in their theology, but by 1560 the leaders were Calvinists, with a strong antipathy to episcopalian authority, who hoped to replace all bishops with superintendents. Moreover, in Scotland the Reformation, having been achieved by armed rebellion against the Crown, was opposed to royal control and in its first decade had largely been allowed to act autonomously. Tensions between Church and monarchy were inevitable and became manifest when the Regent Morton in the 1570s and James VI in the 1580s tried to impose royal authority through the bishops. The struggle continued throughout the reign of James VI, but he was too good a diplomat to push things too far. Charles I, however, seemed determined to extend royal power so that Scots feared that their national identity was being eroded. His attempt to impose an Anglicised form of worship on the Scots through the imposition of *The New Prayer Book* met with widespread resistance, and as no concessions were granted, the result was a national protest which took the form of The National Covenant of Scotland, first signed in Greyfriars Churchyard, Edinburgh, on 28 February 1638. This expressed loyalty to the Crown, but also the determination to maintain the national religion.

Fife can claim a leading role in so far as one of the co-authors of the covenant document was Alexander Henderson, minister of Leuchars. Fife's part, however, in the formulation of a covenant mentality predated 1638. When the General Assembly, alarmed at the attempts of James VI to limit the power of the Presbyterian Church, had spoken of renewing the Covenant of Mercy in 1596, it had been the Synod of Fife and the presbytery of St Andrews that had taken this up and declared a new covenant between God and his ministers. Lay people had been invited to join, and it had been promoted in many Fife parishes. In the new Covenant of 1638, covenanting zeal flourished in the Lowlands rather than the Highlands, and Fife was among the counties in which it was strongest. Special mention should be made of Samuel Rutherford who has been named 'the saint of the Covenant'. In 1638 he was appointed Professor of Divinity in St Mary's College, St Andrews, and thereafter was a member of covenanting assemblies, taking an important part in their deliberations. Often he took the part of rigid Covenanters in disputes with moderates, even siding with western remonstrants who condemned the treaty with the king as sinful. In this, however, he did not represent the whole of Fife. In fact he was the only member of the presbytery of St Andrews to hold this position, and was often in opposition to all his university colleagues. At the restoration of Charles II, Rutherford's political work *Lex Rex* was ordered to be burnt in Edinburgh and St Andrews, and he himself was charged with treason. He was, however, too ill to appear in court, and died in St Andrews the following year.

It was in the second phase of the movement, which is generally described as that of the Later Covenanters, that one of the most outstanding incidents of Covenant history occurred in Fife. Archbishop James Sharp, who had once been on the side of the Covenanters, had procured troops for the suppression of conventicles in Fife. These soldiers had gone beyond their remit, and were guilty of robbery and violence. Therefore a group of nine, led by David Hackston of Rathillet in Fife and including John Balfour of Kinloch with six tenant farmers from Fife and a weaver originally from Dundee, set out on 3 May 1679 to frighten, and possibly to beat up, the sheriff depute of Fife, William Carmichael, who was, however, given a warning to stay clear. Disappointed at losing their prey, the covenanting zealots were about to return home when they heard that Archbishop Sharp's coach was heading their way. Quickly they took their decision (though Hackston disapproved of it), pursued the coach, and brought it to a standstill. Before his daughter's eyes, the Archbishop was dragged from his coach and murdered on Magus Muir. This ugly incident sparked off further rebellion, and at Drumclog in Lanarkshire, a small party of Covenanters was successful in defeating a detachment of troops led by Graham of Claverhouse. Significantly, one of the covenanting officers was David Hackston of Rathillet. The military success of the Covenanters was, however, short-lived, and their forces were defeated at the Battle of Bothwell Bridge. After the battle, five captured men, Thomas Brown, James Wood, Andrew Sword, John Weddell and John Clyde, were taken to Fife, and executed as a reprisal for the murder of Archbishop Sharp, an act as atrocious as the murder itself, since none of those executed had taken any part in the assassination of the prelate. The place of execution is today marked by a monument to their memory close to Strathkinness. (Nearby is a cairn to the memory of Archbishop Sharp.) Amongst others captured at Bothwell Bridge were six from Fife, James Beal, Andrew Prie, James Kirk, John Kirk, Thomas Miller and Robert Boog, who were banished to America, but were shipwrecked off the coast of Orkney. Thomas Miller from the parish of Ceres was the only one of the six to escape with his life.

David Hackston was later captured after a skirmish at Airds Moss, and put on trial for his part in the murder of Sharp. He was condemned to be hanged, and was afterwards quartered. One of his hands was buried in the graveyard of the parish church in Cupar. In the same grave the heads of two other executed Covenanters are buried; Laurence Hay, a weaver from Fife, and Andrew Pitullagh, a land labourer from the parish of Largo. They bear witness to the ardour of Fife Covenanters as they had been members of a society in Fife, which had riled the authorities by issuing a paper entitled *A Testimony against the Evils of our Times*.

Later in the same year as Hackston's execution, 1680, and undeterred by the defeat at Bothwell Bridge, the preacher Richard Cameron founded the group that was to be known as the Cameronians with the 'Sanquhar Declaration' which went so far as to declare that Charles II should be deposed and to declare war against the Crown. His preaching was not delivered in Fife, but he had come from that county, and had been converted to the Covenant by the preaching at field conventicles near his home in Falkland, which again points to the strength of the covenant movement in Fife. Although Richard Cameron was soon killed in battle, the Cameronians were formed into a regular regiment which was to play a part in the last stages of the struggle. Before that, further sufferings awaited the Covenanters. When James VII came to the throne and the Earl of Argyll returned from exile to lead a rebellion, 224 covenanter prisoners were taken from various prisons in May 1685 and sent to Dunnottar Castle. On their way, they were stopped in Fife and for one night the tolbooth at Burntisland became the prison for the greatest number of Covenanters ever incarcerated together. They were lodged in two rooms of the tolbooth while John Wedderburne, the Laird of Gosford, was sent over from the Privy Council to escort to Edinburgh as many as would swear to the oath of allegiance with the supremacy in it. Thirty-eight complied, and the others were taken to Dunnottar where they were imprisoned for eleven weeks. Events, however, were changing quickly. The Revolution ousted James VII, and although his supporters under Bonnie Dundee won a victory at Killiecrankie in 1689, the stout defence of the city of Dunkeld by the Cameronians prevented the Jacobites gaining from their victory. When William of Orange was accepted as ruler, a Presbyterian majority in Parliament was able to demand the abolition of prelacy. Although this was not the mind of the king, the failure of the bishops to support him led William to give way, and Presbyterianism was established in Scotland in 1690. The covenanting movement in Scotland had played a major role in this final settlement.

FIFTEEN

THE AGRICULTURAL TRADITION

Fife's agricultural traditions rest on its geography and history. Geographically, the peninsula of Fife has a very short landward boundary with its neighbouring shires of Clackmannan, Kinross and Perth, and a very long natural water boundary – the last stretch of the mighty river Tay, the North Sea from St Andrews Bay to Fife Ness, and the Firth of Forth up to Kincardine. Fife is a lowland area with a backbone of higher ground that runs from west to east through the middle of the county; the west and east Lomond hills (the Paps of Fife), along the limestone escarpment – the Riggin o' Fife – which overlooks the Howe of Fife and south-east to the volcanic plugs of Largo Law and Kelly Law. In the north of Fife the fertile Tayside strip known as the Barony rises steeply to Fife's other upland ground which culminates in Norman's Law.

The average rainfall of Fife is low: 50 cm in the east to 90 cm in the west. The county has few rivers. The Eden follows the line of the 'backbone' from Kinross-shire to flow into St Andrews Bay at Guardbridge. In the south the Leven drains Kinross-shire's Loch Leven which was much reduced in area when the 'Cut' was dug last century. The Leven flows into the Firth of Forth under the Bawbee Brig which connects Leven to Methil.

It is reputed to have been King James VI who described the Kingdom of Fife as 'a beggar's mantle fringed with gold'. The coastal strip is free draining, with good soil depth, and has been cultivated from earliest times. South of St Andrews, for example, grain was grown and stored in barns belonging to the King. It was then taken along the ancient highway from the village of Kingsbarns to feed the Court when the King brought it to his hunting Palace of Falkland. Gradually, over the centuries, reclamation and enclosure progressed inward from the fringe. Scrub and stone removal and the new skills of stone and tile drainage were all done by sweat of the brow. Most of the county is now capable of being ploughed to sustain arable crops and much of the higher ground has had its grazing improved by lime and now carries sheep and cattle at reasonable stocking rates.

Land tenure a hundred years ago was mainly through landlords granting 7- or 14-year leases to tenants. Today, more farms will be owner-occupied than tenanted. The Fife estates were never as large as in many other Scottish counties. Their owners must have had a reputation for argument as a Fife laird was described as one having 'a wee puckle land, a doo'cot and a law suit'.

For the first half of the 20th century, agriculture in the British Isles had to rely on rotations to sustain cleanliness from weeds and maintain fertility. Fife's commonest rotation on the good ground that did not require a 'rest' in grass was known as the 'sair six' of oats, poats, wheat, neeps, barley and hay. The oats were always called corn. They were largely consumed on the farm, bruised for the horses, cattle and sheep, and milled at the local mill into oatmeal for farmers in the 'big hoose' and their employees in the 'cotton'. The surplus corn was of course readily saleable and left the farm in very heavy hessian sacks, which held four bushels (32 gallons). These sacks were hired from the railway company and weighed a mere 1½ cwt (80.74 kg) when filled with oats. Barley tipped the scales at 2 cwt (101.6 kg), A sack of wheat (2¼ cwt, 114.3 kg) on your back fairly shoved you into your boots.

The oat straw was feeding straw for the cattle and being the cleanest and least prickly was always used for filling the straw tykes or mattresses. Most farms with their own built-in threshing mill would thresh corn on a frequent basis as cattle were deemed to 'do' better on fresh straw.

The 'poats' were never called anything other than 'tatties' except when trying to remember the rotation! Potatoes have always been the big variable, the main cash crop. Always the most expensive crop to produce with yield and price much more variable than grain, they have the potential to make a good financial contribution or equally give a crushing disaster. The government's creation of the Potato Marketing Board in the early 1930s put a floor in the market and helped to level out the yo-yo effect. This was done mainly by allocating a fixed area to each producer. A fair number of the Fife potato growers produce seed for the English market and this ties in with the the 'sair six' as Scottish Department of Agriculture rules controlling seed potato production insists on a minimum of six years' separation from the previous potato crop. To maximise the potato yield at the peak of this six-year cycle, liberal dunging was required. This farmyard manure was produced by autumn-bought fattening cattle, often of Irish origin, housed in the traditional Fife pantiled 'reeds'. In October the Fife schools closed for a fortnight. The tatties were then gathered by bairns, and winter coats, football boots and new bikes were purchased 'wi' ma ain money'.

In November the potato fields were ploughed and wheat sown tight behind the ploughs. It would be next September before the wheat was cut by binders, stooked, then lead to the corn-yard where it was mainly built on platforms of sparred wood supported on stone or glazed tile columns about 75 cm high. These were known as 'staithles'. Their purpose was to try to keep the stack free from mice and rats, as it would probably not be threshed until the following April or even May when wheat prices were traditionally higher.

The travelling mill would be drawn alongside a staithle and the sheaves forked straight on to the mill. The mill man fed the wheat into the drum lengthwise, very carefully, to keep the threshed straw as unbroken as possible. Unlike the sheaf of unthreshed wheat tied in the middle with one string by the binder, the threshed straw was packed in a much bigger 'bunch' tied with two strings. These bunches of wheat straw were used to thatch the cereal stacks to keep them dry all winter, but more especially they were required to thatch and frost proof the potatoes which were all stored in long narrow pits along a field edge. A big staithle of wheat could hold about 4 acres (1.6 ha). With a good crop and everything going well, the 12–15 people required round the mill would probably thresh four staithles which would produce 200 bags, 22½ tons, in a good day.

Neeps followed wheat. If there was a surplus of dung, after the potato land was well spread, it would go on the neep ground. Early ploughing to achieve the maximum frost mould was the aim; as turnips required the finest seed bed of all the crops and with only harrows and rollers for cultivation tools, all Jack Frost's assistance in breaking down clods was gratefully appreciated. In Fife neeps meant the swede turnip. However, the softer Aberdeen yellow turnip was also grown. This was the second cleaning crop in the rotation and had many summer hours of labour spent on it weeding out both annuals and the dreaded 'wrack' i.e. couch grass. The neeps were all hand pulled, topped and tailed. Those for the cattle were carted off to fill the neep sheds while those to be fed to sheep were pitted across the field in 2–3-ton pits. These neeps were cut into jumbo-sized chips and filled into long flat-bottomed wooden troughs. The rows of these neep troughs, and the lighter V-bottomed troughs which held the cereal and concentrate sheep feed, were turned on to fresh ground each day. Thus the whole field was evenly manured with the droppings and the 'golden hoof'.

The barley, which followed, was the main cereal cash crop. The small village maltings gradually closed but two large family maltings, Kilgour's and Hutchison's in Kirkcaldy, were ready buyers of all Fife's malting quality grain. Barley stooks were supposed to hear the kirk bells twice before being lead and built into ground stacks, as were oats. A generous layer of straw was laid as a bed to keep even the lowest layer or 'gang' sweet and dry. The carter was able to fork the sheaves right up to the builder on the top of these conical beehive stacks. This was unlike the large staithles where a second forker called 'the craw' caught on his or her fork the pitched sheaf and placed it both pointing the correct way, and right way up, to the builder as he crawled round on his knees. The builder's heavy corduroy breeks would have a large second corduroy patch on the knees to try to ease his labour.

In late spring, when the barley was nicely rowed up, the seeds for the final crop were broadcast, lightly harrowed and rolled up. In the autumn, after the barley was cleared, the young grass would likely be fit to be lightly grazed by feeding lambs. It was then left to produce one heavy crop of hay in June. Before the days of the pick-up baler the swathes were turned until ready to build into tramped and roped heaps called 'rucks'. The rucks dried out for a further two to three weeks and then with the aid of various horse forks or elevators were built into large stacks. In the east of Fife at that time hay could be an excellent cash crop too. Dundee had a huge population of heavy horses pulling raw jute up the steep hills from the docks. They created a steady demand for hay. The hay was baled on piecework in a heavy wooden hand baler. A man jumped into the large box and tramped the loose hay as tight as possible till the box was full. A heavy lid was securely fastened and two men pumped handles, which lifted the baler's false bottom ratchet-wise upwards, till the bale was fully compressed. The bale was then tied with wires, side doors knocked open, the bale extracted and the whole process repeated. The re-growth after the hay was taken off was called 'foggage'. Purchased lambs from upland farms grazed this foggage enclosed by temporary nets, which would later be used to contain the sheep on the turnip field where they finished their fattening period.

That was a general blueprint of Fife's agriculture for the first half of this century.

Fife's adaptable soils and climate have allowed other crops to be grown to advantage as the economic or political will has dictated. There was once a thriving linen industry with mills all over Fife. Probably the last to close was in Freuchie. A special type of cloth got its name from the old name of the Fife village of Dairsie – Osnaburg cloth. All these mills would be supplied with Fife flax. However, the crop which caused most variation to the 'sair six', partly in the first and also into the second half of this century, was sugar beet. The British Sugar Beet Corporation was one of the earliest examples of that fashionable word 'quango'. From around the turn of the century factories were established up the arable east coast of England. In the early 1920s the feasibility of a Scottish factory was considered. After trial, areas were grown in Fife with the produce being railed to Selby in Yorkshire for testing and sugar extraction.

It was decided to build a factory at Cupar. The site chosen was central to the growing area, located on a main railway line and with a plentiful water supply from the River Eden. Vast quantities of water were used to wash the beet out of the delivery wagons and lorries into the silo and then via the flumes into the factory. Beet brought a great deal of employment to Fife as, in its early days, it was a very labour intensive crop. The sugar beet seed looked like crumbs of cork; each crumb produced two or more seedlings. These seedlings had to be thinned out to leave a single plant every 250 cm along the drill. This was done with the farm staff in echelon fashion, each with a long shafted hoe. The crop was always hand hoed a second time and sometimes a third. For many years, from the opening of the factory, harvesting the beet was very laborious. Beet grew *in* not *on* the ground like turnips and had to be slackened with a plough before they could be pulled out by hand. One beet was pulled with each hand and they were then knocked together to remove as much earth as possible. They were then laid down in rows with the tips of the large, thin parsnip-shaped roots touching and the leaves and crown 'outside left and outside right'.

After a reasonable break, the next task was to chop off the crown. Many different types of heavy machete knives were tried but the most successful was made from a 30 cm piece of a scythe blade with a handle at 45° to the blade. This very heavy work was almost invariably done on piecework at so much per 100 yd (91 m) by Irish men who lived very rough in the basic bothies each farm provided. There were many disputes between these workers and the farmer regarding the quality of the job and the poor rate being paid. Too much earth left on or too many green shaws left on and the farmer was complaining. But if the workers cut off an over-large slice of the crown they really heard complaint, because this was losing the poor farmer tons per acre! The regular farm staff then hand-loaded the beets to be carted to a clamp in the farmyard or railway station, there to be graiped straight into wagons. The beet graip or 'herp' is a weapon now only found in agricultural museums but at one time the entire tonnage of each factory would be manhandled one or more times with graips. They were like a large shovel in size but with six curved spring-steel tines, each with a ball on its point so that it did not pierce into the beet.

Cupar factory opened each year for the 'campaign'. The factory was much more efficient if it had a steady throughput 24 hours per day. To achieve this, careful calculations were made of the yield in the entire area serving the factory; hence, how many days the campaign would last. Then, each grower was supposed to deliver his crops uniformly throughout the season. This was achieved by issuing each grower permits for every load. And as these permits were dated and had to be handed into the weighbridge, control was achieved. Each load had a sample bucketful taken before being emptied. This was analysed in the tare house for earth content, leaf content and for sugar content. Thus, with the total weight known, the value of each load was ascertained. The price paid was agreed before each season mainly by government and the British Sugar Beet Corporation in consultation with the National Farmers Union. It was a profitable crop to grow and the demand for sugar beet area was enough for the corporation to dictate a quota to each grower.

The early growing methods were gradually replaced by mechanical methods, which greatly reduced the backbreaking hand-labour hours. A method of breaking up the clusters of seed into single ones which were then coated with a degradable clay allowed these 'monogerm' seeds to be sown by precision seeders at their final required spacing. That, along with the introduction of chemical weed killers, virtually eliminated hand hoeing. As tractors replaced horses, lifting machines became more and more efficient. The crowns were cut off and the roots delivered into trailers. These crowns were valuable livestock feeding, usually for sheep, but there were some machines available to allow carting of the crowns for cattle feeding. The sliced and dried residue of the beet was a popular feed for both sheep and cattle; it could be bought back by the grower at preferential rates. One tonne of dried beet pulp was allowed for approximately every 14 tons clean beet delivered. Sugar beet is very intolerant of acid growing conditions and the principal task of the excellent beet fieldsmen employed by the factory to advise growers was to ensure that the pH of the soil was correct before drilling. To achieve that, vast quantities of the waste lime used in the sugar purification process were applied to the land. Unfortunately for Fife, after 50 years the machinery at Cupar was worn out. Replacement policy in its sibling factories in England was to centralise with one super-factory. It would have been uneconomic to attempt to amalgamate Cupar with other factories, as the nearest was at Selby in Yorkshire. Sadly, the British Sugar Corporation or government refused to allow the capital expenditure necessary for Cupar's survival; 1972 was the last 'campaign', and the end of sugar beet growing in Scotland.

For centuries the controlling factors in Fife's farming have been more political and economic than climatic and geographic. For instance, in previous times, large areas of Fife grew flax for its thriving linen industry. Cheap imports of other fibres killed that, just as Cupar succumbed to bolster a sugar cane economy elsewhere. No one crop replaced sugar beet but from around that time others have appeared. There is, for example, a co-operative owning its own self-propelled vining machines whose members are growing peas to be frozen for human consumption.

The not easily concealed oilseed rape, whose vivid yellow brightens (or desecrates?) the patchwork pattern of fields in May, is grown to a varying degree; that degree is mainly price controlled. The desire to grow field vegetables, however, is another factor in deciding on oilseed rape or not. Watered from the Eden and mainly centred round Kettle in the Howe of Fife, field vegetables have had a major impact on the Fife farming scene in the recent past. Lettuce, carrots, swedes, cabbage, white cauliflower and green broccoli can all be seen. Like oilseed rape many of these are brassicas and, as rape self-seeds the ground to great profusion, it is well nigh impossible to follow rape with any vegetable because the closeness of their botanical relationship makes weed control chemically impossible.

While Fife could never be described as a dairying county, milk has always been produced. For the needs of the farmhouse and staff every farm kept a cow or cows; they were the first to disappear. Next, the small herds which retailed all their production in the nearby village or town had to give up as hygiene regulations increased. Compulsory pasteurisation meant selling wholesale to the creamery or installing pasteurisation plant. Very few took up the latter alternative and many more decided to quit. Today, the few dairy herds left in

Fife are fairly large ones. Specialisation and simplicity of enterprises has taken over from the days when 'a wee puckle o' a' thing' was the rule. Ham and eggs now come from the supermarket. The farmer's wife used to have her own income from the scratching corn-yard hens. And the ploo'mans wife fed two pigs per year in the stone-built pan-tiled pigsty called the pig's crave. Each farm toon had a row of 'cotton' – the cottages – every one with a perfectly kept vegetable garden at the bottom of which was a crave, an ash midden, and a dry toilet for the use of females only!

Poultry units either for egg or broiler production are not numerous in Fife. Those in operation are in large specialised units as is the production of pig meat. Here the cycle is on the move again. European legislation against sow tethers or stalls has lead to the appearance of pigs being seen out doors each making for their own 'Anderson shelter'.

Beef cattle farming and sheep breeding and feeding are still found in Fife, but less so since the horrific consequences of the totally unnecessary media driven hysteria of BSE. The ensuing beaureaucratic legislation governing traceability, tagging and accountability will drive even more of the small units out of livestock production. Unless, of course, the remuneration escalates. As has been said before, the Fife farmer can produce many crops if the rewards are there. The decline in livestock numbers has resulted in reductions in the ancillary services. There were once many livestock auction marts in Fife, now there are none. Formerly, most butchers had a slaughterhouse at the back of their premises. This ultimately changed to every town providing a municipal slaughterhouse. Now there is only one slaughterhouse left in Fife, at St Andrews.

The potato is still as important as it was in the 'sair six' days. Early this century Finlay from Auchtermuchty was Fife's famous name in potatoes. He was the breeder of many successful varieties with the prefix 'Arran'. Today's famous Fife potato name is unsung; it should be Wm Raeside, Dunino. The mechanisation of the potato crop as we handle it today owes its origin to a germ of an idea pursued by Raeside. In spring, when the field was sufficiently worked down to start planting potatoes, he experimented with a modified two-row potato digger which put the stones and remaining clods in the valley between the free soil. He then planted his potatoes in the (nearly) stone-free drill of earth. Come autumn the harvester dug the potato drill, the earth fell free, and potatoes and only potatoes were deposited in the trailer travelling alongside. That principle lead to a whole series of spring 'de-stoners' and autumn harvesters being produced by all the manufacturers of potato equipment in the UK. Today, most potatoes are stored and moved around in one-ton boxes. The boxes are stored in insulated, environmentally controlled stores at a low temperature, just above freezing, to inhibit growth for the seed element. Potatoes for processing into crisps require to be stored at a warm temperature to prevent starch changing to sugar and affecting the taste. It is a long way from the wheat straw and earth-happed pit at the back of a dyke. To justify the huge capital requirement of the potato crop, specialisation has taken place here too. The non-potato grower will often rent the rotational field for potatoes on his farm to the farmer still equipped to handle them.

And so we are left with the biggest specialist of all in Fife farming today: the grain farmer. To a certain extent grain is always the goal. Even with the 'sair six' half the area was grain. The other three crops were primarily cleaning and feeding crops, although producing cash as well. For over forty years it has been possible to keep grain clean from annual weeds with the hormone weed killers of MCPA and successors. More recently the scientists gave farmers glyphosate which controls the worst cereal weed of all in Fife: 'wrack' (couch grass). With these cleaning aids, near continuous cereal growing is possible, and many are virtually farming that way in Fife today. The sequence is ploughing and then sowing with cultivator and seeder combined – the 'one pass seeder'. The crop is sprayed through the summer to kill weeds and avoid fungal disease. Nowadays, many combine harvesters are capable of harvesting more per hour than the threshing gang achieved in a day. The straw is either chopped by the combine for incorporation in the soil or baled for sale. The stubble is sprayed for couch grass and the land is ready to be ploughed again.

The common size of an east Fife farm was around 365 acres (147 ha). Beyond that size, no matter how centrally the stable was placed, it became uneconomic as the horses spent too much time travelling to and from work in relation to time spent working. This size of unit supported 10 to 12 people in various families staying on the farm. On one of these units today just the farmer and one other is not uncommon. The three cereal crops of old are still grown, but today oats are very much a minority crop; even barley has reduced in acreage. Wheat predominates. The breeders have supplied the farmer with earlier ripening short-strawed varieties capable of high yields in response to manurial feeding, elimination of weed competition and being kept free from disease. Much of Fife's wheat goes to the enormous broiler unit just over the Forth Bridge and to the grain distillers at Cameron Bridge, Leven.

The final 'crop' influencing Fife farming as it struggles into the 21st century is the golf course. Tourism for caravans or chalets takes out fields here and there around our beautiful Fife coastline, but golf courses take out whole farms. Will their influence be sair!? The developers are most certainly hoping the rotation will be longer than six! At least there is a slight chance they could become food producing again if all went tapsalteerie – which is more than could happen to the farms covered over with motorways, factories and new housing.

Fife's farming is varied; given half a political chance it will not be the first to go under. It has many natural attributes, not least its people. Do not believe all that nonsense about needing a long spoon to sup with the De'il – or a Fifer!

Sixteen

The Fisheries of Fife

'The sea is their familiar neighbour, their great benefactor, their ruthless enemy'
John Geddie, *The Fringes of Fife*

Introduction

Of all the parts of Scotland, in none has fishing been more important throughout history than in Fife. This is related both to the available resource base and to the location of the county; and it is related also to the enterprise of the fishermen. On the south side of Fife the Firth of Forth is effectively set within the heart of the area of Scotland that was richest and most populous. Moreover, waters were sheltered and provided good opportunities for inshore fishing. On the north side of the county the Tay estuary provided some of the best salmon fishing in a country famed in the European context for its salmon; and it was also a main source of shellfish (especially mussels) which served as food and an important source of bait for line fishing. While fishing has been practised throughout history around all the coast of Fife, the area which has for centuries been outstanding is the East Neuk at the outward extremity of the shore fronting the Forth. From an early date, fishermen of the communities of the Fife coast, as well as supplying their own local areas, have been involved in bigger scale efforts, with their catches entering into commerce which extended outside the county. This early involvement in commerce helps explain how most of the fishing communities of Fife acquired burgh status on a pattern that is unusual in the rest of Scotland. They became major suppliers to the national capital of Edinburgh on the opposite shore of the Forth, and in herring fishing especially played a pioneer role in catching fish for more distant markets, including the main ones in continental Europe. For centuries fishermen have shown a willingness to go long distances to the best fishing grounds. One of the results of this activity is that records of the last two hundred years for landings in Fife show only a restricted part of the work of Fife fishermen, many of whom have operated from many different bases in Scotland and elsewhere in the British Isles.

170

HISTORY OF THE FISHERIES

The importance of fishing in Fife can be traced to the earliest phases of Scottish prehistory. The earliest known settlement of Scotland from *c.* 7000 BC onwards was by hunter-gatherers, and coastal communities living largely on fish were prominent. An important site is that of Morton in north-east Fife, where a Mesolithic community made great use of a variety of fish, especially of the easily gathered sessile shellfish like oysters and mussels. Even when farming had begun after *c.* 4000 BC fish continued as an important diet component.

Although, as is usual in Scotland, the historical record is sparse, there can be little doubt that fish from the rivers and estuaries as well as the sea continued to be important through the whole of the timespan. In the Medieval period salmon was an important national resource and was exploited, especially at the mouths of the bigger rivers. The abbey of Balmerino had control of many of the salmon fishings in the Tay estuary, as is on record from a charter by Robert the Bruce (Campbell 1867:95), and these fishings continued to be profitable in lay hands after the Reformation. In the late 18th and early 19th centuries, when salmon reached an unprecedented level of demand because of transport of the fresh article in fast sailing ships to the London market, the fishings substantially increased in value, and the Tay fishings have been the subject of the most detailed study yet done in Scotland into the history of salmon fishing (Robertson 1998). This fishery became the subject of a major Scottish test case on the use of 'fixed engine' nets. The litigation dragged on for years before the stake nets in question were declared illegal in 1812, a decision confirmed by the House of Lords in 1816 (NSA Fife:590). Behind this dispute was the issue of how many fish were to be allowed to pass through the estuary to ascend the river, and the banning of stake nets was claimed to have reduced the annual catch from the stations in Balmerino parish by around 90%. Comparable disputes featured on many Scottish salmon rivers. There were also salmon fishings on the Eden estuary; and with the development of coastal netting stations in the 19th century, there was salmon fishing at a number of points on the shore of the Firth of Forth.

Documentary evidence from a number of sources indicates the existence of various settlements around the coast from the Medieval period onwards, and while places like Crail, Anstruther and Pittenweem had interests and activity in fishing, most of the surviving evidence for this pertains to who had the rights to the fishing or to shares in its proceeds, rather than to its scale of output or how many people it involved. It is clear that by the 16th century almost all of the fishing settlements known later were already in existence. For sea fishing the burgh of Crail was noteworthy from as early as the 14th century: it had burgh status from the 12th century, it capitalised on the 'Lammas drave' herring, and was involved in export to the continent. It is on record in the 16th century as having a system of indentured training for fisher boys, and the town also retained charter rights to token payments in fish from the boats; at the same time it was sending its half-decked 'crears' to fish for herring at Lewis and for cod at Orkney (Gourlay 1879, 4–5). Although enough is known to show that the yield of the 'drave' was highly variable, Crail was the main centre for fishing until the 18th century, and for the 'drave' season it drew fishermen from north-east Scotland to join the local men. Cellardyke is first specifically recorded in the 16th century (Watson 1986, 29); and although recorded as a long continuous street along the shore till the middle of the 19th century, it was to become the foremost centre. Its near neighbours Anstruther, Pittenweem and St Monance were active from the same time, and Buckhaven was also of front rank until the late 19th century, after which its men went more into coal-mining in the local pits. Fishing and mining have long been recognised as two of the most hazardous occupations in Scotland, and it is only in Fife that the two overlap. Buckhaven is an interesting case, where the men found mining less hazardous, and more reliable in income, than fishing.

By the start of the 18th century Sibbald records ten places on the Fife coast as being involved in the 'drave'; the biggest boats had crews of seven or eight men: there were 104 of these boats manned by a total of 746 men, with 'countrymen' supplementing the regular fishermen in the crews for the drave season (Sibbald 1701, 50–52). This anticipated a prominent characteristic of the later bigger-scale herring fisheries, in that the proceeds were divided into a number of shares between boat, gear and crew; and the making up of crews with seasonal hired labour. Although the 18th century was a long lean period for the Forth herring fisheries, there were also developments in the white fisheries. As well as disposing of these locally by fishwives and merchants in Fife, the fishermen also provided on a big scale for the growing Edinburgh market on the opposite side of the firth.

FISHING IN THE MODERN PERIOD

The major expansion in fishing came from the 19th century with expanding population and commercial opportunities in the modern economy. A factor that aided the developments was that Fife was favourably placed for access to markets in Scotland and beyond, and this was enhanced with the easier communication provided by the growth of the railway network after the middle of the 19th century. As well as supplying the landward area of Fife, by the latter 19th century fish landed were sent fresh to more distant markets, and this included not only Glasgow and Edinburgh and elsewhere in Scotland, but also the major centres in England as well. This also entailed an early development of fish auctions, replacing earlier systems of engagement or contract between fishermen and curers or merchants. Although this meant more variable prices to the fishermen, it did mean considerably higher average returns; and it helped keep Fife men in the van of development in Scotland. As well as a marked increase in both boats and fishermen, there was a proportionate increase in the related shore trades of curers, merchants, coopers and other workers.

THE DEVELOPMENT OF HARBOURS

Since time immemorial fishing boats had had to be drawn up on the beaches: although there are records of some early attempts to build harbours, limits of technology and finance meant that these were always subject to storm damage and could not guarantee shelter for boats. Serious harbour construction in the main had to wait till the 19th century when expanding fishing activity and the increase in boat size generated the necessity of harbour development. There was considerable harbour construction along the Fife coast, although it tended to lag seriously behind need, and for long there was inadequate harbourage for the fleets. In 1856 at Cellardyke it was observed that the harbour was capable of holding only about a third of the boats based there (SRO 19/3/4:177). In the fishing ports harbours were built or improved partly by money supplied by the Fishery Board; some resources were also contributed by burghs, but funds subscribed by fishermen played a larger part in Fife than anywhere else in Scotland. The improvement to Cellardyke harbour in 1829 was one of the first to be helped by the Board, and the fishermen raised nearly 30% of the cost. The original building of Buckhaven harbour between 1835 and 1840, also aided by the Board, was a bigger project at what was already a major fishing settlement; and when this was enlarged between 1850 and 1853 the fishermen collected the then remarkable sum of £3000 towards the cost. The prime example of fishermen's initiative in developing the essential harbours was at St Monance where a harbour costing £15,000 was built unaided. The biggest harbour development in Fife was that of the Union harbour at Anstruther, a major project of the Board built between 1866 and 1876 to give shelter to the increasing number of big boats and to provide a main base for the winter herring fishery. This was so important that the Board's own limited funds were supplemented by other public sources and the total outlay eventually reached almost £48,000. The Board also provided money for improving the harbour at St Andrews at the end of the 19th century, while improvements at Pittenweem were aided in the early 20th century (Coull 1995, 25–42).

THE HERRING FISHERY

Fife men played a leading part in the main national success story of the Scottish herring fishery, which by the late 19th century was the world's biggest fishery. On most of the Scottish coast herring were little fished before modern times, but on the Forth there appears to have been herring fishing from Medieval times onward, even if on a limited scale. Fife men were unusual on the east coast of Scotland in being able to engage in both the Lammas (late summer) and winter 'draves' for herring off their own coast; summer herring were fuller, but winter herring, although leaner, often brought better prices at a season when the market was short supplied.

In the peak years after the middle of the 19th century there might be over 500 boats at the Lammas 'drave', and upwards of 300 at the winter fishing. Both fishings attracted boats from other parts of the coast to join the home fleets. Much of the winter fishing especially was within the firth. Burntisland was a major landing point at the start of the 19th century, and it had one of Scotland's first fishery offices which operated for most of the first half of the 19th century. Anstruther, however, became the principal fishery office.

The main method of catching herring was the drift-net, in which the boat put out her nets attached in a line to a main rope. However, when shoals were close to the coast, anchored nets were also used, and in the 20th century some boats began to copy the Clyde fishermen and use the ring-net which employs the encircling principle.

If the herring fisheries were always unpredictable, they were overall successful and prosperous, especially in the second half of the 19th century when they were at the forefront of development. It was at this time that Scottish cured herring rose to a position of dominance in the main market on the North European Plain. The fishery provided a key impetus to the improvement of the fishing fleets. Also, from the late 1850s Fife men were in the lead in substituting the more efficient and lighter cotton nets for those of the earlier hemp.

In the herring fisheries in most parts of Scotland engagements, which bound crews to fish for curers for the season at fixed prices, were the rule until the late 1880s. However, from mid-century it became possible to send herring from Fife by railway to market in England as well as Scotland. Around 1860 at the Lammas 'drave' the increased level of demand saw boats coming to depend on day prices, and engagements rapidly going out of use. In 1863 it was recorded that the whole fleet now sold its catches at day prices (SRO AF9/3/5:113). This development was largely due to the ability to supply the market with fresh and smoked herring, and also to supply great-line boats (English as well as Scottish) with fresh herring as bait. In the 1880s the market for winter herring was to suffer from the large-scale import into Britain of herring from Norway in steam freighters; there was to be some compensation for this from the 1890s with the development of 'klondyking' by which herring were lightly salted and exported in bulk to Germany for processing.

THE DEVELOPMENT OF MOBILITY

For centuries there had been fishermen in Fife who were prepared to go long distances away from home to search out opportunities. From the late 18th century a feature of the expanding pattern was that fishermen might go to distant bases for a season, and Fife fishermen and curers had some involvement in the rise of Wick in Caithness as a main centre of the herring fishing from the late 18th century. As the 19th century rolled on, and especially from the 1870s, poorer catches in the Lammas 'drave' meant that the leading boats fished more and more from the better located ports on the north-east shoulder of Scotland. They were engaged for the fishing from early July to early September, often to Fife curers who went to places such as Stonehaven and Montrose, and also to the main herring ports of Peterhead and Fraserburgh. The home summer fishing in Fife became of minor importance in Fife itself. However, boats from Fife were conspicuously active in seeking out herring off other coasts at other seasons. In the second half of the century it became established practice for the Buckhaven fleet, as well as making a major contribution to the fishing effort at Dunbar, to work from north-eastern English ports like Shields in the early summer, while at the same season there were boats from the East Neuk which fished at the Hebrides or at Howth in Ireland. On occasion, too, some boats went through the Forth and Clyde Canal to take part in the Loch Fyne herring fishery. It was Fife boats which in the 1860s began the practice of fishing at East Anglia in autumn – a fishery which by the end of the century became a major one for the whole Scottish herring fleet. From the 1880s, too, they went in force to the Shetland Islands for the early summer fishing in May and June. Also, the general adoption in Scotland of the auction system of selling towards the end of the century gave boats a new freedom of movement between bases during the season.

In the early stages of this development of mobility it was necessary for crews to find accommodation on shore when they worked from bases away from home; but the move to bigger and decked boats in the latter part of the century, along with the building of cabins and proper bunks on board, made it possible for them to live on the boats. In the long run this gave them more freedom to move from one port to another, depending on where the fishing was best.

OTHER FISHERIES

There were also other important fisheries, including the offshore great-lining for cod and ling. Although the main thrust of development was in the herring fishery, some of the first fully decked boats were built for the great-line fishery in the mid-1860s, and in the 1890s it was in this fishery that the great bold step of investing in the much more costly steam boats was made.

However, there was from around 1860 a reduction in the great-line fishing effort for cod and ling along with a substantial increase in the inshore small-line fishery for haddock. This fishery was especially stimulated by the extension of the railway network, when with easier access to markets there was a strong demand-led price rise. As well as haddock being marketed fresh there was a big rise in the preparation of the smoked 'finnans'. Haddock lines were baited on shore by the women before the boats sailed, and mussels came from the Eden estuary and the Firth of Tay; they later came too from the Clyde by railway. There was also some beam trawling for flat fish on the Traith ground off Pittenweem. From the end of the century there was a considerable use of anchored cod nets close inshore. This was a method which dispensed with the tedious work of line-baiting, and could take advantage of the waters of the firth which were put out of bounds to trawling after 1885.

On the more outlying part of the coast at Crail and Kingsbarns there was an increase of the fishery for crab and lobster: this was also a response to demand as distribution to market improved. For crabs and lobsters, which are more subject to spoilage, the more flexible auction systems were not feasible, and engagement systems continued into the 20th century.

TRENDS IN FISHERMEN AND BOATS

In the modern period there is available more precise statistical information relating to the fisheries, thanks to the work of government agencies. Total numbers of boats and fishermen for fishery districts exist from 1825 onwards, and numbers of men and boats at each 'creek' were recorded from 1855 through to 1980.

Figure 16(a) shows the recorded numbers of fishermen since 1825. The strong increase is evident – from 1825 to the recorded peak in 1885 the number of fishermen increased four times, and the numbers of boats by the same factor. During this period, as well as the full-time majority, the numbers of fishermen included 'half-dealsmen', who helped crew the boats at the main herring seasons: they came partly from Fife, but also included 'hielan' men from the West Coast and Hebrides. Since the late 19th-century peak there has been a big contraction in employment, mainly associated with the increasing efficiency of boats; it has also occurred at a time when there has been an increase of alternative opportunities, whereas formerly in fishing communities the great part of available work was fishing or fishing-related.

Figure 16(b) shows the trend in numbers of boats and is broadly parallel to numbers of fishermen. In the 19th-century build-up, as well as the increase in numbers, the principal development was the improvement in the boats used for the main fishery of herring. While it was only in the latter part of the century that the bigger boats (1st class ones, i.e. longer than 30 ft (9 m)) were

Figure 16a & b
Numbers of Fishermen and Fishing Boats in the Anstruther Fishery District 1825–1996

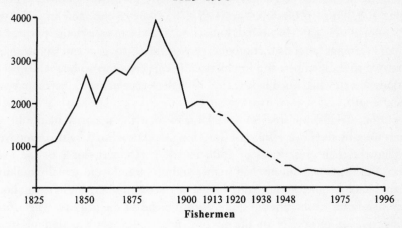

Fishermen

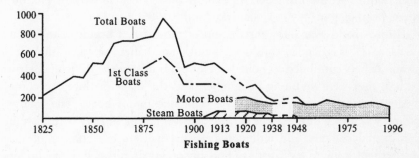

Fishing Boats

distinguished, it is clear that the majority of the fleet were in this category. Moreover, by that time they had passed from being open to half-decked and then fully decked boats; they had also become carvel as opposed to clinker built. During the century there was also an increase in smaller boats: a familiar design in the later 19th century became the 'bauldie', an improved and decked version of the traditional 'fifie' style. There were always fishermen who used such boats locally all year; and smaller boats were also used by partly retired older fishermen, as well as (between main seasons) for line fishing by men spending most of the year in bigger boats.

Important as the investment in boats was, even more significant was the investment in gear, especially of herring nets. During the century, as well as increasing greatly in number, nets had gone from being home-made to factory-made, and from hemp to the lighter and more effective cotton. With their usual involvement in a series of herring fishings, crews would have acquired two or three sets of gear, and at the end of a fishing one set could be brought ashore for mending by their wives while another set was put aboard. The Fishery Board recorded the total value of boats and gear from 1866 but did not separately itemise the gear value till 1875; all this time the total value was in the range £90,000 to £100,000; but of £97,785 in 1875 the value of boats was £27,806, of nets £55,164, and of lines £14,922. The usual practice of dividing a boat's earnings (after deduction of expenses) into boat, gear and labour shares is related to these values; and in practice the core crew owned boat and gear in various shares, while hired labour (in Fife 'half-dealsmen') made up the crew to full strength.

Further details available from 1895 show that the majority of the bigger boats were by then over 45 ft (14.7 m) long, and new boats by this time were costing the then great sums of £300 to £400. However, some of the most successful fishermen already had higher ambitions and were actually building steam boats, despite the substantial increase in cost. Investment in steam boats was mainly for offshore long-lining until the end of the century, when, on a rising tide of prosperity in the herring fishery, the construction of steam drifters began; and although these cost around £3000 each by World War I they dominated the main herring fishery. By 1913 there were in Fife 60 of them, belonging mainly to Cellardyke (Smith 1985, 84).

Before World War I the installation of motors had begun in the smaller boats, and this expanded considerably during and after the war. Although the steam drifters continued to hold pride of place during the difficult inter-war period, they were declining in number; and the shape of things to come is evident in the increase in the more economic motor boats. The inter-war period was a very difficult one for the Scottish herring fishery with disrupted continental markets, and although persisted in by a big number of steam drifters which found it difficult to find any other enterprise, it went into long-term decline. Fife fishermen at this period started to turn to seine-netting for white fish, a trend that continued through World War II and afterwards.

After World War II there was a thorough-going reconstruction of the fleets, stimulated by government grant and loan schemes, and diesel-powered craft rapidly became the norm. The early post-war boats were still of wooden construction, but from the 1970s there has been the adoption of steel construction for the main part of the fleet. Since World War II Fife has shared in the great increase in the efficiency of fishing, boats being equipped with modern gear along with fishing and navigation aids. Inevitably this has been accompanied by substantial increases in capital and operating costs, and with a big decrease in the manpower needed on the boats. By no means now do all fishermen's sons follow their fathers to sea, and the old involvement of the womenfolk in baiting lines and mending nets has disappeared.

Although the drift-net fishery continued with diesel boats into the 1970s, Fife men abandoned it in the early post-war years mainly in favour of full-time

Figure 17

**Numbers of Fishermen and Fishing Boats in the Fishing 'Creeks' of the Anstruther
Fishery District 1855, 1888 (peak), and 1980**

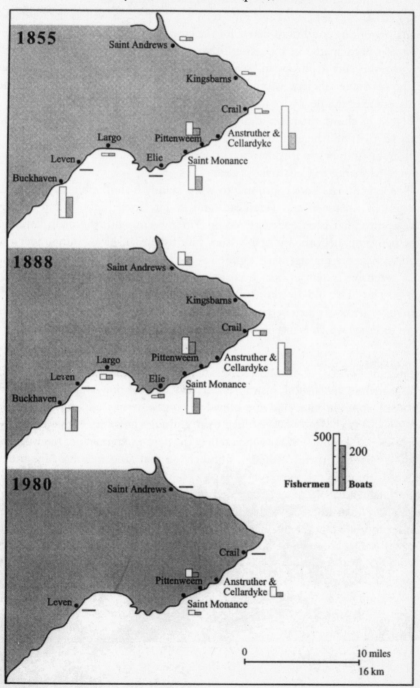

seine-netting. However, a few of the boats persisted into the 1970s in great-lining, mainly at Faroe. In seine-netting the Fife men continued to show their flair for innovation and were the leaders in Scotland in introducing such improvements as rope-bins and rope-reels for the gear, as well as shelter decks to make working conditions better for the crew. Since the 1960s the fishermen have also participated in the rising fisheries for previously little-utilised shell species, especially nephrops and scallops, which find a ready high-value market in the consumer society. More recently, with more powerful engines in the boats, some of the fleet have turned to white fish trawling.

Figure 17 shows the boats and men recorded at each 'creek' or base for the years 1855, 1888 (the peak situation) and 1980. Although fishing was engaged in from St Andrews to Buckhaven, the sustained dominance of the East Neuk from St Monance to Cellardyke is clear.

The larger boats have continued to work mainly from the bigger white fish markets of Aberdeen and Peterhead, and in Fife itself harbour and market development has been concentrated on Pittenweem, with the main landings now being of shellfish. Inevitably, too, Fife fishermen have come under the modern fisheries management regime in which for conservation reasons there is an extensive system of boat licensing along with quota limits for the main fish species. The old freedom of fishing has gone for good, and although fishermen are now much better equipped than ever before, they have to operate in an industry which is heavily regulated.

CONCLUSION

The maritime and fishing history of Fife has made a powerful impact on its seaboard communities, and the crowded narrow streets adjacent to its old harbours have an atmosphere of their own; although now modernised, many of the houses still show features which reflect the days when much of the work on gear was done in them. Although numbers of boats and men are now much reduced, some of the foremost Scottish fishermen still come from Fife. It is fitting that the Scottish national fishery museum has been located at St Ayles beside the Anstruther Union harbour. In this era of consciousness of heritage, it is appropriate that the distinctive legacy of the fisheries should be maintained here for public access and instruction.

Seventeen

Industries in Fife

Fife has seen the introduction of a range of industries over the past 300 years. Some, including one of the oldest, coal-mining, still survive. Almost all accounts up until well into the 20th century list the four main industries of Fife as farming, fishing, coal-mining and linen manufacture, though the balance between them, and their location, has varied over time. Following these in importance are variously cited the manufacture of salt, quarrying, lime-burning, and shipbuilding.

The first book to give an overall picture of Fife is probably Sibbald's *History of Fife*, written in 1710. He gives the impression that trade and industry were concentrated in the south and west, along the south coast as far east as Dysart. The *Old Statistical Account* gives a snapshot of Fife in the early 1790s, a period which saw some older industries, such as the making of girdles in Culross, extinct or on the point of collapse. At the same time new industries were being set up or contemplated, and the first stages of the mechanisation of existing industries being embarked on. The second half of the 18th century was a period of rapid change. The opening of the Carron iron-works near Falkirk in 1759, for example, killed off small-scale iron production in Fife, but at the same time created a market for Fife's coal and ironstone.

The *New Statistical Account* provides another picture for the 1830s and 1840s. By this time the 18th-century enthusiasm to try new industries had been replaced by a greater economic realism, and a concentration on industries which had been proved to be viable. But industrial enterprise was still limited by the high cost of overland transport. This was largely overcome by the second half of the 19th century, with the development of canals, railways and improved roads. Until then water transport was many times more cost-effective than overland transport, and industry was concentrated on or near the coast.

Many industries were interdependent. Salt-making, lime-burning and iron-founding used coal as fuel, while many other industries used coal to power steam engines. For an industry to flourish a number of features had to come together – geographical location, natural resources, easy access to a transport network or a large market, and available labour, quite apart from entrepreneurial skills and finance. Some places had more natural advantages than others. The minister of Markinch in 1840 wrote that:

Local facilities for the establishment of all those branches of productive industry which require the aid of machinery, are peculiar and numerous. The most remote part of the parish is but an inconsiderable distance from the coast. It is traversed by excellent roads in all directions . . . The water power supplied by two considerable streams, the Leven and the Orr, is unlimited and inexhaustible. Coals are abundant and cheap, and excellent stone for building is found in all directions, and at trifling depth below the surface; while seven populous villages furnish an abundance of hands . . .'

At Dunino, by contrast, the minister lamented that the parish had fine sandstone, but no market for it: 'Were these Dunino quarries placed within the county of Middlesex, near the great southern metropolis, their value would be incalculable'. Another writer in 1855 pointed out that 'wherever fuel is most abundant, there the population is greatest, and manufactures, commerce and agriculture, mutually aid and stimulate each other'.

By 1895 Millar described the principal industries as 'weaving, mining, fishing, bleaching and shipbuilding. All these occupations have been greatly extended during the past hundred years by the application of steam as a motive power, and by improvements in machinery'. By the 1950s one in five men was employed in the coal-mining industry, which was concentrated in west Fife. In east Fife agriculture was still the main employer, and there were no large industries. Kirkcaldy was the industrial heart of the county, with a range of manufacturing industry. New industries in the 20th century included the aluminium plant established at Burntisland in 1917, the naval dockyard started at Rosyth in 1916, and more recently the oil rig fabrication yard established at Methil in 1972, and the petrochemical plant at Mossmorran started in 1981.

The promotion and finance of industry has also changed over the centuries. In the 18th century developments were in general led by landowners, who were concerned to promote the use of the resources of their estates. The 19th century saw industry run mainly by private companies, and by the 20th century an increasing number of firms were owned by large companies based outside Fife.

The earliest recorded industry in Fife is the extraction of coal. In 1291 the monks of Dunfermline Abbey were given the right to work the coal on the lands of Pittencrieff, for their own use, not for sale. Throughout the next four centuries coal was extracted where it was near the surface or could be reached by tunnelling into a hillside, and, at least on the south coast, coal was in general use as domestic fuel. By the middle of the 18th century most of the coal which could be reached by existing technology and was economically viable in terms of the nearness of markets or of water transport had been worked out. After about 1750 the industry was revived by the introduction of steam engines to pump water out of pits and so enable deeper seams to be worked. Their introduction was gradual at first, as the capital cost was high, but they came into widespread use in the 1790s.

Coal was traditionally mined by the 'stoop and room' method, leaving pillars of coal to support the roof. Men dug the coal, and women carried it to the pit head. From the early 19th century there was a gradual change to 'longwall' working, where all the coal was removed, the roof being supported with wooden pit props, and then allowed to settle. The 1842 Mines Act banned the employment underground of women, girls, and boys under ten, leading in the short term to economic hardship for many families.

Almost half of the 63 parishes of Fife were reported in the *Old Statistical Account* to have coal workings active or only fairly recently closed. By the time of the *New Statistical Account* coal working was more industrialised, and concentrated in far fewer parishes. From the mid-18th century the market for coal increased rapidly. The population was growing, and other industries were developing which used coal as fuel. By the middle of the 19th century this market was enormous. By this time the eastern end of the Fife coalfield was exhausted. The coming of the railways, however, allowed the exploitation of parts of the coalfield which lay inland and had previously been uneconomic because of the cost of transport. Rapid growth after 1870 meant that by 1914 one in ten of the population was employed in the industry, which was concentrated around Kelty, Cowdenbeath and Wemyss. Coal produced here was exported to northern Europe from the rapidly developing ports of Methil and Burntisland.

The Fife Coal Company, founded in 1872, was a latecomer on the scene, but it grew and absorbed a number of other small companies. It also sank new pits, such as the Mary Pit at Lochore in 1902. By 1911 it was employing over 14,000 people, and by 1914 was responsible for half the coal produced in Fife. The next largest company was the Wemyss Coal Company, which opened several new mines in the 1860s and 1870s, and in 1898 the Michael Pit, at one time the largest colliery in Scotland. The company connected Methil to the railway network, and built three large wet docks there between 1887 and 1913, by which time Methil was regularly handling three million tons of coal a year.

The First World War created industrial demand for coal, but destroyed the export market. Some men were taken away from the industry, and capital investment was delayed. After the war some markets disappeared as depression hit and industries closed. There was a slow revival in the 1930s. In 1935 the Fife Coal Company made a major investment in a new colliery at Comrie, and developed plans for another at Rothes. Then the outbreak of war increased demand again.

The sinking of the Rothes pit was started in 1946. The following year the 33

collieries and one drift-mine in Fife were nationalised, with the area
headquarters in Cowdenbeath, and high hopes for the future of the Fife
coalfield. Major investment was put into the Rothes, Bowhill, Michael,
Valleyfield and Seafield collieries. Fife was still heavily dependant on mining.
By the l 950s one in five men was employed in the coal mining industry, and
Fife was expected to become 'Scotland's premier coal producing area'. Coal-
fired power stations were built at Kincardine in 1960, Methil in 1963 and
Longannet in 1966. But the Fife coal industry declined rapidly. The Bowhill
and Rothes collieries were failures, the Michael was closed after a fire in 1967,
and the last shipment of coal from Methil docks was made in 1970. Valleyfield
was not very productive and was closed in 1978, the Frances closed in 1985,
and Comrie and Seafield, the only real success among the post-war pits, in
1987. The only deep mine left in Fife is at Longannet, though there are several
open-cast mines.

Technological developments from the second half of the 18th century also
included the laying of wooden railways along which horses drew wagons of
coal to the harbour and to salt-pans. In 1770 Henderson of Fordell laid a
wagonway from Fordell to his newly created harbour of St David's 4 miles
(6.4 km) away. There were several others, including Halbeath to Inverkeithing,
and St Monans to Pittenweem. Most wagonways had a fairly short life, but the
Fordell wagonway was given iron rails in 1833, and steel rails and steam
locomotives in 1867, and remained in use until 1946.

The manufacture of salt by using coal fires to evaporate sea-water has been
carried on along the coast of Fife from at least the 15th century. Salt was never
economic to make if the coal cost too much or had to be transported too far.
But the process used the lowest grade of coal which was otherwise difficult to
sell – 'panwood' – and when salt prices were reasonably high combined coal
and salt works could be profitable. It could take as much as six tons of coal to
make one ton of salt, depending on several variables including the salinity of
the water. It was a skilled occupation, each pan worked by a master salter with
one or two assistants. The process was often disrupted by bad weather, breaks
in the coal supply, or the need for cleaning or repairs to equipment or
buildings.

The salt produced was mainly sold for domestic purposes though it did have
some industrial uses, in the manufacture of pottery and glass, and in tanning.
It was also used for preserving meat and fish, though Scots salt was not of good
enough quality to be ideal for this. But as long as it was cheaper than imported
salt it was marketable. Between 1665 and 1823 Scottish salt paid lower
customs duty than imported salt, except that necessary for industries such as
fish curing. In the 16th and 17th centuries salt was exported to the Baltic and
the Low Countries, though higher quality salt was also imported. During the
18th century exports fell but this was compensated for by a developing

domestic market in the growing cities, with the salt being transported by sea up and down the east coast.

Pans are recorded at Dysart from the 15th century, and at Kirkcaldy, St David's, Pittenweem and West Wemyss in the 16th century. Between 1575 and 1625 Sir George Bruce had 44 salt-pans at Culross, and there were pans in the 17th century at various other sites from Kincardine to Pittenweem, but with the bulk of the production in the westernmost parishes. During the first half of the 18th century, half the salt output of Scotland was from Fife. By the 1790s the industry had almost died out in Tulliallan and Culross; the main centre of production was Methil and Wemyss, and there were new works at Preston Island, Largo and St Monans.

Demand and prices fluctuated, particularly when wars disrupted imports, and so demand for Scots salt increased, and its price rose. The nine pans at St Monans, for example, were built between 1771 and 1774 as a result of high prices, but by the time the complex was completed prices had fallen. In 1773 the salt producing landowners along the Forth formed an association to restrict output to try to stabilise prices. After the removal of tariff protection in 1823, most works declined rapidly. At St David's, where sea salt was mixed with imported rock salt, work continued until about 1850. Salt making also continued on a reduced scale at Inverkeithing, Kirkcaldy, Leven, Limekilns and Wemyss, and in 1900 a new works was opened in Kinghorn. The last working pans, at Limekilns, closed in 1946.

Salters, like colliers, were traditionally serfs, bound to their place of work. But by the 18th century salters were relatively well paid, and as skilled workers had at least some bargaining power with their employers. Salt-making was a messy process. According to the minister of Dysart in 1792 'the engines and salt pans occasion much smoke, which is very disagreeable, destroying vegetation in the gardens and penetrating the inmost recesses of the houses'.

Two types of ironstone are found in Fife, clayband and blackband, but it was only with the opening of the Carron works near Falkirk in 1759 that its exploitation really became economically viable. It was mostly extracted as a by-product of coal-mining, though some was gathered along the coast. Iron-working was carried out in various parts of Fife, but usually with imported iron, sometimes recycled. By the 1790s girdle-making at Culross had almost died out, but at Pathhead, outside Dysart, 43 smiths were making nails from scrap iron from Holland. Inverkeithing had an iron foundry where 'they make beautiful chimney grates, waggon wheels and all kind of cast iron work for machinery', while one in Aberdour made spades and shovels using a water-driven hammer.

The *New Statistical Account* reported the export of ironstone from six parishes between Kingsbarns and Dysart. From Anstruther Wester it was shipped to Newcastle, and from Dysart 'is generally shipped for Carron; and it is understood that a ton of it yields about 12 cwt of iron'. Nail-making had ceased at Dysart, but there were foundries at Aberdour, Balgonie, Dunfermline, Inverkeithing and Scoonie. By 1890 the centre of iron founding was in Kirkcaldy, making machinery for other industries. Other places with foundries in the past 100 years include Auchtermuchty, Dunfermline, Kirkcaldy, Leven, Oakley and Tayport.

Another early industry in Fife was quarrying. Stone from Nydie, near St Andrews, was said to have been used for St Rule's Chapel in 1070, and for Holy Trinity Church in 1412. It was still being used for the best buildings in St Andrews right up to the construction of St Leonard's Church in 1904. Stone from Fife Ness was said to have been used for repairs to St Andrews Cathedral in 1455, and for Cromwell's citadel at Perth.

Many parishes in the *Old Statistical Account* reported plentiful supplies of freestone (sandstone) or whinstone (trap) for general building purposes, though a few, such as Forgan, had to import building stone. Whinstone breaks into jagged shapes, and if used for buildings needs the addition of sandstone facings for doors and windows. Sandstones vary greatly, some being unattractive and weathering very easily, while others have an attractive colour and are harder. Good quality sandstone, as well as other more specialist stones such as marble, were worth quarrying commercially, particularly if situated close to the sea. Stone from Newburgh and Inverkeithing was shipped to London for paving stones during the 18th century. Burntisland had several good quarries, including one of a particularly hard stone 'which is used for oven soles, and chimney grates', and there was a marble quarry at Grange. In Kirkcaldy 'The best houses are built from the quarries of Burntisland, Long-Annet, or Culello – which last, though but lately opened, promises, on account of its superior texture, colour, and solidity, to be in much request'. Dunfermline parish had several quarries of granite and good sandstone 'extremely white, durable, and susceptible of a fine polish'.

By the time of the *New Statistical Account* whinstone had come into its own not only for field walls and farm buildings but for road metalling, and later as ballast for railway tracks. Good sandstone was increasingly in demand for building in the expanding city of Edinburgh, particularly from the quarries around Burntisland and Inverkeithing, such as Grange and Cullaloe. And the minister of Inverkeithing in 1836 attributed the increase in the population of his parish mainly to an influx of labourers in about 1831 'to work in the greenstone quarries supplying materials for the extension of Leith pier, and the erection of the new bridge at Stirling'. When these jobs were completed, the quarries were abandoned. Unlike coal-mines, which flood, quarries are easy to close and re-open, depending on demand.

In the 1860s stone from Grange and Cullaloe was used for Fettes College, and the restoration of St Giles. The new harbour constructed at St Monans in

1863 was built of local sandstone, with a coping of bluestone from a quarry near Inverkeithing, carried in the sloop *Blossom*. There are still several working quarries in Fife, and also a number of companies extracting sand and gravel.

Limestone was crushed and burned with coal in kilns to make lime which was then used either as an agricultural fertiliser or in the building industry, in mortar or in lime wash which covered soft sandstone to protect it from weathering. In the 18th century, limestone was quarried and processed locally wherever possible, because of transport costs. The *Old Statistical Account* reported lime quarrying and processing in 15 parishes, with activity centred around Charlestown and Ceres.

By the time of the *New Statistical Account* there were still 13 parishes producing lime. As land transport improved, however, areas with poorer quality stone were increasingly choosing to import lime from centres of industrial production such as Charlestown or Sunderland, rather than import coal to make their own. But if the stone was of high enough quality it was apparently worth not only importing coal but using road transport for the finished product. The minister of Cults in 1838 recorded that a third of the lime produced there was shipped at Newburgh for Dundee and Perth. It was in great demand, and as well as 43 men directly employed at the works, in summer there were 'upwards of a hundred carters' from adjacent parishes 'conveying coals to the kilns and lime to the port of Newburgh'. Most of these carters were small tenant farmers who but for this extra work 'would not afford sufficient work for their horses'.

Charlestown was a major centre of production, replacing the older lime processing village of Limekilns. Charles, Earl of Elgin, built nine kilns in 1770, and a further five in 1792. The process used one part coal to four parts limestone. In 1837 Charlestown employed over 200 men; 'The quarry is traversed by railways in every direction, by which the limestone is conveyed to the kilns and quays in wagons'. Quarrying ended in 1937, but the plant continued processing imported lime until the late 1950s. In the early 20th century limestone was still quarried between Burntisland and Aberdour, and at Roscobie, Leslie, Kingsbarns and Ceres, with larger works at Burntisland and Cults, both producing about 1,000 tons of lime a week in the 1950s. Lime is still being produced at Cults.

Wherever there was a good local source of clay, it was used to manufacture bricks, roofing tiles, floor tiles, and coarse earthenware. Perhaps the first in Fife was the Linktown Brick and Tile Works, established in 1714 by William Adam, architect and father of Robert Adam. In the 1790s there were brick-works at Cupar, Kincardine and Leven, and a clay bed had been identified at Culross 'equal, if not superior in quality, for pottery and glasshouse purposes, to that which is brought from Stourbridge, in Worcestershire'. The number of brick-works had increased to seven by the time of the *New Statistical Account*,

and those at Cupar and Linktown were also producing earthenware. In around
1850 a brick-works replaced the salt-works at St David's. Seams of fireclay were
often found while mining coal, and used on site to make bricks and pipes for
the collieries. Some colliery brick-works did however produce for a wider
market. The early 20th century saw perhaps the widest spread of brick-works
in Fife, along the coast between Leven and Seafield (just beyond St Andrews),
and inland at Falkland and Cupar.

The kelp industry is usually associated with the western highlands and
islands, but the *Old Statistical Account* records the last remnants of the industry
in Fife, as prices had been high during the American war (1775–83), but
dropped thereafter. Kelp was harvested occasionally at Dunfermline, annually
in Aberdour and Pittenweem, every two years at Anstruther Wester and
Burntisland, and every three years in St Monans and Wemyss, yielding
between 8 and 15 tons per harvest in each place.

Other minor industries with a relatively brief life in Fife include the
production of vitriol (sulphuric acid) at Burntisland in the 1790s and
Thornton in the 1830s. Soap was made in Dunfermline in the 1790s and well
into the 19th century. The production of glass was introduced into Scotland in
the 17th century. There was a glass factory in one of the Wemyss caves in
c. 1740, but after this the production of glass for bottles, window glass and
crystal was all concentrated in or near Glasgow and Edinburgh. The exception
was a small works at Pettycur in around 1900.

During the 18th century lead was mined or investigated in the parishes of
Falkland, Inverkeithing and Kemback, but none of these enterprises lasted very
long or made much profit. Scotland's only ever ochre mine operated in Letham
Glen, near Leven, between about 1830 and 1865. A 'new and ingenious
method of extracting tar from coal' was invented by the Earl of Dundonald at
Culross in 1781, but the industry subsequently moved to the central belt. In
the late 19th and early 20th centuries shale-oil was manufactured as a by-
product of coal mining, at various places from Burntisland to Pitcorthie, near
Crail, but the local product could not compete with cheap imports.

Flax had for centuries been grown in Fife, and linen produced for domestic
use, but in the 18th century linen manufacture was developed on an industrial
scale. The production of linen was a complex process. First, flax stalks were
gathered in bundles, stacked or hung up to dry for about two weeks, then
retted, to separate the fibres from the rest of the plant. This was done by
soaking the bundles in water for about another fortnight, a smelly process
which polluted the pond or stream used. Then the bundles were dried again,
and hammered to break the outer sheath, which was then removed by the
process known as scutching. The flax was then heckled to remove any
remaining debris and align the fibres, which could then be spun, a process best
done when they were slightly moist. Hand-spinners used saliva, and the lack of

this was a problem with early attempts at mechanical spinning.

The linen industry was stimulated by the Act of Union, and in 1727 the 'Commissioners and Trustees for Improveing Fisherys and Manufactures in Scotland' were established. In the words of Sir John Sinclair, 'This board has since continued in constant activity, and regulated the trade in all its branches – from the sowing of the flax-seed, to the measuring and finishing of the bleached cloth'. The Board tried to increase the percentage of home-grown flax, and encouraged technical improvements, setting up spinning schools, and paying subsidies to set up bleachfields, including an early one at Cupar. By 1772 there were 13 bleachfields in Fife. In 1746 the British Linen Company was established, to aid the marketing of linen. It gradually changed into a bank, one of its first branches being in Dunfermline.

Bleaching involved soaking the linen in an alkaline solution, laying it out to dry, and then soaking it in a weaker acid solution as a neutraliser. Over the 18th century the chemicals used improved greatly, producing a whiter cloth with less risk of damage. The final process was beetling or beating the cloth, a process performed in the 19th century by calendaring machines with large metal rollers.

The industry was organised by 'manufacturers'. Some acted as middlemen, supplying the yarn to self-employed hand-loom weavers and buying the finished cloth. Others employed weavers, either in their own homes or in 'loom-sheds'. Most manufacturers started life as weavers, though a few started as merchants. Hand-loom weaving was not always a full-time occupation and many weavers worked in fishing or agriculture during the summer.

During the 18th century the linen industry developed a variety of specialisations in different locations. Dunfermline came to specialise in fine linen damask for items such as table-cloths. The making of damasks had been introduced in the town in 1718, but it was only with the introduction of the Jacquard loom in 1825 that the industry really took off. The *Ordnance Gazetteer* of 1894 claimed that 'The damask manufacture of Dunfermline is probably unequalled in the world for excellence of design and beauty of finish'. The rest of Fife made coarser linens, including canvas in the Kirkcaldy area.

By the end of the 18th century the industry was developing fast and becoming concentrated in Angus, Fife and Perthshire. It was also becoming centralised within Fife. In 1810 'The chief seats of these manufactures are Kirkcaldy, Dysart, Leslie, and Dunfermline'. Scutchings was the first process to be mechanised, from the 1730s, and by 1772 there were 11 lint (scutching) mills in Fife, all powered by water. The next process to be mechanised was heckling, then spinning. Power spinning was introduced in Kirkcaldy in 1792. By 1800 there were 11 spinning mills, by 1828, 34, and by 1836, 47. The first power loom was introduced in Kirkcaldy in 1821. The 1820s and 1830s saw great growth in the industry, and as it became increasingly mechanised hand-loom weaving declined rapidly and virtually disappeared by 1860.

A slump in 1841 was followed by 20 years of stagnation, but the 1860s saw further development, boosted by the new railway network. By 1864 there were 51 linen works in Fife, with over 5,000 power looms, and employing 11,500 people. A few years later there were 69 works, over 11,000 looms and over 13,000 employees. In 1890 there were 14 power-loom factories in Kirkcaldy alone. By 1915 the industry was employing about 6000 people, half of them in Kirkcaldy. Other places with a significant linen industry up to the First World War included Auchtermuchty, Cupar, Freuchie, Kinglassie, Leslie, Newburgh, Strathmiglo and Tayport, with a jute and linen spinning mill and two linen factories. Between the wars the industry declined, especially with the loss of the American market.

Another use of flax or hemp was making ropes, both for maritime and for agricultural use. In the 1790s there were roperies at Dysart, Elie and Leven and by the 1830s there were also works at Cupar and Anstruther Easter, and three sites in Dunfermline. A fishing net factory was set up in Lower Largo in 1869, providing work for unemployed hand-loom weavers. Another industry related to seafaring was the manufacture of oilskin clothing in Cellardyke from the late 19th century and in Newburgh from 1913. One of the main exports of Fife in the Middle Ages had been woollen cloth. Wool went on being produced into the 20th century, though on a very small scale. Cotton and silk were also worked in a few places.

The malting of barley on a small scale for local consumption was widespread, but there were a few places where larger breweries were established. The *New Statistical Account* lists several, mostly in agricultural east Fife. The brewery in Auchtertool supplied 'private families, inns, and alehouses in various places, but the greater part of its ales are usually shipped at Kirkcaldy for London'. Malting and brewing continued in the 19th and 20th centuries in the main towns of Dunfermline and Kirkcaldy, and at various places in the Howe of Fife.

Another use of barley was in distilling, a process which also used coal as fuel. In the 1790s there were distilleries at Burntisland (Grange), Dunfermline, Dysart, Inverkeithing, Kincaple and two in Kincardine, which imported barley from England and the Carse of Gowrie, and exported their spirits to Edinburgh and Glasgow. By the time of the *New Statistical Account* there was also one in Markinch. In 1910 there were three, at Auchtermuchty, Burntisland and Cameron Bridge. By 1951 Cameron Bridge was the only one left, but it is now one of the largest distilleries in the world.

In the Middle Ages Fife had exported animal hides. By the 18th century tanneries were established in Cupar, Inverkeithing, and Kirkcaldy, which used over 200 tons of bark imported from Germany, and sold the finished products 'in the neighbouring towns, in the north of Scotland, in Perth, Glasgow,

Edinburgh, and occasionally in London'. Fifty years later there were seven tanneries in Fife; by 1910 only three remained at Anstruther, Cupar and Dunfermline.

By the end of the 18th century demand grew for paper for packaging, books and newspapers. The industry started in Fife in the early 19th century, with the first three works all in Markinch parish, using the power of the River Leven. Later, mills were built at Guardbridge, Inverkeithing, Leslie, Leven, and several in the Markinch area, processing esparto grass and cotton rags from North Africa and wood pulp from Scandinavia. Fife was the third county in Scotland for papermaking after Midlothian and Lanarkshire. In the 1950s there were seven mills, employing 3000 people. Today there are five, in Dunfermline, Guardbridge, Leslie and Markinch, employing over 2500 people.

Michael Nairn, a manufacturer of canvas in Kirkcaldy from 1828, established the first floor-cloth factory in Scotland at Pathhead in 1847. The canvas was treated with several layers of oil paint, then dried and a printed design added. The company flourished, and by 1870 had warehouses in Manchester, London and Paris. At the height of the industry, in about 1890, there were eight floor-cloth manufacturers in Kirkcaldy, and much of their output was exported. In 1881 Nairn's started the manufacture of linoleum, made from a mixture of cork fibre and oil paint, and in 1891 the Tayside Floorcloth Company started production in Newburgh. The 1960s saw a decline in sales in favour of carpet, though Nairn's survived after diversifying, making vinyl tiles from 1953 and cushionfloor vinyl from 1979.

'The peninsular form of the county of Fife . . . has given it considerable advantages over most other counties in Scotland in respect to the facilities of shipping agricultural produce – most of the best land lying within five miles of a shipping port'. The first published survey of shipping in Fife was carried out in 1656 by Thomas Tucker. He listed fifty ships, of which twelve were in Kirkcaldy, ten in Anstruther and seven in Burntisland. All the ports in Fife, both large and small, suffered a decline in the second half of the 17th century, exacerbated by the Act of Union. Daniel Defoe in 1723 commented of Burntisland, 'what is the best harbour in the world without ships?' The trade which did survive consisted of importing iron, timber, lime, flax, lint seed, and manufactured goods, and exporting coal, salt, lime, ironstone, sandstone, grain, potatoes and finished linen cloth. The *Old Statistical Account* recorded activity at 26 ports in Fife, including a growing trade in coarse linen to America and the West Indies.

By the time of the *New Statistical Account* trade was concentrated in fewer ports. Some belonged to towns such as Kirkcaldy, which had 91 vessels registered, trading with 'North and South America, the Mediterranean, France, the Baltic, and occasionally beyond the Cape of Good Hope'. Others were built for specific industries, such as Guardbridge for its distillery or St David's for coal. Cargoes were much the same, with the addition of whisky. By the later 19th century Burntisland had become the second port in the Forth after Leith, with the building of a wet dock in 1872, and another one less than 20 years later. Wet docks were also constructed at Dysart, Kirkcaldy, Methil and West Wemyss. The railways made many smaller ports redundant, and by 1910 the main ports were Burntisland, Kirkcaldy and Methil.

Ship and boat building has been carried on in Fife for many centuries, but the scale and locations have varied. A yard established at Dysart in 1764, for example, lasted about 150 years, then did only repair work before closing in 1912. Other places where ships were built in the 18th century included Anstruther, Burntisland, Kincardine, Kirkcaldy and West Wemyss. Several of these yards were in decline or closed by the second quarter of the 19th century, but new yards opened to build metal ships. Abden yard, near Kinghorn, was established in 1865, and built steamers for the P & O company. By 1910 there was still a little work being carried out at Kincardine, Inverkeithing, Kinghorn, Tayport and Newburgh. The yard at Burntisland was restarted in 1918, and flourished until 1969. But Fife yards never competed with Dundee or the Clyde. The largest vessel built at Burntisland was 11,000 tons. Some yards, such as Miller's of St Monans, founded in 1747, specialised in small wooden boats. With metal ships came the new industry of shipbreaking, carried out at Charlestown *c.* 1930 to 1960, and at Inverkeithing and Rosyth.

As cities grew during the 18th century, so did a desire to escape from them occasionally. In the 1790s Elie was described as 'remarkably well adapted for sea bathing' and 'of late, much resorted to for that purpose'. In 1836 the minister of Burntisland wrote that 'For a number of years, the town has been a favourite watering-place. The pure air, the good bathing-ground, the agreeable and extensive walks, the rich and varied scenery . . . attract annually a great number of visitors'. And in perhaps the first reference to tourism taking over from previous industries, he noted that 'The vitriol work . . . has been long suspended, and the premises have been converted into cottages for the summer visitors'.

Once the railway came the East Neuk of Fife became more accessible, and a popular place for seaside holidays, while the 20th century has seen an increase in cultural tourism, with the growth of museums and historic buildings open to the public. The tourism industry now employs over 7000 people in Fife.

One of the early attractions for tourists was the game of golf, then played almost exclusively on coastal links courses, thereby, in the words of Sheriff Mackay in 1890:

> turning to profitable use the barren margin of the coast between the sands and the arable land, and filling the little houses of the coast towns with summer lodgers, who gain health and relaxation from business in an

exhilarating exercise, in which they find as much zest as children in playing on the sands or swimming in the sea.

By the first half of the 19th century golf balls were being manufactured in St Andrews. In the 20th century golf clubs were manufactured at Anstruther, Kinghorn, Leven and St Andrews. There are several golf-related industries in Fife today, making everything from hand-made putters to electric golf trolleys.

Some of Scotland's main industries such as steel and cotton never developed in Fife. But there were and are industries in which Fife has played a leading role, including coal, salt, linen, floor-cloth and linoleum, while the potteries of Kirkcaldy, though small, produced very distinctive decorated wares which are collected and reproduced today. Pennant in 1772 described Fife as 'happy in collieries, in iron stone, lime and freestone, blest in manufactures'. Today 23% of employees in Fife still work in manufacturing. And although coal-mining and linen manufacture are no longer represented among the 23 major employers in Fife, there are still three paper mills, one floor-covering manufacturer and one distillery.

EIGHTEEN

TOWNS AND VILLAGES

Fife emerged from the Medieval period still dominated by the more successful of its royal burghs, established when agriculture was the predominant industry, and Scotland's trade was conducted predominantly with the countries bordering the North Sea. During the 18th century, however, patterns of trade changed, partly as a result of the Act of Union, and partly due to the growth of trade with America and the West Indies, reducing the importance of the small ports on the east coast. From about the middle of the 18th century agricultural practices also changed, and the cities of Glasgow, Edinburgh and Dundee grew rapidly, providing markets for surplus agricultural produce and employment opportunities for surplus agricultural labourers. The royal burghs had also gradually lost their privileges. The monopoly on export trade had been abolished in 1672, and the burghs' rights over their surrounding areas had been restricted by the creation of more burghs. Crail, for example, had for nearly 400 years controlled an area stretching from the River Leven to Boarhills, until the creation of the burghs of Pittenweem, Anstruther Wester, Anstruther Easter and Kilrenny between 1541 and 1592.

The 18th century also saw the development of new industries, first of all in areas with good water power, even if this meant building new settlements in rural areas, such as the paper mills on the river Leven, or the linen mills in Dura Den. Public transport networks also developed and changed, with steam ferries replacing sail, roads being improved and realigned and the development of a railway network which first of all used ferries then replaced them with bridges, and finally the construction of the Kincardine, Tay and Forth road bridges.

Although the planning of road and railway networks was influenced by existing settlement patterns, there were some communities which were bypassed, and some new places where settlement seemed appropriate. Both Kinghorn and Lower Largo are dominated by railway viaducts, one in use and one redundant, which symbolise the changing patterns of transport, towering over the little harbours the railway made redundant. As travel became faster there was less need for the old posting inns where horses had been changed and travellers had stopped for rest and refreshment. All these developments led to changes in the pattern of settlement in Fife, changes which continue to this day.

Some of the old burghs stagnated, while others grew beyond the imagination of their founders. At the beginning of the 18th century there were 18 royal burghs in Fife, all but four of them on the coast, and 24 burghs of barony, ten of which were inland. Some of the royal burghs, such as Auchtermuchty and Newburgh, had never become more than small local market towns, and the string of East Neuk burghs were only beginning to recover from over 100 years of stagnation, but some of the burghs of central and west Fife, particularly Dunfermline and Kirkcaldy, were more prosperous. Some burghs of barony prospered, especially where they became industrial centres, such as Markinch, Methil and West Wemyss. Others, such as Dunbog, made little impact, and never fulfilled the ambition of their founders. The Hopes of Balcomie, for example, created a burgh of barony at Fife Ness in 1707, but the 'little village' was in decline by 1790 and disappeared within the next 50 years.

From about the mid-18th century the population balance of Fife changed, with agricultural east Fife growing far less quickly than west Fife with its coal reserves and other industries which developed, fuelled by coal. Between 1750 and 1950, the population of east Fife increased by 50%, and that of west Fife by 500%. By the mid-19th century the leading towns in Fife were Dunfermline, Inverkeithing, Burntisland, Kirkcaldy, Cupar and St Andrews. 'The greater part of the towns and villages are in a thriving condition, the dullest and most backward being those on the coast east from Dysart'. By this time some of the old burghs, such as Culross and Earlsferry, were effectively small villages.

Cupar, the old county town, was in the 1790s the third largest town in Fife, after Dunfermline and Kirkcaldy. Today it is the ninth largest, overtaken by St. Andrews and five newer towns, three of which did not exist in the 1790s. Burntisland and Inverkeithing, like Cupar, have grown but not very fast, and all three old royal burghs are now smaller than Dalgety Bay. Dunfermline and Kirkcaldy have been the most successful of the old royal burghs. The weaving industry in Dunfermline was said to have been 'the first important step in the prosperity of the burgh'. The manufacturers of the town concentrated on the production of fine linen, especially damask for table linen. The concentration on quality helped the industry to survive well into the 20th century, and brought prosperity and growth to the town. Kirkcaldy was also a centre for the manufacture of linen, but of coarser fabrics, including sail-cloth. From the production of canvas developed the production of floor-cloth and later linoleum (see Chapter 17). Kirkcaldy had been an important port until the economic collapse of the mid-17th century. Industrial growth from the second half of the 18th century meant that trade grew as well, with exports of coal, salt and linen cloth, and imports of timber, flax and hemp. As a result a wet dock was created in the 19th century. Both of these towns also had access to plentiful supplies of coal, without which their industries would not have been so competitive.

By the mid-19th century new towns were being created. Ladybank, an early 19th-century weaving village, grew into a town after the coming of the railway in 1847, and acquired burghal status in 1878. In central Fife, with the rapid growth of the mining industry, Lochgelly, a planned village dating from the late 18th century, was made a burgh in 1877, and Cowdenbeath in 1890. A garden city was started at Rosyth in 1915 for workers at the naval dockyard. The village of Kennoway had part of a planned new town built adjacent to it after the Second World War, and a completely new town was built at Glenrothes from 1948, originally to house workers for the newly-opened Rothes colliery. A large area of housing has been built at Dalgety Bay since 1962, a dormitory town for commuters to Edinburgh, but lacking the community facilities of a true new town. The relative growth of the main towns in Fife over the past 200 years is shown in Table 4.

Table 4
Population of the Main Towns in Fife between *c.* 1790 and 1991

Town	1790s	Rank	1841	1881	1911	1951	1991	Rank
Buckhaven & Methil	915	8	c. 2000	4207	15,149	20,152	16,821	4
Burntisland	c. 1000	7	1859	4271	4708	5668	5808	12
Cowdenbeath	0		127	2769	14,029	13,151	11,842	6
Cupar	3135	3	5137	5010	4380	5530	7382	9
Dalgety Bay	0		0	0	0	0	7571	8
Dunfermline	5192	2	13,296	19,915	28,103	44,719	54,814	1
Glenrothes	0		0	0	0	1682	37,214	3
Inverkeithing	1330	5	1827	1653	3291	3695	5856	11
Kirkcaldy & Dysart	6003	1	16,835	34,206	43,798	49,050	46,728	2
Leven	1165	6	1827	3067	6559	8868	8127	7
Lochgelly	342	9	770	2601	9149	9103	6848	10
Newport	0		260	2311	3643	3274	4200	13
St Andrews	2739	4	4449	6458	7851	9457	14,599	5

At the other end of Fife, New Dundee was founded in 1713, but (renamed Newport-Dundee, then Newport-on-Tay) only developed after a steamboat pier was built in 1823. Newport became a burgh in 1887, and in 1902 was extended to include Wormit, another suburb of Dundee which had been established with the coming of the railway. Other burghs were also officially united, in recognition of the fact that they had physically grown together. Buckhaven, Methil and Innerleven became one burgh in 1891, Anstruther Easter, Anstruther Wester and Kilrenny in 1929, Elie and Earlsferry also in 1929, and Kirkcaldy and Dysart in 1930. All these burghs, large and small, new and old, were self-governing until local government reorganisation in

1975. Long before that, however, they had increasingly become dependent on the wider local government framework of the county council for the provision of services such as roads, education and health.

Three hundred years ago villages on the English model did not exist in Scotland. Some people lived and worked in burghs, of which there were a large number in Fife. Those who worked in the countryside lived in scattered farmtouns, in simple thatched cottages of one or two rooms. Most rural churches stood in isolation. Many later provided a focus for the growth of a village, but some, such as Abdie and Cameron, still stand alone. Changes in agriculture during the 18th century meant that fewer people were needed to work the land, but at the same time employment opportunities were developing in other industries, both in towns and in the countryside. Sometimes, especially in the case of geographically isolated industries such as salt-pans or some rural flax mills, rented housing was provided for the workers. But in many other cases villages were designed by landowners, to provide a focus for work and other activities. It has been calculated that between 1745 and 1845 over 450 villages were deliberately created in Scotland. Once a settlement had a basic core of residents in employment, then it would attract a range of tradesmen such as bakers and blacksmiths, and if the village was a success, eventually a school and a church might be built. Some villages, such as Springfield, had a 'preaching station' as an interim measure before a proper church was provided. Once a village developed a reasonable infrastructure it could usually survive the collapse of the original industry on which it was founded.

The 18th century did see the deliberate removal of a few rural settlements. Sir John Anstruther of Elie removed the settlement of Balclevie, near Kilconquhar Loch, in 1771, to 'improve' the view from his house. At about the same time the village of Dalgety, near Donibristle House, was removed by the earl of Moray and the area landscaped. In 1810 the inhabitants of the village of Kinloch were moved to a row of 24 cottages at Monkstown, soon itself to become part of the new village of Ladybank. Some villages which consisted wholly of rented cottages, provided for workers in industries in rural locations, also largely disappeared when the works closed. Coaltown of Callange, for example, now consists of only two cottages.

However, most of the villages established in the 18th and 19th centuries proved permanent. They were usually laid out on an accessible site, such as a turnpike road, and on poor land, thus providing more income for the landowner than he had previously gained from agricultural use. Plots were laid out and often advertised in newspapers or on handbills which were distributed in the surrounding area. An advertisement in the *Caledonian Mercury* of 13 December 1792, for example, advertised plots at Prinlaws, just outside Leslie:

Manufacturers, Weavers and Mechanics will be accommodated with Ground for Houses, Work-Shops, and Gardens, at the very easy rate of Fourpence Halfpenny per Rood of Feu or Ground Rent; and as the proprietor wishes to give encouragement, no feu or ground rent will be expected for seven years. These favourable terms, with the advantage of good stone, sand and water on the ground, and lime and coal in the near neighbourhood, render it a very eligible situation . . . Within a few hundred yards of the ground to be feued, there is a COTTON and FLAX SPINNING MILL where young People of either sex, from eight to twenty years of age, will find constant employment.

Purchasers of feus usually had to build a house of a standard size on a common building line, to minimum specified standards such as a slate roof. It was the act of feuing such plots rather than building houses for rent which made such a difference to rural life. Feuing gave the purchaser a permanent stake, in contrast to agricultural labourers or tenant farmers. Feuing was a form of leasehold, whereby the feuar paid a lump sum equal to an agreed number of years' rent, then continued to pay an annual rent (feu duty), but had bought the right for him and his heirs to live in the property in perpetuity, or to sell that right with the property. When a site was being newly feued advantageous terms were often offered to attract settlers. The act of feuing fixed the annual payment, so that, after a period of inflation, the feu duty became less of a burden, though the feu-superior still retained certain rights, such as to restrict the type of buildings erected and the type of business carried out on the plot, and the right to exploit any minerals beneath the land. Some planned villages were not feued but offered on leases of 99 years or even longer. Leslie New Town, for example, was founded in 1798 on 200 year leases.

The period between the writing of the *Old Statistical Account* in the 1790s and the *New Statistical Account* in the 1830s and 1840s saw the creation or expansion of a large number of villages in all parts of Fife. The parish of Dunfermline, for example, had eight villages in 1791 and 13 in 1844. Cupar had none in 1793 and two in 1836. Villages created for hand-loom weavers included Cults, where new cottages were built in 1838, and the old ones used as loom-shops: Dairsie, Freuchie, Gauldry, Gladney (now part of Ceres), Kinglassie, Kingskettle, Ladybank, Springfield, and Kirkland (of Wemyss). When the linen industry became more industrialised, other villages were built around spinning mills, such as Prinlaws (from 1798) and Milton of Balgonie (from 1807).

The second most common industry for which villages were established was coal-mining. Eighteenth-century mining villages include Coaltown of Balgonie, and Halbeath, Townhill and a number of others in the vicinity of Dunfermline and Inverkeithing. The 19th century saw the founding of settlements such as Boreland (Dysart), Kelty, Thornton and Coaltown of Wemyss. The coming of railways allowed the exploitation of coal resources farther inland, and mining villages continued to be created well into the 20th century, with Crosshill and Lochore in the first decade, and Ballingry from 1947. Some villages which had been built for hand-loom weavers later became mining villages. These include Kinglassie and East Wemyss, where the Michael Pit was opened in 1895.

Other industries for which villages were founded include quarrying, distilling and iron-founding. Charlestown was established in 1761 by Charles, 5th Earl of Elgin, for lime workers and colliers on his estate, with rows of cottages around a green, on the hill above his lime-kilns and harbour. This created a new centre of the lime industry on the estate, replacing the older village of Limekilns. In Strathkinness in the second half of the 19th century quarrying took over from hand-loom weaving as the main industry. Windygates and Auchtertool both grew up around 19th-century distilleries, and Guardbridge around a distillery built in about 1810, which was converted to a paper mill in 1872. Oakley was built for workers at the Forth Ironworks, established in 1846, but later became another mining village.

Some planned villages were simply community centres, without being dependant on any specific industry. In this sense they were like burghs of barony, but without their formal structure. Colinsburgh, for example, created a burgh of barony in 1707, had been founded by Colin, Earl of Balcarres, mainly to provide a second community centre in the very large rural parish of Kilconquhar. Later planned villages were often more successful than the minor burghs of barony, as they were more independent of landowners. The minister of Logie in 1837, for example, reported that three small villages had grown up in the parish 'by the encouragement given to feuing by some of the proprietors'.

Plots at Lundin Links were feued in the mid-19th century for holiday or retirement homes. An advertisement claimed that 'as a sea-bathing station and resort for valetudinarians, the locality cannot be excelled. The sites are contiguous to the beautiful Links of Lundin and Leven, which bid fair soon to surpass the far-famed Links of St Andrews'. Other places also offered fresh air and sea bathing. Towns such as Aberdour and Burntisland offered an escape from the noise and pollution of Edinburgh, while Newburgh, Newport and Tayport offered holiday homes for the middle classes of Dundee. Plots advertised for sale near Tayport in the *Fife Herald* in 1823, for example, offered 'a country residence and bathing-quarters to families generally resident in Dundee'. This trend for building along the coast for holidays and retirement continued after the era of planned villages.

By the end of the 18th century some of the new villages were larger and better placed for development than some of the old royal burghs. It was no longer size which distinguished these burghs. What did and still does differentiate the old burghs from the newer villages are their public buildings. Churches and schools were provided in each parish, maintained by the landowners or heritors, but the larger burghs had their own grammar schools. Burghs had tolbooths where the council met, weights and measures were checked, justice dispensed and prisoners confined. The style and date of the tolbooth can tell us much about the fortunes of the burgh. Those with the oldest surviving tolbooths, such as Crail, Culross, Strathmiglo and West Wemyss, are often those which stagnated, though Dysart is an exception. Tolbooths were later replaced by Council Houses or Burgh Chambers, and separate court houses and jails were built. Replacement local government offices generally signify growth and prosperity. County Buildings in Cupar, the central building in a new street built around 1815, is the only attempt in Fife to imitate the style of the New Town of Edinburgh. St Andrews Town Hall was built in 1858, part of a major rebuilding and expansion of the town tied in with the coming of the railway and the election of a dynamic provost. Dunfermline's ornate City Chambers were built in 1875. Kirkcaldy Town House was designed in 1937, soon after the merger of the burgh with Dysart. The largest local government offices are now in Glenrothes, the new centre for a unified Fife.

As well as cells in tolbooths, Fife has two surviving separate prison buildings, both in Cupar, one of 1813 and one of 1842, both later used by the county militia. The militia and local volunteer regiments were raised during the Napoleonic wars, and drilled on open public spaces such as Volunteers' Green in Kirkcaldy. Public open spaces became increasingly important during the 18th and 19th centuries as towns became more overcrowded. Some parks were traditional open spaces where fairs had been held, but the later 19th and early 20th century saw the donation of large parks by wealthy individuals or their purchase by town councils. In Kirkcaldy, for example, Beveridge Park was financed by a legacy from Provost Michael Beveridge in 1890, Ravenscraig Park gifted by Sir Michael Nairn in 1929, and Dunnikier Park purchased by the town council in 1945.

The traditional grammar schools were gradually replaced in the late 18th or early 19th century by 'academies' with a broader syllabus, and often with new buildings. No specific academy building survives in Fife, though Cupar Academy was housed in the newest part of the older grammar school, built in 1806 on Castle Hill, and in use as a school until 1975. St Andrews had no academy but in 1832 the foundation stone was laid for the Madras College, the first large public building in the town since the Reformation. It was financed by a legacy from Dr Andrew Bell, born in St Andrews, the promoter of the monitorial system of education which he had developed in Madras (southern India), whereby the older pupils are used to teach the younger. As the town grew later in the 19th century, so did the school, attracting many boarders.

The late 18th and early 19th centuries also saw the founding of the first public libraries, though the surviving purpose-built libraries in Fife are all of a later date, such as Cupar's Duncan Institute of 1870, Dunfermline's Carnegie Library of 1883, and Anstruther's Murray Library of 1908. As the names imply, library buildings were often financed by benefactors who had left the town and made their fortunes elsewhere. The best known of these is Andrew Carnegie, whose generosity was felt not only in his birthplace of Dunfermline but all over Scotland. Having made a fortune in iron and steel in America, he gifted the estate of Pittencreiff to the town in 1903, and paid for the building of public baths and a technical college as well as the library. Other examples of smaller benefactions include almshouses, bandstands, statues, drinking fountains and horse troughs, as well as restoration work, and they can be found in almost every town in Fife, from the Valleyfield Almshouses in Culross to the Livingstone Fountain in Newburgh.

Other facilities which tended to be established in the older burghs were those catering for travellers, such as the great posting hotels of the first half of the 19th century, and financial facilities. Some of the most distinctive urban buildings of the 19th and early 20th centuries were the offices of the various banks. Several examples can be seen in the High Streets of Dunfermline and Kirkcaldy, and also in smaller towns such as Anstruther. Fife's two local banks, the Fife Bank (1802–25) and the Cupar Bank (1802–11) had simpler offices. The headquarters of the Fife Bank in the Bonnygate, Cupar, survives as a private house.

The burghs had an income from the 'Common Good', which consisted of land the town rented out, customs dues, harbour and shore dues if it was a port, and other odd items. From this income the town had to pay its share of the salary of the minister and the upkeep of the church, the whole of the salaries of its schoolmasters and the maintenance of school buildings, and the salaries of any other employees such as drummer or gaoler. The town council had to maintain the town house and the streets and, if they could afford it, provide extras such as lighting, or even a piped water supply. The old burghs relied on their traditional income from the common good, and were reluctant to introduce any compulsory taxation of inhabitants. The ten police burghs established in Fife between 1865 and 1892, however, were formed for exactly that purpose, to be allowed to collect local taxes in order to pay for public services. Outside the burghs, provision of public services was the responsibility of the county landowners and later the County Council.

The old burghs may have had impressive ground plans, but at the beginning of the 18th century many buildings were of dry stone or wood, with thatched roofs; they were damp, insecure, and a great fire risk. The *Old Statistical Account* in the 1790s records major rebuilding within the previous 30 years in places as diverse as Cupar, Leuchars, Newburgh and St Monans. Standards of building and of fitting out houses were changing, as was the whole townscape. 'Kincardine is a pretty large village . . . containing 312 houses, substantially built, and are generally finished neatly in the inside', and roofed with tiles. At Newburgh 'Formerly, the generality of houses . . . were low built, and covered with thatch of straw, or of reeds. Of late years a better style of architecture has prevailed . . . ' Most houses there now had ceilings rather than being open to the rafters and 'On the same spot, where 12 years ago a board was placed in the window, to exclude the winter storm, now may be seen, a Venetian blind . . . for blunting the rays of the summer sun'. And around towns such as Cupar 'buildings of a more magnificent form, elegant and stately villas, tower on the rising grounds'.

Improvements in building style are noted by many writers in the *New Statistical Account*. In Leslie, for example, 'The improvement that has taken place in the building of the houses is very decided. The walls are built of neat squared whin, and rybats, corners, skews, and chimney-tops of ashlar work of freestone, the roof either tile or slate, the interior of four apartments, very comfortable and substantially finished'. And Cupar 'wears now the appearance of a clean and comfortable English town'. In the countryside as well, 'In cottage architecture there has been a very marked improvement', with three or four rooms instead of one or two. The first half of the 19th century saw most farmhouses rebuilt with two storeys and slate roofs, and after that the construction of larger and well-designed steadings.

For a long time towns managed to expand within their original boundaries, by building taller houses, and squeezing houses in along closes. But by the end of the 18th century suburbs were beginning to develop. Many were deliberate creations, often called 'Newtown', as in Abbotshall, Cupar, and Sinclairton (Dysart), providing housing for weavers and others and profits for their developers. St Andrews in 1838 had 'considerably enlarged its boundaries, by modern erections at its south-east and north-west extremities, and by the filling up of a number of blanks in the streets and lanes'. Once towns had expanded beyond their boundaries, the process continued, with boundaries being adjusted, sometimes several times, to take account of new developments. This expansion continues to the present day, boosted for much of this century by the building of local authority housing, deliberately laid out with plenty of public and private space in contrast to the confined town centre dwellings it was replacing. Thus some towns have increased greatly in area without any significant increase in population.

The building industry was one which grew fast after the middle of the 18th century. Numbers of wrights and masons increased, and specialist trades such as plumbers gradually developed. There were also more people who described themselves as surveyors, architects, builders or developers. The demand for new buildings and the refurbishment of old ones, both for domestic and for industrial use, has hardly faltered in the past 250 years. Within both towns and villages life inside the new buildings has also changed almost beyond recognition. Since the mid-18th century there has been a continuous growth in consumer spending. Houses are larger, with more specialised rooms within them. They are more solid, lighter and warmer, furnished with carpets, curtains and upholstered furniture, and equipped with cleaner and simpler means of heating, lighting and cooking.

Urbanisation brought problems as well as benefits. The *New Statistical Account* contains many comments on the number of public houses, and the consequent effect on morals. In Dunfermline, for example, 'the cases of extreme indigence and misery arising mainly from intemperance, with its concomitant evils, idleness, profligacy, carelessness of persons and dwellings, neglect of education of children and of divine ordinances, are often very appalling and heart-rending'. The minister of Kennoway regarded the large number of licensed premises in his parish as unnecessary and 'a powerful temptation to the worst of all vices', while in Auchterderran, 'drunkenness, formerly rare, is now lamentably frequent'. Even rural areas were affected by the increasing secularisation of society. In Leuchars 'the enlargement of our villages . . . has not been attended with an improvement in the morals of the people', and in Monimail 'family worship is not so generally observed; and the religious instruction of children and domestics is not so carefully attended to as in former times'.

Leisure time has also increased and ways of using it have changed. Two hundred years ago the availability of fresh air and sea bathing within easy reach of Edinburgh or Dundee made some Fife towns such as Aberdour, Burntisland and Newburgh very attractive to the growing middle classes. Now people can travel much farther afield for better beaches and more exotic scenery. But a new tourism has developed based on historic buildings and landscapes. A guide book of 1882 claimed that:

There is something touching in the sight of such old towns as Pittenweem, Anstruther, or Crail, left as they were two hundred years ago, as if the spirit of progress had overlooked them – not unlike old maiden ladies shut up in their garrets, unwilling to forget the days of their early beauty, although the bloom has faded long ago – still able to boast of their royal degree, and ever thinking to themselves what might have been were it not for their more fortunate rivals Dundee and Glasgow, and even Kirkcaldy, luring the young men all away. ('Kilrounie')

But it is these burghs, together with Culross at the other end of Fife, which have, precisely because of their lack of development, now become both tourist attractions and places where people choose to live, while commuting to work in more developed but less obviously attractive towns both in Fife and beyond its boundaries.

Royal burghs
Dunfermline (1124–47), Crail (1150–52), Inverkeithing (1153/62), Kinghorn (1165/72), Cupar (1327), Falkland (1458), Auchtermuchty (1517), Pittenweem (1541), Burntisland (1541), Anstruther Easter (1583), Anstruther Wester (1587), Earlsferry (1589), Culross (1592), Kilrenny (1592), Dysart (1594), St Andrews (1620), Newburgh (1631), Kirkcaldy (1644).

Burghs of barony
Leslie (1458), Aberdour (1501), Strathmiglo (1509), West Wemyss (1511), Largo (1513), Drummochy (west of Largo, 1540), Pitlessie (1540), Newbigging of Auchtertool (1541), St Monans (1596), Elie (1599), Ferryport-on-Craig (1599), Leven (1609), Milton of Auchtertool (1617), Ceres (1620), Innergellie (Kilrenny, 1623), Methil (1662), Kennoway (1663), Kincardine (1663), Linktown of Abbotshall (1663), Valleyfield (1663), Markinch (1673), Dunbog (1687), Colinsburgh (1707), Fifeness (1707).

Nineteen

Place-Names of Fife

Since most of the place-names discussed in this chapter were formed before the boundary changes made from the 17th century onwards, in the following chapter 'Fife' will represent the Medieval sheriffdom (for which see Chapter 6).

Place-names offer a unique insight into many aspects of the history of Fife, illuminating early settlement, agricultural practices, roadways, flora and fauna, languages and their interaction, as well as ecclesiastical, administrative, industrial and social history.

'Fife' itself is probably connected with the Pictish royal personal name *Vip-*, and its earliest recorded form may be in the 3rd-century Colchester inscription VEPOGEN- ('of the clan or kindred of *Uepo-* or *Vip*'). If this clan already held sway in Fife at this time, then this name might mean 'Fife-born' (Koch 1980, 89). 'Fife' (modern Gaelic *Fìobh(a)*) is a Gaelicisation of this Pictish name, and must have been generally applied to the area now known as Fife when Gaelic became firmly established in eastern Scotland by around AD 900.

An early territorial name for west Fife is the now obsolete 'Fothrif', which still existed in the late 18th century in *Fatrick Moor*, according to *OSA* (Dunfermline) an area north of Dunfermline. It is also found on Blaeu (Gordon) as *Forthridge Muirs*, which appears as a large area north of Inverkeithing. Fothrif was retained for administrative purposes until the Reformation as the name of a deanery within St Andrews diocese, covering west Fife from the mouth of the Leven to Auchtermuchty on the east and including Kinross-shire and Clackmannanshire on the west. The deanery which covered east Fife was known simply as Fife. The meaning of Fothrif is unclear, but the second element may represent the genitive of Old Gaelic *Fìb* 'Fife' (pronounced 'feev'), while the first element may be Gaelic *foithir*, itself a loan-word from Pictish **uotir* 'district, (administrative) region', found in several important place-names in eastern Scotland, such as Fettercairn, Forteviot, Dunotter and Fetteresso.[1] It would thus mean 'the district of Fife', perhaps suggesting a different administrative status from east Fife. Within Fothrif *foithir* is found in the place-name Kinneddar[2] SLN 'at the end of the district', perhaps referring to the district known as Fothrif: it is telling that Kineddar is not far from the boundary between Fothrif and Strathearn. It

Figure 18
Medieval Parishes of Fife and Kinross *c.* 1300 with Part of Clackmannshire and Perth

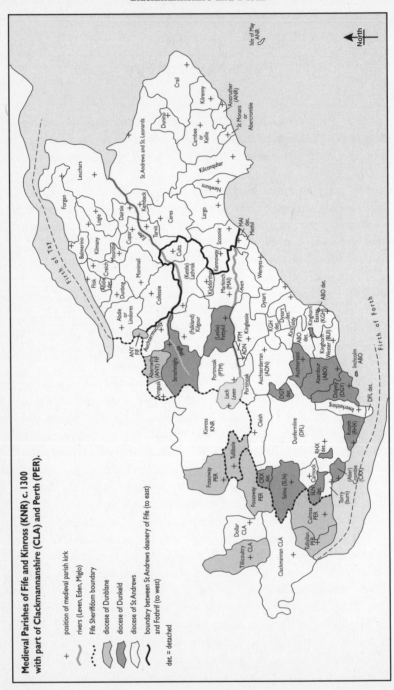

would appear from the Gaelic place-name Rosyth, *ros Fìbe*, 'promontory of Fife',[3] which lies in Fothrif, that Fothrif was seen as part of Fife, and this is further suggested by the description *Fif cum Fothreue* ('Fife with Fothrif') in a source which as it stands was compiled around 1200.[4]

LANGUAGES

Any account of place-names must also be in part a linguistic history, since place-names bear witness first and foremost to past languages spoken in any given area. Our very oldest place-names in Fife, the river name Tay, and possibly the Ore, can be assigned to an Indo-European language which pre-dated the arrival of Celtic, also an Indo-European language, which itself arrived in Britain and Ireland between around 700 and 500 BC.[5]

The first language spoken in Fife which can be identified with any certainty is Pictish, a p-Celtic language closely related to the British spoken in the early Medieval period in Lothian and Strathclyde. It was replaced by Gaelic, a q-Celtic language from Argyll deriving originally from Ireland. This process of replacement of Pictish by Gaelic probably began in the 9th century, and was completed by around AD 1000. Apart from the Pictish carved stones, the Picts' most tangible legacy are the place-names adopted directly from them by Gaelic speakers, with minimum adaptation. These include place-names which contain the Pictish **abor* 'river or burn mouth' (e.g. Aberdour ABO, Aberdollo † LAR, Abercrombie SMS and TOB, now Crombie); **pren* 'tree', perhaps referring to a tree with special local significance (e.g. Prinlaws LSL, Pirnie WMS, Primrose DFL and DNO); and **coet* 'wood(-land)', found in the burn name Keithing, 'wood burn', which later became incorporated into the Gaelic place-name Inverkeithing 'Keithing burn mouth'.[6] To these can be added Cupar, which derives from a Pictish word meaning 'confluence'; also the river name Miglo, found in Strathmiglo 'broad valley of the Miglo'. This contains a Pictish word related to Welsh *mign*, 'bog, marsh'.[7]

It is not clear why some place-names survived into the post-Pictish era, whereas others were renamed, or Gaelicised. One dynamic seems to be that the more important a place, the more likely its name would survive the political, cultural and linguistic changes of the 9th and 10th centuries. This is borne out by the survival of the Pictish names for key places in eastern Scotland such as Aberdeen, Abernethy, Arbroath and Perth. Within Fife, the names of several medieval parishes, which reflect early territorial units probably dating back to Pictish times, show strong Pictish influence, e.g. Aberdour, Abercrombie, now St Monans, and Abercrombie (later Crombie), now part of Torryburn. It is possible that some of the minor Pictish names mentioned above, such as Prinlaws or Aberdollo, were of much greater local significance during the period in question than they subsequently became.[8]

Other important names probably dating from Pictish times are Crail and Kirkcaldy. Both contain Pictish *cair 'fort', closely related to Welsh caer and found south of the Forth in place-names from Cardiff via Carlisle to Cramond, while north of the Forth it occurs in such names as Cargill PER, Carpow PER and Kirkbuddo ANG. It has a high correlation with Roman fortifications, either real or perceived, and this may well lie behind its usage in Crail and Kirkcaldy. The second element in Crail is cognate with the British and Gaelic word a(i)l 'rock', no doubt referring to the cliff above the harbour, the site of medieval Crail castle; while the second element in Kirkcaldy is perhaps a personal name or epithet based on Pictish *caled 'fierce' (Taylor 1994a, 8–10 and Breeze 1997, 99).

Another group of names showing Pictish influence contains elements borrowed into Gaelic as common nouns, which could then be used to form new place-names. The biggest group of such names contains the place-name element Pit- (Pictish *pett 'land-holding, estate'), which occurs in 78 Fife place-names.[9] The second element of many of these names is Gaelic rather than Pictish, so it is impossible to say whether these represent completely new coinings, or whether the second element is a Gaelicisation of a related Pictish word: Pictish and Gaelic were after all both Celtic languages, and so had many words in common, or words which differed from each other only slightly. One of the problems in deciding whether a place-name in this category is Pictish or Gaelic is that our knowledge of Pictish is severely limited, coming as it does almost exclusively from place-names and personal names. For example, Pittencrieff occurs twice in Fife (DFL and CUP), and means 'holding or estate of the tree', from Gaelic *pett na craoibhe.[10] However, Pictish seems to have had a word for tree closely related to Gaelic craobh,[11] and it may well be that this place-name is basically Pictish. On the other hand several Pit- names contain Gaelic personal names such as Pitconochie DFL (Donnchadh/Duncan) or the now lost St Andrews place-name Pitoutie,[12] (Ultan), and so in the form in which we have them they probably date from the Gaelic-speaking period i.e. not earlier than around AD 900. Furthermore Pitlochie KGL[13] ('estate of the stone' [Gaelic clach]) can scarcely be any earlier than the late 9th century, since the stone in question is most likely to be the Class III Dogton Cross, which art historians date to the mid- to late 9th century.

Other place-name elements which were probably borrowed into Gaelic as common nouns, but which have not survived into modern Gaelic, are *gronn 'bog, marsh' and *carden 'wood, forest'. The former is found in the parish names Forgan,[14] 'above the bog' and Kinghorn,[15] head/end of the bog'. It is also found in Pitgorno[16] SLO. The latter is found in Carden[17] ADN and Kincardine TUL.

Although the Pictish contribution to Fife place-names is greater than has hitherto been recognised and remains to be more exactly defined, there is no doubt that the bulk of the more important settlement-names are Gaelic, or at least Gaelicised. Apart from some ecclesiastical place-names (for which see below), Gaelic place-names would have been coined from around 900, and were still being coined in the later 12th century (see Taylor 1994, 108–9 and 111–13). This period must be regarded as Fife's major place-naming era. It has given us, for example, the 108 Fife place-names beginning with *Bal-* (Gaelic *baile* 'estate, farm'),[18] such as Balcolmie CRA ('Colm or Colmán's estate'), Balmule ABO[19] ('estate of the sons of Maol') and Balfour MAI ('estate of the arable land'). Our earliest recorded *Bal-* name in Fife (as well as in Scotland) is Balchrystie NBN (*Ballecristyn* 1070 x 93 *St. A. Lib.* 115; 'estate belonging to Christ or to a man called Gillechrist').

Another important Gaelic word found as a generic element in around 23 Fife place-names is *dùn* '(fortified) hill, fortification'. These include such high-status places as Dunfermline,[20] Dunbog,[21] Dunino[22] (all parish names) and in many cases places at or near discernible fortified remains, such as Dunearn BUI, Dumglow in the Cleish Hills (now KNR) or Denork CMN, earlier *Dunorc*.[23] It is also found as a specific or qualifying element in Bandon MAI (*baile an dùin*), Pitdinnie CNK (*pett <an> dùin*) and Auchindownie LAR.

This last illustrates the importance of collecting early forms of place-names. On the surface it would appear to contain the common Gaelic element *achadh* 'field, (secondary) farm'. However, early forms clearly show that it contains Gaelic *aodann* 'face, hill-slope' (*Edindony* 1459 *RMS* ii no. 665, *Edindownie* 1517 *Fife Ct Bk* 398), with the more unusual generic element being replaced by a more familiar one long after the meaning of the words had been lost.[24] Despite the fact that *Auch-* from *achadh* is a widespread and familiar Scottish place-name element, there are no certain examples in Fife, contrary to the impression given by W. F. H. Nicolaisen's distribution map of names containing *achadh* (1976, 140 and *Atlas*, 60). On this map there is a cluster of three dots in central Fife. One represents Auchmuir KGL, one Auchmutie MAI, both of which lie on the River Leven, and both of which contain Gaelic *àth* 'ford'. There is in fact no place-name containing *achadh* in that area. The only place-name in Fife which may contain *achadh* is Auchinchochin † CMN, now lost, which appears relatively late in the record (1599) and must therefore remain suspect. This means that Fife is curiously empty of this otherwise common place-name element. Why this should be is unclear: it may be that the naming vocabulary of Fife Gaelic did not have this word, or that the conditions in which *achadh* place-names grew up in other parts of Gaelic-speaking Scotland were somehow different in Fife.

Easily confused with *Auch-* from *achadh*, but in fact stemming from a completely different word, Gaelic *uachdar* 'upland', are the *Auchter* place-names: the parish names Auchtermuchty, Auchtertool, and Moonzie, formerly

Auchtermoonzie; and the settlement names Auchtermairnie KWY, and Struthers CER formerly Auchterutherstruther. Auchtertool and (Auchter) Moonzie both contain burn names, and represent the upland areas in which the Teil and Moonzie Burns rise respectively. Auchtermuchty may well follow the same pattern, with the second element a burn name containing Gaelic *muc* 'pig', rather than referring to the actual animal.[25] Struthers (*Uchteruthirstruthire* 1440 *RMS* ii no. 240) represents Gaelic *uachdar eadar sruthra* 'upland between burns'.[26] Auchterderran, the large west Fife parish which once included Ballingry, is not originally an *Auchter-* name, the earliest forms containing an unexplained element **urchan* or **urken*, which occurs several times on its own.[27]

Old Norse

Probably in the 10th century a handful of Scandinavian names were coined in Fife: these are Corbie (now Birkhill) BMO, Gedbys † KDT (NT260922), Humbie ABO, Weathersbie † ADN (NT235948), Weddersbie CLS, all of which contain Old Norse *b´y(r)* 'farm'; several of the specific elements point to animal-rearing activities of these name-givers viz *geit*, 'she-goat' (Gedbys); *hundr* 'dog' (Humbie); and *veðr* 'wether, castrated ram' (Weathersbie and Weddersbie). Another early Norse place-name is Kirkness PTM (now KNR).[28]

Scots

The mould in which all the above place-names, Pictish, Picto-Gaelic, Gaelic and Old Norse, have been cast, giving them the form in which they are familiar to us today, is supplied by the next language which arrived in Fife from the late 12th century onwards: Scots, a Germanic language, descended from Northern Anglo-Saxon, with a strong admixture of Scandinavian.[29]

Not only have all Fife's Celtic place-names been adapted to the Scots sound-system, Scots has also generated many settlement names, as well as the names for the bulk of our minor topographical features. The main Scots element indicating settlement is *toun* 'farm, estate', the equivalent of Gaelic *baile*. The formation of several *toun* names containing personal names can be accurately dated because the individuals concerned occur in dateable contexts. For example Otterston DGY is named after a man with an Anglo-Scandinavian name, Other or Ottarr, who held the land which later became known as Otterston in the late 12th century (*Inchcolm Chrs.* no. 7). Wormistone CRA is the *toun* of Winemar, who was given the land by the king *c.* 1180 (*RRS* ii no. 196). Both Gillemuire and Gillegreig, who gave their names to Gilmerton CMN and Greigston CMN respectively, were alive around 1200, while Gillanders, the eponym of Glanderston TOB, appears in a charter of 1231 (*Dunf. Reg.* no. 196). The eponym of Masterton DFL is the mason Master Aelric, who worked on the abbey kirk of Dunfermline around 1150. Masterton was not a new settlement, as it had the Gaelic name *Ledmacdungal* 'the hillside of the sons of Dúngal'.* This tells us also that a settlement can be older than its name; however, it is only very rarely that we are afforded a glimpse into an older stratum of nomenclature.

Toun also combined with Scots words such as *coal, kirk, mill(n)* and *muir* ('rough grazing') to signify settlements which grew up on or round these various features, such as Coalton of Wemyss WMS, Kirkton BUI, Milton of Balgonie MAI and Morton of Blebo KMB.

Toun, or its later unstressed form -*ton*, remained productive until at least the early 19th century. Other Scots elements such as *side, hill*, and *burn*, which first appear in charters around 1200, are still productive 800 years later.

There are two place-names in Fife which contain an element derived from Anglo-Saxon *wíc* '(dependent) farm'. These are Heatherwick, now obsolete, SLO (NO163077)[30] and Pusk LEU (NO439207).[31] This element is rare north of the Forth, and is best seen as having been introduced by Older Scots speakers from the later 12th century onwards.[32]

In the early modern period Scots gave rise to many humorous, often self-deprecating names for minor settlements, usually on poor, marginal land. Several of these names contain verbs, giving them extra punch and vividness. Because of their unflattering meanings, many have now disappeared or have been 'improved'. Examples of those which have disappeared are: Coldbrose SLN, Hungerabaid, also known as Hungerhimout KTT (Hungerhimout is also the old name for Hayfield KDT); and Pilkembare or Pilkiebare, Scots *pilk them bare* 'strip or rob them bare',[33] found in FGN, KTT, KDT (Abbotshall) and ATL (on the site of the Mossmorran Shell–Esso liquid gas complex; the name survives in the Pilkham Hills to the south of the site). An example of a name which has been improved is Maukinrich 'make him or them rich', now the name of a plantation in KGL. This is no doubt the same as the lost name in KTT which appears as *Mak em rough* (Ainslie/1775) and *Mackimrugh* (1809 Sasines) 'make them rough'. The transition between the two is seen in the KTT name already in 1816, where the lands are called '*Mackimrich* or *Mackimrough*' (Sasines). A name which was improved, but which did not survive, first appears as *Lowsie Hall* (Ainslie/1775) ('lousy hall'), but by 1827 is *Louisahall* (Ainslie/1827).[34]

Another category of name which stems primarily from the 17th century, and no doubt reflects covenanting traditions, is taken from the Old Testament. This, like the previous category, has to a large extent disappeared; for example Ramoth Gilead, which appears on Ainslie/1827 in FLK; and Zoar KDT, another name for Wester Gallatown, recorded in 1793.[35] But such names did not always express solemn piety. There were at least two places in Fife called Sodom, one CLT, the other CER, while the neighbouring steading of the latter was called Gomorrah (Ainslie/1775). The only such name to have survived into modern times is Gomorrah Plantation by Dundonald ADN, which

* Or 'half <holding> of the sons of Dúngal'.

appeared on the OS 1:25,000 map of 1964. Whether these names referred to the poor quality of the land, or entailed some kind of judgment on the inhabitants is not entirely clear. Similar disapproval may be behind the now obsolete place-name Babylon CER (NO 377082).[36]

THE CHURCH

Names which are rooted in organised religion are not confined to the Biblical names of convenanting times. The Church has given rise to place-names since at least the 7th century. Navitie BGY contains a word related to Gaulish *nemeton*, an element which may have been adopted and adapted by Christianity from pagan usage.[37] The same element is also found in a now lost place-name in the St Andrews area which appears in the late 12th and early 13th century as *Neuethinendoreth* etc. (e.g. 1165 x 78 *St. A. Lib.* 141). The last two elements are probably *an deòraidh*, giving 'Navitie of the dewar or relic keeper'.** Another very early stratum of church place-names is that containing the element *eglés*, a Pictish word for 'church' (borrowed from Latin *ecclesia*). There are four such names in Fife: Ecclesmaline or Legsmalee † KGH (*Ecclesmaline* 1162 x 69 *Inchcolm Chrs* no. 1), Eglesnamin † now Hallow Hill, by St Andrews SSL,[38] Eglismarten † SLO and Inchmarten ABO (*Eglismarten* 1347 x 55 *Inchcolm Chrs* no. 33). These names were coined in the Pictish period, either in the earliest period of conversion to Christianity, or later once the Pictish Church had been fully established.[39]

There is no doubt that by the 8th century a mature and well-organised Pictish Church had developed, fusing together influences from Dál Riada (Argyll, especially Iona) and Ireland to the west and Northumbria to the south. The beginning of the 8th century was a complex time in Pictish Church history, and it is probably during this period that the eleven Fife place-names were coined which contain the Gaelic *cill* 'church'. They form a remarkable cluster centred on east Fife, the only area on the whole east coast of Scotland south of Inverness to contain *cill*-names. Two (Kilconquhar KCQ and Kilduncan SSL) contain the saint's name Duncan. The most likely candidate for this saint is Duncan or Donnchad, abbot of Iona, who died in 717, and under whose auspices Roman usages were introduced into that abbey, and it is likely that the other *cill*-names in Fife were formed at a similar period.[40] Of these eleven names, seven were Medieval parishes, which shows their ecclesiastical significance. These are Fettykill [now LSL], Kilconquhar, Kilgour [now FAL], Kilmany, Kilrenny, Kinglassie and Methil [now part of WMS]), while an eighth, Kinglassie (*Kilglassin*) SSL, had certain parochial rights around 1200 (see *St. A. Lib.* 318). If this dating is correct, it would mean that Gaelic place-names, at least in an ecclesiastical context, were being coined around 150 years before a Gaelic-speaking dynasty established itself on the Pictish throne.

** It may be represented by Arnydie, now Bankhead, CER (formerly SSL).

Figure 19
Ecclesiastical Place-Names

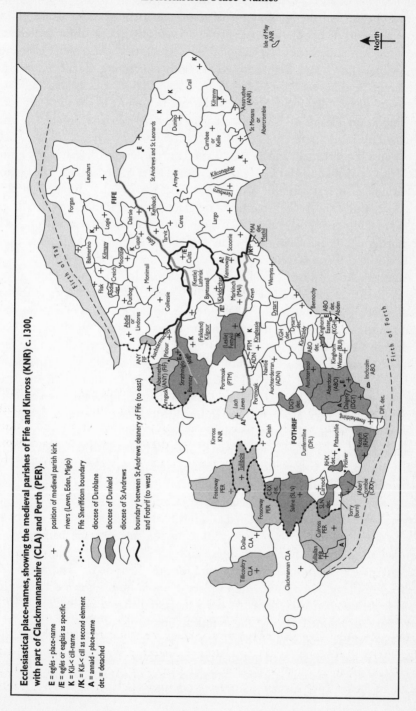

Ecclesiastical place-names, showing the medieval parishes of Fife and Kinross (KNR) c. 1300, with part of Clackmannanshire (CLA) and Perth (PER).

E = eglés - place-name
/E = eglés or eaglais as specific
K = Kil-< cill-name
/K = Kil-< cill as second element
A = annaid - place-name
det. = detached

+ = position of medieval parish kirk
~ = rivers (Leven, Eden, Miglo)
⋯⋯ = Fife Sheriffdom boundary
= diocese of Dunblane
= diocese of Dunkeld
= diocese of St Andrews
∿ = boundary between St Andrews deanery of Fife (to east) and Fothrif (to west)

This is not surprising given the known influence of the Gaelic-speaking Iona-based church in Pictland, especially in the 7th century.

This means that the window for dating Gaelic-derived ecclesiastical place-name elements in Fife[41] is wider than the one already discussed for settlement and topographical names. Typical of these ecclesiastical place-name elements are Bannaty SLO and Bennochy KDT, both containing Gaelic *beannachd* 'blessing', in this case 'place blessed by a saint'. Both places may refer to otherwise unrecorded incidents or associations belonging to the life of St Serf, the important Pictish or British saint who may have lived around 700, and who had his headquarters at Culross, with strong links to Dysart and the Loch Leven area. Dysart itself, a loan-word from Latin *desertum* ('desert, waste') into Old Irish (and thence into Gaelic), was named after St Serf's traditional place of hermitage. It was certainly a place of retreat for an early church centre in west Fife, and if the St Serf traditions are genuine, then it may well have been linked to Culross or Loch Leven.[42] The importance of Dysart as an early church or minster centre is underlined by the fact that both the adjacent parishes of Kirkcaldy and Wemyss were subordinate to it in the early 13th century.

Another church-related Gaelic word which has left two important place-names is Gaelic *apainn* 'abbey lands', Old Irish *apdaine* 'abbacy', found in Abdie (parish) and Abden KGH. Despite the monastic origins of this word, it seems in the later Gaelic-speaking period in eastern Scotland to mean any land belonging to the church (see Barrow 1989, 77). Abdie must refer to the fact that it was part of the pre-12th century lordship of the old church at Abernethy PER, a territory which stretched into Fife along the Tay to include the later parishes of Abdie, Dunbog, Flisk and Coultra (later Balmerino).[43] For a group of settlement-names around Dunfermline which have strong ecclesiastical connotations, such as Pitbauchlie and Pitliver, see Taylor 1994a, 5–7.[44]

The ecclesiastical place-name element *annaid* has given rise to two minor Fife place-names: Craigannet (NT155865) and Annets Hill (NO343043), topographical features in outlying parts of the parishes of Dalgety and Kennoway respectively.[45] A Gaelic word, from Old Irish *andóit* meaning 'mother-church', it has been defined as 'a flexible technical term for a church in a superior relationship to others, possessing the relics of the patron saint, entitled to a share of pastoral dues, and having a responsibility for the maintenance of subordinate churches and for the provision of pastoral care.'[46]

Because many *annat* names are in places remote from known ecclesiastical centres such as parish kirks, it has been suggested that it meant 'old church site', one abandoned during the political upheavals of the 9th and 10th centuries, occasioned chiefly by Scandinavian incursions.[47] More recently, however, it has been pointed out that certain of the *annat* names could simply indicate that the place in question had some fiscal or tenurial connection with the local centre of pastoral care, the *annaid*. Thus an *annat* place-name does not necessarily imply the site of an early church, although it does mean that one existed in the wider vicinity.[48] This is the most likely explanation for the relatively remote and peripheral situation of both Craigannet and Annets Hill.

ROUTE-WAYS

Many place-names refer to the Medieval road network, especially those places where a route-way had to negotiate an obstacle such as a river, a bog or difficult hills. Such place-names can be seen almost as the Medieval equivalent of our modern road-signs, helping the traveller to complete his or her journey safely. As long as the language in which the place-name was coined was understood, the name would act as a constant reminder of the hazard or other feature ahead.[49] The two settlement names in Fife called Starr (MAI and KLM) derive from Scottish Gaelic *stair* 'path over a bog',[50] indicating ways across the large bog or fen which lies beside each of these settlements. Ballo FAL, the estate in the Lomond Hills, is Gaelic *bealach* 'pass', referring to the important route-way which crossed the Lomonds from Glenvale (*gleann a' bhealaich* 'glen of the pass') in the north-west past Ballo towards Leslie and Markinch to the south-east.

From at least the late 11th century St Andrews, with its relics of the apostle Andrew, was the most important pilgrimage centre in Scotland, with roads and ferries converging on the shrine from north, south and west. Both Queen Margaret (d. 1093) and the earls of Fife (12th century) established important ferries with this pilgrimage traffic in mind, and both are still commemorated in place-names viz (North) Queensferry DFL and Earlsferry ELI. The third ferry which was especially connected with pilgrimage to St Andrews was at the place known originally as *Portincrag*, from Broughty Ferry ANG to Tayport FPC FIF. This is Gaelic *port na creige* 'harbour of the rock', the rock in question no doubt the rock on which Broughty Castle now stands, and which protected the harbour on its east side.[51] Through the ferry this name has moved across the Tay to Fife, and is found in Ferry-Port-on-Craig, the name of the parish in which Tayport is situated.[52]

MODERN NAMES

Although many place-names in Fife are over 1000 years old, new names are still being coined to refer to new features and settlements. The most conspicuous example in recent years is the name of what has become Fife's 'capital', the home of Fife Council since 1975: Glenrothes. This name was decided upon by Fife County Council's planning Committee in 1947, amidst considerable controversy, to designate the new town that was then being planned to be built on the rolling farmland between Markinch and Leslie. It derives from the title of the chief laird of the area, the Earl of Rothes, combined with the element *glen*, with scant regard for actual local topography. There were several other contenders, the strongest being 'Westwood', the name of the then Secretary of State for Scotland.[53] The precincts of the new town itself, however, are named after the farms on whose fields they stand, and several (Auchmutie, Pitteuchar, Finglassie and Caskieberran) date back to the Gaelic-speaking period. Dalgety Bay, the other big new town in Fife, which was begun in 1964, took its name from a genuine topographical feature, the large bay beside which the first houses were built, the name 'Dalgety' itself being the name of the parish, first recorded as *Dalgathin* in 1179[54], and probably containing Gaelic *dealg* 'thorn', meaning 'place of thorns'.[55] Amongst young people in the area there is a tendency to refer to the town simply as 'The Bay'. Names, however deep their roots, are organic parts of our social and linguistic world, and as such are never static.

PARISH ABREVIATIONS

ABE Abdie
ABO Aberdour
ADN Auchterderran
AMY Auchtermuchty
ANE Anstruther Easter
ANR Anstruther Wester
ATL Auchtertool
BEA Beath
BGY Ballingry
BMO Balmerino
BUI Burntisland
CBE Carnbee
CER Ceres
CLE Cleish (KNR formerly FIF)
CLS Collessie
CLT Cults
CMN Cameron
CNK Carnock
CRA Crail
CRC Creich
CRX Abercombie, now Crombie, part of TOB
CUP Cupar
CUS Culross (FIF formerly PER)
DAE Dairsie
DBG Dunbog

DFL Dunfermline
DGY Dalgety
DNO Dunino
ELI Elie
FAL Falkland
FGN Forgan
FLK Flisk
FPC Ferry-Port-on-Craig
IKG Inverkeithing
KBS Kingsbarns
KCQ Kilconquhar
KDT Kirkcaldy and Dysart
KGH Kinghorn
KGL Kinglassie
KLM Kilmany
KMB Kemback
KRY Kilrenny
KTT Kettle
KWY Kennoway
LEU Leuchars
LSL Leslie

LOG Logie
MAI Markinch
MML Monimail
MNZ Moonzie

NBH Newburgh
NBN Newburn
PIT Pittenweem
PTM Portmoak (KNR formerly FIF)
RHX Rosyth, now part of DFL
SCO Scoonie
SLO Strathmiglo

SMS St Monans
SSL St Andrews and St Leonards
TOB Torryburn
SLN Saline
TUL Tulliallan (FIF formerly PER)
WMS Wemyss

COUNTY ABBREVIATIONS

ANG	Angus
FIF	Fife
KNR	Kinross-shire
PER	Perthshire

NOTES

1. For a full discussion of the extent of Fothrif, and other possible meanings, see Taylor 1995, 20–6. The meaning proposed above, however, was not included there. See also Watson 1926, 114; and Clancy and Taylor, forthcoming. An early form is *Fotherif c.* 1128 *Dunf. Reg.* no. 1.

2. *Kynedyr* 1312x1329 *Dunf. Reg.* no.358.

3. *Rossiue* 1162 x 64 *RRS* i no. 256; *Rossive* 1179 *Inchcolm Chrs.* no. ii. The promontory was no doubt the headland from which the Forth Bridges go out on the north side.

4. Anderson 1980, 242.

5. For a full account of this earliest stratum in Scottish place-names, see Nicolaisen 1976, chapter 9 and, more generally, Kitson 1996.

6. For more examples of this place-name element in Fife, see Taylor and Henderson 1998, 238.

7. For more examples of this element in eastern Scottish place-names, see Watson 1926, 374–6.

8. For the suggestion that these *Aber-* names may originally have been important in a pre-Christian water-worshipping religion, see Nicolaisen 1996, 21–2.

9. For a full list, see Taylor 1995, appendix 9. Almost one third are now obsolete.

10. Or possibly **pett nan craobh* 'holding of the trees' (*Petyncreff* 1291 *Dunf. Reg.* no. 323 DFL; *Pettencreif* and *Pettincreiff c.* 1395 *RMS* i app. 2 no. 1734 CUP).

11. Battle fought at Moncrieff (south-east of Perth) in 728, recorded as *Monidcroib* in the Annals of Ulster.

12. *Pettultin* 1144 *St. A. Lib.* 122; it lay roughly where Rufflets Hotel now stands (NO485160). See Taylor 1995, 413–14.

13. *Petclochin* 1204 x 28 *Dunf. Reg.* no. 146.

14. *Forgrund* 1198 x 1202 *St. A. Lib.* 260.

15. *Kingorn'* 1127 x 31 *Dunf. Reg.* no. 1.

16. *Petgornoc* 1227 *Balm. Lib.* no. 11.

17. Best known in the name Cardenden, which incorporates the Scots *den* 'ravine, deep valley'.
18. For a full list, see Taylor 1995, appendix 8.
19. *Balmacmol* 1214 x *c.* 26 *Dunf. Reg.* no. 168.
20. Perhaps with two burn names as specific, the Ferm † and the Lynn; see Taylor 1994a, 12 (note 7).
21. Specific (second) element is Gaelic *balg*, earlier *bolg* 'bag, belly', in place-names often referring to a rounded, belly- or bag-like hill. Besides Dunbog (*Dunbulc'* 1189x95 *Arb. Lib.* i no. 35) it is found in the Fife place-names Balbougie IKG, Blebo KMB (*Bladebolg* 1165x69 *RRS* ii no. 28) and Bogie KDT.
22. Specific is Gaelic *aonach* 'assembly, market-place'.
23. See Taylor 1995, 241–2, 149 and 371–2 respectively. Even with the element *dùn*, however, we must reckon with Pictish influence, since there must have been a very similar, if not identical, Pictish word with the same range of meanings.
24. The earliest record of the change of the first element is *Auchindowny* 1540 *RMS* iii no. 2167. However *Edin-* forms are still appearing in the late 17th century. Such substitution or confusion of elements is a common feature of Scottish toponymy; see Taylor 1997, 7–8, 18–19.
25. Gaelic and Welsh burn names often contain animal names. See Watson 1926, 441–2.
26. The two burns in question are now called the Glassy How Burn and the Craigrothie Burn.
27. *Hurkyndorath c.* 1059x93 *St A. Lib.* 117; *Urechehem c.* 1147x59 *St A. Lib.* 43; *Wrchane* 1165 x 69 *St A. Lib.* 175; the second element contains Gaelic *daire* 'oak', or its Pictish cognate.
28. For a full discussion of Scandinavian personal and place-names in Fife, see Taylor 1995a.
29. Known as Older Scots until the 18th century; for a full definition of 'Older Scots', see *CDS*, xiii–xvi. The more modern variety of this language is known variously as Lallans, Scots, or, especially in the North-East, 'the Doric'.
30. *Hetheruik* 1590x1654 Pont (Blaeu) East & West Fife. Of the six certain *wíc*-names benorth Forth, three contain the elements *heather + wíc*. It is therefore likely that this was a compound noun meaning 'dependent settlement on heather-covered land'.
31. *Pureswic* 1209 *St A. Lib.* 86, *Pureswjch* 1240 ibid. 164. The first element seems to be related to Anglo-Saxon *pur* 'bittern or snipe' (cf. Scots *pirr* 'common tern').
32. This is more likely than the suggestion put forward in Proudfoot and Kelly 1996 that these names belong to a much earlier period. To their useful list of *wíc-* names benorth Forth (ibid. 7) might tentatively be added Glenuig ANG (NO32 63: *Glennowik* 1483), as well as the two Fife names mentioned here.
33. Denoting either land difficult to gain a living from, or a holding whose rent was considered extortionate.
34. KCQ (NO469071).
35. Sasines no. 3709.
36. SGF/1828.
37. See Barrow 1998, 56–9 and Barrow 1998a passim.

38. See Barrow 1983, 7–8.

39. See Barrow 1983 and Taylor 1998

40. See Taylor 1996 passim for more details of this and the other ecclesiastical place-name element *both*, as in Tullibole (now KNR).

41. For a full list, see Watson 1926, 244–69 and Taylor 1998, 10–13.

42. For a good edition and translation of the late twelfth-century *Life of St Serf,* see Macquarrie 1993.

43. See Barrow 1973, 51; refined and expanded by Rogers 1992, 216–32. Creich, from Gaelic *crìoch* 'boundary', would seem to refer to its position on the southern boundary of this important early territorial unit.

44. Note also the obsolete Bantuscall (*Pettuscall* 1590 *RMS* v no. 1775; *Bantuscall* 1594 *RMS* vi no. 94) for Gaelic *pett an t-soisgeil* and *baile an t-soisgeil* both meaning 'estate or holding of the Gospel'. As with Pitliver DFL, which means 'estate or holding of the book i.e. Gospel' (also the probable meaning of Pitlour SLO, formerly in the Fife part of Abernethy parish), this most likely signifies that the revenue from the estate went either to the keeper of a special copy of the Gospel, or to the production of some such copy or copies. An unprinted 1590 charter (SRO C2/3712 no. 447) allows us to locate Bantuscall around NO297068. Its ecclesiastical character is still evident in the post-Reformation period, as it is always described as kirklands of the parish kirk of Lathrisk (which parish later became known as Kettle). See Taylor 1995, 272 for more details.

45. A third is Longannet TUL, in Perthshire until 1891. It is first mentioned as the name of a rock (*Langannand'*) in (1586 *RMS* v no. 1270). The first element may be yet another Gaelic church-related word, *lann.* Its basic meaning is 'enclosure', but its cognate has given rise to Welsh *llan* 'church', and it often has ecclesiastical associations in eastern Scottish place-names. For more on this, see Taylor 1998, 8–10.

46. Clancy 1995, 101.

47. MacDonald 1973, 139.

48. Clancy 1995, 114.

49. For an excellent discussion of place-names and Medieval route-ways, see Barrow 1984/92.

50. This fairly common Scottish place-name element is unknown in Ireland. See Watson 1926, 120, 200. It can also indicate a way through other types of difficult terrain, such as hills; the best known example is Stormont, the area north and north-east of Perth. The second element is *monadh* 'hill', referring to the southern limits of the Grampians.

51. This feature is referred to as *Crag* at Portincrag in a charter of *c.* 1200 concerning the grant of land at Portincrag on the north side of the Tay to Arbroath Abbey made by the earls of Angus so that the abbey might build a hospital or inn (*RRS* ii no. 456).

52. This parish was created out of the northern part of Leuchars parish in 1606. The relevant act of Parliament reads '. . . and als understanding ane kirk laitlie to be biggit within the towne of the Eist Ferrie of Portincrag quhilk is the northmaist part of the . . . parrochin [of Lucharis] to be callit the paroch kirk of Portincrag' (*APS* iv p. 302).

53. The details of this fascinating and often amusing debate can be found in Wood 1989, 15–20.
54. *Inchcolm Chrs* no. 2.
55. See Watson 1926, 517 (note to p. 250). This element is certainly found in Dalginch MAI.

Twenty

Communications

Jutting out into the North Sea and with the lowest fording or bridging points well up the Forth and the Tay, Fife has stood aside from the main land routes for many centuries. While the peninsula could quickly be bypassed by those seeking to control the eastern seaboard by land, it was of course eminently accessible by water. Roman troops, based in their supply port at Cramond, could easily cross to Fife directly, to near Kinghorn, or by the Queensferry narrows, then head for the Tay shore near Carpow. Although traces of other Roman camps at Edenside near Cupar and at Auchtermuchty suggest at least precautionary patrols into the peninsula, we are not aware of a serious confrontation with the local people, who may have felt too exposed to cause trouble. From their defensive refuges on such hills as Dumglow, the Lomonds or Norman's Law they would have been able to keep most of Fife in view, passing signals to friendly neighbours when threatened, just as celebratory beacons are used today.

With easy coastal navigation a string of harbours had developed by Medieval times, particularly along the Forth shore, from which ships traded not only with the eastern seaboard of Britain but with the whole of northern Europe. Backed by a belt of fertile coastal farmland, populations expanded as their harbours exported hides, wool and surplus grain, joined later by coal and salt. The more enterprising settlements became recognised for their commercial and craft skills, several ports of the East Neuk acquiring the trading privileges of burghs in the 15th and 16th centuries. St Andrews, although its harbour was small and more exposed, was the centre of a diocese including Aberdeen, Dundee, Perth, Stirling, Edinburgh and Berwick, and had been an ecclesiastical burgh since 1144.

The journey to the nearest market would then be as far as most people would need to travel, itinerant cadgers and carriers supplying specialised household needs to the more landward settlements. However, the holy shrine of St Andrew attracted far-travelled pilgrims who mostly arrived in Fife by the short crossing at the Queen's Ferry and by that from North Berwick to Earlsferry, a passage traditionally established by Macduff, a 12th-century earl.

Rulers, their representatives and soldiers, prelates and their clerks were obliged to pay regular visits to such centres as Dunfermline and St Andrews. Those close to the king also visited Falkland Palace with its hunting grounds.

Figure 20
Roads Shown on Maps up to 1750

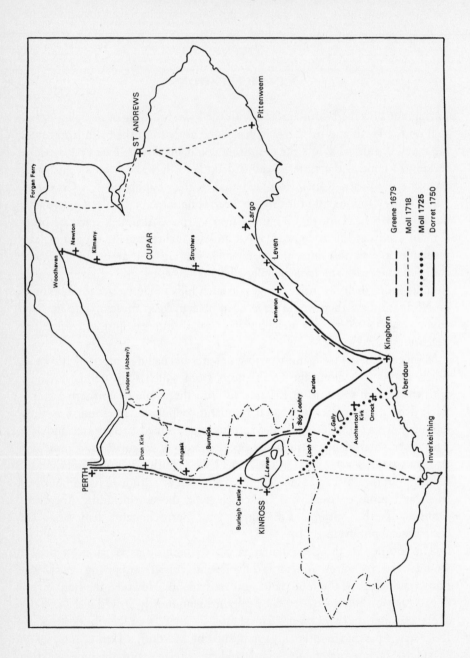

Figure 21
Roads on Fair Copy from Roy's Military Survey 1747–50

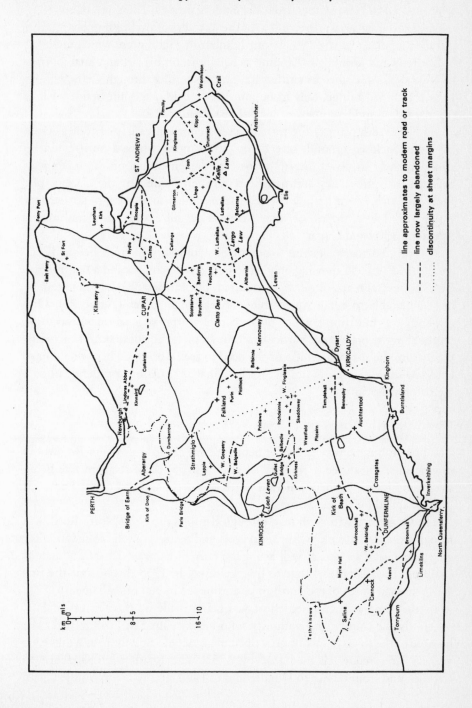

James VI on his return in 1617 was to illustrate the logistical problems of travelling on the highways of his day, large numbers of horses having been requisitioned in Fife parishes, from the landing point at Kinghorn onwards.

More specific routes are recorded for the journeys of Archbishop Sharp, who travelled regularly in the 1660s from Edinburgh to a diocese which included St Andrews and Dunblane. Landing at Kinghorn on his last and fatal journey in 1669, he is described as visiting Kennoway, passing through Ceres with its narrow humped bridge, only to be murdered on Magus Muir beside what is still named on modern maps as the Bishop's Road.

Until the 18th century the traveller could choose a variety of routes across largely unenclosed ground, several trails converging where a burn could be safely crossed. To travel directly across Stratheden meant picking one's way between the hummocky and marshy terrain left behind by the glaciers, but from the Loch Leven basin a col near Burnside led to a string of settlements along the lower slopes of the North Fife hills such as Strathmiglo, Auchtermuchty and Cupar.

Few printed maps showing roads in Scotland survive from before 1700, *Blaeu's Atlas* of 1654 showing only settlements, watercourses and a few bridges. By 1750 several maps of Fife had appeared, but cartographers do not seem to have been able to agree which were the principal routes (Figure 20). One difficulty was in defining which of the complex array of local tracks was to be regarded as the main road, particularly since a preferred route would vary with the season, the size of a vehicle or the need to seek a bridge. There would have been few or no sign posts and Archbishop Sharp's coachman prudently hired a guide for a visit in 1663.

IMPROVING THE ROADS

The first comprehensive survey of Scotland was carried out under Roy whose draughtsmen produced a 'military sketch' in 1755, those roads in Fife being shown in Figure 21, the Y-junction north of the col and east of the Lomonds being mapped for the first time.

The Queensferry to Perth road through Kinross, the Great North Road, was recognised as a vital link by Roy's surveyors and required a solid foundation for guns and heavy wagons as well as for the current commercial traffic, such as coal from the Blairadam estate to Inverkeithing. In 1753 this became the first turnpike road north of the Forth to be authorised by Act of Parliament.

By this time a determined effort was being made by the heritors of Fife, effectively the county road authority, who met at Cupar in 1748 to make the best use of the six days' labour prescribed in an Act of 1669 for road works each year. A later report claimed that by 1753 'The Road from Kinghorn to Cowper, and from thence to Dundee and to Faulkland . . . were finished', and

Figure 22

Main Turnpike Roads Authorised up to the 1797 Act

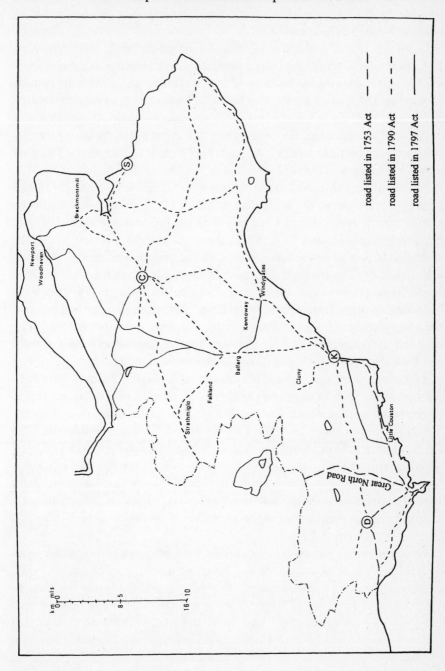

praised the heritors' skilful management (Silver, 1984, 320; see Appendix to this chapter.) Another commented: 'The statute work in some champaign counties, by the attention of the gentlemen, has answered every purpose of its intention' (Silver 1987b, 144).

In the new era of political stability and economic growth developing after 1746, commercial traffic was bound to increase rapidly and personal travel was also being popularised, as by Boswell in his account of of his journey with Johnson in 1773, when he wrote of hiring a chaise at Kinghorn and travelling through St Andrews to Woodhaven. Since the days when Romans had crossed from Carpow, ferries had developed along the shore to the mouth of the Tay and along the Forth as far as Crail, and these were to dominate the Fife road network (Duncan, 127–134).

It is significant that the leading figures at the Cupar meeting in 1748 had been two coal owners, the lords Rothes and St Clair, whose heavy coal carts needed reliable road surfaces. Coal as a domestic fuel was now carried all over Fife from the pits around Kirkcaldy to the coalless north. The last half of the century was also to see a rapid increase in the adoption of new agricultural practices, including liming and protected cropping through enclosure. As a result, highways were carrying heavier traffic at the same time as they were becoming confined by new field boundaries. Whereas a traveller had hitherto been free to choose his route from a variety of more or less parallel tracks, he now had no option but to share a narrow strip of ground between two walls and hope the horses would not drown in the resulting morass.

The initiative shown by the road authority at Cupar in 1748 may have been prompted by a wish to postpone the alternative remedy, road tolls, as much as a need to bring the principal roads up to a suitable standard, for it was not until 1790 that another turnpike act for Fife was passed. This time, unlike the 1753 Act for the Great North Road which involved Kinross and Perth, the 1790 Act, together with a supplement in 1797, was specifically for Fife and effectively laid out most of the road network we use today (Figure 22). Most important were the direct route from New Inn to the Tay ferries, its branch through Falkland towards Newburgh and the upgrading of the road between Cupar and Strathmiglo towards Kinross.

Once the money had been subscribed by local investors, the expensive work of draining the valley bottoms for new routes with easier gradients could begin, notably the glacially widened valleys of the Motray and the Fernie Burn north-west of Cupar. Hillside and ridge tracks on naturally drained ground that had been used for centuries could now be abandoned, and some, such as that between Parbroath and Glenduckie, were deliberately closed to prevent evasion of tolls.

One 1790 Act road which conspicuously failed to be built was that from Dunfermline through Crossgates to Kirkcaldy. Alternative routes from west to east across Fife were mooted, but apathetic absentee landowners failed to subscribe and it was not until two hundred years later, in 1990, that its modern equivalent, the East Fife Regional Road, was completed (Silver 1987a, 154).

POSTAL SERVICES AND THE STAGECOACH

Although the most rapid means of information transmission remained the postboy at the gallop, with 'posts' or 'stages' for a change of mount, increasing quantities of mail demanded fast wheeled transport. At first local carriers and then passenger coaches carried mail under licence, but when in 1786 a specially designed fast Royal Mail coach ran from Edinburgh to London it set a pace in efficiency which affected other coach services, for the few passengers permitted could reach their destinations sooner. By 1813 two hundred such mail coaches ran in Scotland.

Competition among private stagecoach companies was intense and the rival Kingdom of Fife and Tallyho coaches raced through Cupar in the 1830s, overtaking one another on the slope down to the ferry quay at Pettycur. Toll receipts at the main turnpike bars had increased when mail coaches lost their exemption privilege in 1813, a badly-needed reform since their heavily loaded narrow wheels severely rutted the highway. The extra money helped to pay for the provision of a higher standard of road construction and maintenance, notably under the supervision of John McAdam's manager, McConnell, who was engaged by several Fife road trusts.

The hub of the Fife road system was now the junction east of the Lomonds where stood the New Inn and an adjacent tollbar. This gathered the highest toll revenue in the county, each turnpike trustee charged with responsibility for a stretch of the road having a share based partly on its length, partly on traffic damage (Silver 1984, 193).

MODERN ROAD STANDARDS

While it was pressure from the army, the Post Office, carters and coach owners that had led to road improvements in the 18th century, it was the owners of private cars and even bicycles who more recently headed the campaign for smoother, dust free surfaces, a policy funded by taxation from 1909. John McAdam ran a tar factory in New Jersey before he began investigating Britain's roads; the use of the product coupled with his name in 1902 might have surprised him.

THE RAILWAYS

By 1800 the benefits of moving heavy loads on rails were apparent to the landowner managers of the Fife road system, particularly in the south where

Figure 23
Fife Railway System

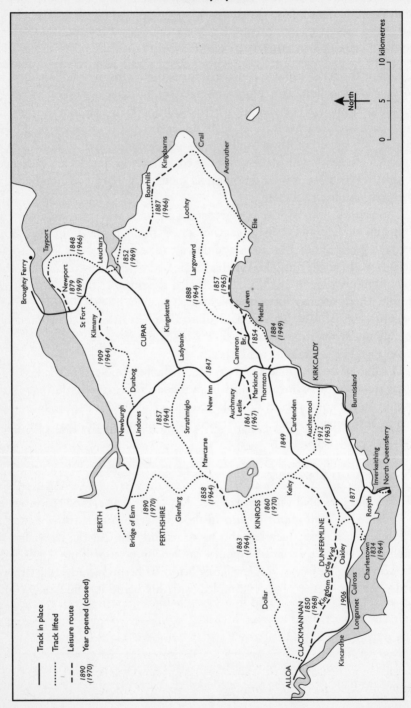

several such owners mined coal carried by wagonways to jetties on the Forth. By contrast the packhorse trains and horse-drawn carts moving coal north from the pits to northern Fife were inadequate and expensive. In 1825 Robert Stevenson was proposing a wagonway to take Balbirnie coal and Forthar lime north to Newburgh. Lord Elgin, whose coal-pits and lime works had been served by horse-drawn wagonways since about 1768, had connected his own line to Dunfermline in 1834, running a passenger service to his port of Charlestown. Thus, although the prospect of new railways may have dismayed coach owners and tollbar tacksmen, many road trustees were positively eager to promote railways near their estates and to buy shares in the new companies.

A railway had reached Edinburgh from Glasgow in 1842 and by 1846 one could travel by a west coast route through Carlisle to London, while a rival company only had to build a bridge at Berwick to complete the east coast line. To continue the railway through Fife it was decided that the Forth would be crossed between Granton and Burntisland, using the ferry acquired by the wealthy Duke of Buccleuch. By 1844 the Duke had built two new harbours with low-water piers, designed to take a ferry carrying loaded railway wagons (Bennett, 31–2, 57). A new railway from near the present Waverley Station in Edinburgh to Leith was extended to Granton in 1846, when work began on the lines across Fife.

The route ran close to the main turnpike road as far as Kingskettle, using a deep cutting to cross the col east of the Lomonds, ominously close to the most profitable tollbar in Fife. After a long embankment, the new railway swung north to a junction at Ladybank, and from there work proceeded north-west towards Newburgh for Perth, and north-east to reach another train ferry at Ferryport-on-Craig.

By 1847 the Perth branch had reached Lindores and the second branch as far as Cupar. The following year the line to the newly-named Tayport was finished, a second vessel being purchased to take goods wagons across to Broughty Ferry, while passengers used the existing steamer and could continue on the same boat to Dundee.

Branches to other parts of Fife were called for, principally by coal owners, with Dunfermline acquiring a link to Thornton in 1849. So great was the output from the Wemyss collieries by the 1850s that at Burntisland there were often queues of waiting ships. The port was enlarged in 1876 and the situation further eased in 1888 when Captain Wemyss completed a dock at Methil. By this time not only had a loop line through Buckhaven from Thornton been built but he had also constructed a comprehensive system of private colliery lines, making Methil the principal coal exporting port in Scotland.

Modifications to both ends of the main line were needed to connect with the railway bridges across the Tay in 1878 and across the Forth in 1890. A new branch from Leuchars to Wormit carried many of the materials for the first bridge; at the time of the the 1879 disaster a line had already been built from Tayport to Wormit. Ferries ran from both Tayport and Newport to Dundee until the bridge was rebuilt in 1887.

At the Forth crossing the choice of Queensferry for the new bridge required connections to the Edinburgh to Falkirk railway on the south side and to Burntisland in Fife. North Queensferry had been connected to Dunfermline since 1877 and had its own ferry pier near the present sailing club. The new connection to Edinburgh now demanded a high-level station and the old line to the pier was closed.

A connection from Leuchars to St Andrews was built in 1852 mainly for passenger traffic, although freight included coal from western Fife and Strathkinness freestone. The coastal line from Leven reached Anstruther in 1863 and was welcomed particularly by the fish merchants who found that the steamer service, governed by the tides, missed valuable markets. The line was completed to St Andrews in 1887 and from 1910 up to 1965 a Fifeshire Coast Express ran from Glasgow to Crail.

The above and subsequent developments in the Fife railway system are shown in Figure 23. The only branches not to connect directly with the lines of 1848 were those around Dunfermline, a line being built to Oakley in 1849. A further link to the west came in 1906 with the completion of the railway from Kincardine to Dunfermline via Culross.

The transport changes outlined above were rapid in terms of human experience, for a ten-year-old boy seeing the first mail coach land at North Queensferry for Aberdeen in 1798 would only have been 60 when the first train puffed its way across Fife in 1848. A child of the same age that year could have lived to see stations being closed in 1930 between Crail and St Andrews, at a time when the former turnpike roads were beginning to take back much of the goods and local passenger traffic they had lost to the railways.

BUS SERVICES

In 1805, when stage coaches ran between Pettycur and Newport, they were patronised mainly by business and professional people; they were too expensive for the bulk of travellers on shorter journeys. One answer for the less well off was the horse drawn omnibus, which had a regular Largo to Anstruther service recorded before 1838.

On the arrival of railways the stage coach was almost eclipsed, although the service between Kirkcaldy and Anstruther lasted until 1854 and that from Milnathort to Burntisland until 1860. William Pagan, the Cupar solicitor and road trustee, predicted that each new railway station would need a local vehicle for passenger connections; indeed, ten years later one surveyor complained that traffic near stations, greater than on some turnpikes, was causing excessive wear on his roads. Between Falkland Road railway station and Falkland itself passengers were carried by such a feeder service for half a century. A horse omnibus could also be used to connect across gaps in the rail network as between Crail and St Andrews where the track was not completed until 1883.

Tramways, at first horse drawn and, after 1903, electrically powered, were developed in the Kirkcaldy area, where Gallatown was connected to Leven in 1906, an example quickly followed at Dunfermline, with tracks to Lochgelly and Rosyth. However, the future of local mass transport clearly lay with the motor bus, the first recorded service running between Largo and Kennoway in 1909. By 1913 the General Motor Carrying Company of Kirkcaldy was using converted lorries as charabancs for weekends; two years later it owned eight purpose-built buses.

Soon motor buses were able to challenge the monopoly of the railways over the longer passenger routes, often at half the fare. This relieved the isolation of more rural areas, bringing country people more directly into a town centre rather than to an outlying railway station. However, the railway companies faced this threat by buying up their rivals. Walter Alexander and Sons, founded in 1923, came under railway ownership in 1929 and by 1936 the company controlled every regular bus route in Fife.

After the nationalisation of railways in 1948, a few independent bus operators remained that had survived the pre-war mergers, such as Williamson of Gauldry, who combined with Moffat of Cardenden to set up a base at Glenrothes which was by that time deprived of a railway line but was still central in the road network.

All bus companies were open to take-over after deregulation in 1986 and in the ensuing free-for-all Alexanders were bought by the felicitously named Stagecoach organisation. There followed a fierce undercutting of fares and picking up of passengers ahead of other companies' buses, but it was perhaps more restrained than in the late 1920s when many suffered 'from the excessive speeding and jockeying of heavy vehicles'. Moffat and Williamson now have a share of the routes between Glenrothes, St Andrews and Dundee, including the school bus runs, but elsewhere Stagecoach has virtually eliminated its competitors and, in the words of a current council report 'there is concern that there are not sufficient operators to tender realistically'. However, the firm can claim significant improvements to the service and is replacing many of its older buses. Minibuses have been introduced for many town runs and for reaching the more remote villages, the latter as a social service supported by Fife Council which also provides the principal bus stations. Fuel sources may change but it seems that horse troughs may not be needed again for some time!

PRESENT AND FUTURE NEEDS

In response to the phenomenal post-war rise in car ownership in Britain (from 2 million vehicles in 1950 to 20 million in 1990), and the shift of freight from railways, road building has seldom kept pace with the increasing traffic. Bypasses round Dunfermline, Auchtermuchty, Cupar and St Andrews proposed in 1946 are still not built, but the 1964 road bridge at Queensferry and the M90 motorway to Perth have reduced traffic east from Kincardine, and the East Fife Regional Road has relieved from traffic a string of settlements between Crossgates and Glenrothes. However, local congestion approaching the Forth Road Bridge has now led to calls for a relief bridge upstream at Kincardine.

Fife's measures to reduce pollution, save fuel and to make the roads safer include new railway stations at Thornton and Dalgety Bay, with proposals to reconnect St Andrews to the main line and support for a rail link to Edinburgh airport.

To reduce the use of private cars to get to work, car-sharing and park-and-ride schemes have been introduced and a network of cycle ways, nearing completion, already incorporates disused railway tracks across Glenrothes and west of Dunfermline through Oakley.

In 1971, 28.5% of people in Fife travelled to work by bus, but by 1991 this had fallen to 10.9%, while car ownership had increased by 84% (Fife, 1997). Recent schemes to link bus services with rail timetables and free travel passes for certain groups have halted this decline. One problem, resulting from the easy access of car owners to town supermarkets, has been the closure of small rural shops, leaving people who do not have cars stranded without a publicly supported bus service.

ROAD/RAIL FREIGHT STRATEGY

In a continuing campaign for the return of some goods traffic to the railways a recent council report (Fife, 1998b) recommends closer integration with the heavy goods network serving Europe. Although Rosyth has adequate port facilities for deep-sea container handling, the present centres at Mossend and Coatbridge in central Scotland still dominate the system and traffic flow to the north of the Forth has shifted westwards to Kincardine where a new road bridge is to be built. The report also points out that greater use might be made of the ports of Burntisland whose present main import is bauxite from West Africa, and of Methil which now handles mostly timber and road salt. The heaviest traffic in coal is to the Longannet power station but it is now planned to reopen the line through Alloa to Stirling, strengthened to take the new 3000-tonne trains. This line could also carry high containers which are prevented from using the Forth rail bridge. The underused branch between

Ladybank and Newburgh could well carry the freight from a railhead in the Rosyth/Halbeath area.

In the Forth a natural gas terminal at Braefoot near Dalgety Bay berths small tankers loading products from the Mossmorran plant, while at Rosyth the naval use of some of the dockyard continues. Part of the remaining area is now being developed as a container transfer depot (connecting with such ports as Zeebrugge) and as a terminal for passenger liners.

COMMUNICATIONS, LEISURE AND LANDSCAPE

Traces of early routes do not rank highly in Fife for preservation, unless as bridges (Ceres) or street paving (Culross). However, enough survive to remind the enquiring visitor of past ways of travel. Remnants of the overland routes abandoned after 18th-century improvements show the limited expectations of early travellers, taking the landscape as they found it and attempting to haul only the smallest, most robust of wheeled vehicles. The more level routes are of course as satisfactory now as then and many simply lie under layers of tarmac. Others may persist only as farm tracks, as field boundaries or are marked by disused fords and bridges. They might be recognised locally as walking routes, but few have the protected status of legal rights of way.

Fife is particularly well endowed with distinctive turnpike milestones and tollhouses. These have been faithfully recorded (Stephen, 1947), but part of the old Burntisland to Perth road over the Pilkham Hills has been swallowed up by industrial development and numerous railway embankments are at the mercy of the bulldozer, as near Kingsbarns and Dunbog. However, as we have seen with the old Dunfermline to Alloa rail-bed, catering for recreational needs can prolong the survival of abandoned routes.

Most of the support for the former Fife Coast railway came from visitors to seaside resorts along the south coast, such as Largo, Elie, and St Andrews. Now car traffic generated by a growing number of golf courses threatens to overload the winding coast road and increase congestion in St Andrews itself. Although Signor Lunardi set a precedent when he landed in his balloon at Ceres in 1787, Fife now has only a small airfield at Glenrothes. RAF Leuchars was used during the 1995 Open Championship by golfers who transferred there by helicopter after jetting into Edinburgh Airport on Concorde.

For most of the year the east of the peninsula is pleasantly detached and, so long as the Forth Bridge holds together, the restless can always glide past the Lomonds on the inter-city train to the busier world. There is now even a chance that St Andrews may be reconnected to the main railway line, reducing car traffic through Guardbridge which is particularly heavy in the summer months.

THE LOUDOUN MANUSCRIPT

(NRAS 631 BUTE PAPERS, ?1767)

The Gentlemen of the County of Fife, having met at Cowper in May 1748, to consider the Condition of the High Roads, and to fall upon some Scheme for the more effectually repairing them in time coming, came to the following Resolutions:

First,
   That the Sum of ten pence be laid upon each £100 Scots of valued Rent within the County, amounting yearly to £150 Sterling
Secondly
   That all Roads be laid asside from geting any of the aforesaid Money, till the most publick Roads in the County be finished *viz* The Road from Kinghorn to Cowper, and from thence to Dundee and to Faulkland, being the Road to Perth.
Thirdly
   They appoint a Committee of Noblemen and Gentlemen upon that Road, to oversee the Work and call out the Day Labourers and Carriages, of which Lord Rothes & Lord St Clair were the Spirit

The Committee having met at Kirkcaldy some days after, came to the following Resolutions, which having been approved of by the County, have been practised ever since with little variation:

That every Person who has a Cart in his Possession in any of the Towns shall turn out to work on the said Roads, for three Days before & three Days after Harvest, or pay two Shillings Sterling for each defficient Day.
Secondly
   That each Farmer in the County being lyable in a Carriage for each Plough of Land in his Possession, or when the Lands are enclosed, and so mostly in Grass, they shall be charged with one Carriage for each Fifty acres, or Twelve Shillings Sterling in default of the Six Days Work of the Carriage. *Allways Providing*, that the aforesaid Composition money both for Day Labourers and Carriages be paid without Trouble, for if they stand a Charge before a Justice of the Peace, the Payment for Deficiencies, to be as the Law Directs.

Thirdly

That all Noblemen and Gentlemen be lyable to pay the Statute Work for Lands in their Possession, according to the foregoing Rule, but when their Grass Parks are set out in Parcels, below fifty acres (as is often the Case), the Gentlemen is to pay twelve Shillings for each 50 Acres and to be relieved by the Tennants according to the quantity they possess

Fourthly

That £50 worth of proper Working Tools be immediately bought for carrying on the Work, &

Fifthly

That each Nobleman and Gentleman give their Attendance in their Turn, from Eight in the morning till five in the Afternoon according to the following List, to be put into the Overseer of the Roads Hands, he being to write to the Gentleman to be on his Attendance three Days before his Turn is.

Sixthly

That the Overseer shall produce a List of the Carriages and Labourers summoned for that Day by the Constable, and show him also before Ten o Clock a list of the Persons who have been summoned for that Day by the Constable, and who are Deficients, which List the Gentleman Overseer for the Day shall subscribe, and which Lists to be sent to a meeting of the Justices of Peace to be held allways at the giving up the Work upon the Roads for that year both before and after Harvest.

I must observe that it was owing to the constant and unwearied Attendance of the Gentlemen who had the Management of these Roads, animated by the Example of the Lords Rothes & St Clair that they were so well and speedily carried on, and to the employing all the County Money on the most publick Roads, and not parceling it out as formerly, which was ate up by the Constables without doing any Good, as it was not worth any Gentleman's while to attend, where so few Men were employed and so little to be done.

In five years the two great Roads were finished, and the People of the Country made so perfectly acquainted with that sort of Work, that ever sine, the Roads of the County which are Six, among which the £150 is divided, are carried on by a Constable and sometimes by an Overseer hired likewise without troubling any of the Gentlemen oftener than once a fortnight to see what has been done.

It must be understood that none was summoned to work upon any Road above four computed Miles from their Dwelling House, all the other Parishes of the County being constantly employed in making more private Roads where they have done a great deal with the Statute Work alone, without any assistance of money, as this County was for the most part well peopled till of late.

TWENTY-ONE

ST ANDREWS UNIVERSITY

The foundation of the University of St Andrews was not an event, it was a process. After the Great Schism of 1378 Scotland remained faithful to the Avignon pope, so Scottish students found themselves barred from almost all the European universities. In May 1410 a group of Scottish masters began to teach in St Andrews and on 28 February 1412 Bishop Henry Wardlaw of St Andrews recognised the group, recounting in his charter that the university's purpose was to 'surround the Catholic faith with an impregnable wall of doctors and masters'. On 28 August 1413, Pope Benedict XIII from Peniscola in Aragon issued the six Bulls erecting the school at St Andrews into a complete university, ceremonially promulgated in St Andrews on 4th February 1414, just in time to validate the first crop of bachelors' degrees.

In the early university of about fifty students, the most distinguished of the masters was Laurence of Lindores, inquisitor of heretical pravity for Scotland, formerly of the University of Paris, with a wide reputation as an expounder of Buridan's commentaries on the works of Aristotle. The earliest teaching probably took place in one or other of the St Andrews religious houses, but the Faculty of Arts met as early as 1416 in a chapel of St John the Evangelist on part of the site of St Mary's College library in South Street, and in 1419 it is styled a 'college' with Laurence of Lindores as its head. In 1435 a proper school, to be known as the Pedagogy, becomes available on an adjacent rig to the west of St John's chapel. Teaching facilities increased in 1450 when Bishop James Kennedy founded a partial rival to the Pedagogy by creating St Salvator's College to teach theology and arts to 'safeguard and strengthen the Catholic faith'. In 1465 Kennedy died and bequeathed a sumptuous list of personal possessions to ensure that the work was finished. Despite dissension and strife between the new college and the Pedagogy, the university was turning out twice as many graduates as in its early days and it was graced by many distinguished teachers and graduates. William Schevez, graduate and master of the university and student at Louvain, gained a European reputation with Jasper Laet dedicating one of his books to him. He later became archbishop and chancellor of the university and is the first Scot of whom there is an authentic portrait. The poets William Dunbar and Gavin Douglas are interesting alumni of this period.

The difficulties between the ill-endowed Pedagogy, the Faculty of Arts and

St Salvator's College were considerably alleviated by the creation of a third force in the university. Archbishop Alexander Stewart and Prior John Hepburn decided in 1512–13 to adapt the hospital adjoining the church of St Leonard within the St Andrews priory precinct as a new foundation 'to steady the rocking barque of Peter' in order that the number of learned men should increase to the glory of God and the edification of the people. The new college succeeded in ways that the founders would not have wished. It became the intellectual fountainhead for Protestantism such that 'drinking at St Leonard's well' became the stereotype of the Reformer. St Leonard's College remained the most lively of the university's colleges and collected a library of impressive excellence from a line of distinguished donors. Gavin Logie is the teacher mainly credited with instilling Reformed ideas, but the subprior, John Winram, who became one of the chief Reformers in Fife, and took, by virtue of his office, a particular interest in the college until days before his death in 1582 at the age of 90 (tombstone in St Leonard's chapel) was notable for 'liberal' views. St Leonard's reforming students include Patrick Hamilton, Alexander Allane, Alexander Seton, Henry Forrest and Robert, the youngest of the three Wedderburn brothers.

After the foundation of St Leonard's, the rival institutions within the university had a sometimes uneasy and unequal relationship. The old Pedagogy was less well provided than the two later colleges. Successive archbishops tried to remedy this. Archbishop James Beaton sent a supplication to the Pope shortly after his translation to St Andrews. However, he procrastinated until prodded by his kinsman, Archibald Hay and his nephew and successor, David Beaton. The legal formalities for the new college of St Mary were completed just a week before Archbishop James Beaton died and it was left to his successor to secure endowments and begin building on the Pedagogy site. Archibald Hay's grand ideas for a trilingual college expounding current continental humanist ideas might have succeeded as he was appointed principal in July 1546, but he perished in the rout at Pinkie on 10 September 1547. His successor as principal, John Douglas, also with Parisian experience, had, in Archbishop John Hamilton, a man determined to complete the foundation. Extra land on the west and further endowments were added. A new staff, some from England, were appointed and the new St Mary's was promulgated in a charter on 25 February 1555, emphasising theological study as the basis of a Catholic reformation. But it came too late; there was too little time before the local and national events of 1559–60 brought the Reformation to Scotland. That this was so swiftly successful and complete can in part be explained by the fact that the majority of the university and the priory chapter joined it.

The Reformers almost immediately put together detailed and well thought out plans for education and the university, but the political will to pay was lacking. It was not until 1579 that the Scottish Parliament passed an act: 'Ratification of the reformation of the Universitie of Sanct-Andrewes'. This allocated arts teaching to the colleges of St Salvator and St Leonard, with the former also having professors of law, mathematics and medicine and St Mary's being the college of higher study, confining itself to theology. There is little evidence that the content or manner of teaching changed much from what was described in the pages of James Melville's diary. Senior students still took turns on Saturday mornings to read out essays in either Latin or Greek on subjects of their choice as diverse as a diatribe on the quality of college meals ('exiguous portions' and 'greasy morsels'), a sycophantic praise of a college master or a deep discussion by an aspiring theologue.

The university was now a vibrant place with two of the most famous Scots of all time on its staff. George Buchanan, poet, playwright, political theorist and historian was Principal of St Leonard's College from 1566 until 1570 and, more importantly, Andrew Melville came back to his old college after a distinguished career to be Principal of St Mary's from 1580 to 1607. During this period he was active locally and nationally as the champion of Presbyterianism.

About the end of the 16th century Fifa or Fife displaced Britannia amongst the four nations into which the students and teachers were organised, partly in response to changing recruitment areas consequent on the founding of universities in Glasgow (1451), Aberdeen (1495) and, especially, Edinburgh (1583), but it is also testimony that since 1410 Fifers have had a much greater opportunity for a university education than people from many other parts of Scotland. The Senatus Academicus emerges now as the main governing body of the university. For the first time the university as distinct from the colleges begins to look for a home for itself to form a central meeting place and a common library. This seems to have been one of the recommendations of a commission of visitation in 1608 and moves were made with the support of Archbishop Spottiswood to bring it about. The royal family and a few other grandees were persuaded to donate books and building began on a site immediately to the east of St Mary's College in 1612, but not until the king's only return visit to Scotland in 1617 was money forthcoming for the roof and it was May 1643 before the building was completed with a donation by a former student and regent, Alexander Henderson. The period from 1590 to 1625 was also important in the history of the university as its first period of international fame. The result was to some extent due to the appointment of the Aberdonians John Johnston and Robert Howie as professor and principal in St Mary's College. It was also a time of exceptional peace in Europe. Students came from the continent to study at St Andrews: English, French, Dutch, Danes, Belgians, Poles, Prussians, Germans, Italians, Norwegians and a Jew. The Faculty of Arts even gave sustenance to a visiting Greek. The Thirty

Years' War and the Civil War reduced foreign students to a trickle.

By the end of the first quarter of the 17th century, St Andrews was coming under increasing competition from the other Scottish universities. Having been founded as the Scottish national university, St Andrews had maintained its pull, but an attempt to remain *the* Scottish centre for theological studies, whereby each Scottish diocese should support two students of divinity at St Andrews, soon failed in the face of developing divinity studies at the much more active commercial centres of Aberdeen and Edinburgh. The fortunes of the university were declining with those of the town, which was no longer the ecclesiastical capital of Scotland. By the end of the century, St Andrews was, like all the Scottish universities, no more than a local university insofar as arts education was concerned. But we should not diminish St Andrews too far or too fast. National figures like Samuel Rutherford, James Sharp and James Gregory served as teachers and the sons of the peerage still came to St Andrews as students. Three of the great figures of the century, Montrose, Argyll and Lauderdale were St Andrews alumni. Although we know a good deal about the courses and the structure of the university in this period through the papers of the university commission of 1642 to 1648, they only tell part of the story. Surviving student notebooks show that they studied much more widely than the basic set texts. A number of distinguished physicians were St Andrews alumni including Dr David Kinloch, Dr John Wedderburn and Dr John Makluire, who states that his *Buckler of bodily health* (1630) 'was hatched in the Universitie of St Andrews'. More than one student was sent to St Andrews to study fortification in preparation for a military career, a subject not documented in the archives of the university. Near the end of the century the Synod of Fife laid a charge against St Leonard's College of teaching Cartesianism (a philosophical system claiming to be independent of scholastic tradition and theological dogma). The college argued that it was the college's duty to take notice of new systems of philosophy. Mathematical studies were revived in 1668 with the appointment of James Gregory, the inventor of a reflecting telescope, to a new Regius chair and in the same year a chair of Hebrew was added to St Mary's College.

The university was deeply involved in the politics of the Revolution and the masters adhered solidly to the losing side. This resulted in the dismissal of the entire staff except for a single individual, who had not been in office long enough to declare his opinions. A unique printed advertisement to fill their places was then sent to every kirk in Scotland. Most of the replacements were elderly Covenanters who had very short periods of office and so the university entered the 18th century with a youngish staff. The commission appointed by parliament in 1690 for visiting the universities ordered both specific and general changes. The intention to have common courses throughout the Scottish university system failed to prosper, but the idea, first mooted at the

Reformation, to have specialist professors in individual subjects to replace the regenting system (where each master taught all the subjects of the arts course on a four year rotation), was revived. In St Andrews, professorships of Greek and later natural philosophy are the first to be established. After this the university was mostly left alone by government for over a century, except for periodic investigations until the early 1720s of political loyalty.

In the early 18th century, St Mary's College had a remarkable period of success, drawing in much enlarged numbers of divinity students, perhaps attracted by the reputation of Thomas Halyburton (posthumously reinforced by publication) and of Principal James Hadow, 'dark and grimly in his appearance', through his vigorous participation in the controversy over the *Marrow Doctrines*. Later, divinity student numbers returned to their previous level of about thirty. However, student numbers fell sharply in the philosophy colleges from 1740 much to the dismay of the professors, who depended on fees from students for a considerable part of their income. Unaware that it was part of a national and temporary trend, they felt that drastic action had to be taken. Their solution, which required and received parliamentary approval, was a union between the colleges of St Leonard and St Salvator concentrated on one site, simultaneously abolishing the regenting system and reducing the number of staff from fourteen to nine. The new college set up in the St Leonard's College buildings in 1747 until a refurbished St Salvator's College was ready to receive the United College ten years later. In 1772, after a chequered existence, St Leonard's College was sold to Principal Robert Watson as a dwelling, with the exception of the chapel, which remains in university ownership.

The only other major building of the century was undertaken in 1764–67 when the library building was heightened. From 1710 until 1837 the university had the privilege of copyright deposit whereby a copy of every book published in the United Kingdom was presented. The intellectual flowering known as the Enlightenment, did not pass St Andrews by. Robert Watson's histories of Philip II and III had as much celebrity in his own time as the more enduring works of William Robertson. Mathematical studies flourished under Nicholas Vilant who employed as assistants James Ivory, John Leslie, James Brown and John West. Interesting people like George Hill, a leading Moderate divine, and John Rotheram, pupil and friend of Linnaeus and assistant to Joseph Black, joined the professoriate. The university continued to be attractive to the aristocracy – the antiquarian Earl of Buchan, the tree-planting Earl of Moray and the Earl of Elgin, who gave his name to the Elgin marbles, were all alumni. From more humble origins Adam Ferguson, philosopher, Robert Fergusson, poet, James Wilson, signatory of the American Declaration of Independence and Thomas Chalmers, pioneer political economist and theologian are a few of the names which are remembered.

The 19th century brought dramatic changes. Like all great conflicts, the Napoleonic Wars brought many discontinuities to national life. After a century of little interference from central government the great period of the parliamentary commission and legislative acts in 1859 and 1889 substantially changed the Scottish universities, making them progressively more bureaucratic and centrally controlled. Here, by the end of the century, the colleges had ceased to be independent corporations and St. Mary's, the divinity college, was no longer the more important partner. After an abortive attempt in 1892, an additional college, University College, Dundee, was added in 1897. Residence ceased in St Mary's College in 1814 and in United College in 1820. Fees were no longer exacted from arts students according to social status and supposed ability to pay. Student numbers did not enjoy the increases of universities in towns of industrial expansion. Just under 200 arts students and about 30 divinity students was the average, rising to a peak of 343 in 1824–25 and a low of 131 in 1876–77, which caused alarm in the university although, with hindsight, it coincided with a period of agricultural depression. Some professors saw women as a source of students. In 1862–63 Elizabeth Garrett matriculated as a medical student, though the reactionaries banned her from classes. But in 1876 a more daring enterprise was launched to allow women to gain an external qualification. The LLA (Lady Literate in Arts) scheme had an extraordinary success – by the time it was wound up in 1932, 36,017 candidates from all over the world had entered and 5117 achieved the diploma. In 1892 women were allowed to enter the university as ordinary students.

For most of the century the buildings of the university and colleges were maintained by the Commissioners of Woods and Forests and from time to time after prolonged pressure additions were made – the university building on South Street gained an extension in 1830 in identical style to the original. In 1831 and 1846 United College gained the quadrangle and cloister which survive. An attempt was made by Principal J. D. Forbes of United College in 1861 to attract the sons of 'persons of the higher ranks' of Scottish society by setting up a wardened residence called the College Hall, but it did not long survive his departure and closed in 1874. More successful was a residence for women students, partly from the profits of the LLA scheme, called University Hall, opened in 1896.

The impact of the university was undoubtedly less in this century, mainly on account of its small size, but it had its able teachers who attracted students like Thomas Chalmers in moral philosophy and political economy and John Tulloch in divinity. Two exceptional scientists were successive principals of United College: Sir David Brewster, inventor of the stereoscope and promoter of science, and James David Forbes, whose demonstration of the polarisation of heat helped the development of the theory of the energy spectrum and who first demonstrated that glaciers flowed like rivers. Towards the end of the century, Sir James Donaldson became, from 1890, the first principal of the university and turned around its fortunes in almost every area through a fortuitous mixture of scholarship, political influence and fund-raising ability. It was a period when universities prospered as a result of private benefaction rather than from the direct funding of government grants. Government funding, which provided only a small proportion of university income at the beginning of the century, has come to provide most of it with inevitable concomitant continuous government scrutiny and control. Donaldson owed his political influence to being private tutor to the young Earl of Rosebery and he had a wide knowledge of Greek and Roman ideas on education. He moved easily and genially in most company, but found the Marquess of Bute, twice rector, a hard man to deal with as chairman of the powerful new University Court. However, he did not forfeit Bute's generosity and two new buildings, a dining hall for the students' union and a building for an expanded medical faculty were secured. An extension to the east wing of United College, a physics building, two chemistry buildings, a gymnasium, two extensions to the university library, a museum with accommodation for the zoology professor and a new marine laboratory were Donaldson-period additions.

Among the distinguished professors of this time were Lewis Campbell and John Burnet in Greek, T. S. Baynes, editor of *Encyclopaedia Britannica* with Andrew Seth and Henry Jones, in logic and William Angus Knight in ethics, who, if he was not a great philosopher, was behind the success of the LLA scheme, a pioneer in Wordsworth studies and a prime mover in setting up Dove Cottage Museum. William Carmichael McIntosh set up the first British marine laboratory and Thomas Purdie pioneered in chemistry.

The principal from 1922 was a romantic figure. Sir James Irvine had first come to the university as a lab boy, and then as professor of chemistry aided the war effort by producing essential chemicals in huts on the United College tennis courts. He had absorbed the lessons of the Donaldson era well and had a clear vision for the future. It seemed to him that if the university was to grow, as it must, the most pressing need was for student accommodation. With the aid of several wealthy friends he added St Salvator's Hall as a residence for men (1930 and 1940) with the Swallowgate as an annex (1937) and McIntosh Hall (1921–39). He added music and chairs of history, botany and geology. There were also developments in the Dundee College, with which relations were and would always be uneasy, as it possessed a council which had been left with powers which never could be reconciled with those of the University Court. An inquiry by Lord Cooper in 1949 followed by a royal commission in 1952 seemed to provide a solution by the University of St Andrews Act (1953) which dissolved all the colleges and made them unincorporated societies, but two new college councils still maintained and emphasised the division between north and south of the Tay. It seemed natural that the greatly increased university provision which flowed from the Robbins Report in 1963 should include a separate Dundee University. This proved a desperate remedy for it left two truncated institutions at the separation in 1967. The new principal, J. Steven Watson, had to preside over an institution which had to expand rapidly to survive. A ready supply of building land from its ancient endowments and the happy acquisition of the North Haugh in 1960 aided developments of a size, range and location unmatched in any of its previous history. More than half a dozen new residences and new buildings for chemistry, mathematics and physics with a new university library were erected in about a decade and student numbers rose from 1900 in 1967 to about 3000 in 1972. Since Steven Watson died in 1986 the emphasis has still been on expansion under his successor and student numbers have risen to 6200. New building has included a large 537-bed residence, a biomolecular sciences wing grafted on to the chemistry building, a large addition to the Gatty marine laboratories, a community sports complex funded with lottery money and a new Gateway building begun in 1999.

This expansion has left the University with a very large portfolio of buildings in many areas of the old town and on a number of outlying sites. These range in date from houses built before the university was founded, though, like all continuously occupied structures, much modified by successive owners, to modern buildings of varying architectural merit As the visitor comes into St Andrews from the west, the North Haugh site lies on the right with undistinguished modern buildings for physics (1965–66), mathematics (1967), computing (1972), and chemistry, with a recent addition to the north (1968 and 1998). To the west of these is New Hall (1993), a large residence which time may dignify, and the remarkable Andrew Melville Hall (1968).

Proceeding eastwards along North Street the visitor passes John Burnet Hall, a converted hotel, on the right and just beyond City Road, again on the right, is the back of a 19th-century domestic crescent, now unified into McIntosh Hall. At this point we turn left down Golf Place, making for The Scores and pass on the corner a striking red sandstone building (1895), another converted hotel, now Hamilton Hall. Farther along the Scores, beyond St James Church, are Victorian mansions, villas and town houses, many of which are owned by the university and are used for various teaching purposes. About half-way along on the left is the Scots baronial University House (1864–66). We return to North Street via Murray Park and continue east. On the left we come to the Adamesque St Katherine's Lodge (*c.* 1812) with the large bulk of the University Library (1976) behind, before passing a group of domestic buildings, now offices. At the corner of Butt's Wynd is the 16th-century house in which the Admirable Crichton is alleged to have lodged while a student. The 'sixteenth-century' house with outside stair immediately opposite is a university reconstruction of 1950 to an approximation of its original design. The first of the colleges is now reached and its tower dominates the street. Built between 1450 and 1470, only the tower and chapel remain of the original buildings – the range to the left having been reconstructed in the 17th century. Within the quadrangle the ranges to the north and east, with the cloister, are pleasantly Victorian. The chapel contains the magnificent Gothic tomb of the founder, Bishop Kennedy, but the interior is otherwise a reconstruction of 1861 and 1930. To the east of the chapel is a house, older than the college, which has been in university possession since 1904 and was extended in 1912. College Gate, the main university offices, was built in 1953. The next imposing building slightly back from the street is the Younger Hall, much criticised at its building in 1929 for its eclectic style, but proving much more acceptable with age. Behind it lies St Salvator's Hall (1930 and 1940) and, to the east, the minimalist Gannochy Hall. At the end of this street on the left are various domestic buildings now in university ownership and, on the right, probably the oldest house in St Andrews, the former dwelling of the Archdeacon, now Deans Court. This has been much altered and restored and probably the only remaining part of the original 12th-century house is the now almost entirely underground vaulted first level.

Market Street, the second of the three main streets of St Andrews, has the smallest University presence with only a few buildings at the west end. The ugly students' union on the north side lies opposite the former studio of the first professional photographer in St Andrews, Thomas Rodger, now occupied by the Careers Advisory Service.

At the east end of South Street the distinctive early house, The Roundel, probably 16th-century although it bears the arms of Prior Haldenstone (1418–43) on its gable, is owned by the university. Through The Pends is St Leonard's College chapel, the only part of the college still retained. Some other parts of the early buildings survive, incorporated into St Leonard's school. About the middle of the street, South Street has two important sites. On the south is the original university building of 1612–43, alongside St Mary's College, with its first building (1542) on the street and the Hamilton buildings of *c.* 1550, with remodelling in 1829–30, behind. The altered date on the royal coat of arms (1542 to 1563) on the street façade may point to the date of the reputed planting by Mary, Queen of Scots, of the thorn still growing in the quadrangle. Successive extensions to the university library, now used for other purposes, and the Bute medical buildings, are built on St Mary's gardens. On the opposite side of the street 69–71 South Street is one of the largest old houses of St Andrews. It also has associations with Queen Mary as one of the houses in which she is said to have stayed on one of her ten visits to St Andrews. The house dates back to at least the 15th century and was the private residence of two archbishops (Stewart and Adamson). Farther west on the south side is another hall of residence (Southgait) which is also a converted hotel (1857).

Off the road through the West Port to Ceres are University Hall (1896) with later additions and the baronial annex of Westerlee (1865–68). Down St Leonard's Road is the sports complex, with playing fields surrounding the university observatory to the west. Beyond these are two residences: David Russell Hall (1970), was an interesting attempt by Kenneth Purdom to design a cheap residence – the 'spire' on the central building is a chimney – and Fife Park (1972) alongside is simply an adaptation of a domestic design to provide student flats. To complete the round of university buildings we should return along South Street to Queen's Gardens, where at the south-east corner is St Regulus Hall (1864–65, with a later addition); farther east along towards Abbey Street we pass the botany building on the south (1984). We now proceed to the East Sands where we find the Gatty Marine laboratory (1896 with later additions) and behind it another residence, Albany Park (1973), which is also an adapted domestic design. Even with many minor properties unlisted it is easy to feel that no university in Scotland so pervades the fabric of the town in which it is situated.

Twenty-Two

Folklore and Traditions

Firm evidence of the earliest human occupation of mainland Scotland is to be found at Fife Ness some 9600 years ago. Another Mesolithic settlement, of some 8000 years ago, on the land now known as Morton Farm, Tentsmuir, offers the clearest roots of the county's folklore. Here amongst the remains of the hunter-gatherers lie clues to that eerie frontier between harsh mortal life and the unseen world of spirits and gods that once held sway in Fife.

In these early days the folkloric beliefs of the inhabitants of Fife depended largely on whether they dwelt on the coast or inland. At the coast the first objects to be invested with a folklore would be shells, marine creatures and seabirds; while inland, the rabbit, deer, hedgehog. and the like would be given individual folkloric powers.

Fife's early inhabitants did not distinguish between mortals and the animal kingdom. They supposed that other living creatures, the rich game and wild fowl of Tentsmuir for instance, were credited with their own powers of speech and understanding and they were thus rendered anthropomorphic. These faculties were thought to be particularly available to animals at potentially ritualistic times, like the changing of the seasons. Such a superstition that animals could assume human speech at festive times remained in folk memory until the Victorian era when Fife countryfolk averred that at Hogmanay domestic animals (particularly cattle) could speak wisdom as one year passed into the next.

In many of Scotland's folk stories in general, and Fife folk-tales in particular, the dividing line between man and beast virtually disappears. Those who migrated into Fife from across the North Sea, around 9000 BC, were later deemed to be children of the sea creatures who lived in the mysterious waters, and gave rise to the folklore of seals and mermaids living and inter-marrying with humans.

As in other parts of Scotland, animals were worshipped in Fife. Cats, cows, pigs, horses, stags, rams, dogs, snakes, bears, hares and boar all feature in Fife folk-tales and superstitions and each played a part in the early religious cults in Fife. In particular, boar had a high profile. A relic of the boar cult was gifted to the cathedral of St Andrews by Alexander I when he regranted the hunting rights known as the *Cursus Apri Regalis*. His donation of a set of 16-inch boar's tusks was fixed with silver chains to the high altar.

From prehistoric sites animal mascots and carved relics have been found to testify to these cult beliefs. Thus the superstitions and folk-tales of Fife are rich in animal imagery. The following are some examples of the Fife folklore of birds and beasts.

To the old folk of Fife a ladybird was a sign of good fortune; the deeper its red colour the greater the fortune, and ants were used in psychosomatic medicine. Fifers used to attempt to cure deafness by mixing ants' eggs with onion juice and dropping the concoction into the troublesome ear. As to bees, should one fly into the house, a visitor might be expected, and it was considered unlucky to drive it out. A bee landing on the hand was a sign of riches to come, and should you capture the first bee of the season in your purse a whole year of good fortune was forecast. Cow's breath was deemed a cure for consumption in parts of Fife. A superstition came to Fife from France – to be extant amongst the French exiles living at Freuchie and serving the court at Falkland – that cows were given sweet breath because they used it to warm the infant Christ.

Lapwings were generally disliked in Fife because of their supposed cry of 'Bewitched! Bewitched!', while the farmyard rooster was always associated with magic. The fact that the bird greeted the day, the old folk said, was a sure sign of psychic power. The lark, with its three black spots under the tongue, was another bird to be wary of because of its power to curse those who might cause it harm. The wren was given lucky credence in Fife as was the swallow whose nest on a window-sill would promote prosperity. The yellow-hammer, called 'yellow-yorling' in Fife, was a bird of ill-omen being dubbed the 'Devil's bird'. The curlew, called the 'whaup' in Fife from the 16th century, was another bird to be wary of as it was deemed to carry off the spirits of the wicked at nightfall. It was feared, too, because it was one of the 'Seven Whistlers' thought to be the wandering souls of those who had been evil in life and who were condemned to walk the earth for ever. Their cries would foretell disaster; so whenever the whistles of the plover, the whimbrel, the widgeon and other associated birds were heard few wished to venture out. Fife soldiers believed that these birds crying out before a battle would indicate slaughter to come.

The most tenacious of all superstitions in Fife belonged to the fisher communities. The most common of these from Crail to Kirkcaldy were associated with times of sailing. Fife seamen would avoid sailing on a Friday, the day, old superstition said, when witches had domain over the waters. Another unlucky day was the first Monday in April, the supposed birthday of Cain, and the day he slew his brother Abel. Likewise the last Monday in December was avoided as the day Judas hanged himself. To avoid bad luck at sea Fife fishermen took with them a variety of mascots: salt, with its magic powers of life protection; iron to thwart evil; and a hare's foot in the pocket to keep storms away.

To encounter a hare before you set sail, though, was considered an evil omen, as was sneezing aboard ship. Fife seamen did not like sailing in a vessel that had changed its name too often since being built, and it was considered bad luck for a fisherman to be asked where he was going before setting sail. And there was a whole range of things that should never be done at sea. Whistling was one, for it was deemed to mock the Devil and raise storms. Again, a drinking vessel should never be tapped with the finger while aboard as that would sound the death knell of fellow crewmen. Lawyers, professional gamblers and clergy were all unwelcome on board too, with women regarded as the unluckiest of all. Yet, set within the figurehead, the spirit of any vessel was considered to be female, for once upon a time tribal shamans had been women.

Over the years Fife fishermen and sailors formed a taboo language of words that should never be uttered on board or in the home. Some old-time Fife fishermen would never mention the word 'eggs', as the shells of these were thought to be used by witches for transportation across the seas. Words like church, chapel and manse were all avoided because of their associations with the clergy, as were the words hare, rabbit, knife and pig. All of these had euphemisms to avoid bad luck. It was a common set of superstitions amongst fishermen in Fife that they could tell the weather by observing sea creatures. The bounding and springing of dolphins and porpoises was deemed a sign of approaching gales, while a dog whining near a ship forecast storms. And a playful cat near a ship meant rain.

Because Fife was an early site for the spawning of Christianity, the county was an area where Christian missionaries grafted their festivals onto already established pagan ones to ensure the continuum of belief. A number of Fife's pre-Reformation churches are built on pagan ritual sites. One clear example is the church of Dunino; in Dunino Den, druid stones, which were 'Christianised' by incising crosses on them, are still pointed out. Such sites bear testimony to the continuation of folklore festivals from Celtic heathendom to Christian times.

Fife's Celtic tribesmen set their festivals and seasonal traditions around four folklore divisions which in turn were given Christian relevance. They were set out in this way:

Imbolc	The feast of the Celtic Spring goddess	St Bride's Day, 1 February
Beltane	The feast of Bel, ruler of the Celtic underworld and Tin the Celtic fire god (Spring equinox and May)	Day of the Holy Cross, 3 May
Lugnasad	The feast of Lugh	Lammas
Samhuinn	The feast of the dead (Autumn equinox; November)	Harvest festival

To these festivals the Christian missionaries added Hallowmass (Hallowe'en; All Saints Day, 31 October) and Christmas during the Norse feast of Yule, 25 December until 6 January. From these folklore roots the old Scots quarter days were evolved:

Candlemas   The Purification of the Blessed Virgin Mary: 2 February
Whitsun   The Season of Pentecost (Old Beltane): 15 May
Lammas   1 August
Martinmas   Old Hallowmass. The feast of St Martin of Tours: 11 November

These were the traditional days on which Scots folk hired servants and paid their rents and quarterly wages.

Two folkloric Medieval traditions associated with the old quarter days survive at St Andrews and Kirkcaldy. For a week in April the Esplanade at Kirkcaldy is thronged with crowds attending the Easter chartered fair known as the Links Market. Today the event is a cacophonous gathering of colourful carousels and the cries of barkers. In former times the tradesmen at this market dealt in weights and measures that were almost unique to Fife.

In Medieval Fife, at least three standards of weight would be used: English pounds (16 oz), Dutch pounds (17.5 oz) and tron pounds (22 oz). English measures were used to weigh out flour, bread and barley; Dutch for meat and meal; and tron weights for butter, cheese and tallow. Gone too are the traditional names for some measures, like *lippie* (2 lbs) and *firlot* (2 stone).

St Andrews' only surviving fair is the Lammas Market, which is likely to be the oldest surviving market in Scotland. This festival, to honour the fruits of the soil, is a delightful anachronism that clogs the set streets of South Street and middle Market Street on the second Monday and Tuesday of August. The market was secured as a privilege for the burghers of St Andrews in 1620 by James VI & I; Charles I also recognised the market by act of parliament. Lammas, or Loaf Mass, was once a one-day hiring fair and an occasion of religious observance which brought to the town a huge influx of people. Until 1800 it was the only place in Fife where people could buy ironmongery. At one time the focal point of the market was a beer tent set up near South Street and Queen's Gardens, where the hiring of farm servants for the ensuing year was enacted. The Town Band played for the delight of the crowds all day, but frequent visits to the beer tent led to increasingly eccentric playing as the day progressed. Another bright occasion for the burghers of St Andrews was the annual Horse Fair which came to an end in the 1950s.

The University of St Andrews maintains three traditions that have become a part of folklore history in Meal Monday, the Kate Kennedy pageant and Raisin Monday. Meal Monday occurs in February and on that day there are no classes within the university. In Medieval times the poorer students went home on this day to collect their mid-term rations of oatmeal which was to last them the rest of the term.

The colourful costume pageant known as Kate Kennedy is thought to have originated around 1848 as a rumbustious end of term romp organised by students from the natural philosophy department. Records show that the students wore a variety of eccentric clothes for the occasion. By the 1860s the romp had developed into a procession through the town wherein the students dressed up as characters from the university's history. A central part of the procession was the lampooning of town and gown personalities and the university threatened to ban it. The survival of the procession was a symbol of student freedom. Eventually, in 1874, the procession came into serious conflict with the burgh authorities and was banned; and apart from a procession in 1881, the ban remained until 1926.

For his address to the university in 1922, the then rector, Sir James Matthew Barrie took 'courage' as his theme, and during his address to the students he mused on the historical characters he would have liked to have walked and talked with. This inspired two students that a revived Kate Kennedy was the nearest that they could get to Barrie's central idea, so today some hundred or so characters associated with the university and town history parade through the streets.

The pageant's link with a character called 'Kate Kennedy' is pure folklore tradition. Founded in 1411 by Bishop Henry Wardlaw, the University of St Andrews developed into three colleges by the mid-16th century. St Salvator's was founded in 1450 by Bishop James Kennedy and is the starting point of the pageant today. Here in the quad the characters assemble with Kate Kennedy as their central figure. Tradition makes her one of the daughters of founder Bishop Kennedy's brother, Gilbert, Lord Kennedy of Dunure and his wife, Catherine Maxwell. It is also averred by tradition that the young Kate was the chatelain of her uncle's household. How Kate became associated with the pageant is obscure, but some authorities have ascribed her procession to a folk memory of a local festival celebrating the coming of spring, or indeed of the founding of the college. This is of course pure speculation.

Traditionally, Kate Kennedy is played by a 'beardless bejant' – that is a male first-year student. She rides in a carriage with her uncle dressed in his full canonicals to process around the town. Today the procession is one of the most vibrant and colourful in Europe and is organised by the Kate Kennedy Club, an organisation bent on fostering good relations between town and gown as well as raising charity monies.

Raisin Monday has developed into a 'weekend' in early November. University tradition avers that the first year students are called bejants and bejantines, a term taken from the French *bec-jaune* indicating a fledgling. Custom decrees that these bejants acquire a 'Senior Man' or 'Senior Woman' student (usually third or fourth year) to act as their mentor during the first year. These students are called 'academic parents' and help introduce the fledgling to the traditions of the university, its society and life.

On Raisin Monday, during Martinmas Term, it is customary for bejants and bejantines to offer their academic parents the equivalent of a pound of raisins in exchange for a ribald receipt in Latin; these days the gift is usually interpreted as a bottle of wine. Custom decrees too, that the students dress in eccentric costumes to receive their receipts and they gather in the quad of St Salvator's College, where in recent years they have squirted each other the with large quantities of shaving cream.

Martinmas was once a time of popular celebration in Fife. It was dedicated to one of Scotland's most popular Medieval saints, St Martin of Tours, who was deemed to be a tutor of St Ninian and was often pictured on a white horse as a harbinger of snow. His feast day was 11 November, when the old folk said winter began with intensity. The eve of St Martin was a time when house parties were held to mark the quarter day of Martinmas, when many took up new employment.

Balwearie Castle lies less than 3 km south-west of Kirkcaldy on an estate that was old when a plain rectangular fortified tower was set up by William Scott of Balwearie on the licence of King James III in 1463. For his namesake, Sir Walter Scott, Balwearie was the focal point of folklore in Fife; for here dwelt Sir Michael Scott, bynamed 'The Wizard', who was to have such a dramatic role in Scott's *The Lay of the Last Minstrel* (1805):

> In these far climes it was my lot
> To meet the wondrous Michael Scott;
> A wizard of such dreadful fame,
> That when, in Salamanca's cave,
> Him listed his magic wand to wave,
> The bells would ring in Notre Dame.
> Some of his skills he taught to me;
> And, warrior, I could say to thee
> The words that cleft Eildon Hills in three.
> And bridled the Tweed with a curb of stone:
> But to speak them were a deadly sin . . .

Born in the late 12th century, Michael Scott had formed around him all of the Medieval aspects of folklore that were attributed to those who studied astrology, alchemy and the arcane arts of the east. Dubbed a 'seer' and a 'wizard', Scott had studied at Oxford, Paris and Padua, the centre of the magic arts, and learned the 'Black Arts', too, as tutor and atrologer at Palermo.

Michael Scott built up an international reputation, which even earned him a mention in Dante's *Inferno* (Canto XX), to make him a larger than life folk character and a person to be summoned up in conversation about superstition in Fife. Whenever the cult of the Devil, familiar demons, black magic and necromancy were mentioned a reference to Michael Scott was inevitable.

Here is a typical folktale about Michael Scott based on Medieval interpretation: on one occasion the King of Scots was angry at the attacks by French pirates on Scots vessels at sea, so he commanded Michael Scott to go to France as ambassador to petition the king to have the outrages stopped. Rather than appoint a diplomatic suite, Scott opened his magic *Book of Might* and read out a spell to conjure up his black demon horse. Mounting the mare, Scott sped through the air to France. Haughtily striding into the French king's presence, Scott relayed the wishes of his Scottish master. The King of France demurred and made to wave Scott from his presence. Scott whistled up his demonic horse and commanded it to stamp its hooves three times. On the first stamp all the bells in the churches of Paris were set jangling. On the second three towers of the palace collapsed, and as the horse was about to make a third stamp, the French king capitulated. Orders were given to the French seamen to end their piracy and Scott left to recount the good news to the King of Scots.

Sir Walter Scott took great delight in taking groups of his visitors on expeditions to Melrose Abbey. There he would point out the supposed site of Michael Scott's tomb in the south transept with the added folklore comment that somewhere beneath their feet lay Scott's magic volume the *Book of Might*.

Fife folklore's richest stories about the Devil concern his presumed ability to hurl great boulders across the countryside to form hills, hazards in river beds and extraneous rocks in fields. By the gate of Crail's parish church stands the Blue Boulder, a rock, legend has it, flung by the Devil from the Isle of May to demolish the church which was being built. The Earl of Hell missed and the boulder split in two, one part landing on Balcomie beach and the other by the kirk gate. The latter is still pointed out as bearing his dark lordship's thumbprint.

As well as the Earl of Hell, Fife folklore tradition can offer a range of nicknames for the Devil, from Auld Clootie and Auld Sandie, to Auld Waghorn and Auld Harry – all euphemisms in case the utterance of the word Devil or Satan brought bad luck. Nevertheless in Fife folklore several sayings and proverbs were remembered that boldly used the taboo words. Here are a few examples:

> The Deil dances in an empty pocket.
> There's a Deil in every mouthful of whisky.
> The Deil is busy in a high wind.
> The Deil is guid to his ain.
> He needs a lang-shankit spoon that sups wi' the Deil.

All witches were considered to be the creatures of the Devil, and, although the

Devil does not appear much in the indictment of Fife witches, what they did was considered Devil's work. Regular meetings with the Devil were thought to be the everyday activities of witches and a few brave Fife folk actually admitted to meeting the Earl of Hell. In the volume *The Royal House of Stuart* there is a reference to John Knox having a conversation with the Devil in the cathedral graveyard of St Andrews. Yet it is the village of Auchtermuchty that enters folklore record as the place once attacked by the Devil.

For many years the folk of Auchtermuchty were recognised and praised for their piety, a fact, the old folk said, which irritated the Devil. In order to tempt the villagers into a more wanton way of life the Devil is said to have visited Auchtermuchty in the guise of a Presbyterian clergyman. As the village had no church of its own at that time the Devil preached to them in the square and so inspired all who listened that he soon had some converts.

On the day that the Devil set up his pulpit a man called Robin Ruthven caught sight of the Devil's feet beneath his cloak. Where one would have expected to see shoes Ruthven saw cloven hooves. In a moment of bravery Ruthven denounced the Devil who rose above the rooftops 'like a fiery dragon in his anger' and disappeared in a trail of flames and noxious gases towards the Lomond hills. And that, said the old folk, is why you can never get an Auchtermuchty person to heed a sermon.

The village of Kilconquhar – pronounced 'kinnucher' locally – can add a little to the county's witchlore and devilry, for here was an execution site for East Neuk witches. As late as 1705 the Presbyterian clergy of Pittenweem were pursuing witches hereabouts and a local balladist recalled the drowning of witches in Kilconquhar Loch:

> They tied her arms behind her back
> And twisted them wi' a pin,
> And they dragged her to Kilconquhar Loch
> An' coupit the limmer in (*threw the villain in*)

The mysterious tumuli and forlorn standing stones which are highlighted on Fife horizons were long invested with their own folklore. Were they the graves of giants and the playthings of fabulous beings? Certainly it was believed that these old burial mounds were the probable sites of hidden treasure, or even the entrances to a strange underground world of demons.

The finding of grave goods on these sites added to the folklore of the places. One such site was Norrie's Law, some two-and-a-half miles (4 km) north-west of Largo. Here in 1819 was discovered a hoard of 7th-century native Pictish and late Roman silver. This gave rise to stories of spectral warriors being seen on the slopes of Largo Law encased in gold and silver armour. It gave rise to the tradition too, that there was so much gold on Largo Law that it turned sheep fleeces yellow.

Fife was to supply one of Scotland's most dedicated ghost hunters and folklorists of the spectral world. When he was not studying the archaeology and architecture of St Andrews cathedral William T. Linskill was in pursuit of the burgh's ghosts. Born in 1858, Linskill had been brought to St Andrews for the school holidays and liked the place so much that he set up his home there in 1897. He steeped himself in the town's history and played a prominent part in its administration as Dean of Guild. He is remembered mostly today for his book, *St Andrews Ghost Stories*, wherein he published one of the most remarkable collections of Scottish ghost stories ever assembled.

Linskill's particular obsession was the pursuit of 'The White Lady'. Her haunt was a tower set in the old precinct wall of the cathedral, a place used in later centuries as a burial vault for the Martines, the Lairds of Denbrae. In 1868 the upper room of the tower had been opened to reveal a collection of coffins and at the time each cadaver was carefully examined. One was the embalmed body of 'a female who had on her hands white gloves'. She was to be Linskill's inspiration for his 'White Lady'.

Linskill carefully assembled a history of what he now called 'The Haunted Tower' and logged the myriad tales of strange lights and sounds which had emanated from its depths and which had been recorded in the tales of the local familes who dwelt in the fisher quarter of the burgh.

By the 1870s, it seems, tales of the appearance of the ghostly 'White Lady' were so common that Linskill vowed to trace her steps himself. At midnight on 21 August 1888, he caused the 'Haunted Tower' to be opened. By the light of hurricane lamps he and his followers examined the jumble of bones in the tower. Alas, to his disappointment there was no sign of the 'beautiful embalmed girl' but the tradition of her walking the precincts of the cathedral persisted in living memory.

Folklore is a living concept and modern industry and commerce has kept folklore traditions alive. Shipbuilders launching vessels with a ritual libation of champagne and sailors carrying a piece of sea coal for good luck, along with craftsmen like blacksmiths, have kept industrial folklore vibrant. Blacksmiths, considered the oldest of all craftsmen because they made the tools of others, have had a long established folklore in Fife. Because they worked in iron, a traditional sure defence against witchcraft, blacksmiths were invested by tradition with skills beyond the scope of their forges. Often sick children were brought to a smith's forge to be cured. The sound of iron striking an anvil was long thought a cure for sustained bleeding, and water saved after cooling iron was deemed to have medicinal qualities. Like farriers, blacksmiths were also considered skilled in dealing with animals. One Fife superstition was that local smiths could calm restive horses by whispering secret words. Fife 'horse whispering' was thought to be an inherited skill.

Fife communities were given a strong sense of custom and tradition from the beliefs of many a workforce from miners to quarrymen. Fife miners had their own set of superstitions. Pit disasters were considered more likely when beans were in flower, others thought washing the back caused a weakening of pit roofs. Some miners would never walk back into their homes if they had forgotten something on their way to a shift. They would stand by the door while someone brought the forgotten item. Others thought it was unlucky to change shifts with someone midweek, while others said it was attracting ill fortune leading to the sack if you counted your pay-packet on mine property.

Apprenticeships and the taking on of novices all had their traditions in Fife industry. This might range from trussing newly chartered coopers in a barrel they had made before passing out a fully fledged craftsman, to baptising young print apprentices with ink. 'Blessings' for good fortune like the 'topping out' ceremonies or 'cutting the first turf' at building sites, or consecrating fishing nets and tools of the trade have ensured that the industrial community played a prominent part in Fife folklore and tradition.

New customs and new beliefs are coming into existence every day. Some of these will survive well into the 21st century to be the foundation of the Fife folk ways of the future.

BIBLIOGRAPHY

A Cloud of Witnesses, 1871. Edinburgh.

Ainslie, 1775. Map of the Counties of Fife and Kinross compiled and engraved by John Ainslie 1775.

Ainslie, 1827. Map of East Part of Fifeshire compiled from the surveys of John Ainslie and John Bell 1827.

Alcock, L. 1993. *The Neighbours of the Picts: Angles, Britons and Scots at war and at home*, Dornoch.

Anderson, J.M. 1905. *The Matriculation Roll of the University of St Andrews, 1747–1897*, Edinburgh.

Anderson, J.M. 1926. Early Records of the University of S Andrews, *SHS* 3rd series vol. viii., Edinburgh.

Anderson, M.O. 1980. *Kings and Kingship in Early Scotland* (revised edition, Edinburgh; first edition 1973).

APS 1814–75. *The Acts of the Parliaments of Scotland*, ed. T. Thomson and C. Innes.

Apted, M.R. 1957–58. Two painted ceilings from Mary Somerville's House, Burntisland, *Proceedings of the Society of Antiquaries of Scotland*, xci, 144–76.

Arb. Lib., 1848–56. *Liber S. Thome de Aberbrothoc*, Bannatyne Club.

Ashmore, P.J. 1996. *Neolithic and Bronze Age Scotland*, Historic Scotland and BT Batsford, London.

Atlas, 1996. *Atlas of Scottish History to 1707*, ed. P.G.B. McNeill and H.L. MacQueen, Edinburgh.

Balm. Lib. 1841. *Liber Sancte Marie de Balmorinach*, Abbotsford Club.

Bannerman, J. 1993. 'MacDuff, Fife'. In: Grant A. & Stringer K.J. (eds.) *Medieval Scotland: Crown, Lordship and Cornmunity*, 20–38.

Barclay, G. (n.d.) *Balfarg. The Prehistoric Ceremonial Complex*, Fife Regional Council, Glenrothes.

Barclay, G. 1998. *Farmers, Temples and Tombs: Scotland in the Neolithic and Early Bronze Ages,* in The Making of Scotland series, Canongate Books with Historic Scotland, Edinburgh.

Barclay, G. & Russell-White; C.J. (eds). 1993. Excavations in the ceremonial complex of the fourth to second millennium at Balfarg/Balbirnie, Glenrothes, Fife. *Proceedings of the Society of Antiquaries of Scotland* 123, 43–210.

Barrow, G.W.S. 1952–53. The Earls of Fife in the 12th Century. *Proceedings of the Society of Antiquaries of Scotland,* 87, 51–62.

Barrow, G.W.S. 1983. The Childhood of Scottish Christianity: a Note on Some Place-Name Evidence, *Scottish Studies* 27, 1–15.

Barrow, G.W.S. 1984. 'Land Routes: The Medieval Evidence'. In: *Loads and Roads in Scotland and Beyond,* ed. A. Fenton & G. Stell, 49–66 (also in Barrow, G.W.S. 1992, *Scotland and its Neighbours in the Middle Ages* London, 201–16, entitled simply 'Land Routes').

Barrow, G.W.S. 1989. 'The Lost Gàidhealtachd'. In: *Gaelic and Scotland,* ed. W. Gillies 67–88 (also in Barrow, G.W.S. 1992 *Scotland and its Neighbours in the Middle Ages,* London 105–26).

Barrow, G.W.S. 1998. 'The Uses of Place-names and Scottish history – pointers and pitfalls'. In: *The Uses of Place-Names,* ed. S. Taylor, Edinburgh, 54–74.

Barrow, G.W.S. 1998a. 'Religion in Scotland on the eve of Christianity' in *Forschungen zur Reichs-, Papst- und Landesgeschichte,* ed. Borchardt K. & Bünz E. Part 1, Stuttgart, 25–32 [a study of *nemeton* place-names in Scotland].

Beatson, R. 1794. *General view of the agriculture of the County of Fife,* Edinburgh.

Bennett, G.P. 1982. *The Great Road between Forth and Tay,* Markinch.

Blaeu (Gordon), Map 'Fife Vicecomitatus, The Sheirfdome of Fyfe', by James Gordon, dated 1645, published in J. Blaeu, 1654. *Theatrum Orbis Terrarum, sive Atlas Novus,* V. Amsterdam. Reproduced in J.C. Stone, 1991. *Illustrated Maps of Scotland, from Blaeu's Novus of the 17th Century,* London, 61, Plate 27.

Breeze, A. 1997. Etymological Notes on *Kirkcaldy, jockteleg* 'knife', *kiaugh* 'trouble', *striffen* 'membrane' and *cow* 'hobgoblin', *Scottish Language* 16, 97–110 [Kirkcaldy 97–9].

Brooks, N.P. & Whittington, G. 1977. 'Planning and growth in the medieval Scottish burgh: the example of St Andrews'. In: *Transactions of the Institute of British Geographers,* New Series, vol. 2, no. 2.

Brotchie, A.W. 1990. *Fife's Trams and Buses,* Dundee.

Bruce, W.S. 1980. *The Railways of Fife,* Perth.

Brunner, C.T. 1929. *Road Versus Rail: The Case for Motor Transport,* London.

Buckroyd, J. 1987. *The Life of James Sharp. Archbishop of St Andrews 1618–1679,* Edinburgh.

Burgess, C. 1974. 'The Bronze Age'. In: Renfrew, C. (ed) *British Prehistory: A New Outline,* London.

Cameron, J. 1984. Aspects of the Lutheran Contribution to the Scottish Reformation 1528–1552. *Scottish Church History Society Records* 22, 1–12.

Cameron, J.K. 1990. Three articles on the early history of St Mary's College in

D.W. Shaw ed. In: *Divers Manners: a St Mary's Miscellany*. St Andrews, 29–72.

Campbell, J. 1897. *Balmerino and its Abbey. A Parochial History*, Edinburgh.

Campbell, J. 1899. *Balmerino and its abbey, a parish history, with notices of the adjacent district*, Edinburgh.

Cant, R.G. 1950. *The College of St Salvator*, Edinburgh.

Cant, R.G. 1976. *Historic Crail*.

Cant, R.G. 1992. *The University of St Andrews: a short history*, 3rd edn, St Andrews.

Carte Monialium de Northberwic, 1847, Bannatyne Club.

Chartulary of the Abbey of Lindores, 1903m Scottish History Society.

Clancy, T.O. 1995. *Annat* in Scotland & the Origins of the Parish, *Innes Review* 46, 91–115.

Clancy, T.O. & Taylor, S. *Fetter-names*. Forthcoming.

Close Brooks, J. 1986. 'Excavations at Clatchard Craig, Fife', *Proceedings of the Society of Antiquaries of Scotland*, Vol. 116, 1986, 117–185.

Coles, J.M. 1971. 'The Early Settlement of Scotland: Excavations at Morton, Fife.' *Proc. Prehist. Soc.*, 37, 284–366.

Corbet, G.B. 1998. *The Nature of Fife*, Scottish Cultural Press/Scottish Wildlife Trust, Edinburgh.

Coull, J.R. 1995. The Role of the Fishery Board in the Development of Scottish Fishing Harbours *c.* 1809–1939, *Scottish Economic and Society History* 15, 25–42.

Coull, J.R. 1996. *The Sea Fisheries of Scotland: A Historical Geography*, John Donald, Edinburgh.

CSD, 1985. *Concise Scots Dictionary*, ed. M. Robinson, Aberdeen.

Cunliffe, B., 1974. 'The Iron Age' in Renfrew, C. (ed.) *British History a new outline*, London.

Dawson, J.E.A. 1991. *The face of Ane Perfyt Reformed Kyrk: St Andrews and the Early Scottish Reformation. Humanism and Reform: the Church in Europe, England and Scotland, 1400–1643*. Oxford, Blackwell.

Dean, P. & A. 1981. *Passage of Time*, North Queensferry.

Dennison, E.P. 1995. *Historic Kirkcaldy. The Archaeological Implications of Development*, Scottish Burgh Survey.

Dennison, E.P. 1996. 'Burgh Trading Liberties: Inverkeithing, Dunfermline & Kirkcaldy'. In: *Atlas of Scottish History to 1707*, P. McNeil & H. MacQueen (eds.), p. 235, Edinburgh.

Donaldson, G. 1960. *The Scottish Reformation*, Cambridge University Press.

Donaldson, G. 1965. *Scotland: James V to James VII*, Edinburgh.

Donaldson, G. 1970. *Scottish Historical Documents*, Edinburgh.

Dow, F.D. 1979. *Cromwellian Scotland 1651–1660*, Edinburgh.

Driscoll, S. 1997. A Pictish Settlement in north-east Fife: The Scottish Field

School of Archaeology excavations at Easter Kinnear, *Tayside and Fife Archaeological Journal*, vol. 3, Tayside and Fife Archaeological Committee, Glenrothes.

Dunbar, L.J. 1997. Synods and Superintendence: John Winram and Fife, 1561–1572, *Records of the Scottish History Society, Vol. 27*, 97–125.

Duncan, A.A.M. 1956–57. Documents relating to the Priory of the Isle of May, *c.* 1140–1313, *Proceedings of the Society of Antiquaries of Scotland*, xc, 52–80.

Duncan, A.A.M. 1978. *Scotland: The Making of the Kingdom*, Edinburgh.

Duncan, A.A.M. 1958. The Earliest Scottish Charters, *Scottish Historical Review*, xxxvii.

Duncan, P. 1999. 'The River Tay' in Omand D. (ed.) *The Perthshire Book*, Edinburgh.

Dunf. Reg. 1842. *Registrum de Dunfermelyn*, Bannatyne Club.

Dunlop, A.I. 1964. *Acta facultatis artium universitatis Sanctiandree, 1413–1588*, Edinburgh.

Feachem, R. 1977. *Guide to Prehistoric Scotland*, London.

Ferguson, K. 1982. *A History of Glenrothes.* Glenrothes Development Corporation, Glenrothes.

Ferguson, W. 1968. *Scotland: 1689 to the Present*, Edinburgh.

Fife Council, 1946. *Fife Looks Ahead*, Edinburgh.

Fife Council, 1997. *Sustainability Indicators for Fife*, Glenrothes.

Fife Council, 1998a. Transport Policies and Progress, 1992–97, Glenrothes.

Fife Council, 1998b. *The Development of a Freight Strategy for Fife*, Glenrothes.

Fife Ct. Bk. 1928. *The Sheriff Court Book of Fife 1515–22*, ed. W.C. Dickinson. Scottish History Society.

Fife Regional Council, Economic reports and Structural Plans. Various dates.

Fife Regional Council, 1989. *Fife's Early Archaeological Heritage: A Guide*, Glenrothes.

Forsyth, K. 1995. 'Language in Pictland, spoken and written' in Nichol, E. (ed) *A Pictish Panorama*, Balgavies, Angus.

Foster, S. 1996. *Picts, Gaels and Scots*, Batsford/Historic Scotland, London.

Foster, S. (ed.) 1998. *The St Andrews Sarcophagus*, Historic Scotland, Dublin.

Fotheringham, N. 1997. *Charlestown: Built on lime*, Carnegie Trust, Dunfermline.

Gardiner, L.G. 1961. *Stage Coach to John o' Groats*, London.

Gilfillan, G. (n.d.) *The Martyrs & Heroes of the Scottish Covenant*, Edinburgh & London (first published 1852).

Gourlay, G. 1879. *Fisher Life, or The Memorial of Cellardyke and the Fife Coast*, Fife Herald Office, Cupar.

Gray, M. 1978. *The Fishing Industries of Scotland 1790–1914.* Oxford University Press, Oxford.

Hall, B. 1825. 'An account of the ferry across the Tay at Dundee', Abertay Historical Society, Reprint No. 1: 1973.

Hall, M. 1998. 'A probable gaming board from Ormiston, Newburgh, Fife', *Tayside and Fife Archaeological Journal*, vol. 4, 74–118.

Henderson, I. 1967. *The Picts*, London.

Henderson, I. 1986. 'The "David Cycle" in Pictish art'. In: Higgit, J. (ed) *Early Medieval Sculpture in Britain and Ireland*, 87–123.

Henry, D. 1997 (ed.). *The worm, the germ and the thorn. Pictish and related studies presented to Isabel Henderson*, Balgavies, Angus.

Herkless, J. 1891, *Cardinal Beaton: Priest and Politician*, Edinburgh & London.

Herkless, J. & Hannay, R.K. 1905. *The College of St Leonard*, Edinburgh.

Hingley, R. 1998. *Settlement and Sacrifice, The Later Prehistoric Peoples of Scotland*, in The Making of Scotland series Edinburgh.

Hunter, F. 1996. Recent Roman Iron Age metalwork finds from Fife, *Tayside and Fife Archaeological Journal*, vol. 2, 113–125, Tayside and Fife Archaeological Committee, Glenrothes.

Inchcolm Chrs. 1938. *Charters of the Abbey of Incholm*, Easson, D.E. & Macdonald, A. (eds.) Scottish History Society.

Johnston, R.C. 1981. *Jordan Fantosme's Chronicle*, lines 471–474, 36–7, Oxford.

Keppie, L. 1998. *Scotland's Roman Remains: An Introduction and Handbook*, 2nd edn, Edinburgh.

Kirk, 1991. *The Religion of Early Scottish Protestants. Humanism and Reform: the Church in Europe, England and Scotland, 1400–1643*, 361–412, Oxford.

Kitson, P.R. 1996. British and European River-Names, *Transactions of the Philological Society* 94:2, 73–118.

Knox, J. 1898. *The History of the Reformation of Religion within the Realm of Scotland*, London.

Koch, J.T. 1980. The Stone of the *Weni-kones, Bulletin of the Board of Celtic Studies* 29, 87–9.

Laing, A. 1876. *Lindores Abbey and its burgh of Newburgh, their history and annals*, Edinburgh.

Lamont-Brown, R. 1988. *Discovering Fife*, John Donald, Edinburgh.

Lumsden, J. 1914. *The Covenants of Scotland*, Paisley.

Lynch, M. 1991. *Scotland: a New History*, London.

MacDonald, A. 1973. Annat in Scotland: A Provisional Review, *Scottish Studies* 17, 135–46.

MacGibbon, D. & Ross, T. 1896. *The Ecclesiastical Architecture of Scotland I*, 193–6, 309–14.

MacGregor, A.R. 1996. *Fife and Angus Geology. An Excursion Guide*, 3rd edn, Pentland Press, Edinburgh.

MacInnes, A.I. 1991. *Charles I and the Making of the Covenanting Movement 1625–1641*, Edinburgh.

Mack, A. 1997. *Field Guide to the Pictish Symbol Stones*, Balgavies, Angus.

Mackie, R.L. 1962. *A Short History of Scotland*, Edinburgh & London.

Macquarrie, A. 1993. *Vita Sancti Servani*: The Life of St Serf, *Innes Review* vol. 44(2), 122–52.

Maxwell, G. 1998. *A Gathering of Eagles, Scenes from Roman Scotland*, Edinburgh.

McRoberts, D. (n.d.) B. Halloran Material Destruction caused by the Scottish Reformation, *Essays* 415–462.

Mercer, R. 1982. The excavation of a late Neolithic henge-type enclosure at Balfarg, Markinch, Fife, Scotland, *Proceedings of the Society of Antiquaries of Scotland*, 111, 63–171.

Millar, A.H. 1895. *Fife, Pictorial and Historical, Its People, Burghs, Castles and Mansions* (no publisher).

Mitchison, R. 1970. *A History of Scotland*, London.

Mitchison, R. 1990. *Lordship to Patronage: Scotland 1603–1745*, reprinted Edinburgh.

Morrison, I. 1985. *Landscape with Lake Dwellings: The Crannogs of Scotland*, Edinburgh.

Muir, R. and Welfare, H. 1983. *The National Trust Guide to Prehistoric and Roman Britain*, London.

National Library of Scotland. 'Discources Anent the Improvements may be made in Scotland for Advancing the Wealth of the Kingdom in these parts by a Well Wisher to his Country.' (Ms 33.5.31), Attributed to Sir Robert Sibbald.

Neale, C. 1985. *Dunfermline Heritage*, Carnegie Dunfermline Trust, Dunfermline.

Neish, J.S. 1890. *History of Newport and the Parish of Forgan and rambles round the district*, Dundee.

Nicol, E. (ed.) 1995. *A Pictish Panorama*, Balgavies, Angus.

Nicolaisen, W.F.H. 1976. *Scottish Place Names*, London (second impression with additional information 1979)

Nocolaisen, W.F.H. 1976. *The Picts and their Place Names*, Groam House Museum Lecture Publications, Rosemarkie.

Oram, R.D. 1997. *Scottish Prehistory*, Birlinn.

Oram, R.D. 1999. 'Prelatical builders' in Oram, A.D. & Stell, G.P. *Lordship and Architecture in Medieval and Renaissance Scotland* (forthcoming).

Oram, R.D. Continuity, Adaptation and Integration: The Earls and Earldom of Mar *c.* 1150–*c.* 1300 in Boardman, S. (ed.) Native Kindreds in Medieval Scotland. forthcoming.

Pride, G.L. 1990. *The Kingdom of Fife: An Architectural Guide*, Royal

Incorporation of Architects, Edinburgh.

Proudfoot, E. 1996. Excavations at the long cist cemetery on the Hallow Hill, St Andrews, Fife, 1975–7, *Proceedings of the Society of Antiquaries of Scotland*, vol. 126.

Proudfoot, E. 1997. Short-cist burials from Fife, Upper Kenly Farm, Belliston Farm and Dalgety Bay' *Tayside and Fife Archeological Journal*, vol. 3, 1–21.

Proudfoot, E. & Aliaga-Kelly, C. 1996. Towards an interpretation of anomalous finds and place-names of Anglo-Saxon origin in Scotland, *Anglo-Saxon Studies in Archaeology and History* 9, 1–13.

Pryde, G.S. 1965. *The Burghs of Scotland: a critical list*, London.

Rea, A.H. 1902. *Lindores Abbey and its Historic Associations*, Dundee.

Register of the Minister, Elders and Deacons of the Christian Congregation of St Andrew's. Edinburgh, 1889.

Reid, M.L. 1993. *Prehistoric Houses in Britain*, Shires Archaeology, Princes Risborough.

Renfrew, C. (ed.) 1974. *British Prehistory: a new outline*, London.

Ritchie, J.N.G. 1974. Excavation of the stone circle and cairn at Balbirnie, Fife, *Archaeological Journal*, 131, 1–32.

RMS, 1882–1914. *Registrum Magni Sigilli Regum Scottorum* ed. Thomson, J.M. et. al., Edinburgh.

Robertson, C.J.A. 1983. *The Origins of the Scottish Railway System 1722–1784*.

Robertson, I.A. 1998. *The Tay Salmon Fisheries since the eighteenth century*, Criuthne Press, Glasgow.

Rogers, J.M. 1992. The Formation of the Parish Unit and Community in Perthshire, unpublished PhD, Edinburgh University.

RRS i, 1960. *Regesta Regum Scottorum* vol. i (*Acts of Malcolm IV*) ed. G.W.S. Barrow, Edinburgh.

RRS ii, 1970. *Regesta Regum Scottorum* vol. ii (*Acts of William I*) ed. G.W.S. Barrow, Edinburgh.

Salmon, J.B. ed. 1950. *Veterum laudes*, Edinburgh.

Scott Bruce, W. 1980. *The Railways of Fife*, Perth.

Scottish Record Office, *SRO*, 19/4/1 to 19/4/8: Letters and Reports of the Anstruther District.

SGF/1828. Map of Counties of Fife and Kinross, surveyed in the years 1826 and 1827, Sharp, Greenwood & Fowler, reprinted by Wychwood Editions 1992.

Silver, O. 1984. *The Development of the Fife Road System 1700–1850*. PhD thesis, University of St Andrews. Fife reference libraries.

Silver, O. 1987a. *The Roads of Fife*, Edinburgh.

Silver, O. 1987b. The Roads of Scotland: from Statute Labour to Tolls – the first phase, 1700 to 1775 *SGM* 103.3.

Sinclair, Sir J. 1978. *The Statistical Account of Scotland 1791–1799: Vol. X, Fife*,

Wakefield (OSA.X).

Smith, P. 1985. *The Lammas Drave and the Winter Herrin': A History of the Herring Fishing from East Fife*, John Donald, Edinburgh.

Smyth, A. 1984. *Warlords and Holy Men The New History of Scotland AD 80–1000*, London.

St A. Lib. 1841. *Liber Cartarum Prioratus Sancti Andrew in Scotia*, Bannatyne Club.

Stephen, W.M. 1967–8. Milestones and Wayside Makers in Fife, *Proceedings of the Society of Antiquaries of Scotland*, 100.

Stephen, W.M. 1967. Toll-houses of the Greater Fife Area, *Industrial Archaeology* 4.

Stevenson, D. (ed.) 1982. *The Government of Scotland under the Covenanters 1637–1651*, Scottish History Society.

Stevenson, D. 1988. *The Covenanters: The National Covenant and Scotland*, Edinburgh.

TAFAC, 1999. St Andrews, *TAFAC* Journal.

Taylor, S. 1994. Babbet and Bridin Pudding or Polyglot Fife in the Middle Ages, *Nomina* 17, 99–118.

Taylor, S. 1994a. Some Early Scottish Place-Names and Queen Margaret, *Scottish Language* 13, 1–17.

Taylor, S. 1995. Settlement-Names in Fife unpublished PhD thesis, University of Edinburgh.

Taylor, S. 1995a. 'The Scandinavians in Fife and Kinross: The Onomastic Evidence'. In: *Scandinavian Settlement* in *Northern Britain*, ed. B.E. Crawford, London. 141–67.

Taylor, S. 1996. 'Place-names and the Early church in Eastern Scotland'. In *Dark Age Britain*, ed. B.E. Crawford, Aberdeen, 93–110.

Taylor, S. 1997. 'Generic-Element Variation, with Special Reference to Eastern Scotland', *Nomina* 20, 5–22.

Taylor, S. 1998. Place-names and the early church in Scotland, *Records of the Scottish Church History Society* 28, 1–22.

Taylor, S. & Henderson, J.M. 1998. 'The medieval marches of Wester Kinnear, Kilmany Parish, Fife, *Tayside and Fife Archaeological Journal* 4, 232–47.

The New Statistical Account of Scotland, Vol. 9, Fifeshire 1845, Edinburgh (*NSA*.9).

Thomas, C. 1981. *Christianity in Roman Britain to AD 500*, London.

Thomas, J. 1971. *A Regional History of the Railways of Great Britain Vol. VI: Scotland: The Lowlands and the Borders*, Newton Abbot.

Thomson, J.H. 1903. *The Martyr Graves of Scotland*, Edinburgh & London.

Todd, A.B. (n.d.) *The Homes, Haunts, and Battlefields of the Covenanters*, Edinburgh.

Torrie, E.P. Dennison, 1984. The Gild of Dunfermline in the Fifteenth

Century, unpublished PhD thesis, University of Edinburgh.

Torrie, E.P. Dennison (ed.) 1986. *The Gild Court Book of Dunfermline, 1433–1594, SRS.*

Torrie, E.P. Dennison, 1988. 'The guild in fifteenth century Dunfermline', in *The Scottish Medieval Town*, ed M. Lynch, M. Spearman, & G. Stell, Edinburgh.

Wainwright, F. 1955. *The Problem of the Picts*, Perth.

Walker, B. & Ritchie, G. 1987. *Exploring Scotland's Heritage: Fife and Tayside*, Edinburgh.

Walker, B. & Ritchie, G. 1996. *Exploring Scotland's Heritage: Fife, Perthshire and Angus*, Edinburgh.

Watkins, T. 1982. The excavation of an Early Bronze Age cemetery at Barns Farm, Dalgety Bay, Fife, *Proceedings of the Society of Antiquaries of Scotland*, vol. 112, 48–141.

Watson, H.D. 1986. *Kilrenny and Cellardyke: 800 Years of History*, John Donald, Edinburgh.

Watson, W.J. 1926. *The History of the Celtic Place-Names of Scotland*, Edinburgh and London (reprinted Edinburgh, 1993).

Whatley, C.A. 1984. *That important and necessary article: the salt industry and its trade in Fife and Tayside c. 1570–1850*, Abertay Historical Society Publication.

Whyte, I. 1995. *Scotland before the Industrial Revolution: An Economic and Social History c. 1050 to c. 1750*, London.

Wickham-Jones, C.R. 1994. *Scotland's First Settlers*, Historic Scotland and BT Batsford, London.

Wickham-Jones, C.R. & Dalland, M. 1998. A small Mesolithic Site at Fife Ness, Crail, Scotland, *Tayside and Fife Archaeological Journal.*

Will, R.S. & Dixon, T.N. 1995. Excavations at Balgonie Castle, Markinch, Fife, *Proceedings of the Society of Antiquaries of Scotland*, 125, 1109–1118.

Wood, A.J.D. 1989. *40 Years New: Glenrothes 1948–1988*, Glenrothes.

Wormald, J. 1992. *Court, Kirk and Community: Scotland 1470–1625*, reprinted Edinburgh.

INDEX